MONEY AND SCHOOLS

Fourth Edition

David C. Thompson
R. Craig Wood
Faith E. Crampton

EYE ON EDUCATION
6 DEPOT WAY WEST, SUITE 106
LARCHMONT, NY 10538
(914) 833–0551
(914) 833–0761 fax
www.eyeoneducation.com

Library of Congress Cataloging-in-Publication Data

Thompson, David C.
    Money and schools / David C. Thompson, R. Craig Wood, Faith E. Crampton. 4th ed.
    p.   cm.
    Includes bibliographical references and index.
    ISBN 978-1-59667-074-7 (alk. paper)
    1. School budgets—United States—Handbooks, manuals, etc. 2. Schools—United States—Acounting—Handbooks, manuals, etc. 3. Education—United States—Finance—Handbooks, manuals, etc. Wood, R. Craig II, Crampton, Faith E. III.
    Title
    LB2830.2.T56 2008
    371.2'060973—dc22

                                    2007041146

10 9 8 7 6 5 4 3 2 1

Also Available from EYE ON EDUCATION

ABOUT THE AUTHORS

Professor **David C. Thompson**'s professional career has spanned classroom teacher, elementary principal, high school principal, superintendent of schools, and the professoriate. A specialist in school finance litigation, his publication record is prolific and encompasses numerous book chapters, monographs, and refereed journal articles. A frequently invited author in respected circles, he has published chapters in four consecutive *American Education Finance Association Yearbooks* and has been widely published in the *Journal of Education Finance*, the National Organization on Legal Problems of Education's *NOLPE Handbook of School Law*, West's *Education Law Reporter*, books by the Association of School Business Officials International (ASBO), and many others. He has served on boards including the Authors' Committee of West's *Education Law Reporter*, is legislative editor for the *Journal of Education Finance*, has written an invited review of finance litigation for West's *Education Law Reporter*, and is chair of the Board of Editors of the scholarly journal *Educational Considerations*. His textbooks include *Fiscal Leadership for Schools: Concepts and Practices* (Longman), *Principles of School Business Management* (ASBO), *Education Finance Law: Constitutional Challenges to State Aid Plans* (ELA), *Money and Schools* (Eye on Education), and *Saving America's School Infrastructure* (IAP) with the foreword by The Honorable Senator Edward M. Kennedy. He also served as author, editor, and consultant to the Core Finance Data Task Force's 2004 rewrite of the U.S. Department of Education's authoritative handbook *Financial Accounting for Local and State School Systems*, which significantly changed how school districts must report financial data to superior units of government. His consulting work has included advisement or expert analysis for state departments of education, state legislatures, attorneys general, and litigants in school finance. His research has been presented to numerous major organizations including the American Education Finance Association, Education Law Association, National Center for Education Statistics, National Education Association, National Conference of State Legislatures, and other keynote addresses to large audiences. He also served as Founding co-director of the University Council for Educational Administration's (UCEA) Center for Education Finance at Kansas State University and the University of Florida from 1989 to 2006. Dr. Thompson is Professor in the Graduate School and Chair of the Department of Educational Leadership at Kansas State University.

Professor **R. Craig Wood** is a leading scholar in the field of education finance as well as education law. His research regarding the methods of distributing school finance aid has appeared in numerous scholarly law and education journals and books. He is a prolific author regarding the financing of elementary and secondary education, having written more than 200 book chapters, monographs, and scholarly journal articles and law reviews, including the American Education Finance Association's *Annual Yearbooks*, *Journal of Education Finance*, and the Education Law Association's *Handbook of School Law* series. His books include *Education Finance*

Law (ELA), *Fiscal Leadership for Schools* (Longman), *Principles of School Business Management* (ASBO), and *Money and Schools* (Eye on Education). His latest text (with David Thompson), *Financing Public Education*, is forthcoming. He has served on the Board of Directors of the Education Law Association, as well as serving as past president of the American Education Finance Association. He serves on the editorial boards of West's *Education Law Reporter*, *Journal of Education Finance*, and *Educational Considerations*, as well as the University of Florida's *Journal of Law and Public Policy*. He designed the current system of financing public elementary and secondary education for the Missouri legislature. Most recently, he measured the cost of educational adequacy for the state legislatures of Montana and Rhode Island. He has served as the lead expert witness for state legislatures regarding education finance constitutional challenges for such states as Florida, Missouri, Montana, South Dakota, and Texas. Dr. Wood is professor in the Department of Educational Administration and Policy at the University of Florida.

Professor **Faith E. Crampton**'s professional career has spanned public education, senior administrative positions in state government, senior research and policy positions in national education and legislative organizations, and graduate faculty positions in public and private research universities. Her current position is associate professor of education finance and policy in the Department of Administrative Leadership at the University of Wisconsin-Milwaukee. She is past president of the Fiscal Issues, Policy, and Education Finance Special Interest Group of the American Educational Research Association and a past member of the Board of Directors of the American Education Finance Association. She is also a past member of the Board of Directors for the University Council for Educational Administration's Center for Education Finance. She has held graduate faculty appointments in education finance at the University of Oregon and the University of Rochester. Outside academe, she has served as a senior researcher with the National Education Association, a senior policy analyst and consultant for the National Conference of State Legislatures, and Deputy Director of the Ohio Student Loan Commission. She is a highly respected expert witness in school finance litigation and consultant to legislatures on school finance reform. She has published widely in leading journals such as the *Journal of Education Finance*, *Educational Considerations*, *National Association of Secondary School Principals Journal*, *Journal of School Business Management*, *Journal of the Council of Educational Facility Planners International*, and *School Business Affairs*, in addition to authoring numerous monographs, reports, book chapters, and policy briefs. She is executive editor of the scholarly journal *Educational Considerations*, and a member of the editorial staff of the *Journal of Education Finance*. In 2003, she published the groundbreaking book, *Saving America's School Infrastructure*, with a foreword by Senator Edward M. Kennedy. Dr. Crampton has presented scholarly papers and given invited presentations to national and international research and policy organizations, such as the American Education Finance Association, American Educational Research Association, British Educational Management and Administration Society, Center for Budget Policy and Priorities, Education Writers Association, NAACP, National Conference of Professors of Educational Administration, and Organizations Concerned About Rural Education. She began her career as a public school teacher.

ACKNOWLEDGMENTS

No book is ever written without the valuable assistance of others. This includes manuscript reviewers and resource people trusted for their ability to discern and clarify a variety of issues that may escape authors during the writing stage.

The authors wish to thank the following people who contributed in important ways to this current edition and to earlier editions of *Money and Schools.* In particular, the authors are grateful to reviewers of the previous three editions, whose advice continues to strongly influence this latest iteration: Eric Bartleson, Mankato State University; Michael Boone, Southwest Texas State University; Dennis Brennan, University of the Pacific; William E. Camp, University of North Texas; Leonard Etlinger, Chicago State University; John Freeman, University of Alabama; Frank Gallant, University of Idaho; Catherine Glascock, Ohio University; Seth Hirshorn, University of Michigan; Larry K. Kelly, Arizona School Administrators Association; Dennis Lauro, Assistant Superintendent, Pelham, NY; T. C. Mattocks, Idaho State University; Joseph Natale, Superintendent, Warwick Valley, NY; Doug Nelson, Washington State University; William Owings, Old Dominion University; Ray Proulx, University of Vermont; Augustana Reyes, University of Houston; Ross Rubenstein, Georgia State University; William Salwaechter, Oklahoma State University; Catherine Sielke, University of Georgia; David Steele, Seattle Pacific University; Ed Stehno, Fort Hays State University; Donald Tetreault, University of South Carolina; Bill Thornton, University of Nevada, Reno; Gary C. Wenzel, State University of West Georgia; and Richard Wiggall, Illinois State University.

Gratitude is especially expressed to reviewers and commentators for portions of this fourth edition: Kathleen Brown, University of Missouri–St. Louis; Gerald Fowler, Shippensburg University; W. B Haselton, University of Louisville; Albert Jurenas, Florida Atlantic University; and P. Allen Whitlatch, South Dakota State University. Additionally, a great debt is owed to final reviewers of the completed book: Carlos Cruz, Texas A&M University–Kingsville; Joe Flora, University of South Carolina; Jack Herlihy, Eastern Kentucky University; and Anthony Rolle, Texas A&M University–College Station.

Finally, the authors are grateful for thoughtful book reviews and other extended commentary from Carla Edlefson, Professor of Educational Administration at Ashland University and Richard King, Professor and Associate Dean of Education at the University of South Florida. We are, of course, humbly grateful for the acceptance of our work by the field, whose opinions we value most of all.

TABLE OF CONTENTS

FOREWORD TO THE FOURTH EDITION

OVERVIEW

Welcome to the fourth edition of this book! To our contemporaries who used the earlier editions, we welcome you back as old friends and trusted colleagues. To new users, we offer a special welcome to this new edition and hope you will be able to satisfy your interest in school finance and resource management through this book. As was true with each previous edition, we have again attempted to shed new light on the critical needs of the field in a way that is clear, precise, and engaging. Our reasoning for this approach is simple: We believe that how schools are funded is of critical importance in today's world of high stakes accountability, and we believe that skilled educational leaders must be highly connected to the relationship between money and the aims of education and highly responsive to public perceptions about how fiscal resources are used. In our view, the topic is vibrant and the need for clarity and preciseness cannot be overstated.

WHO WE ARE

Our approach in this book is, in meaningful part, a result of who we are as authors. Our own personal histories as practitioners and university professors permeate the entire book by reflecting on how we believe new generations of school leaders should be trained. Thus who we are says a great deal about what readers should expect from this fourth edition of *Money and Schools*. Plainly put, we are very experienced scholars and public school practitioners, and we believe the impact of our collective history is important to readers' willingness to accept what we say in this book. We are scholars because we now work in major research universities, carrying out scholarly agendas and teaching courses in educational leadership, specifically in school finance-related issues. Equally important is that we have deep and timeworn practitioner roots. Collectively, we have served as superintendents, assistant superintendents, school business managers, grant managers, principals, and classroom teachers in public school systems across the United States. We have also provided extensive consulting work on behalf of school districts, and for more than a decade we've been involved in legal battles in more than a dozen states as expert witnesses on behalf of plaintiffs or defendants seeking improved funding for schools. The especially critical aspect of our professional histories is that we have not written this book solely from a theory base, nor have we used the book as a bully pulpit to advance any political views about how national, state, or local units of government fund schools. Instead, who we are relates to this book at the most basic level by virtue of the fact that we are practitioners who have done the things our readers are most interested in—in other words we've built budgets, cut budgets, raised taxes, faced angry constituents, hired and fired staff, experienced the accountability and student achievement wars, and so on. As a result, we believe our readers' experience with this book will be enhanced by knowing us for who we are—for the most part, we are school people like most of our readers.

THE NEW CONTEXT

As we go to press with this fourth edition, the context of schooling continues to change greatly. The federal *No Child Left Behind* (NCLB) law of 2001 that brought great change to the American education landscape continues to force state legislatures into both proactive and reactive roles, and many states themselves have separately and additionally demanded new pupil performance accountability in exchange for school funding. Not surprisingly, school leaders continue to be subjected to enormous pressure in this regard, and the profession itself has brought scrutiny upon its own ranks through other reforms aimed at testing the competencies of licensed school leaders. Although our profession has always believed that education is a high stakes enterprise in which children deserve the best opportunity regardless of individual circumstance, the result of these many changes to the context of schooling has been to engage leaders at a higher level of understanding about just how critical leadership is to guaranteeing the universally coveted (and now mandated) student performance outcomes.

As a result, the die is already cast only a few years into the new millennium. The context of schools today demands that school leaders must be highly skilled, and a critically important skill is understanding the relationship between not only opportunity and money but also outcomes and money. The widely adopted Interstate School Leaders Licensure Consortium's (ISLLC) standards for school leadership preparation, authored by the Council of Chief State School Officers, goes to exactly this issue as ISLLC declares that all leaders should be competent in six standards, wherein fiscal resources can make or break schools' ability to produce acceptable student outcomes:

- ◆ *Standard 1:* A school administrator is an educational leader who promotes the success of all students by facilitating the development, articulation, implementation, and stewardship of a vision of learning that is shared and supported by the school community.

- ◆ *Standard 2:* A school administrator is an educational leader who promotes the success of all students by advocating, nurturing, and sustaining a school culture and instructional program conducive to student learning and staff professional growth.

- ◆ *Standard 3:* A school administrator is an educational leader who promotes the success of all students by ensuring management of the organization, operations, and resources for a safe, efficient, and effective learning environment.

- ◆ *Standard 4:* A school administrator is an educational leader who promotes the success of all students by collaborating with families and community members, responding to diverse community interests and needs, and mobilizing community resources.

♦ *Standard 5:* A school administrator is an educational leader who promotes the success of all students by acting with integrity, fairness, and in an ethical manner.

♦ *Standard 6:* A school administrator is an educational leader who promotes the success of all students by understanding, responding to, and influencing the larger political, social, economic, legal, and cultural context.

Although some measure of these standards might be accomplished by simply working harder, there is a strong belief that neither the spirit nor the detail of school reform can be met without financial resources in significantly greater supply than exists in public schools today. To meet NCLB's demands—including new demands imbedded in NCLB's reauthorization—at the level of required academic performance means to bring all children literally to the same outcome, and school leaders are regarded as key to meeting such accountability. The ISLLC standards on which school leaders' training is to be judged clearly supports the same end, and in equally clear fashion the standards call for school leaders to understand the economic context of schools and its connection to the outcomes of teaching and learning. As a result, the context of this fourth edition of *Money and Schools* is that federal law now demands equality of educational outcomes for all children; that school performance accountability expectations at other levels of government continues to increase; and that the education profession itself has embraced rigorous performance accountability and has targeted school leadership in its sights by demanding school leaders who understand the complex nature of schooling and the relationship of money to educational opportunity and outcome.

WHO SHOULD READ THIS BOOK

From its title, it is clear that this book is intended for both broad and specialized audiences. Choosing this book indicates that readers have a connection to schools that causes them to demonstrate a high level of interest in education's costs. Specifically, this book reaches out to school administrators, classroom teachers, school boards, and laypersons in the broader public. Although that sounds like everyone, each of these audiences has a different value for the book. Administrators will find that the material confirms their existing knowledge, reminds them of things not considered recently, and extends their knowledge by engaging recent federal and state reform movements. We also have long advocated that the first group of people who should know more about school funding is classroom teachers. Teachers often complain about limited school budgets and instinctively understand that new requirements are stretching inadequate dollars even thinner, but they usually have little knowledge of how school budgets work—for example, sources of revenue and permissible expenditures. We also believe school board members will benefit from this book. Although it is popular to bash school boards as insensitive to the financial shortcomings of schools, it is altogether too easy to forget that board members are asked to make difficult and unpopular decisions, usually without being professionally trained in recognizing education's needs—a reality made more complex by increasingly stringent federal and state accountability requirements. Finally, laypersons can benefit from this book, in that we are all taxpayers. So, in the end, this book truly is for nearly everyone, subject only to the limitations on what the book does and does not try to do.

WHAT YOU SHOULD EXPECT FROM THIS BOOK

This book continues to be organized around three broad parts: an overview of funding concepts, an overview of daily funding operations, and a look into the future. Moving through these parts is like an inverted pyramid, starting with the broad social context of schools and continuing into specialized examinations of various elements of school budgeting in each individual chapter.

At the broadest level, it is important for everyone to understand that money and student achievement are related (Chapter 1). It is also critical to know that education's current condition is a product of a long history that involves the interplay of complex aspects of our cultural and governmental heritage (Chapter 2). The next logical step is to review sources of revenue and expenditure (Chapter 3), in that people's frustrations and misunderstanding of school budgets often can be traced back to these complex issues. After this broad overview, the book launches into a detailed view of daily funding operations. The focus is on our audience, however, seeking readability without the clutter of academic language or heavy research citation. We begin with the view that accountability, regulation, and ethics are the watchwords for the future, so that understanding the flow of money into schools and its proper handling is the basis for all good decision making (Chapter 4). School budget planning (Chapter 5) is next addressed from the perspective of how budgets are built, with subsequent chapters looking in greater detail at the major elements of budget construction. Specifically, issues of budgeting for personnel (Chapter 6), budgeting for instruction (Chapter 7), and budgeting for student activities (Chapter 8) are elements that cut across wise budgeting behaviors at both district and school levels. The same can be said about budgeting for school infrastructure (Chapter 9), budgeting for transportation and food services (Chapter 10), and the need to budget for liability and risk management (Chapter 11). Clearly issues of site-based leadership under new performance accountability standards have strong budget implications (Chapter 12), with activities that occur at all levels in a school system. Finally, a look to the future is essential (Chapter 13) because schools continue to face radical change.

WHAT THIS BOOK DOESN'T DO

We also want to be clear about what this book does not do. Specifically, it does not cover each topic to its greatest depth; given limitations of space and purpose, this is not within the scope of the book. It also does not intend to create skilled practitioners. Again, space and purpose do not lend themselves to teaching specific skills at the level of practice. It also does not intend to represent the range of all necessary elements of good budgeting in schools. Although the premise of this book is that budgeting can be made less murky, it remains a highly complex activity when anyone attempts to actually carry it out. As a result, knowledge rather than skills is the goal of this book—knowledge needed by everyone because everyone pays taxes, sends children to school, or benefits from an educated citizenry.

HOW SHOULD YOU READ THIS BOOK?

The best way is to read the chapters sequentially because there is a logical progression. However, experienced administrators to whom the concepts are already familiar will have no difficulty choosing chapters in any order. School board members, teachers, and laypersons may also read the chapters in any order, although they might find it necessary to dip back into earlier chapters if some point seems unclear.

HOW CAN YOU LEARN MORE?

If you find your interest piqued by issues in this book, there are many ways to learn more about school budgeting. Obvious ways are reading other books and taking classes relating to school funding. Several excellent textbooks are available that go more deeply into the issues introduced here—we've authored several such books. Courses at a good university can be helpful in refreshing your knowledge or extending your grasp of these issues. Depending on your current employment and career goals, internships with practicing administrators can be a great learning aid, as no one has ever really experienced budgeting until it has become a "do-or-die" activity. Other ways to learn more include attending state department of education budget workshops, as well as seminars conducted by state professional groups such as administrator organizations and school board associations. Valuable resource people also exist right at home, such as your school district's business manager or school principal—each of these persons is required to carry out budgeting as a daily activity. Finally, you can contact us.

Overview of Broad Concepts

SCHOOLS, VALUES, AND MONEY

THE CHALLENGE

The fear of economic and social decline is so great that education reform has become a national agenda wherein critics link America's preeminence in world markets, gainful employment, and the survival and stability of democracy to the education system. As school leaders, it is important to understand that school finance is at the heart of schooling because it requires much money to pay for either the successes or failures of education.

Thompson, Wood, & Honeyman (1994)

CHAPTER DRIVERS

At the close of this chapter you will have reflected upon these questions:
- What is the context of public education today?
- What is the emerging nature of schools?
- Where did schools come from?
- What should schools be doing?
- What are schools "capable" of doing?
- What is the effect of money on schools?
- Does money make a difference in student achievement?
- What happens when schools get more (or less) money?
- Where might public schools be headed?

THE CONTEXT OF PUBLIC EDUCATION

In each of the previous three editions of this book we began with the statement that the context of public education is undergoing dramatic change. We argued in each edition that education—indeed, all of global society—is being relentlessly restructured on a massive scale equal to many events from our past that history books now record as having reshaped the fate of entire nations. That statement and argument continue to be absolutely true and the pace of change has not only failed to slow, but instead gives every appearance of accelerating with no end in sight. As a result of such a seemingly eternal truth, we should consider the context of such change as we begin our study of *money and schools*—that is, schools are not immune to today's economic and social upheaval, and many observers would assert that the public education system is in very real danger.

The assertion that schools might be endangered is rooted in issues that have been raised at all levels of society over the past several decades. Although the past is often subject to a certain romanticism that fails to objectively ask whether the world was ever more rational and gentle than it is today, the past few decades have fomented a new tendency toward hostile challenges over a wide range of real and imaginary injustices—a confrontiveness that has led to a national personality that no longer seems to care much about modeling civility or working collaboratively for a common social goal. Recent national elections provide excellent examples of how critics from the political right harshly ridicule what they view as forsaking traditional American values, arguing that governmental activism spawns laziness, ingratitude, and immorality while simultaneously punishing law-abiding, industrious, and upright citizens—a view that seeks to criminalize any opposing view. In response, critics from the political left approach frenzy in making their diametrically opposed views known by shouting down anyone they judge as intolerant, while demonstrating a remarkable level of intolerance themselves for views disagreeing with their own. The breakdown of civility is evident in election results so tightly drawn as to divide the nation along stark ideological lines, so that it has become normal to challenge the outcome of national and local elections through the courts. At its most fundamental level, the rift in society is based in vastly different views of the role of government in individuals' lives, and as people have come to see verbal aggression as a socially acceptable way to present their beliefs. That same rift has come to dominate the news and suggests that the disagreements are too deep to be resolved. In many cases, the rift has both social and economic roots—a dangerous mix when fundamental social values and huge amounts of money are the key elements in an arena where aggression—with ultimate winners and losers—is in play.

The implications of such turmoil for schools are great. Schools are an integral part of modern society, transmitting culture and winning approval (or scorn) for their success in preparing future generations for living in an increasingly national and international world. But because the splinterings in society are increasingly irreconcilable, education today is caught more than ever among competing demands that propound the mission of schools from starkly opposite ends of the political and social continuum. The questions arising from such a context are profound. For example, what are public schools becoming? For that matter, where did schools come from, and what does that say about what schools are today? Of profound importance are the contentious questions: What *should* schools be doing? What are schools *capable* of doing? Difficult enough to answer objectively, these questions are dramatically loaded by the strident political agendas from the left and right that adopt these same questions as causes, raising new questions that imply what each set of advocates would "transform" if they could capture unlimited political power. The struggle is grandly illustrated in contemporary terms by the *No Child Left Behind Act*[1] (NCLB, 2001), which asserts confident answers to earth-shaking questions such as: What is the impact of money on schools? What actually happens when schools get more money? NCLB effectively raises the even more difficult questions of whether schools really need more money and whether schools are broken. All these questions, in a social and political context that seems eager to fight and never to seek commonality, raise the ultimate specter of where public education may be eventually headed if it stays the present course.

These are worrisome issues as we face a combative future—issues that school leaders must be prepared to address with wisdom and strength for reasons of national prosperity and survival. As a result, the rest of this chapter, along with Chapter 13, sets the stage for the critical importance of schools and money in a new and politically unstable era. But as we launch that discussion, we admit upfront to an important value orientation: *That is, we strongly favor adequate and equitable support of every kind for public schools.* We admit that our orientation derives at least in part from our being "insiders" to the education "establishment," as we have collectively spent more than a century as educators, researchers, and leaders in this massive industry. We recognize the criticisms we face as a result of our insider views, and we ourselves have at times perceptively referred to public education as a growth industry that secures its own future by creating an unending demand cycle—both by constantly raising standards and by the ever-constant need to remediate our professional failures. But at the same time, our 100+ years of experience as school leaders at high levels of responsibility have caused us to truly believe that schools are America's last and finest hope, if for no other reason than the individual and collective well-being (including our own retirement prospects!) of the nation and world depend on preparing each new generation to take the economic and social reins of leadership. As a result, we warn our readers that this book holds an honest and sometimes unflattering view of schools and money—a view uncluttered by political correctness. With that said, our journey begins with the context of public education because it is within that setting where school monies are obtained and spent.

WHAT ARE SCHOOLS BECOMING?

A burning question on the minds of many people across the political spectrum is: *What is the emerging nature of schools?* Although the question is too complex to fully answer in this book, it is useful to raise the issue of change because speculating

---

1   P.L. 107-110, No Child Left Behind Act of 2001. Billed by Congress as an act to close the achievement gap with accountability, flexibility, and choice.

about the answer is fundamental to understanding schools and money as far into the future as we can see.

Where Did Schools Come From?

The battle for control of education is by no means new, although it has shown recent signs of intense escalation as the stakes for winners and losers have shifted over time in an increasingly knowledge-based society. But it is important to recognize at the outset that part of the current struggle for control of schools stems from our national history in that people as a rule are resistant to change, particularly when change is perceived as threatening to their way of life. Consequently, it is an important insight to recognize that nothing, including resistance to change, exists without historical roots, and the past gives many clues into a vast array of otherwise loosely connected realities.[2]

The unique history of the United States contributed much to current struggles over schools, in that the structure of education today is the product of a long and tense evolutionary process. Most of us know the brief history of American education, beginning with establishment of schools in the original colonies. The first law formally requiring schools came into existence in 1642 with adoption of a law in Massachusetts requiring the town fathers to determine if children were being given adequate religious and occupational training. Similar action followed in several other colonies, so that by 1720 laws mandating some amount of schooling were in place in Connecticut, Maine, New Hampshire, and Vermont. These laws were destined to be broadened as the idea of enlightened self-government was added to the defense for requiring public education, giving birth to the now familiar democratic principles as argued by Thomas Jefferson, William Penn, and others who wielded great influence on the emerging nature of schooling in the new nation.

In addition to the practical reasons for encouraging public education, the intense isolation of the colonies and the later westward expansion were powerful contributors to the evolving structure of public schools. The original colonies were fiercely independent, even to the point of deciding separately whether they each would give financial support to the American Revolution. In the post-Revolutionary War era, the early Congress struggled with its lack of funds to pay war debts, much of which stemmed from intense resistance to any centralized government, and it was a harbinger of a politically mistrustful future that the early nation witnessed a bitter war of contrasting ideologies, such as those of Hamilton and Jefferson regarding establishment of a strong federal government. Westward expansion, with its geographic isolationism, only exacerbated the independent streak of the new breed of Americans, leading to tightly held local views on how schools should be organized. Yet at the same time, the nation's makeup was shifting dramatically in other ways, with soaring immigration, establishment of great cities, and growing sentiment against child-labor abuse. Through a long series of complex events, the Common Schools Movement arose

---

2   For a more detailed discussion, see Chapter 2 in David C. Thompson, R. Craig Wood, and David Honeyman, *Fiscal Leadership for Schools: Concepts and Practices* (New York: Longman, 1994), 76–87.

under early advocates like Horace Mann, so that public education somewhat resembling the structure of schools today began to emerge by 1840.

Probably the most striking features of public schools in the growing nation were the frequency with which they were established and the parochialism on which they were run. The empty vastness of the nation led to the need for countless thousands of tiny schools. Although no one knows how many schools existed across the nation before a trend toward consolidation began, the number had to be at least equal to the number of towns in the states and territories at any given time. The only meaningful way to understand the staggering proliferation of schools is to look to the first formal attempts to tally public schools, with U.S. Department of Education data showing that in 1929, there were 238,306 elementary schools; 149,282 one-teacher schools; and 23,930 secondary schools—a total of 411,518 schools—all within slightly more than 119,000 school districts! The parochialism stemming from such isolation goes far in explaining the fiercely local nature of schooling, and it speaks loudly to why today we still find schools only two or three blocks apart with low enrollments all across the United States. After all, if there were more than 100,000 school districts, it stands to reason that there must have been an equal number of different preferences for how schooling should be carried out, especially because states did not seek to regulate schools until only recently.

The evolution of public schools in the United States is, of course, far more complex than is presented here. But historic roots easily illustrate current realities. Just as children predictably internalize some of the same values taught to them during their own upbringing, the customs and culture of local communities are deeply held values that affect the nature of schools, and the stubborn pride of Americans in creating and preserving local traditions for schools is legendary. The desire for local control is well expressed by the continual fear of many modern rural school districts, as citizens hasten to charge, "…as the school goes, so goes the town." Indeed, we've served as senior administrators in communities where countless school district patrons repeatedly told us with great anxiety, "If the school goes, the post office and the churches will follow close behind"; in other words, schools make up the heart of the community in many people's minds, so much so that the strongest pillar of a community is perceived lost if schools close. Consequently, a long sense of local tradition produces a fierce struggle at any cost to save schools, and the entirety of the struggle over education—be it racial integration, local taxes, curriculum, or school budgets—is rooted in the American tradition of local control and resentment toward outside interference.

What Should Schools Be Doing?

Where schools came from is part of the answer to what schools are becoming, at least in the sense of understanding how hard it is to agree on anything about schools. But another part of the question about what schools are becoming is wrapped up in the subquestion: *What should schools be doing?*

Although we have come a long way from the political and social isolationism of the past, the stubbornly parochial nature of schools in the United States continues to stand as a reminder of the great difficulty of trying to reach consensus on what schools should be about. Almost any news report today chronicles some new dispute about schools, ranging from threats to withdraw fiscal support to angry calls for more reforms because of some newly perceived breakdown in schools' effectiveness. Almost daily, administrators lose their jobs because of arguments over what schools should be doing. Teacher unions and professional negotiations become deeply mired in either restricting educational activities or in promoting programs of special interest. School board candidates often run on platforms of educational reform, and legislators are subjected to tremendous pressures from groups specifically organized to force (or prevent) changes in what schools are doing. No one is immune to such pressure, in large part because people instinctively understand that schools are a key player in the nation's future—so much so that control of schools is tantamount to control of the future.

Historic opinions on what schools should do have centered mostly on issues relating to teaching morality, democracy, and equality. Intense interest among the early colonies in preparing children for a morally upright life was noted in our earlier discussion. Ideas from Thomas Jefferson, Horace Mann, and many others weighed in, extending the grasp of education and arguing that an enlightened citizenry is the most effective curb against tyranny—as Benjamin Franklin said, "Government is not reason; it is not eloquence; it is force. Like fire, it is a dangerous servant and a fearful master." Franklin's statement succinctly captures the historic attitude of many Americans toward governmental control and paints a vivid portrait of a central purpose for schooling in earlier times. More recently, a concern for human equality has been added to the aims of schooling. The earthshaking effect of the *Brown v. Board of Education*[3] decision in 1954, overturning the race-based doctrine of "separate but equal" as a legitimate social order, is clear evidence of expanded concern about equality in education and all other aspects of the human condition. The Civil Rights Act of 1964 and the expansive civil rights laws that followed have had enormous educational implications, giving rise to a huge body of federal and state case law and statutes controlling expansive and far-reaching concepts, including gender equality, rights of students in special education, rights of citizens under equal access provisions, and so forth. As time has marched on, the volume and tenor of special interest legislation has only intensified, accompanied by increasing willingness to aggressively advocate for controversial positions.

The ever-increasing likelihood for ideological conflict is a poignant window on current views regarding what schools *should* be doing, especially in context of the nature of equality and social justice. Little disagreement exists about education for basic economic productivity, although ensuring access provides fertile ground for disputes relating to true equality. Critics charge that many students have very unequal access to economic-enhancing opportunities such as technology or higher education, which is then posited to ensure the perpetuation of disadvantaged populations far into the future, a position immediately attacked by their philosophical and political opponents who forcefully invoke local choice to exceed—or only offer—a minimum educational program. Even greater disagreement exists today about education for morality, particularly when issues infringe on parental beliefs, as with mandated sex education, creationism, and other issues perceived to restrict parental control. Hysteria

---

3   374 U.S. 483 (1954).

often rules, with dissenters threatening to abandon public schools and proponents of compulsory education angrily shouting back. But it is still the broader issue of attempts to force uniformity on schools in social and academic equality that produces the greatest conflict regarding what schools should be about. Is it the role of schools to provide a *minimum* educational opportunity? Is it education's role to provide *exactly* equal educational opportunities? Is it the role of education to provide equal educational *outcomes*? Reformers have tended to argue at least for exactly equal opportunity, whereas the precedent of American history promotes some minimum opportunity with the freedom to exceed by local preference. Reformers emotionally argue that such local freedom ensures racially and economically segregated schools, an outcome in direct conflict with the U.S. Constitution's guarantees of equal protection.[4] Defenders of local choice, however, hotly reply that communism is dead and that America is still all about individual initiative. The debate is carried out at all levels—courts struggle with lawsuits over school funding, legislatures receive intense pressure from political advocates of all stripes, and taxpayers engage in passive or overt revolt, while school boards, teachers, administrators, and children are caught in a tug-of-war, ultimately resulting in diminished resources because of expensive litigation and lack of cooperation. In the end, there is no one voice speaking for what education *should be doing* because the many voices seek different and fundamentally incompatible ends.

What Are Schools Capable of Doing?

At least a piece of the current debate currently overlooked is recognizing what schools are actually capable of doing. Partisan politics confidently act as if schools are capable of fully satisfying each side's goals. Social reformers point to the gains of the last century and argue that a combination of legal and social reforms has created a better, though still imperfect, society. Advocates for restoring a more traditional society are just as confident that rebuilding basic education and traditional values in schools would solve every social ill now afflicting the nation. With such strident noise, it is difficult to know who is right, but the overriding conclusion is that each side fervently believes schools are *the* major vehicle to some essential outcome. Yet the question must be asked as to what schools are actually *capable* of doing? That is, can schools achieve the aims of either side, and—importantly—at what price? This generates subquestions, to which data offer some insight. For example: What is the effect of money on schools? What happens when schools get more money? Do schools really need more money? What will happen if schools receive less money? These questions envelop the larger question of what schools should be doing by accelerating the stakes as partisan factions simultaneously compete to increase or decrease spending on schools. Although the questions are painfully clear, the answers are unsatisfying, especially relating to what schools are capable of doing.

---

4   U.S. Constitution, Amendment XIV.

What Is the Effect of Money on Schools?

An increasingly testy issue is the impact of money on schools. Many questions form around this kernel, primarily inquiring at the most basic level whether money has any measurable effect on student achievement. Obviously, people asking the question have their own reasons for seeking the "right" answer. Educators generally believe their right answer would empower many things not now possible given current funding levels because they assume the answer would inevitably spur new money. Legislators asking the same question are driven by complex goals, uppermost among which is that limited public resources must be shared with other essential government roles such as social services, public safety, roads, arts, and so forth—all in the context of finite tax revenues gathered from increasingly surly taxpayers. School boards often share many of the same goals as educators, but with the added burden of making policy decisions in the context of local politics. At its root, however, the question about the impact of money on schools always asks: Does money make a difference in student achievement? The stakes are high, as advocates for higher funding may suffer a devastating setback if no clear effect is readily available, whereas education's critics will have gained a powerful reason to reduce funding for schools, or at least a reason to allow funding to stagnate at current levels—a risk scenario exponentially heightened as other intensely political student achievement agendas, such as the federal *No Child Left Behind* law, roll ahead unstoppably.

Unfortunately, the answer to the question is very incomplete and unsatisfying. Much research has been done on the relationship between money and academic achievement, but with limited—although significant—results. A sizable limitation springs from relative inexperience researching such complex issues, in that formal interest is only about 40 years old, a fact leading to complaints about inadequate methodologies used in assessing the complex relationships between money and achievement. Additionally, at times bias has affected research results, in that some investigators may have approached the question in search of a preferred answer. Although we cannot provide a conclusive answer to the effect of money on schools in this book, much can be learned by summarizing what is regarded with reasonable respect at this time.

A significant body of literature on the relationship between student achievement and money is known as *production–function* research, and efforts to extend this line of inquiry and to find new avenues of exploration are constantly pursued. Various sources have chronicled the development of this line of inquiry. Production-function studies began with the Coleman Report,[5] which was funded by the federal government as part of the Civil Rights Act of 1964. The study focused on questions about racial inequality, indicators of quality such as curriculum, teacher qualifications, and student learning as measured by standardized tests, all within the context of socioeconomic status. The Coleman Report's findings were pessimistic about both the impact

---

5   James Coleman, Ernst Campbell, Carol Hobson, James McPartland, Alexander Mood, Frederic Weinfeld, and Robert York. *Equality of Educational Opportunity* (Washington, DC: U.S. Government Printing Office 1966).

of resources and the school's ability to overcome the effects of genetics and the home environment.

Response to the Coleman Report was swift and dramatic. Educators were incensed at the notion that education had limited impact, particularly for disadvantaged children, and reformers chose to view the study skeptically because it did not promise much educational benefit for disadvantaged children. A spate of counter-studies sprang up after the Coleman Report, typified by the Summers and Wolf[6] study, which examined 627 sixth-grade students in the Philadelphia schools, finding that certain variables, such as better teacher preparation, presence of high achievers, smaller class size, and so forth, did have a positive effect on achievement for all children. The Effective Schools Movement, initiated soon after the Coleman Report, similarly was based in ideological protest and sought to identify traits of effective schools that could be emulated to boost student achievement. Although all such studies yielded useful insights into improving student achievement through resource allocation, all were based at least partly in a desire to counter the Coleman Report, an observation that weakened the objectivity of their findings because researchers were seeking to refute data they found objectionable.

Although the foregoing description only lightly touches on a large body of very complex literature, it is the case that the dust has never settled, with researchers continuing to pursue approaches to the productivity equation. There is little to be gained by considering individual studies leading up to the present time; more can be learned by looking at criticisms and the generalizations sought by meta-research, including new developments since the last edition of this text, since what is currently on researchers' minds represents the best thinking on productivity to this time.

The gist of criticisms of production–function research is captured by examining various attacks on the Coleman Report. Although considered at the time to be a good study, the Coleman Report has been subjected to intense criticism for methodological flaws. Chief among criticisms have been *nonresponse* and *stratification* of variables resulting in noncomparable data, *errors* in data entry, and *misinterpretation* of interaction effects. Simply put, nonresponse refers to the misleading impression of a very large dataset when in fact the number of respondents was far smaller than intended, raising questions of generalizability. Stratification refers to data being examined in separate sets, perhaps wrongly constructed, so that effects of variables such as race, religion, and so forth might have been exaggerated or misleading. Errors in data entry plague all large datasets and may make the results suspect. Finally, misinterpretation of interaction effects refers to a lack of sophistication in research design, in which causal relationships are inferred that were not really verified in the data. These criticisms have been helpful in limiting misapplication of the Coleman Report, although some would argue that subsequent research has not improved greatly and has suffered equally scathing criticism.

A second useful tool for examining the effect of money on student achievement is meta-analysis. At some point, the body of literature on any topic becomes so large

---

6   Anita Summers and Barbara Wolfe, "Do Schools Make a Difference?" *American Economic Review* 67, no. 4 (1977): 639–52.

that it obscures the underlying question because each study appears to have yielded the final answer—a situation worsened when each "final" answer contradicts other "final" answers. In production–function research, this tendency is accentuated by the large number of studies yielding seemingly opposite results, with thousands of studies in the available database. Meta-analysis seeks to find commonality of results among studies, so that the weight and direction of total evidence can be evaluated. Representative studies from opposite views provide a summary of the debate.

The case against appreciable impact of money generally is associated with Eric Hanushek's work. Through a series of studies with provocative titles such as *Throwing Money at Schools*[7] and *The Case for Equalized Mediocrity . . .*,[8] Hanushek has made a case that some readers have interpreted to dismiss the importance of money in schools. On separate occasions, Hanushek published meta-analyses of existing studies finding in sum that the relationship between school resources and student achievement is not directional, or is at least not strong and consistent given current funding practices. The essence of his argument against assumptions about the relationship between money and achievement is that the ways in which education's costs have increased should not have been expected to yield achievement gains. The assertion takes two forms. First, Hanushek argued that expenditures apart from direct instructional costs have increased more than costs for direct instruction. He concurrently argued that such costs should not be expected to produce gains, even when held to be valid instructional expenditures such as for improved teacher retirement plans. Second, he argued that attempts to spend more for direct instruction have been ill-advised. For example, schools have rushed to spend more to reduce class sizes, hire better educated teachers, and improve teacher salaries, all in the face of weak evidence that massaging such variables leads to true achievement gains. On the other side, several studies have found favorable impact of *selected* resources on student achievement.[9] One of the more comprehensive meta-analyses finding for positive impact was conducted by Laine, Greenwald, and Hedges[10] in which they reviewed a set of carefully selected studies. They concluded that resources *are* related to achievement, so that variables such as per-pupil expenditure, smaller classes, smaller school

---

7   Eric A. Hanushek, "Throwing Money at Schools," *Journal of Policy Analysis and Management* 1 (1981): 19–41.

8   Eric A. Hanushek, "The Quest for Equalized Mediocrity: School Finance Reform Without Consideration of School Performance," in *Where Does The Money Go? 16th Annual Yearbook of the American Education Finance Association*, ed. Lawrence Picus and James Wattenbarger, 20–43 (Thousand Oaks, CA: Corwin Press, 1996).

9   See, e.g., Bettye MacPhail-Wilcox and Richard King, "Production Functions Revisited in the Context of Educational Reform," *Journal of Education Finance* 12, no. 2 (1986): 191–222; see also Bettye MacPhail-Wilcox and Richard King, "Resource Allocation Studies: Implications for School Improvement and School Finance Research," *Journal of Education Finance* 11, no. 4 (1986): 416–32.

10   Richard Laine, Rob Greenwald, and Larry Hedges, "Money Does Matter: A Research Synthesis of a New Universe of Education Production Function Studies," in *Where Does The Money Go? 16th Annual Yearbook of the American Education Finance Association*, ed. Lawrence Picus and James Wattenbarger, 44–70 (Thousand Oaks, CA: Corwin Press, 1996).

size, teacher ability, teacher education, and teacher experience have positive measurable impacts. The debate has recently taken a new direction, as researchers have increasingly called for disaggregation of data at the student level (in contrast to traditional interdistrict comparisons) and greater discernment and analysis in evaluating research results in hopes of finding better answers to these perplexing questions.[11] Raymond and Hanushek,[12] for example, recently held that biased search for evidence relating to student outcomes still persists and that the emerging data in fact tend to support the idea that reform (as expressed by states having strong achievement accountability systems) is more consistently related to improved student achievement than is true in states where accountability systems are less rigorous. Similarly, Grissmer[13] recently argued that the confusion over results in the literature likely relates to poor research methodology. His own reanalysis of experimental, nonexperimental, and historical data held that the evidence increasingly leans toward the view that targeted expenditures can raise achievement scores, especially for disadvantaged students.

Seemingly countless other studies exist, with current emphasis engaging in ever-increasing sophistication, but frequently resulting only in cautious encouragement that money well placed is money better spent. The most recent research continues to be frustrated by the lack of clear linearity of manipulable variables that produce precise productivity equations, but simultaneously fruitful enough to sustain the line of inquiry. No doubt vexing to fiscal conservatives is the preliminary finding that higher achievement needs to be buttressed by higher spending—even conditioned thereon—so that one event necessarily follows from the other.[14] Encouraging to spending advocates, however, is a current trend that seems to favor the assertion that virtually all money matters, as recently illustrated by one of the most sophisticated

11 See, e.g., Allan Odden and Carolyn Busch, eds. "Special Issue: Collection of School-Level Finance Data," *Journal of Education Finance* 22, no. 3 (1997) entire issue; Margaret Goertz and Leanna Stiefel, eds. "Special Issue: Collection of School-Level Finance Data," *Journal of Education Finance* 23, no. 4 (1998) entire issue; Lawrence O. Picus and Ed Robillard, "The Collection and Use of Student Level Data: Implications for School Finance Research," *Educational Considerations* 28, no. 1:26–31 (Fall 2000); William E. Camp, David C. Thompson, and John Crain, "Within-District Equity: Issues of Desegregation and Microeconomic Analysis," in *Microlevel School Finance. 1989 American Education Finance Association Yearbook*, ed. David H. Monk and Julie K. Underwood (Cambridge: M. Ballinger, 1989), 273–92.

12 Margaret Raymond and Eric Hanushek, "Shopping for Evidence against School Accountability," in *Developments in School Finance: 2003. Fiscal Proceedings from the Annual State Data Conference of July 2003*, 117–129 (Washington, DC: National Center for Education Statistics, 2004).

13 David Grissmer, "Research Directions for Understanding the Relationship of Educational Resources to Educational Outcomes," in *Education Finance in the New Millennium. Yearbook of the American Education Finance Association*, 139–55 (New York: Eye On Education, 2001).

14 Bruce Baker, Lori Taylor, and Arnold Vedlitz, "Measuring Educational Adequacy in Public Schools." Report to the Texas Legislature Joint Committee on Public School Finance, The Texas School Project. www.capitol.state.tx.us/psf/reports/htm (2004).

studies in which spending effects were found to matter even after controlling for the highly impactful—and highly variable—effect of teacher performance.[15]

Under these general conditions, the answer to questions about the effect of money on schools is still emergent and even confusing. History reveals some inexpert attempts at disentanglement, although such studies may have been the best possible efforts at the time. To make matters worse, different answers can depend on one's political beliefs. For example, educators are justified in thinking more could be done with extra money. Legislators are justified in knowing that they must divide a finite pie among competing audiences. Taxpayers are correct in asking why they should pay more, especially in the context of years of national reports bemoaning declining student achievement. School boards and administrators are faced with the hard task of making painful resource decisions, knowing that some aspects of schools will be deemphasized as a result of spending in other areas, while feeling pressured to support all groups and knowing that increased spending might only result in higher taxes. For all constituencies, asking if money makes a difference in student achievement yields no definitive answers. Yet the question continues to reverberate with deafening proportion: If there is no conclusive answer, then more will make no measurable difference—a question that inevitably raises logical speculation that less money might not initiate some catastrophic result.

What Happens When Schools Get More (or Less) Money?

On the bright side, the answer to the question of what happens when schools get more (or less) money has moved almost imperceptibly forward since previous editions of this text. As noted in earlier editions, one possible answer continues to come from the long-standing perspective that it is difficult to know the limits on the impact of more money. Childs and Shakeshaft[16] made this point long ago in an earlier meta-analysis when they wryly noted that there have never been any public schools with enough money to be able to see what might happen when schools have enough to spend. Although some would rush to argue that a small number of public schools are very wealthy indeed, it remains that no longitudinal systematic studies of this specific question have been conducted. Such a study would maximally benefit from manipulation of fiscal inputs for the express purpose of measuring the impact of money on student achievement—a task difficult to carry out in schools because the scientific method would intentionally withhold resources from one group in order to compare to another group—an ethically unacceptable proposition.

A second possible answer relates to the absence of data on experimental control. As we just noted, by virtue of ethical prohibitions we are largely left to speculate as to the impact of more money. Carrying a step forward, experience and intuition predict

---

15 Sarah Archibald, "Narrowing In on Educational Resources That Do Affect Student Achievement," *Peabody Journal of Education,* 81 no. 4 (2006): 23–42.

16 Stephen Childs and Charol Shakeshaft. "A Meta-Analysis of Research on the Relationship Between Educational Expenditures and Student Achievement," *Journal of Education Finance* 12, no. 2 (1986): 249–63.

that one immediate effect of a sudden and massive infusion of new resources would be the most logically possible response by schools—that is, the purchase of more (or at least more costly) human resources, in that most school budgets are largely consumed by personnel costs. In other words, increased funding for schools typically buys more staff or simply results in higher salaries for existing staff. Although such a scenario is not without merit, the argument for more funding is difficult to make because no corresponding achievement gain can be confidently promised, whereas higher salaries can almost surely be predicted from a resource influx.

A third possible answer also relates to what can be intuitively known. Even granted that most new money would go to higher salaries, it is reasonable to believe that some portion of new funds would be used to address nonpersonnel costs. Schools have many unmet needs, possibly because they have tried to resolve their staffing shortfalls first, knowing that instruction is their raison d'être. Among the unmet needs are a decaying physical infrastructure, such as antiquated buildings unable to support new technologies, unsafe buses and other soaring transportation costs, and outdated curriculum materials and teaching aids. Even assuming for a moment no direct link between how money is currently being spent and increased achievement, no sensible person could argue against using new money to reduce class sizes, provide safe school buildings, purchase new instructional materials and textbooks, and so forth.

An equally interesting question is raised by asking what would happen if schools were to receive less money. Here again, voices on either side of the debate predict very different outcomes. In fairness, few (if any) inside education would advocate for reduced spending merely because desired linkages between expenditures and student achievement are not settled. Such a call is more likely the response of taxpayers who believe that, because money is "wasted" absent a profitable bottom achievement line, the proper punishment is to withhold resources from schools. In contrast, most scholars argue for increased scrutiny of *how* money is spent, although Monk long ago captured the pitfall in such behavior when he noted that this might demand more psychoanalytic expertise than the discipline possesses if it is to understand the extremes of such microanalysis.[17] Notwithstanding, some elements of sophisticated microlevel inquiry have begun to develop, partly in response to the fact that relative expenditure levels have dropped in some states over recent time[18] and as scholarly interest in analyzing school level data has taken on new strength.

Unfortunately, like the effects of more money, the answer to what happens if significantly less money were available is largely speculative. However, intuition and observation of current realities again have to play an important role in estimating the effect of revenue losses. Intuition tells us that many districts already are skating near the edge of disaster, as in some states support for education has stagnated or has not kept up with rising costs. Costs have soared as liability has increased, as teacher

---

17 David H. Monk, *Educational Finance: An Economic Approach,* 345 (New York: McGraw-Hill, 1990).

18 See, e.g., David C. Thompson and Faith E. Crampton, "The Impact of School Finance Litigation," *Educational Considerations* 28, no. 1 (Fall 2000): 1–12.

unions have succeeded in raising salaries and benefits, and as nonpersonnel operating costs have skyrocketed. Schools are not immune to markets, including costs for products *and* the force of patrons who vote at the polls on local option school taxes and vote with their feet in other ways that cause enrollments and school revenues to move about, sometimes unfavorably. Intuition says that many districts cannot survive much more pressure, already having been forced into equipment and maintenance deferral, program and staff reductions, closure of attendance centers, consolidation of entire school districts, and even bankruptcies. Experience tells us that districts in some states have been faced with such actual scenarios, including academic or fiscal receivership under new and aggressive state and federal accountability laws. On the other hand, the lack of crisis in any given district on any given day should not make school leaders feel that there is no need to critically examine spending patterns and long-term fiscal health. In this era of social and economic unrest, education is obligated to examine itself carefully, which may include admitting that it is too easy to obtain and spend tax dollars without asking hard questions about efficiency and effectiveness of school operations. All school districts would do well to recognize the danger of the flip side of the more-money-is-better argument; that is, if there are no indisputable data to predict an increase in achievement for each additional dollar invested, neither are there clear data to support a view that fewer dollars would spark a corresponding drop in achievement. In other words, less money is a reasonable option for many people, especially those who strongly champion alternatives to public education.

On balance, however, few schools are faced with excess funds, and most schools are not faced with financial ruin, although money has become more difficult to secure and its distribution increasingly more contentious. But on the other hand, it is a stark reality that accountability, both achievement based and fiscal efficiency driven, has become a powerful weapon in the hands of state legislatures, as states have demanded sweeping reforms and as courts have ruled on a wide array of issues under the aegis of equal education. All these events serve to underscore fierce competition for fiscal resources and an increasingly fragmented society that is unwilling to silently pour vast sums of new money into schools in exchange for the lofty and imprecise educational jargon of the past.[19]

---

19   See, e.g., Allan Odden and Sarah Archibald, *Reallocating Resources: How to Boost Student Achievement Without Asking for More* (Thousand Oaks, CA: Corwin Press, 2001). Odden and Archibald argue rather persuasively that significant new resources will not be forthcoming, as there is a formidable sentiment at policy-making levels that all the necessary resources are now in place—it is a matter of better and more responsible utilization. To secure the seriousness of this claim, they argue that policy makers expect student proficiency to reach high standards as defined by the National Assessment of Educational Progress (NAEP), where current proficiency is pegged at only 25%. Odden and Archibald believe that policy makers expect proficiency to reach as high as 90%—a staggering task when realizing that an increase to only 50% would require doubling educational productivity from today's performance standard. As the authors put it, these are ambitious goals, all in a context that expects this outcome with no great influx of new resources.

WHERE PUBLIC SCHOOLS MAY BE HEADED

At the outset of this chapter, we drew attention to several important concepts. First, we admitted to certain strong biases, arguing that no one could expect us to offer a compelling defense for why public school funding should be scaled back. We also revealed our personal attitudes for a moment, admitting we deeply believe that public schools are America's finest hope, although our view quickly proved utilitarian in that we see education as the key to preserving American economic and social prosperity, including our own personal prospects. We also said we would be straightforward, presenting a view of money and schools that refuses to approve the shrillness of either political left or right, although in this chapter we focused heavily on presenting the arguments that clamor from various political angles. In fact, that is an appropriate point to make now: Our view of schools and money was well expressed by Saul Alinsky when he said, "It is a world not of angels, but of angles."[20] Although we strongly support a tolerant world in which everyone truly cares for everyone else, we are realists who know well that schools, money, and politics are indivisible—altogether too often along very selfish lines.

These realities affect what we see as we look to the future and wonder where public schools may be headed. We return to this theme in the final chapter in some greater detail, and we continue this line of thinking in Chapter 2 when we consider the broad historical trends that have led to how we currently fund education in the 50 states. But as we prepare to look more specifically at the operational elements of schools and money in upcoming chapters, we are convinced that schools—through their leaders—must do a much better job of communicating strategic plans, including voicing clear budget goals and processes, to an increasingly critical and vocal public. Make no mistake: patrons have the power to cause many changes in schools, and although they have always had that power, it is a weapon that only recently has been developed with sophistication. And it should not be forgotten that today's clients are tomorrow's taxpayers. In other words, schools must begin to promote their virtues, take the lead in performance accountability, and engage their constituents where they are—a theme that runs through this book. If public schools fail, it is clear where education is headed—into a world that includes ever-expanding alternatives to public schools, with loss in support for public education of every kind.

---

20   Saul Alinsky, *Rules for Radicals* (New York: Random House, 1971), 13.

pointcounterpoint

Point

The lack of adequate funding for public schools has long hampered progress in student achievement. Everyone knows that money matters in schools. If elected officials and private citizens are frustrated by declining test scores, the right answer is to step up to the plate and spend for education—in other words, to remain the world's leader requires spending for schools at the level of other advanced nations.

Counterpoint

Only five years after enactment of *No Child Left Behind*, the president announced in his State of the Union address that NCLB has worked because reading and math scores are at all-time highs and achievement gaps are closing. According to critics, however, insufficient funding has been aimed at reform. If critics are right, NCLB should not have produced such results. As a consequence, federal and state governments should be reluctant to pour more resources into schools because reform is not nearly so resource dependent as critics wish to claim.

Questions

♦ What has happened to both funding and achievement levels in your own state and school district since enactment of recent federal education reforms?

♦ In your own view, why do you think student achievement has increased in recent years?

♦ Do any arguments presented by either side fail to make sense? Why?

CASE STUDY

As the newly hired high school principal in your district, you were surprised when the superintendent called you into her office to talk about student achievement profiles. As the conversation progressed, you learned that two previously enthusiastic school board members had raised red flags at last night's board meeting about the district's upcoming special election, in which local voters would be asked to approve an increase in property taxes to fund program improvements throughout the district. Important to those plans were the following: that the district's standardized achievement test scores were among the state's best; that the district's fourth graders were ranked third in the state on National Assessment of Educational Progress (NAEP) mathematics assessments; that the district's eighth graders ranked first in the state on NAEP reading assessments; that last year the district's high school posted a mean SAT writing score 47 points above the national mean; and that more than 50% of the district's graduates completed college degrees within four years after high school. The superintendent indicated that she was impressed with these achievements, but followed up with a discussion that two board members had been cornered by citizens who were forming a taxpayer organization and had begun asking questions about current levels of school funding, dollar amounts to be generated by the proposed tax increase, intended uses of those monies, and how funding levels in their home district compares to surrounding districts and to statewide averages.

At that point, the superintendent pulled out a graph that the taxpayer group had provided to the two now-nervous board members. She indicated that the initial evidence showed local district spending had far outstripped the Consumer Price Index for more than a decade. She added that the taxpayer group had promised more charts by month's end showing that the district's property taxes were already the highest in a ten-county area and sixth highest in the state. She concluded with the observation that both board members were powerful business owners in the community and had complained, albeit privately, about high taxes and that she feared these data might convince other board members to also rethink their commitment to the upcoming tax referendum. The bottom line, she confessed, was how to protect the district's strategic goals in the face of data that showed no urgency to increase spending and might even boomerang into a grassroots attempt to sharply reduce local taxes.

The superintendent finally explained your anticipated role. True, she said, the district's referendum planning activities had included some analysis of how new tax dollars would be spent on programs. But she added that the district had had a very long history of approving tax increases and had never had to defend its goals. Given these new developments, the superintendent had embarked on a fast track to charge each school principal with developing a set of action-specific, outcome-oriented plans that would justify the tax increase and—importantly—identify the programmatic damage resulting from a failed referendum. Although the vote was still four months away, moving ahead now was important in that significant time would be needed to carry the message to the board and the community.

Below is a set of questions. As you respond, consider the context of this chapter and apply your new knowledge to the situation:

Questions

- ◆ What are your overall observations about the community in this case study?
- ◆ What questions do you anticipate will be raised by the community's skeptics?
- ◆ What data will be needed to defend new resources in a community like this one?
- ◆ How will you go about carrying out your charge?
- ◆ How does this community's experience compare to your own place of residence?

FOLLOW-UP ACTIVITIES

+ Write a brief reflection paper in which you identify your personal beliefs and values about what schools are capable of doing. Present your reflection in class, and discuss your views in relationship to other students.

+ Interview five educational stakeholders in your community on their attitudes about money and schools. Draw these persons from various walks in life: for example, a school board member, a business owner, a teacher, a member of the clergy, an administrator, a retired person, a student, a local elected official, and so on.

+ Talk to the person(s) in your school district who are responsible for assessing school performance. This might include central office and school-site personnel such as directors of assessment or curriculum, principals, counselors, and so forth. Ask about district or school performance profiles and trends and determine how the district and individual schools go about raising student achievement levels. Ask if any formal attempt is made to link money and achievement, and, if so, how.

+ Develop a list of the 25 most influential or powerful persons in your community. Profile these influencers, identifying why you included them on your list. Describe their attitudes toward money and schools and state the basis for your thinking. Bring your list to class and reach consensus on your community's power structure.

+ Research newspapers in your community for the last year, tracing the general attitude toward schools. Especially look for reporting on school funding or school performance data. Try to identify the general attitude of the press, the issues deemed newsworthy, and any community opinions you can glean. Use your findings to estimate your community's support level for education.

WEB RESOURCES

American Association of School Administrators: www.aasa.org
American Federation of Teachers: www.aft.org
Council of Chief State School Officers: www.ccsso.org/
Education Commission of the States: www.ecs.org
National Association of State Boards of Education: www.nasbe.org
National Center on Education and the Economy: www.ncee.org
National Center for Education Statistics: www.nces.ed.gov
National Conference of State Legislatures: www.ncsl.org
National Education Association: www.nea.org
National Governors Association, www.nga.org
National School Boards Association: www.nsba.org
U.S. Department of Education: www.ed.gov

RECOMMENDED READINGS

Anthony, Patricia, and Stephen L. Jacobson, eds. American Education Finance Association. Annual Yearbook. *Helping At-Risk Students: What are the Educational and Financial Costs?* Newbury Park, CA: Corwin, 1992.

Benson, Charles S. *The Cheerful Prospect: A Statement on the Future of Public Education.* Boston: Houghton-Mifflin, 1965.

Berne, Robert, and Lawrence O. Picus, eds. American Education Finance Association. Annual Yearbook. *Outcome Equity in Education.* Thousand Oaks, CA: Corwin, 1994.

Chaikind, Stephen, and William J. Fowler, eds. American Education Finance Association. Annual Yearbook. *Education Finance in the New Millennium.* New York: Eye On Education, 2001.

Chubb, John E., and Terry M. Moe. *Politics, Markets, and America's Schools.* Washington, DC: Brookings Institution, 1990.

Coleman, James S., Ernst Campbell, Carol Hobson, James McPartland, Alexander Mood, Frederic Weinfeld, and Robert York. *Equality of educational opportunity.* Washington, DC: U.S. Government Printing Office, 1966.

Crampton, Faith E., and Terry N. Whitney. "The Relationship Between Educational Expenditures and Student Achievement: When Does Money Matter?" An Education Partners Working Paper of the Foundation for State Legislatures. Denver, CO and Washington, DC: National Conference of State Legislatures, 1996.

DeMoss, Karen, and Kenneth K. Wong, eds. American Education Finance Association. Annual Yearbook. *Money, Politics, and Law: Intersections and Conflicts in the Provision of Educational Opportunity.* New York: Eye On Education, 2004.

Gardner, James W. *Excellence: Can We Be Equal and Excellent Too?* New York: Harper & Row, 1961.

Jacobson, Stephen L., and Robert Berne, eds. American Education Finance Association. Annual Yearbook. *Reforming Education: The Emerging Systemic Approach.* Thousand Oaks, CA: Corwin, 1993.

Kozol, Jonathan. *Death at an Early Age.* New York: Penguin Books, 1967.

Kozol, Jonathan. *Savage Inequalities.* New York: HarperCollins, 1992.

Levin, Henry M., and Patrick J. McEwan, eds. American Education Finance Association. Annual Yearbook. *Cost-effectiveness and Educational Policy.* New York: Eye On Education, 2002.

Picus, Lawrence O., and James L. Wattenbarger, eds. American Education Finance Association. Annual Yearbook. *Where Does the Money Go? Resource Allocation in Elementary and Secondary Schools.* Thousand Oaks, CA: Corwin, 1995.

Plecki, Margaret L., and David H. Monk, eds. American Education Finance Association. Annual Yearbook. *School Finance and Teacher Quality: Exploring the Connections.* New York: Eye On Education, 2003.

Stiefel, Leanna, Amy Ellen Schwartz, Ross Rubenstein, and Jeffrey Zabel, eds. American Education Finance Association. Annual Yearbook. *Measuring School Performance and Efficiency: Implications for Practice and Research.* New York: Eye On Education, 2005.

Theobald, Neil D., and Betty Malen, eds. American Education Finance Association. Annual Yearbook. *Balancing Local Control and State Responsibility for K-12 Education.* New York: Eye On Education, 2000.

Thompson, David C., R. Craig Wood, and David S. Honeyman. *Fiscal Leadership for Schools: Concepts and Practices.* New York: Longman, 1994.

Ward, James G., and Patricia Anthony, eds. American Education Finance Association. Annual Yearbook. *Who Pays for Student Diversity? Populations Changes and Educational Policy.* Newbury Park, CA: Corwin, 1991.

Zimmerman, Jonathan. Whose America? *Culture wars in the Public Schools.* Cambridge, MA: Harvard College, 2002.

FUNDING SCHOOLS: A POLICY PERSPECTIVE

THE CHALLENGE

Citizens of Western nations will more readily support their government if its policies are seen by most people as benevolent, and if it makes moderate fiscal demands. In such circumstances governance approximates market exchange; taxes, as Justice Holmes said, are the price citizens pay for civilized government. A long history of punitive taxation...will have long-lasting effects on citizens' attitudes...remembering past injustice, reluctant taxpayers search for ways to evade.

Webber & Wildavsky (1986)

CHAPTER DRIVERS

At the close of this chapter you will have reflected upon these questions:

♦ What is the scope of education finance in America?

♦ How are education and economics related?

♦ What is the structure of school governance in America?

♦ Where do schools derive financial support?

♦ What constitutes adequate and equitable funding for schools?

♦ Can schools at once serve economics, equality, productivity, and liberty?

A MORE EXPANSIVE VIEW

We ended the previous chapter with a warning that there is a growing belief in the United States that public education's performance is at least lackluster, if not suffering a crisis of confidence. Clearly, research on linkages between student achievement and school funding levels is mixed, but there is more to the issue than pure economics. At the same time, it is never as simple as a "bottom line," because the whole discussion revolves around fiscal considerations in tandem with other important social principles that cannot be ignored if we are to sustain a civil democracy.

We need to widen our discussion to other issues that both complicate and drive how school leaders should act (and react) in today's intensely sociopolitical climate. The benefits and costs of education are never as easy as looking only at growth in revenue and spending for schools—that is, we must also give time to looking at the broader scope of funding schools from a *policy* perspective. The concept of *investment* in education, versus an attitude of *expenditure control*, is important too because spending for schools should take into account the value of education to the economy and to society itself. Certainly, a key part of spending on children's educational needs is affected by whether federal, state, and local governments are appropriately sharing the duty to fund schools. And of course, issues of adequate and equitable funding have become thorns in the side of educators, politicians, and taxpayers alike. In essence, then, the debate about money for schools is more than just thinking about good test scores: it also includes considering the ethics of civic responsibility, at least as long as we wish to believe in opportunity, equality, and liberty for everyone.

WHAT IS THE SCOPE OF EDUCATION FINANCE IN AMERICA?

Every text on funding schools in the last 50 years has remarked that education is big business. Although we are accustomed to hearing about huge costs relating to every aspect of society, the enormity of demands of modern life on human and fiscal resources is still shocking (Fig. 2.1, p. 25). Most of us know our nation is deeply in debt, but the sum of $9 trillion estimated for Fiscal Year 2007 (up from $7.4 trillion in the last edition of this book) seems unfathomable. This abstract number takes on more meaning when restated to say that the national debt has increased by $1.49 billion per day since 2006, and it becomes personally meaningful when it is understood that *each* American citizen's share of the national debt hit $28,423 in that year (Fig. 2.2, p. 26). At the same time, Americans raised vast sums for public schools—estimated at more than $500 billion in 2006. In contrast to the national debt, however, funding for schools is mostly paid on a current basis, meaning that revenues must cover expenditures. Inasmuch as most government spending goes to domestic and international programs, including schools, the scope of public financial sacrifice in the United States is sizable. Under these conditions, it is not surprising that Chapter 1 was entitled *Schools, Values, and Money*.

Figure 2.1. How Congress Spends Your Money: 2004–2007

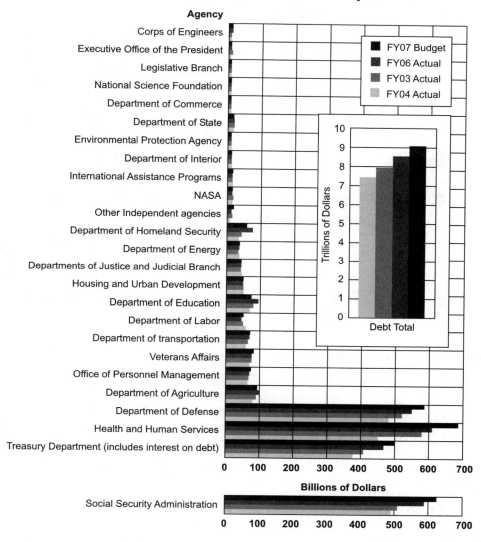

Source: www.federalbudget.com

Figure 2.2. Federal Government Debt per Person 2006

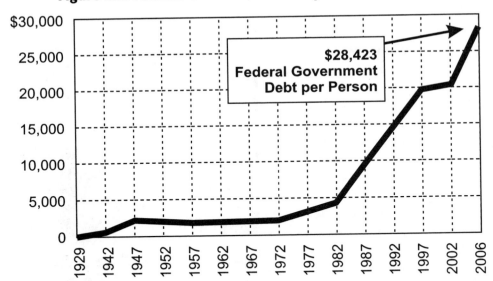

Source: Department of Debt, U.S. Treasury. *Grandfather Economic Report*. Available at: http://mwhodges.home.att.net.

Revenue Growth for Schools

Skyrocketing growth in school revenue has been long-standing, even in earlier times when needs were simpler. Although consistent data collection has not taken place until recently, revenues from 1920 to 2003 reflect the increasing importance of education to our nation (Fig. 2.3, p. 27). In 1920, total revenues for K–12 schools were $970 million. By 1930, revenue had increased to $2.09 billion (+215%). A useful observation is that despite the huge costs of World War I, school revenue rose steadily, partly as a result of the need for training a fighting force and partly to postwar prosperity.

Growth in school revenue experienced only brief lags over the ensuing years. The first 30 years of the last century saw rapid growth, with only the Great Depression forcing visible slowing of revenues. Funding nonetheless grew from 1930 to 1940, despite severe economic times following the stock market crash of 1929. From 1930 to 1940, school revenue grew only slightly from $2.09 to $2.26 billion (+8%), yet the increase was remarkable in light of the economic horrors in the nation, leaving the conclusion that school revenues have been stable, even in times of economic distress.

Figure 2.3. Summary of K–12 Revenues 1920–2003

Revenues for Public Elementary and Secondary Schools by Source of Funds

School Year	Total (000s)	% Federal	% State	% Local	School Year	Total (000s)	% Federal	% State	% Local
1919-20	$970,121	0.3	16.5	83.2	1977-78	$81,443,160	9.4	43.0	47.6
1929-30	2,088,557	0.4	16.9	82.7	1978-79	87,994,143	9.8	45.6	44.6
1939-40	2,260,527	1.8	30.3	68.0	1979-80	96,881,165	9.8	46.8	43.4
1941-42	2,416,580	1.4	31.4	67.1	1980-81	105,949,087	9.2	47.4	43.4
1943-44	2,604,322	1.4	33.0	65.6	1981-82	110,191,257	7.4	47.6	45.0
1945-46	3,059,845	1.4	34.7	63.9	1982-83	117,497,502	7.1	47.9	45.0
1947-48	4,311,534	2.8	38.9	58.3	1983-84	126,055,419	6.8	47.8	45.4
1949-50	5,437,044	2.9	39.8	57.3	1984-85	137,294,678	6.6	48.9	44.4
1951-52	6,423,816	3.5	38.6	57.9	1985-86	149,127,779	6.7	49.4	43.9
1953-54	7,866,852	4.5	37.4	58.1	1986-87	158,523,693	6.4	49.7	43.9
1955-56	9,686,677	4.6	39.5	55.9	1987-88	169,561,974	6.3	49.5	44.1
1957-58	12,181,513	4.0	39.4	56.6	1988-89	192,016,374	6.2	47.8	46.0
1959-60	14,746,618	4.4	39.1	56.5	1989-90	208,547,573	6.1	47.1	46.8
1961-62	17,527,707	4.3	38.7	56.9	1990-91	223,340,537	6.2	47.2	46.7
1963-64	20,544,182	4.4	39.3	56.3	1991-92	234,581,384	6.6	46.4	47.0
1965-66	25,356,858	7.9	39.1	53.0	1992-93	247,626,168	7.0	45.8	47.2
1967-68	31,903,064	8.8	38.5	52.7	1993-94	260,159,468	7.1	45.2	47.8
1969-70	40,266,923	8.0	39.9	52.1	1994-95	273,149,449	6.8	46.8	46.4
1970-71	44,511,292	8.4	39.1	52.5	1995-96	287,702,844	6.6	47.5	45.9
1971-72	50,003,645	8.9	38.3	52.8	1996-97	305,065,192	6.6	48.0	45.4
1972-73	52,117,930	8.7	39.7	51.6	1997-98	325,925,708	6.8	48.4	44.8
1973-74	58,230,892	8.5	41.4	50.1	1998-99	347,377,993	7.1	48.7	44.2
1974-75	64,445,239	9.0	42.0	49.0	1999-2000	372,943,802	7.3	49.5	43.2
1975-76	71,206,073	8.9	44.4	46.7	2000-01	401,355,325	7.3	49.7	43.0
1976-77	75,332,532	8.8	43.2	48.0	2001-02	419,501,976	7.9	49.2	42.9
					2002-03	440,157,299	8.5	48.7	42.8

Source: United States Department of Education, NCES. *Digest of Education Statistics 2005.* (Washington, DC: United States Department of Education, 2006).

The surge in money for schools resumed with the recovery spurred by World War II. From 1940 to 1950, revenue rose to $5.4 billion (+241%). The pattern continued from 1950 to 1960, aided by the space race and triggered by the launch of the Soviet satellite Sputnik and giving rise to a national education agenda under the *National Defense Education Act* (NDEA) in 1958. NDEA led to unequaled growth in school funding, as fears of a Soviet menace led Congress to react with massive federal funding directed at math and science education and fueling an era in which an information economy would become the replacement for a fading industrial economy.

National awareness of global issues brought about by Sputnik was accompanied by rapid change in the social order of the United States, especially between 1950 and 1970. As the nation moved out of rural America to become an economic and political world power toughened by economic depression and war, social problems were reshaping the nation and its schools. Two events forever changed education and its fiscal patterns. The first was *Brown v. Board of Education*,[1] when the U.S. Supreme Court ruled that racial segregation as "separate but equal" was not allowed under the federal Constitution. The second event was the social revolt of the 1960s, typified by the War on Poverty under President Lyndon Johnson. *Brown* reshaped the fundamental nature of public schools via desegregation, with massive costs to taxpayers, while the War on Poverty marked the beginning of a vast list of federal entitlements to schools. Although the federal government had long tried to aid schools, these two events sparked a revolution that would alter the face of education in America. Although these events did not account for all growth in school funding during that time, the 1950 to 1970 era remains unmatched as revenues grew to $14.7 billion (+271%) by 1960 and to $44.5 billion by 1970 (+819% more than 1950). Although inflation mattered, revenue grew at historic rates during these years of social progress and economic prosperity.

The Great Depression proved that school funding responds to economic conditions. Yet short of world wars or total economic ruin, school monies have shown great resilience without fail. The era from 1970 to 1980 was marked by more social reform and high inflation, as many states had their systems for funding schools ruled unconstitutional and as costs soared due to inflation. By 1980, revenues hit nearly $106 billion (+238%). Although public education's share of gross domestic product (GDP) began wavering in 1980, revenue growth was continued because massive redistribution of wealth and funding increases followed the court-ordered restructuring of many state school finance systems. The resiliency of school revenues was also apparent in the economic slump of the 1980s, more than doubling to $223 billion in 1990, and continuing throughout the roaring economy of the 1990s to more than $401 billion in 2001 and topping $440 billion for fiscal year 2003.

Although these data suggest that education has prospered, another view is worth considering as there are at least three factors that may have limited schools' ability to sustain or increase services to children. First, the data speak only to national totals, with each state facing different social and economic situations tied to the state's fiscal abilities and voter preferences. Second, some data suggest that schools' ability to serve may have been weakened despite fiscal growth, particularly during the economic downturn of the new millennium and inasmuch as test scores have lagged despite more resources. Third, some educators argue that funding increases may wrongly portray reality because schools are undergoing vast demographic change—an expensive population is now in school that must be served if the nation is to flourish. An embarrassment of riches for schools thus seems open to sharply divided interpretation.

---

1   374 U.S. 483 at 493 (1954).

Based on reams of data, both sides have held strong views that make real solutions difficult. Two points emerge, however, that are key to an accurate view of the social and economic context of money and schools. First, Americans have long regarded education as the key to economic and social mobility, as they have fought hard for good schools under strong local control. Second, Americans have historically directed vast resources to schools, a fact that underscores how much they value education because people resist paying for what does not have personal meaning. But as critics have noted, the United States now sees itself in a crisis of increasing costs and declining educational productivity. So it is wise to ask whether the public will continue funding a school system that some say is losing ground. As a result, we should consider views that see schools as an investment, rather than as a failing business throwing good money after bad when other educational choices are readily available.

HOW ARE EDUCATION AND ECONOMICS RELATED?

Debate over the value of education has not been limited to recent fears about student test scores. For many years, economists have held that education makes a positive contribution to national economic and social wellbeing, and there have been attempts to quantify the value of schooling. The work of economists is helpful to anyone who faces criticism when trying to make a case for adequate and equitable school funding.

Economics Defined

Although it is hard to reduce a complex field like economics to a brief discussion, it is useful to think of economics as the production, allocation, and consumption of goods and services for the satisfaction of human needs and wants. Economics is interested in goods and services in relation to supply and demand. Rogers and Ruchlin captured it well: "Economics is concerned with two primary phenomena, desires and resources. The confrontation is brought into being…because desires are infinite, whereas resources are finite."[2] Economics in a society where commodities must be bought means that some goods and services are scarce or unequally available, whereas others are plentiful and less valued.

This definition is a problem for a capitalist democracy like the United States. Capitalism needs markets, whereas democracy expects equal access to essential commodities that aid freedom and promote economic productivity and social mobility. The problem arises because public education in a capitalist democracy must be purchased with tax dollars, raising questions about how to fairly fund and distribute education to people in different circumstances.

---

2   Daniel C. Rogers and Hirsch S. Ruchlin. *Economics and Education* (New York: The Free Press, 1971), 5.

Education as an Economic and Social Good

Because economics deals with goods and services and the supply of commodities to individuals and society, it has a direct relationship to education. Among the most important relationships are that education produces human capital, contributes to economic health, and drives the economic and social welfare of entire nations. These benefits accrue at individual and societal levels—as such, they are central to understanding whether education is an investment or an expense.

Education and Human Capital

A series of national reports starting in the 1980s on the condition of education serves as a reminder of the enduring belief that education produces human capital. Economists have explored the link between economic prosperity and education, holding that although linkages are not fully explained, education and economics are highly interdependent. Renowned economists, including John Kenneth Galbraith, Milton Friedman, and Theodore Schultz, have found a positive relationship, arguing that the historic elements of land, capital, and labor must be expanded to include human capital. Schultz captured this well when he said, "Human capital has the fundamental attributes of the basic economic concept of capital; namely, it is a source of future satisfactions, or of future earnings, or both of them. What makes it human capital is the fact that it becomes an integral part of the person."[3]

By this view, education takes on real worth. Whereas ownership of land, growth in capital assets, and costs of unskilled labor were the old bases of economic analysis, the addition of human capital views the costs of unskilled labor as a true *cost*, whereas the expense of creating skilled workers becomes an *investment*. Because capital is used to create new wealth, human capital is an important step in knowing whether education is an expense or an investment because creating highly skilled workers becomes key to stimulating economic growth.

Education and National Economic Health

The justification for capitalist society is freedom to gain private wealth by competing in a free market. The justification for democratic society is based partly on the abuses in a survival-of-the-fittest economy where wealth grows unchecked. Thus a capitalist market in a democratic society demands controls to prevent extreme wealth imbalances. Applied to education, schooling in a free market would favor only those able to buy it. The ultimate test of the idea of education as human capital has played out in the United States, where one of the most powerful wealth generators has been universal access to public education so that more people can create a greater store of private wealth (education), and, in turn, sell their skills in an open market at higher prices. This constraint of freedom reflects a belief that education results in wide individual and societal benefits. Rather than the negative effects of competition and high

---

3   Theodore Schultz. "The Human Capital Approach to Education," in *Economic Factors Affecting the Financing of Education,* eds. Roe L. Johns and others (Gainesville, FL: National Educational Finance Project, 1970), 31.

labor costs hurting production, distribution of education at public expense is seen to create a stronger economy, a higher quality of life for individuals and families, and a more stable society.

Belief in a link between economics and education has been strong in our nation's history, especially over the last century. In 1918, the Commission on Reorganization of Secondary Education declared the need to prepare students for work as one of its *Seven Cardinal Principles.* In 1938, the Educational Policies Commission named economic efficiency among its aims for schools. In 1951, the *Ten Imperative Needs of Youth,* issued by the National Association of Secondary School Principals, gave emphasis to job training. In 1955, the White House Conference on Education promoted various goals for schools, among which good work habits were prominent. Also in 1955, the U.S. Chamber of Commerce said, "People who have a good education produce more goods, earn more money, buy and consume more goods, read more magazines and newspapers, are more active in civic and national affairs, enjoy a higher standard of living, and in general, contribute more to the economy." More recently, the many national reports on education have confirmed a deep belief in the direct link between economic and social productivity and schools.

Whether there is proof of a link between education and national economic health seems less arguable when comparing developed and underdeveloped nations. Few would argue that education widely disbursed does not aid economic and social goals. As the World Bank noted long ago, "The emphasis in low income countries is on development of low-cost basic education... In middle-income countries, where first-level education is already widely available, educational quality is emphasized and with it the expansion of facilities to meet the needs of an increasingly sophisticated economy...As absorptive capacity...grows, the priority shifts toward providing higher level technical skills, as well as developing skills in science, technology, information processing, and research."[4] No defense of this claim is needed, as Americans have long recognized that education feeds itself as an industry by creating jobs and feeds the job market by creating more and better products and the consumerism to acquire those commodities. If human capital development was a first step in seeing the investment represented by education, linking schools and national economic health was a second step because the economy would stumble without the demand education creates for itself.

Education and Individual Benefits

Another way of knowing whether education is an investment or an expense rests in examining the individual benefits of education. Individuals are prime beneficiaries of schooling because others are excluded from direct and equal use of each person's unique skills. Individuals benefit by enjoying greater social mobility, better pay and higher status, and more cultural opportunities. Benefits spill over to society too because salaries are returned to the economy as affluence leads to more consumerism

---

4   Habte Aklilu. *Education and Development: Views from the World Bank* (Washington, DC: World Bank, 1983), 8.

and higher lifestyles. This yields other benefits, as better-educated people are healthier, have less unemployment, are more open to change, and work more efficiently.

Individual benefits are dramatic. Figure 2.4 shows that a person with more years of schooling enjoys higher wages, whereas less education leads to a lifetime of lower returns. The gap is large; in 2005, for example, four or more years of college led to median weekly earnings nearly 2.5 times higher than for a high school dropout and nearly a 1.5 differential between a high school graduate and a dropout. Projecting such differences onto a lifetime of work, education clearly has a powerful impact on individuals.

Figure 2.4. Education Pays: 2005

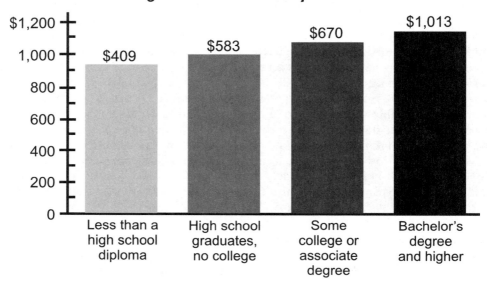

Median weekly earnings of full-time wage and salary workers 25 years of age and over.

Source: www.bls.gov/cps/labor2005/home.htm

Social and Economic Efficiencies of Education

Our discussion of *spillover* effects shows how illogical it is to claim that educational opportunity does not benefit all of society. People who claim schooling is a commodity that should be free of social controls are claiming that education does not merit equal distribution because they see it as solely individual in value. These people likely agree that a minimum level of education is needed, but they miss a fourth step in evaluating whether education is an investment or an expense by not seeing that society and the economy would suffer far greater costs were it not for efficiencies inherent to public education.

The *exclusion principle* is the basis for arguing against broad social services in favor of the view that high spending for schools is inefficient. As with everything, there is a grain of truth within, and it rests in whether social spending (including for schools) yields a positive return or whether it drains off money to pay for low achievement scores. This view ignores that social services are intended to prevent even greater social misfortune and that spending for public aims is actually more efficient because it would fall to charity to pay such costs absent taxation, but that it is inefficient (even impossible) to provide all such services on a charitable basis. A couple of illustrations make this clearer.

The exclusion principle sees individuals as the sole beneficiaries of an expenditure or a good or service. Implicit is the belief that exclusion is at least neutral in its impact on others and—importantly—economically efficient for the recipient. In other words, for the exclusion principle to work, depriving others of a benefit cannot result in great harm, and the cost should be attractive to the beneficiary. However, highway taxes are a good example of the illogic arising from strict application of the exclusion principle. It might be argued that failure to provide public roads would not cause unreasonable harm to others. But even if we accept that doubtful premise, applying the exclusion principle to roads leads to economic *inefficiencies* as most people could not provide their own roads because of prohibitive cost. Analogously, depending on charity to provide critical social services is automatically inefficient and introduces the risk that society would stop providing services if the force of taxation were absent. In other words, many critical services are more efficiently produced in the public sector at a relatively minimal individual cost, so that small sacrifices by many make up a collective benefit that otherwise would be very difficult to provide and would be seriously missed.

Like many tax-funded services, education's efficiencies compete against other ideas in a capitalist democracy. For example, arguments to privatize schools to improve performance and enhance individual freedoms weigh against proof that education does not neatly fit the exclusion principle. Critics falter when they claim students are the sole beneficiaries of schooling because spillover in social mobility, higher pay, socioeconomic status, more employment, cultural opportunities, and other byproducts show that taxing and spending for schools improves everyone's wellbeing. Likewise, democracy requires an informed citizenry; that is, because most people could not privately pay for education, equality among individuals would vary greatly absent public schooling. For many reasons, the benefit of investing in public schools cannot be efficiently gained by any exclusionary mechanism.

Returns on Educational Investment

In Chapter 1, we examined a more skeptical view of spending for schools, allowing that critics have had much ammunition when attacking school productivity. Achievement *is* a formidable challenge, and it *is* sensible for taxpayers to ask if pouring more money into schools is efficient when apparently higher-performing alternatives exist.

In this chapter we've taken the opposite view, arguing that although school revenues and expenditures are vast, there is an investment return that test scores overlook. Our discussion has focused on broad concepts, and we should now consider studies that have taken a deeper look at the cost-to-benefit question. The field of economics has provided studies of returns on educational investment that can be grouped into at least two kinds. The first group looks at relationships between education and economic growth, while the second examines returns on investment to individuals and society. It is useful to think of the latter as rate-of-return studies.

Education and Economic Growth

We said earlier that Americans have long believed in education's impact on personal economic prosperity. Although the student achievement literature has been unable to show the level of return that critics seek, a few classic studies have assessed the contribution of school spending to economic growth. These studies generally have examined changes in gross domestic product (GDP) to estimate the impact of education (i.e., the added value of human capital).

Questioning returns on investment in a society that currently provides about a half-trillion dollars annually for public K–12 schools is reasonable. Answering such questions is more difficult. Although economists like to work with exact quantification, they are sometimes forced to settle for estimates. Because no way exists by which to measure exact output of educational investment relative to dollar inputs, economists have estimated residual effects in the economy.

A *residual* effect can be likened to the analogy of a sum and its parts, where a series of values are added to reach the conclusion that the whole is greater than the sum of its parts. Although application of that analogy to economics is not exactly correct, it illustrates the approach taken by some economists in assessing the dynamic contribution of education to the economy. Economics has usually considered growth to be a function of changes in land, labor, and volume of physical capital. If one variable changes, production will change in response: that is, changes in GDP depend on changes in land, capital, and labor. Where the equation fails is in relation to changes in the "educational stock" of employees (i.e., human capital) because labor traditionally has not included a value for workers' qualifications. Failure to account for human capital has resulted in an unexplained residual effect. In other words, solving the equation results in the analogy of a sum and its parts, as land, labor, and capital sum to *less* than 100% of dynamic increase in GDP, with the unexplained residual being human capital.

Formal studies have supported the concept of residual effect. Schultz argued that people acquire a stock of knowledge and skills that is useless until put to work. As worker knowledge grows, productivity increases. Schultz examined data on the labor force, looking at distribution of education by years of schooling and the cost at each level after adjusting for increases in length of the school year over time.[5] He found that the "stock of education" as measured by the cost of producing that same education had increased from $180 billion (adjusted to 1956 prices) in 1929 to $535 billion in 1957. He also found that only $69 billion in costs could be tied to the 38% growth in labor force size. From this, he imputed that the remaining $286 billion represented a net increase in the stock of education. At the same time, labor income grew $71 bil-

5   Theodore Schultz. "Education and Economic Growth," in *Social Forces Influencing American Education, 16th Yearbook of the National Society of Education*, ed. N.B. Henry (Chicago: University of Chicago Press, 1961), 63.

lion beyond where it would be if earnings had stayed constant at 1929 levels. The $71 billion was termed residual. After annualizing returns, Schultz held that the increase in education per person from 1929 to 1957 explained 36% to 70% of residual economic growth—in essence, Schultz concluded that the economy improved by 36% to 70% as a consequence of investing in schools.

A second approach is seen in Denison's classic work as he studied the impact of 20 variables in the United States from 1909 to 1957.[6] Using changes in worker age, gender, hours, and so on, he calculated increases in labor productivity and found a residual of 0.93%, with 0.67% of that amount attributable to education—a net effect attributing 23% of increased productivity to schooling. In a later study, Denison showed that increases in education explained 33% of growth in GDP from 1973 to 1981. A third Denison study was even more positive, in which he examined the economies of nine Western nations, concluding that the value of education is highest for the United States.

Rate-of-Return Studies

The impact of education can also be seen at smaller levels by considering the relative value of schooling at elementary, secondary, and postsecondary levels. These studies have followed two models: calculating the present discounted value of education, and individual rates of return for added schooling. Both methods imply that consumers' decisions about how much education to buy have an effect on personal income.

The *present-discounted-value* (PDV) method takes actual present value of schooling and multiplies by a discount rate to estimate its future value. PDV is like a price deflator to hold dollars constant for purchasing power over time. For example, the average teacher salary in 1970 in current dollars was $8,626. By 2006, the figure had risen to $50,932. Although factors like seniority and advanced degrees account for some of the increase, a large part of the change is a result of inflation. Holding prices constant and deflating salaries to the same year permits comparison of true gains or losses. The price deflator analogy helps in understanding the PDV method of assessing the worth of education to an individual.

The *individual rate-of-return* (IRR) method also has been used. Its advantage rests in not having to predict an accurate discount rate by using a zero interest rate: that is, what is education worth in *today's* market? The IRR looks at the cost of each level of education compared to benefits at each level. The principle is that the higher the expected income and the lower the cost, the higher the rate of return will be. Figure 2.4 (p. 32) earlier showed weekly earnings based on dropping out, completing high school, and several levels of college. It also showed that the differential is significant at each level of educational attainment. By such data, the rate of return is highly favorable.

Of course, the cost varies for different levels of education. Elementary schooling costs less, if for no other reason than facility costs are lower than for the specialized

---

6   Edward Denison, *The Sources of Economic Growth in the United States and the Alternatives Before Us* (New York: Committee for Economic Development, 1962).

program needs in high schools. But there are other costs for different levels of education that affect profitability of extra units of schooling. For instance, in more advanced nations child labor is nonexistent. Yet as children grow, the cost of education should include loss of earnings from being in school instead of in the workforce. Similarly, at postsecondary levels, costs are increased by tuition, subsistence, and so on. Additionally, more years of school do not yield uncapped earnings because career choice affects income. For example, a public school teacher with a doctorate degree will not match the income of a physician, although the value to society is at least equal. In other words, elementary, secondary, and postsecondary education have intrinsic traits affecting the ultimate rate of return.

Only a few studies have tested returns on elementary schooling. In more advanced nations, logic has held that there is a moral duty regardless of cost and that a minimum skill level is needed for employment. Studies have calculated high returns on elementary schooling, mostly because opportunity costs (foregone earnings) and actual costs (set off against a person gainfully employed) are nearly zero. Hansen found infinite returns,[7] and Hanoch argued for a 100% return.[8] Other studies vary widely; Schultz, rejecting the high return in most studies, held that return on elementary schooling was 35%.[9] Although lower than other studies, Schultz argued that the return is still high because it exceeded returns for investment in physical capital.

Far more studies have examined returns on secondary schooling. Returns have been lower than for elementary education, mostly because of opportunity costs. Becker studied returns in the twentieth century, finding an IRR for high school graduates of 16% in 1939, 20% in 1949, and 28% in 1958.[10] His estimates were close to Schultz's, who estimated the return on high school at 25%. Other studies have agreed, with the added note that human capital has grown at the same time.

Returns on postsecondary education are murkier. Career choice has a strong bearing on earnings, and the point of diminishing returns affects higher levels of education by reaching a point where more school does not yield more income. There is an argument that the United States is overinvested in higher education, creating a glut of overqualified people because the nation's job market cannot keep up with the supply of college graduates. Postsecondary studies show returns on undergraduate degrees varying by career field, with graduate degrees even more dependent on field. Yet despite variation, all returns on education are sizable because when all options are weighed, history shows that poorly educated people are left behind in a nation that has steadily escalated its social and economic standards at a dizzying pace.

---

7   Lee Hansen, "Total and Private Rates of Return to Investment in Schooling." *Journal of Political Economy* 71 (1963): 128–40.

8   Giora Hanoch. "An Economic Analysis of Earnings and Schooling." *Journal of Human Resources* 3 (1967): 310–29.

9   Schultz, "The Human Capital Approach to Education."

10   Gary Becker. *Human Capital: A Theoretical and Empirical Analysis, with Special Reference to Education.* (New York: National Bureau of Economic Research, 1964).

Education and Socioeconomic Investment

Arguments that many services are best served at public expense are well founded, especially from an efficiency perspective. Other benefits accrue too, including freedom, lower crime, less need for other public support, and aiding socioeconomic mobility. These benefits have led scholars to claim that society pays many such costs as a way to stem an adverse tide, while the "cost" of schools actually reverses the tide and pays long-term dividends.

At the most basic level, the greatest return on education is survival of democracy itself. Democracy may be described as government by consent, with the freedom to decide to be led and to decide for oneself the leaders to be chosen. These decisions are not made lightly because they require defenses against abuse: namely, a level of thinking and literacy to prevent class-based greed and to foster wise voter behavior. This view has been embraced by liberals and conservatives alike. Long ago, Adam Smith noted in *The Wealth of Nations*[11] that education is necessary to prevent people from becoming incapable of self-enlightenment and devoid of all charity; and Thomas Jefferson, a great champion of public schools, argued eloquently that the most basic needs of a free people include the ability to discern corruption and to choose leadership wisely.

The relationship between education, democracy, and self-reliance thus cannot be overestimated, and from these roots flow other benefits as people are empowered to productive lives. Much research, for example, points to reduced crime and welfare as a result of education. If the cost of schools is high, the cost of crime is higher because that money could have better uses. Economists and criminologists alike take a dim view of how society might misspend its resources, arguing that locking up two million Americans on any given day badly misses the investment mark when comparing the United States to other developed countries; that is, those nations most inclined to incarcerate their citizens typically engage in the lowest welfare spending, whereas those nations most inclined to support welfare spending typically have the lowest incarceration rates.[12] And it has long been widely known that far too many prison inmates are juveniles and therefore prime candidates for education, so that when the cost of education is compared to the cost of locking up young offenders, the loss to society is enormous. The data run in entangled directions: In 2006, the federal government spent $199 billion for payments to the poor, of which $36 billion (an increase of $21 billion since the last edition of this text) was for food stamps. The proposition is irrefutable—even the harshest critic should agree that money is better spent on education and job training because mopping up schools' failures will always be more counterproductive than spending upfront for good schools. Perhaps the greatest accolade to investing in education was stated by Marshall, as he said:

---

11 Adam Smith. *An Inquiry into the Nature and Causes of The Wealth of Nations.* (New York: Modern Library, 1937), 734–35.

12 See, for example, David Downes and Kirstine Hansen, "Welfare and Punishment in Comparative Perspective," in *Perspectives on Punishment. The Contours of Control*, eds. Sarah Armstrong and Leslie McAra (Oxford: Oxford University Press, 2006), 101–18.

We may then conclude that the wisdom of expending public and private funds on education is not to be measured by its direct fruits alone.... [O]ne new idea, such as Bessemer's chief invention, adds as much to England's productive power as the labour of a hundred thousand men.... All this spent during many years in opening the means of...education to the masses would be well paid for if it called out one more Newton or Darwin, Shakespeare or Beethoven.[13]

Whether society will continue to embrace such grand expressions seems highly questionable. Today's society is less willing to invest uncritically in schools, and the latest trends in education legislation seem more focused on a market model with a burning purpose to measure the direct fruits of investment. *No Child Left Behind* (NCLB) is the most current example of that questioning mode in that it presents a model that pays close homage to consumer preferences and with huge implications for how investment in schools occurs. The net sum is that all things change, and the ebb and flow of economic thought and purposes of schooling are meaningfully swayed by the times. At press time, our society has been undergoing decades-long radical change in how it sees money and schools, thereby raising the question of how schools have historically been financed and where it may all be headed—a question that requires some basic understanding of school governance structures.[14]

WHAT IS THE STRUCTURE OF SCHOOL GOVERNANCE IN AMERICA?

Americans accustomed to the vast educational system of our time may be surprised to learn that formal public education is a recent event in this country. Yet even ancient civilizations often had good education systems for their day. The ancient Greeks saw education as the cornerstone of democracy, holding that the mark of a free man was the ability to read, write, think, and speak. Americans today likely would argue that the nation's founders foresaw an entitlement to education when they declared that the right to life, liberty, and the pursuit of happiness are secure only in a nation governed by consent of an intelligent people. Surely, today's American would

---

13 Alfred Marshall. Education and Invention. In *Perspectives on the Economics of Education, ed.* C. S. Benson (Boston: Houghton Mifflin, 1963), 83.

14 Despite the views of some that education is in dire straits, it is the case that the United States has the luxury to engage self-criticism at a level unavailable in much of the world. One has only to consider the plight of developing nations to see the benefits of schooling. Nowhere is belief in the power of education more evident than at the United Nations Educational, Cultural, and Scientific Organization (UNESCO). Using its world conferences as a forum for massive educational initiatives in nearly 200 countries, UNESCO's ambitious goal of "Education For All By 2015" points up the vast unmet need worldwide. UNESCO's World Education Forum in 2000 analyzed progress on its "Education For All Assessment," which was the most in-depth evaluation in history of basic education services. The prognosis was grim, indicating that despite efforts since the first World Conference on Education for All a decade earlier, some 113 million children remained unschooled; nearly a billion adults—mostly women—were illiterate; and that the lack of qualified teachers and learning materials was the reality in many nations. For more on this topic, see www.unesco.org.

say, the nation's most precious documents have since the founding of the nation promised everyone the educational wherewithal for self-governance. Whether that guarantee was actually intended is not clear, but it is true that education resembling how we know schools today did *not* exist prior to the nineteenth century. This is not to say there were no schools, but the current nature of educational systems is in vivid contrast to the historic structure of schools in America.

Brief Historical Roots of American Education

Only a cursory understanding of American history is needed to picture the struggles of settlers in a vast and hostile wilderness. Simply surviving and creating a new way of life was hard enough without the problems of setting up broad government services. In the earliest days of our nation, little in the way of schooling occurred because settlers were too busy feeding themselves and ensuring their personal safety. And there was little motivation for schooling, as the skills needed to survive under these conditions had little to do with books.

Whenever schooling did occur in early America, it was the exclusive province of the home or church. But concern for education was evident early on, as the first school law was passed by the Massachusetts Legislature in 1642, requiring towns to see if children were being taught to read in order to understand religion and to learn a vocation. Formal interest began to grow, and in 1647 the *Ye Old Deluder Satan Act* was passed in that same state and was aimed at strengthening the teaching of morality to children by reading the *Bible*. As the colonies grew, compulsory education for morality gained popularity as Connecticut, Maine, New Hampshire, and Vermont all passed similar laws by 1720.

As nations move beyond survival mode, they seek higher order forms, such as formal education systems. Toward the end of the eighteenth century, interest in formal education had taken shape in most colonies. The Revolutionary War in 1776 had been hard, and the reasons for the war brought about new concern in a young nation that had chafed under British rule. Although education for morality had been the aim of early school laws, new concern emerged based on a call for enlightened government to secure the freedoms that had first led to war. Thomas Jefferson, the great champion of liberty, was among the loudest voices calling for an end to ignorance through education for the common people. In a radical shift from centuries of elitist political control, Jefferson argued that ordinary citizens must be taught to elect good leaders and to keep guard on government. These skills, he said, could only be developed by education for the commoner—a new idea in a world inexperienced in self-determination.

Despite a need to foster morality and self-rule, government-sponsored education progressed slowly for many years after the Revolutionary War. Caught up in westward expansion, there was no time for luxuries like schooling. Nor was there much desire, as liberal education had left a bad taste in the mouths of colonists whose experiences had associated education with aristocracy. Moral and economic education could be taught at home, and in the mind of the colonist morally literate and politically wise voters were a luxury that must wait.

Survivalism and expansionism, however, did not last forever. Not everyone wanted to go west, and some were too poor to leave. With droves of immigrants land-ing in America, great cities sprang up in the early 1800s. These groups were both the beginning and the result of industrialization in the new nation as they provided the labor by which great industries could be built. As cities grew, more industry arose, fueling a need for more labor, which in turn caused cities to grow again. As the cycle fed itself, industry began to recognize that not all growth was good because the vast throngs of workers lacked skills. The "solution" was to call for a new role for education by demanding vocational schooling. Although industrialists argued about whether education solved a need or whether it increased labor costs, the effect was to add economics to education's emerging role.

Rapid growth, especially in great cities, had the effect of increasing the demand for formal education systems. Although the nation had opened its doors to rapid growth in order to aid settlement and expansion, the dizzying speed was unexpected. By 1840 immigration had skyrocketed—from 1820 to 1840, the nation grew by only 751,000, whereas from 1840 to 1850 more than 1.7 million people entered the country. Immigration continued to soar, as more than 16 million people came to the United States between 1840 and 1900. The nation was unprepared to deal with the influx, and social problems were severe as unskilled immigrants clustered into cities. Problems worsened as rural Americans migrated to industrial centers too, either because they had tired of frontier life or were driven from the land. From 1820 to 1900, the U.S. population grew from ten million to 76 million, resulting in cities beset with problems of poverty and illiteracy.

Solutions had to be found. Educating for morality and self-government were still important, but leaders, including Horace Mann and Henry Barnard, argued that education for economic productivity was needed too. Under their leadership, the roots of a uniform public school system emerged in the Common School Movement. Spurred by immigration, the Common School Movement reached its peak between 1840 and 1880 and was driven by education for economic productivity. But the movement held a fourth thread that would imbed itself in the mind of America. Because it had its roots in people who had fled injustice in search of the American dream, the movement embraced a commitment not only to morality, self-determination, and economics, but also the seeds of loyalty to justice and equality.

The Common Schools Movement was nothing short of miraculous and laid the basis for refinements that would profoundly shape the nature and scope of American schools. One refinement forever altered the face of education. Although much of the nation's prosperity was brought about by a favorable climate for commerce, an unsavory aspect of industry before 1900 was the presence of child labor. The United States had followed the European model of exploiting children, but with industrialization came labor unions, which in the last half of the nineteenth century worked to improve wages of adults with the side effect of advocating for child labor laws. The Common Schools Movement was jointly benefited because child labor laws had the effect of removing children from the workforce, making schools an obvious caretaker.

By the dawn of the twentieth century, public education only faintly resembled colonial schools. But though resemblance was small, the roots were deep. Education for morality had moved from religion to humanism based on the views of social reformers, but the expectation that schools would build character remained. Likewise, as the nation won its freedom, education for self-governance held strong to preserve democracy. As industry and commerce grew, education for economics was spurred by massive immigration, setting the stage for the alarms and calls for reform that critics would issue throughout the twentieth century. In sum, schools had been given a key role in a nation that had become vast and diverse—a role reformers struggle with today as wars over morality, democracy, economics, and equality still rage.

Development of School Organization in America

Not surprisingly, the history of schooling in the United States has had a powerful influence on modern educational governance. Within the broad picture of growth we just noted were other distinct trends spanning more than 200 years. For instance, the tendency of people to cluster on the basis of religious, political, or ethnic heritage led to strong views about education and how it should be governed. In early New England, attitudes led to a religious state with strong regulation and taxation for schools. The middle colonies, including Maryland, New Jersey, and Pennsylvania, also were settled by religious groups that disfavored state control. Still another model arose, as other middle and southern colonies leaned toward the view that public schools were for paupers, thereby eschewing state control or tax support. Attitudes were deeply rooted and are still evident today, as geographic regions are notable for the prevalence or absence of private schools and where state school funding schemes may show sympathy for those same views.

It is equally unsurprising that westward settlement led to school governance designs having little commonality. Scholars have long decried the problems of tracing educational history as a consequence of settlers' fierce resistance to any government control. Katz captured the tension well when he noted:

> The conflicts between the democratic localists and the bureaucrats often assumed the atmosphere of an undeclared guerrilla war of sabotage and resistance, as local school districts refused to comply with state regulation and parents refused to comply with the state's representative, the teacher. Insofar as most of the resistance came from inarticulate people, it is the hardest and most maddening aspect of nineteenth century educational history to document. That it existed is, however, beyond doubt, as the frustrated testimony of local and state reformers testifies in almost every document they wrote.[15]

Although reformers long tried to impose a standardized educational system, many years passed before the design emerged that we see today. As the population center of the nation shifted westward, political preferences formed as people settled in and built schools. Intolerant attitudes led dissidents to move on when local traditions did not satisfy their will. Aided by long distances because of sparsely settled lands, the result was creation of thousands of tiny schools serving equally tiny settlements. Although there is no record of the exact number of schools in early America,

---

15   M. Katz, "From Voluntarism to Bureaucracy in American Education," in *Power and Ideology in Education,* eds. Jeremy Karabel and A.H. Halsey (New York: Oxford University Press, 1977), 394.

the disunity of school organization was neatly phrased by Henry Morrison, an early twentieth century school finance scholar, as he referred to modern school organization as "…late New England colonial…a little republic at every crossroads."

Figure 2.5 shows the number of school districts from 1870 to 2004, making several points. First, citizens today can find schools in their communities that seem inordinately close together, but which hark back to times when travel was difficult, making neighborhood schools a necessity. Second, in almost every earlier time each small town had its own school, a truly vast number given all the towns that lived and died. Third, the number of school districts has been far greater than for any other duplicate units of government because school district boundaries in many states are not coterminous with other governments such as counties. Fourth, although no one knows the highest number of school districts that existed before the turn of the twentieth century, the number far exceeded the 117,108 districts found in 1940. Finally, the relationship between growing state control and the number of districts is clear, as the more than 117,000 districts in 1940 fell to 14,383 in 2004—a number that includes the loss of 422 school districts since the first edition of this text, and 176 fewer since the last edition of this text!

Figure 2.5. Number of Public School Districts in Selected Years: 1870–2004

			Public Schools			
School Year	Regular Public School Districts	Total, All Schools	Total, Schools with Reported Grade Spans	Schools with Elementary Grades		Schools with Secondary Grades
				Total	One-teacher	
1870	---	116,312	---	---	---	---
1880	---	178,122	---	---	---	---
1890	---	224,526	---	---	---	---
1900	---	248,279	---	---	---	---
1910	---	265,474	---	---	212,448	---
1920	---	271,319	---	---	187,948	---
1930	---	248,117	---	238,306	148,712	23,930
1940	117,108	226,762	---	---	113,600	---
1950	83,718	---	---	128,225	59,652	24,542
1960	40,520	---	---	91,853	20,213	25,784
1970	17,995	---	89,372	65,800	1,815	25,352
1980	15,929	87,004	---	---	---	---
1990	15,367	83,425	81,880	60,699	630	23,461
2000	14,928	92,012	90,538	68,173	423	26,407
2004	14,383	95,726	93,977	71,195	376	28,219

Source: U.S. Department of Education, NCES. *Digest of Education Statistics 2005* (Washington, DC: Author, 2006).

Although thousands of school districts have closed over the years, a high degree of organizational uniformity has not followed. The U.S. Constitution has permitted wide variation by leaving control of schools to the individual states, which in turn have responded by creating school systems differing greatly in structure, operation, control, and fiscal support. The effect has been to create a system rooted in strong local control, although earlier discussion accurately suggested that local control is weakening as states have adopted an education reform agenda over recent decades. The total picture is best described as a patchwork quilt, as education is highly state-specific in many ways, with vast organizational differences among and within states (Fig. 2.6 shows the diversity in school organization within the 50 states as late as 2004). But most importantly, the struggle over the purpose of schools has endured—a struggle not only over the aims of education and about who is in control, but also about who is responsible for education's costs, and at what level it should be funded.

Figure 2.6. Number of Public School Districts by State: 2004

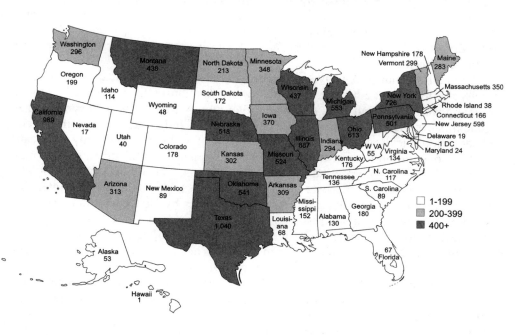

Source: U.S. Department of Education, NCES. *Digest of Education Statistics 2005* (Washington, DC: Author, 2006).

FROM WHERE DO SCHOOLS DERIVE FISCAL SUPPORT?

We have looked only briefly at the links between economics and schools and the development of school organization, but it is easy to see that our national history has a connection to how education is funded. Fiscal support for schools has traced a diffi-

cult path, marked by uncertainty about who should bear the costs. Although education has long interested federal, state, and local governments, the types and amounts
of support from each have varied. In fact, how schools are funded today is a direct
function of how federal, state, and local governments have accepted (or denied)
responsibility for education.

Federal Support for Schools

If we were to ask almost anyone today about the extent of federal involvement in
funding public schools, we would likely get an unsure response. But most people
would say that even if the amount of support is questionable, the federal government
has had a profound impact on schools. That answer would correctly reflect the federal
government's role in education, as it indeed has exercised influence in many ways.

Beginning with the *Northwest Ordinance* of 1787, which surveyed lands and
granted the sixteenth section of each township for educational uses, the federal government embarked on a threefold mission of aiding schools in the name of national
interest. One thrust meant to enhance national defense. A second thrust meant to aid
higher education. A third thrust sought to influence economic and social justice via
education. An additional, but indirect, thrust has been by appointments to federal
judgeships, which have impacted rulings on lawsuits involving schools. At times
these thrusts overlapped, so that the federal role has been greater than otherwise
would have been true.

Although scholars often advocate a stronger federal hand in education, they agree
on why the federal role has been limited. Many founding fathers opposed a strong
national government, and even Alexander Hamilton, virtually the lone sympathizer
of federalism at the Constitutional Convention in 1787, did not argue for a strong federal education role. Resistance to central government was so high that only two years
after the Constitution was ratified, Congress passed a set of amendments, known as
the *Bill of Rights*, with profound impacts on education. The Tenth Amendment was
important to education because its curbs on federalism spoke to the framers' intent by
saying, "The powers not delegated to the United States by the Constitution, nor prohibited by it to the States, are reserved to the States respectively, or to the people."
With these words, the doctrine of sovereign limits was formed, so that the federal
government was *forbidden* a direct role in education because the Constitution is silent
on schools—that is, education by default is a state responsibility.

Although the die was cast making education a state function, Congress has managed a long history of federal influence on schools through other direct authority and
indirect avenues. Direct authority has been derived in two ways. The first has been
through the Powers of Congress in Article 1 of the Constitution, which requires Congress to provide a strong national defense—a duty that Congress has used to send
large sums of money to schools. The second has been by creative interpretation of
Article 1, Section 8, wherein lies the General Welfare Clause, which reads that Congress shall have power to "…lay and collect taxes, duties, imposts and excises, [and]
to pay the debts and provide for the common defense and general welfare of the
United States." National defense has been an easy way for Congress to be involved in
education, but—more importantly—the General Welfare Clause has been construed
by Congress and the courts to allow broad federal interest in schools, particularly in

the social and economic justice arenas. Aiding that path has been Congress's indirect influence, as it has used persuasive ways such as withholding federal funds from programs unrelated to schools unless states embrace federal education goals.

Federalism and Defense Education

Education for defense has a long history, with its beginnings generally marked by establishment of the U.S. Military Academy in 1802. Designed to train military leaders, the academy gave rise to other defense colleges, with the Naval Academy in 1845, the Coast Guard Academy in 1876, and the Air Force Academy in 1954. The Reserve Officer Training Corps (ROTC) also was created at universities so that future leaders could link civilian education with military training. Other education aid followed, some of which was meant to enhance defense or to help veterans reenter civilian life.

Although a full list of federal interests in defense education is too lengthy, a sample gives the flavor and breadth. In 1918, the *Vocational Rehabilitation Act* provided disabled veterans with job training, and similar aid to World War II veterans was given in 1943 in the form of Public Law 78–16. In 1944, Congress created *the Serviceman's Readjustment Act* (PL 78–346), known as the G.I. Bill, providing educational benefits to millions of servicemen. In 1941, a change to the *Lanham Act* granted federal aid to construct and operate schools in areas impacted by federal facilities. In 1950, Congress passed PL 81–815 and PL 81–874, which enhanced this aid, a program that sent millions of dollars to local school districts that lost tax base to military installations. Immediately after World War II, the military established American schools overseas for the children of soldiers in foreign lands. These schools continue today as Department of Defense Schools (DODS).

Some of the largest outlays for defense education were sparked by cold wars and the technology race. In 1950, Congress created the National Science Foundation, which first served defense by training math and science teachers. In 1958, the *National Defense Education Act* (NDEA) under PL 85–865 was enacted to further improve education in math, science, and foreign language in response to the launch of the Soviet satellite Sputnik. The NDEA also provided higher education loans and job training for defense occupations. More recently, PL 95–525 extended the G.I. Bill to persons entering the military after 1985. Many other programs followed, such as the *Education for Economic Security Act* (PL 98–377) of 1984, reflecting new thinking on defense in the modern world—a continuing interest as typified by the *National Defense Authorization Act* (PL 106–398) of 2000; the *Higher Education Relief Opportunities for Students Act* (PL 107–122) of 2001 providing financial waivers to deal with student and family situations resulting from the September 11, 2001 terrorist attacks; and the *Higher Education Relief Opportunities for Students Act* of 2003 (PL 108–76) dealing with student financial aid to address student and family situations resulting from wars and national emergencies.

Federalism and Higher Education

As seen in the last paragraph, a corollary of federal defense has been aid to higher education. Generally, there is an attempt to separate federal interest in general higher education, with the debut of the federal government in nonmilitary higher education affairs marked by the *Morrill Act* in 1862, which established agricultural and mechanical colleges through land grants or direct payments to all states. A second *Morrill Act* followed in 1890, and in some instances these schools became the land grant universities of their respective states, with missions of research, teaching, and service in a practical tradition.

Federal interest in higher education did not end with the *Morrill Acts*. The 1935 *Bankhead Jones Act* (PL 74–320) made grants to states for agricultural experiment stations, a program that spilled over to public schools as the *Agricultural Adjustment Act* (PL 74–320) of 1935 authorizing farm commodity supports, which later developed into school milk and lunch programs. The 1950 *Housing Act* (PL 81–475) authorized loans to construct college housing. Likewise, the *Higher Education Facilities Act* of 1963 (PL 88–204) granted aid for classrooms, libraries, laboratories, and other facilities.

With the vast social reforms of the 1960s, the federal government plunged headlong into various aids and entitlements under the *Civil Rights Act* (PL 88–352) of 1964, some of which aided higher education. The Civil Rights Act granted funds for inservice training in higher education, especially dealing with desegregation. Other grants, such as the *Health Professional Educational Assistance Amendments* (PL 89–290) provided scholarships for needy students; likewise, the *Higher Education Act* (PL 89–329) of 1965 funded community service and teacher training programs and created the National Teacher Corps and graduate fellowships aimed at aiding disadvantaged groups. A long list of involvements also has accumulated over the last several decades, with the most recent actions reflecting contemporary concerns such as the *Taxpayer–Teacher Protection Act* (PL 108–409) of 2004, which increased the amount of loans that may be forgiven for highly qualified math, science, and special education teachers who agree to serve in high-poverty schools for five years; the *Student Grant Hurricane and Disaster Relief Act* (PL 109–67) of 2005, which waived repayments for students receiving federal grant assistance if they were residing in, employed in, or attending an institution of higher education located in a major disaster area; and the *Hurricane Education Recovery Act* (PL 109–148) of 2005, which provided funds for states affected by Hurricane Katrina to restart school operations, provide emergency aid for displaced students, and assist homeless youth. By 2005, federal investment in higher education was large, as Congress was providing $36.4 billion in on-budget funds to higher education exclusive of research funds. Although K–12 education has been left to the states, the federal government has supported higher education aggressively.

Federalist Justice and Education

Federal interest in economic and social justice has not been neatly severable from other federal aims, but it has been the most pervasive and sustained of all federal goals for education. Overlap between federal thrusts has been most apparent for K–12 schools because of the Tenth Amendment's silence on education, leading Congress to become very creative in order to exert influence. The legal basis for federal intervention rests in the General Welfare Clause, which has been held to grant broad powers up to the point of Congressional free will unless overturned by a court. In *United States v. Butler*,[16] the U.S. Supreme Court ruled that the General Welfare Clause could be broadly construed unless Congress acted arbitrarily, a difficult judgment that is made on a case-by-case basis. A further test came in *Helvering v. Davis*,[17] as the Court held that the General Welfare Clause need not be confined to constitutional framers' intent, but could shift with needs of the nation.

Social justice has long been at the core of federal education goals. *Brown v. Board of Education* (1954) changed the entire nature of public schools by ruling that segregation denies equal opportunity. But it was not until the *Civil Rights Act* of 1964 that serious federal entry into education took hold. The events that followed would have a lasting effect by sparking a massive influx of federal aid to a variety of programs aimed at fundamental fairness in the nation's schools.

Although the list of federal interests is again vast, only a few are highlighted here. *The Civil Rights Act* of 1964 channeled significant aid to public schools. Smaller programs followed, such as the 1965 *Disaster Relief Act* (PL 89–313), the 1968 *Handicapped Children's Early Education Assistance Act* (PL 90–538), and the 1970 *Elementary and Secondary Education Assistance Programs* extension (PL 91–230). Two Congressional acts, however, especially accounted for changing the federal relationship to schools: the *Elementary and Secondary Education Act* (ESEA; PL 89–910) of 1965, and the *Education of the Handicapped Act* (PL 94–142) in 1976.

One of Congress's greatest plunges into social activism through education came via the ESEA. Much of the ESEA was aimed toward disadvantaged children because the law was a direct outgrowth of the *Civil Rights Act*. ESEA made grants to elementary and secondary school programs for low-income children and provided library funds, texts, and money for other materials. ESEA also aided educational centers, strengthened state education agencies, and provided funds for research and training. The original ESEA had more than 40 entitlements, each addressing specific interests of Congress.

In fiscal outlays, the most far-reaching provisions of ESEA lay in Title I and were meant to provide supplementary services to low income and culturally disadvantaged children. Children could qualify if they met certain criteria, such as the $2,000 family income limit. Entire schools could qualify for Title I status if the school met threshold numbers of qualifying children in a single school. Schools qualified on three criteria: number of low-income families, number of children with Aid to Families with Dependent Children (AFDC), and a formula taking into account the statewide expenditure per pupil. Title I grew rapidly from $746.9 million in 1965 to its peak of $3 billion in 1980. In 1981, Congress repealed the ESEA in response to President Reagan's efforts to streamline the bureaucracy and to reverse erosion of state control that was said to have occurred under an activist Congress. In 1982, Congress passed the *Education Consolidation and Improvement Act* (ECIA), which continued ESEA while restructuring federal involvement; for example, Title I continued as Chapter 1, but many other programs were collapsed. Chapter 1 changed, too, as more local discre-

---

16   56 S. Ct. 312 (1936).
17   57 S. Ct. 904 (1937).

tion came via block grants. More than 40 other programs were collapsed into Chapter 2, and new provisions relating to administration were made under Chapter 3, reducing the role of the federal government and returning many powers to the states. ECIA did allow several other programs to remain freestanding, including Vocational Education, Education of the Handicapped, National School Lunch, Higher Education, Impact Aid, Title VII Bilingual Education, and Title IX Women's Educational Equity.

Congress also plunged deeper into social justice by enacting PL 94–142, *Education of the Handicapped Act* (EHA) in 1976 in response to intensive litigation seeking to ensure the rights of handicapped children. The challenge that drove PL 94–142 was the 1972 lawsuit in *Pennsylvania Association of Retarded Citizens (PARC)*.[18] Although many states provided special services, provisions often were minimal, permissive, or nonexistent. Decided for plaintiffs, *PARC* unleashed a series of lawsuits aimed at forcing states to provide special services to all children. With Congressional passage of the EHA, states failing to provide services were denied federal aid to schools. To help states provide services, Congress granted $300 million and authorized itself to provide up to 40% of special education costs. Although federal support has never come close to the 40% goal, federal aid and pressure by courts have discouraged states from refusing to provide services. Special education laws have undergone periodic revision, including changes to the *Individuals with Disabilities Act* (PL 105–17) in 1997 that have been termed the most significant since its inception.

Federal interest in K–12 schools has continued to the present day. Recent laws include the *Civil Rights Act* (PL 102–166) of 1991, the 1994 passage of *Goals 2000: Educate America Act* (PL 103–227), the *School-To-Work Opportunities Act* (PL 103–239) of 1994, the *Safe Schools Act* (part of PL 103–227) of 1994, and the *Improving America's Schools Act* (PL 103–382), which revised the ESEA. Topping the list of recent laws having significant impact is, of course, the *No Child Left Behind Act* (PL 107–110) in 2001, which reauthorized the ESEA and mandated high-stakes testing, accountability, early reading programs, and parental choice programs—requirements later heightened in intensity by proposed reauthorization in *Building on Results: A Blueprint for Strengthening the No Child Left Behind Act* (2007). These efforts show that while the federal government has no direct duty to education, it has taken great interest and at times has even commandeered a central role. The only reasonable conclusion is that if the K–12 services funded in part by the federal government were left to local or state units of government, the impact would be enormous—an impact summing in 2005 to nearly $24 billion and comprising an average 9.6% of school districts' revenues (Fig. 2.7, pp.54 –55).

State Support for Schools

If people might be unsure of the federal role in funding schools, they are far more certain that the state is heavily involved. Much of that view stems from the highly visible role played by states in the overall school aid scheme. In the absence of a federal duty to education, states have had to create aid plans to fund the services demanded

18 *Pennsylvania Association of Retarded Children (PARC) vs. Pennsylvania*, 334 F. Supp. 1257 (E.D. Pa. 1971).

by citizens or risk telling local communities that they must rely on local taxes to pay for schools. The inequalities of local ability to pay have been so great, however, that most states over the last century have assumed a key responsibility for funding schools.

Education as the State's Responsibility

Our earlier review of the Tenth Amendment laid out why states have had to bear a big part of education's costs. Although now more accepted, it has been a battle that has caused a huge and still unsettled shift in the balance of power and funding ratio among local and state governments. The fiscal interplay of federal, state, and local governments is a striking feature of Figure 2.7 (pp. 54–55) where, on national average, states have moved from funding only approximately 16% of school costs in 1920 to nearly 50% in 2005.

Figure 2.7 is a terse portrait of constitutional duty to schools that draws three stark lines of historical change. First, as there are only three levels of government available to share schools' costs, it follows that all costs fall in some ratio to this triad. Second, as a direct federal role is forbidden, the federal branch will not accept the lion's share. Third, because local ability to pay varies greatly and because the Constitution grants plenary powers to states, a major portion of school costs has fallen to the states. Although slow to accept, states have increasingly assumed greater proportions of these costs out of necessity and because the courts have found a weighty duty to fund education within the individual states' constitutional provisions.

Individual states have accepted a major funding role quite unevenly. State costs rose to an average 49.9% by 2005, but experience in individual states underscores how enthusiasm for funding schools has varied widely. It is relatively simple to describe how one federal government has aided education—but in contrast there are 50 states, so that a nearly equal number of ways to fund schools has emerged. Although some innovation has been seen, the results have not been equally good in every instance.

Notwithstanding, each state has provided aid for schools to some extent. Amount and method have depended on several factors. The first factor usually has relied on the wealth of each local school district and—in most instances—states have tried to equalize school spending by granting more aid to poorer districts; politically, however, this has been difficult. A second factor has relied to some extent on the amount of federal school aid flowing to a given state. A good example is federal impact aid. In some states, the amount of land exempt from local taxes because of federal installations is high; in such cases, state aid has been important, but the presence of impact aid may have moderated state aid amounts. A third factor has been the operation of political philosophies that have driven the design of state aid plans. For example, some states have adopted equalization aid formulas that inversely link local wealth and state aid. Other states have chosen minimum foundation plans to help districts reach a base expenditure level before leaving the balance of costs to local taxpayers. Only a few states have even proposed full state funding (Chapter 3 provides a full discussion of state aid formulas). A fourth factor of growing importance has been the force of law via school funding lawsuits. The bottom line is that the choice of a state aid plan is a function of political, legal, and economic realities. The other bottom line, though, is that the level of state support for schools has developed unevenly through-out the nation, resulting in wide mixes of federal, state, and local revenues; that is, state aid to local districts varied from a low in 2005 of 27.1% in Nevada to a high of 87.4% in Hawaii.

The fragmentation brought about by state sovereignty over many years, restrained mostly by politics and courts and fitful surges in federal interest, has left a patchwork effect in terms of how each state funds public schools. The result has been that state aid to schools mirrors the economic and political realities of each state. It is unfortunate in some ways that such variability has been able to develop because—to whatever extent money buys quality—the value of an education may be highly unequal across states since the range of expenditures and programs is great. Not all states have made school funding a high priority, while other states have given it great emphasis and have even declared education to be a fundamental right. Consequently, beliefs about the value of education have had a powerful impact on the amount of money invested in state aid plans, and it is often correct to say that states with low educational priorities are among the lower spending states. Although it can be argued that needs and costs differ among states, it is hard to see how wide expenditure differ-ences per pupil are a result of careful analysis of educational needs. Inversely, it is also hard for school leaders to explain why spending for schools should increase when the public often is convinced that pupil achievement is not doing well. And it is ultimately harder to explain these realities when expenditure levels differ greatly not only across states, but across districts within single states as well. But regardless, the record shows an ever-increasing state role in funding schools, and it is likely that recent attempts by states to take greater control of education will result in even more cost shifting to the states.

Local Support for Schools

If citizens are more aware of state aid in schools, they are convinced that educa-tion is a locally funded enterprise. Their opinions arise from a range of views, all relating to the fact that schools are highly visible in every community and have been regarded as locally "owned" from the earliest days of the nation. It is difficult to live and work today without being aware of the turmoil surrounding local school boards, the high profile of local school leaders, and the tensions affecting local school taxes. Although we have made a case in this chapter that states have assumed a much larger role in educational issues, especially via mandating accountability, we have also made a case that states have not assumed equal responsibility for school costs so that wide variance in method and amount of fiscal support continues to affect education. Thus, we next examine local cost-share issues to gain a complete snapshot of funding schools.

Features of Local Support

According to Figure 2.3 (p. 27), decreasing reliance on local funding for public schools is a relatively recent event. Beginning in 1920, with the first reported divi-sions of costs, 83% of the total $970 million in available funding fell on local dis-tricts. The first big shift came in 1940, as the local share of the $2.26 billion dropped to 68%. By 1970, the local share of the $40.27 billion available to schools had dropped again to 52%. By 1990, the local share made up 47% of the $209 billion cost for public K–12 schools. By 2003, the local share stood at about 43% of the $440 billion available for K–12 education.

Although the local share as a percentage of the total expenditure fell over the last century, the picture is actually unstable. For example, it is true that local support for schools in the nation's earlier days was high as a percentage of total costs compared to today. But by many accounts, local dollars have not declined, either in total or in aggregate burden. Locally, gross dollars supplied by taxpayers have increased as a result of inflation and as a result of increased costs tied to other factors such as expanded programs arising either by local choice or in response to federal and state mandates. Likewise, aggregate tax burden has not declined much overall and actually may have increased, as the additional dollars needed in modern complex school organizations have soared and as other governmental units have increased taxes simultaneously. Although the term *municipal overburden* was coined to depict demand on urban taxpayers from multiple taxing units such as cities, counties, police and fire departments, central water and sewage systems, schools, and other services, tax overburden in rural and urban settings alike has led tax critics to charge that there has been very little easing of taxpayer burden.

A second feature of local responsibility lies in recognizing the different realities of school funding in the 50 states. As we said earlier, states have been free to create funding systems except for the pressure of politics that can force similarities between states and because of the demand by courts for funding reform that has occurred over the years. But despite such events, experience in individual states has not led to equal shifts in local districts' share of school costs. Although local shares have dropped (compare Figs. 2.3, p. 27, and 2.7, pp. 54–55) to approximately 40% in 2005, actual local shares in that same year ranged from 65.3% in Nevada to a low 2.2% in Hawaii (excluding the unique District of Columbia). Even if Hawaii's unique school system were excluded, the range would still be great, as in 2005 Vermont required only a 7.6% local share by individual school districts. It is obvious that tax burdens are very different among states, and that national averages do not speak well to the differences among states.

A third feature of local responsibility rests in the basic nature of how local shares are determined. School districts typically derive revenue from a local *tax base*. Although some states tax more than one type of object to raise school revenue, most states rely on *real property* to define a district's tax base. This means that real estate is often the main source of tax revenue at the local level. No two districts contain exactly the same property values, so that highly unequal *tax capacity* may be evident from one school district to the next. A simple illustration makes this clearer. Urban properties are often quite valuable, with businesses, homes, vacant lots, and other land commanding high prices. Rural land is often less costly because it is farther from commerce centers and less attractive for development. Unless rural land has other attributes such as natural resources to make it valuable, urban centers will have much higher *property wealth*. That wealth, or *assessed valuation*, is generally the basis for deriving school revenue by assessing taxes against each property. For example, an acre of urban land might sell for $1 million or more depending on location. In a rural area, a one-acre home site might sell for $3,000—far less if it is remotely located. A *tax rate* of ten *mills*[19] on the urban acre would yield $10,000 in school tax revenue, while the rural home site would yield only $30—a vast difference, with implications for the ability of a local district to provide adequate funding for schools.

Even the implications are complex. Although the data we just saw might suggest a clear rural disadvantage and unfair high urban wealth, the opposite may be true. For example, it is certain that one feature of an urban area is population density. Thus, high property wealth spread over a large population may actually yield low *per capita* wealth. The urban condition may bring high costs associated with disadvantaged populations and tax base competition (i.e., municipal overburden). Many urban property owners are absentee individuals or businesses, having no community loyalty and interested only in taking profits without reinvesting. Rural conditions are equally complex. Although property may be less costly, ownership rests in fewer hands, increasing tax loads for influential citizens who may also be local voters. The lack of urban problems in rural areas does not always result in lower school costs, as smaller populations result in higher per-pupil costs due to diseconomies of scale. Likewise, the reality of vastly unequal tax bases is a vexing problem that creates disparities in districts' ability to levy local school taxes.

A fourth feature of local responsibility is actually a complication of how local school districts determine their cost shares and, to some extent, their total spending levels. This wrinkle takes several forms and is made more complex by how district budgets are determined and the interdependency of tax bases and intergovernmental competition. The idea of municipal overburden was raised earlier, and the broader concept of *tax overburden* applies in some way to almost all schools, including rural areas. A byproduct of overburden has been the hostility encountered by almost all local school districts when seeking to increase funding. In a number of states, patrons must vote on school budgets. In other states, budgets rest with individual school boards, but any politically astute person knows that a board's enthusiasm for adopting budget increases is affected by local taxpayer attitudes. Additionally, many states allow for *local option leeway*, that is, giving local districts the option of additional local *tax effort* for schools. As state aid plans limiting voter leeway have come into existence, and as overall tax burdens have grown, voter approval has become harder to obtain. All these considerations are aggravated by the issue of *fiscal dependence* on other governmental units: In some states, local school budgets are submitted to a higher authority in tandem with budgets of other taxing units such as cities and counties. In these circumstances, fiscal dependency creates problems because local schools may have trouble securing adequate revenue when competition for a finite tax pool is raised to the level of direct conflict between local governmental units.

The issues driving local responsibility and ability to pay for schools are endless, but our discussion shows that it is hard to tell simply from raw percentages whether the local share has declined as much as it appears because there are other issues that

---

19   A mill is 1/1,000 of a dollar, so that 1 mill is $1 tax revenue per $1,000 assessed value (AV). The formula calculates as: AV × mills = tax yield, so that $1,000,000 × 0.001 = $1,000. Likewise, $3,000 × 0.001 = $3. This does not consider fractional assessment, a practice in many states that takes only a portion of the market value of a piece of property.

muddy the waters. What is clear is that districts differ in ability to pay and that experience in the individual states varies widely. It is also clear that if local districts depended entirely on local tax bases, unconscionable disparities would follow. And it is finally clear that the federal, state, and local partnership has been both variable and essential—variable because there is a natural tension among these three levels of government in our fiercely independent nation, and essential because none of these units should be allowed to assume full control of schools. Education has long been a partnership in America; the real issue is refinement of that partnership in ways that enhance fiscal adequacy and equity for every child.

WHAT CONSTITUTES ADEQUATE AND EQUITABLE FUNDING FOR SCHOOLS?

The importance of adequate and equitable funding is heightened by the vast scope and costs of education, changing demographics, and links between education and economic and social progress. Even though research cannot measure the exact link between student achievement and money, there has been a long-standing belief that we must guard against underinvesting in schools to avoid destructive economic and social consequences. In this uncertain context, policy makers have been challenged to fund education at an appropriate level.

The result has been a unending struggle over money and schools. While some struggles have dealt with what schools mean to different members of society, perhaps the greatest war has been over how school money is distributed. Part of the struggle has arisen because there has never been enough money, so that distribution becomes even more critical. By all accounts, the war has escalated as a result of greater willingness to pursue confrontational remedies such as legal challenges to state school-aid formulas. Unhappy reformers have been quick to assert that more money makes better schools, arguing that schools distribute economic and social opportunity and that equal opportunity depends on the quality of schools children attend. They further contend that despite lack of a tight link between money and outcomes, school quality is powerfully affected by purchased resources such as teachers. Reformers then offer the challenge that people who argue for the irrelevance of money still prefer more money for their own children. Under these conditions, litigants have aggressively chased fair and adequate funding, believing that how states fund schools has a direct effect on social and economic justice.

Origins of School Funding Challenges

For more than a century, school finance has been a deep concern for courts and policy makers. Although school finance as a discipline only emerged during the early twentieth century, issues of school taxation have been a flash point since the early days of the nation. Likewise, schools have long been the object of intense feuding regarding equality of educational opportunity as it relates to discrimination, and it is easy to link beliefs about discrimination to differences in amounts of funding for schools.

Figure 2.7. Federal, State, Local Cost Share for Public Elementary and Secondary Education by Source and State: 2005

State or Jurisdiction	Total	Local	State	Federal	Percentage Distribution Local	State	Federal
United States	$487,761,164	$214,389,438	$228,562,195	$44,809,532	44.0	46.9	9.2
Alabama	5,861,380	1,906,607	3,253,486	701,287	32.5	55.5	12.0
Alaska	1,679,646	418,199	957,820	303,626	24.9	57.0	18.1
Arizona	8,151,688	3,301,561	3,898,118	952,009	40.5	47.8	11.7
Arkansas	4,034,796	1,235,669	2,349,685	449,442	30.6	58.2	11.1
California	59,481,350	17,588,882	35,234,574	6,657,894	29.6	59.2	11.2
Colorado	6,911,807	3,475,507	2,954,905	481,395	50.3	42.8	7.0
Connecticut	8,015,309	4,527,506	3,062,150	425,653	56.5	38.2	5.3
Delaware	1,376,724	395,278	851,355	130,091	28.7	61.8	9.4
District of Columbia	1,285,489	1,126,022	--	159,467	87.6	--	12.4
Florida	22,633,476	10,720,541	9,533,209	2,379,726	47.4	42.1	10.5
Georgia	14,726,455	6,848,011	6,466,311	1,412,133	46.5	43.9	9.6
Hawaii	2,274,165	50,578	1,986,614	236,974	2.2	87.4	10.4
Idaho	1,816,509	576,766	1,043,927	195,816	31.8	57.5	10.8
Illinois	21,281,907	12,683,909	6,758,417	1,839,581	59.6	31.8	8.6
Indiana	11,278,665	5,214,024	5,326,048	738,593	46.2	47.2	6.5
Iowa	4,481,531	2,055,162	2,051,947	374,422	45.9	45.8	8.4
Kansas	4,468,190	1,582,904	2,431,195	454,091	35.4	54.4	10.2
Kentucky	5,379,257	1,671,516	3,049,129	658,612	31.1	56.7	12.2
Louisiana	6,057,201	2,337,820	2,878,017	841,364	38.6	47.5	13.9
Maine	2,308,518	1,135,119	946,282	227,117	49.2	41.0	9.8
Maryland	9,886,032	5,496,485	3,729,271	660,276	55.6	37.7	6.7
Massachusetts	12,735,802	6,525,322	5,442,172	768,309	51.2	42.7	6.0
Michigan	18,365,247	5,776,655	11,043,486	1,545,106	31.5	60.1	8.4
Minnesota	8,687,246	2,069,248	6,050,153	567,845	23.8	69.6	6.5
Mississippi	3,642,050	1,099,730	1,965,158	577,162	30.2	54.0	15.8
Missouri	8,373,954	4,768,959	2,859,179	745,815	56.9	34.1	8.9
Montana	1,293,161	514,077	584,289	194,794	39.8	45.2	15.1
Nebraska	2,800,202	1,633,416	877,246	289,540	58.3	31.3	10.3
Nevada	3,393,152	2,215,988	920,244	256,921	65.3	27.1	7.6
New Hampshire	2,242,384	1,236,214	879,428	126,743	55.1	39.2	5.7
New Jersey	21,738,449	11,331,905	9,450,496	956,048	52.1	43.5	4.4
New Mexico	3,049,760	413,289	2,133,707	502,763	13.6	70.0	16.5
New York	43,649,605	21,682,869	18,768,008	3,198,727	49.7	43.0	7.3
North Carolina	10,446,941	2,760,943	6,552,886	1,133,112	26.4	62.7	10.8
North Dakota	920,566	431,813	340,259	148,495	46.9	37.0	16.1

State or Jurisdiction	Total	Local	State	Federal	Percentage Distribution		
					Local	State	Federal
Ohio	19,912,038	9,633,419	8,752,118	1,526,501	48.4	44.0	7.7
Oklahoma	4,621,537	1,520,859	2,466,399	634,278	32.9	53.4	13.7
Oregon	4,999,669	2,052,095	2,439,989	507,585	41.0	48.8	10.2
Pennsylvania	21,439,695	11,937,783	7,717,500	1,784,412	55.7	36.0	8.3
Rhode Island	1,878,044	1,002,573	725,609	149,862	53.4	38.6	8.0
South Carolina	6,267,520	2,768,595	2,837,312	661,614	44.2	45.3	10.6
South Dakota	1,061,844	526,012	355,969	179,863	49.5	33.5	16.9
Tennessee	6,942,997	3,153,736	2,998,090	791,171	45.4	43.2	11.4
Texas	36,798,422	19,466,061	13,214,827	4,117,534	52.9	35.9	11.2
Utah	3,227,340	1,126,268	1,775,126	325,946	34.9	55.0	10.1
Vermont	1,283,411	97,823	1,090,538	95,050	7.6	85.0	7.4
Virginia	11,990,159	6,292,194	4,871,156	826,809	52.5	40.6	6.9
Washington	9,266,940	2,761,736	5,629,205	875,999	29.8	60.7	9.5
West Virginia	2,779,795	766,318	1,684,324	329,154	27.6	60.6	11.8
Wisconsin	9,432,162	4,036,880	4,789,269	606,013	42.8	50.8	6.4
Wyoming	1,130,977	438,594	585,593	106,791	38.8	51.8	9.4

Source: U.S. Department of Education, National Center for Education Statistics, Common Core of Data (CCD). *National Public Education Financial Survey (NPEFS), fiscal year 2005* (Washington, DC: Author, 2007).

The history of school finance litigation has played out in federal and state courts. At the federal level, litigation has focused on the U.S. Constitution in context of interpreting federal responsibility for education, hoping to read a *guaranteed right* into the Constitution. At the state level, litigation has focused on both the *constitutional* and *statutory* demands of each state. Pursuit of justice has been nerve-wracking, as constitutional interpretation is swayed by the times and attitudes of courts, particularly when there is wide variance among states in their constitutional and statutory provisions for school funding. In both federal and state cases, litigants have sought rulings on the meaning of equal opportunity and sought to test the strength of constitutional and statutory language regarding education. Traditionally, attacks have followed three claims: education as a *fundamental right,* the *equal protection* of laws, and the *education articles* of state constitutions. Each of these can be traced from their federal and state origins into modern school finance litigation strategy.

Federal Origins

Although school finance litigation is largely regarded as state specific, the federal case actually predates all other strategies. Plaintiffs first sought equality in funding by seeking a favorable U.S. Supreme Court ruling as the supreme law of the land. The logic was that if a ruling were favorable, states would have to follow federal law.

Bringing a federal lawsuit was a sensible act. Equality had been important since the days when the colonial charters sought freedom from British rule. Equality was a key part of the Bill of Rights, and the Fourteenth Amendment to the Constitution guaranteed equality under federal law. The Fourteenth Amendment was critically important because its provisions applied to the individual states:

> No State shall make or enforce any law which shall abridge the privileges or immunities of citizens of the United States; nor shall any State deprive any person of life, liberty, or property, without due process of law; nor deny to any person within its jurisdiction the equal protection of the laws.[20]

A case for school funding fairness was laid in a series of suits testing the limits of equality under the federal Constitution. Earlier cases had laid a groundwork, including overturning of racial separatism where the practical implications included the costs and organization of schools. The next step was to ask whether unequal money in schools is a type of impermissible inequality under law.

This strategy was actually an extension of judicial sympathy that already existed for other assured fundamental rights. In addition to named rights in the Constitution, the Supreme Court had previously ruled on other rights that it found so basic that they could not be denied except by due process of law. The importance of establishing a fundamental right could not be overstated, in that the equality requirement was so strong that these rights must be protected at all costs—a guarantee reformers hoped would link school funding and equal rights under the Fourteenth Amendment's *equal protection* clause. This line of thinking produced two litigation thrusts. One thrust came from defining unequal treatment of *suspect classes*: School funding litigation might win, plaintiffs thought, if they could show that money was tied to a protected social class in schools. The second thrust came from seeking ways in which some other fundamental right might be violated by unequal funding. The strategy was risky: if neither a fundamental right to education nor a suspect class (e.g., poor people) could be established, lawsuits would have to focus on individual states.

The Early Federal Case

Although federal racial equality litigation actually spanned many decades, it was in the *Brown* case in 1954 when equality of educational opportunity found its footing as the U.S. Supreme Court overturned "separate but equal" provisions, which had allowed racially segregated schools. Overturning the entire social and economic history of the United States, the Court held that separate but equal is inherently unequal, and that education is vital to the health and well-being of the nation. The Court stated:

> …[E]ducation is perhaps the most important function of state and local governments.…It is the very foundation of good citizenship.…In these days, it is doubtful that any child may reasonably be expected to succeed in life if he is denied the opportunity of an education. Such an opportunity, where the state has undertaken to provide it, is a right that must be made available to all on equal terms.[21]

---

20 Proposed by the 39th Congress, June 13, 1866 and ratified July 28, 1868.
21 *Brown v. Board of Education*, 347 U.S. at 493.

Emboldened by *Brown,* reformers turned to fiscal inequality, believing that same analysis could apply to school funding because it was easily proposed that money and educational opportunity vary greatly based on residence in school districts of unequal wealth. Of great value to this theory was a line of argument that unequal district wealth made a case for wealth discrimination, so that the happenstance of residence could be interpreted as a wealth-based suspect class. By this logic, wealth-disadvantaged children by virtue of their accident of residence in poor school districts were a perfect case in point.

The first federal suit took shape in 1969 in Virginia as *Burruss.*[22] Plaintiffs based their claims on the Fourteenth Amendment, arguing that state aid was not given to school districts on the basis of educational needs. The U.S. District Court, however, held that whereas "...deficiencies and differences are forcefully put by plaintiffs' counsel...we do not believe they are creatures of discrimination by the State....We can only see to it that the outlays on one group are not invidiously greater or less than that of another." The court added that, "the courts have neither the knowledge, nor means, nor the power to tailor the public monies to fit the varying needs of these students throughout the state."

The tone of *Burruss* foretold much of the potential failure of a federal case. Over the coming years, plaintiffs experienced the same logic, often as federal courts repeatedly drew on the words of sister courts to express their own limitations. The nearly lone exception came in 1972 in *Van Dusartz,*[23] as a Minnesota federal court held that wealthy districts not only had greater revenue per child but also paid lower tax rates—conditions tied to the child's residence. *Van Dusartz* was hardly the rule, however, as other federal courts complained that their hands were tied by a lack of judicially manageable standards. Equality in federal court was stated negatively, in that absence of money was not the same as discrimination.

The *Rodriguez* Case

Reformers realized, however, that a U.S. Supreme Court ruling was not yet in place, and a test case was carefully planned. A case styled as *Rodriguez*[24] was chosen, in which a U.S. District Court had earlier upheld plaintiffs' claim that the state must be neutral in aiding schools. The district court ruling had encouraged reformers, as it also held that education is of fundamental interest to the state. The case was appealed to the Supreme Court, where plaintiffs argued that the Texas funding system violated federal equal protections by discriminating against a suspect class of poor and that students making up that class were denied the right to equal education. The Supreme Court rejected the suspect class argument, however, as it saw only students living in poor school districts, rather than being poor themselves. The Supreme Court noted that individual income did not correlate exactly with district wealth, and that even if the link had been strong, the Supreme Court's view of wealth suspectness is limited to

---

22 *Burruss v. Wilkerson,* 310 F. Supp. 572 (W.D. Va. 1969).

23 *Van Dusartz v. Hatfield,* 334 F. Supp. 870 (U.S. Dist. Minn. 1971).

24 *San Antonio Independent School District v. Rodriguez,* 411 U.S. 1 (1973).

absolute deprivation. Because no student was deprived of an education, fiscal inequalities were of only relative difference.

The Supreme Court also rejected education as a fundamental right. Plaintiffs had argued that education was so prerequisite to other rights that it created a nexus to other established fundamental rights. The Supreme Court disagreed, seeing no link between education and other rights. Although the Supreme Court criticized the disparities among Texas school districts, only a *rational basis* for the funding formula was required to defend the state-aid plan absent invidious discrimination. A rational basis could be found in Texas's goal of promoting local control of schools, and the Supreme Court refused to intervene in such a complex and political arena.

Subsequent Federal Litigation

Although *Rodriguez* had a chilling effect on new federal lawsuits, other cases were brought to keep the question alive, especially in light of the fact that the Supreme Court did not completely close the door on future claims. Three cases illustrate the importance of the federal courts to defining a federal role in educational equality.

Thirteen years after *Rodriguez*, plaintiffs in Mississippi sued in *Papasan*[25] for equal protection on revenue disparity based on Section Sixteen lands lost during the Civil War. Although the state provided aid to offset losses in affected school districts, by 1981 state funds were only $0.63 per pupil compared to $75.34 per pupil in districts where land had not been taken. Dismissed in federal district court, the Fifth Circuit Court held on appeal in *Papasan* that although the Eleventh Amendment to the U.S. Constitution did not bar equal protection claims, *Rodriguez* was the standard regarding fiscal disparity. The U.S. Supreme Court affirmed, but it also sent the case back for further development. *Papasan* was notable for two reasons: First, the complaint was narrowly taken, never drawing the issue of fundamentality into the claims. Second, a small window of federal interest in school funding was opened by remanding to the lower court, as the Supreme Court noted that unreasonable government action would attract the Court's interest.

A second important case arose in Texas a few years later, as the U.S. Supreme Court ruled in *Plyler*[26] that refusal by a state to educate illegal aliens could invoke federal equal protections. Although the Court stopped short of declaring education a fundamental right, it did approve a higher level of scrutiny in cases of absolute educational deprivation. The Court pointed to its hesitancy to slam shut the federal door, as it stated:

> Education provides the basic tools by which individuals might lead economically productive lives to the benefit of us all. In sum, education has a fundamental role in maintaining the fabric of our society. We cannot ignore the significant social costs borne by our Nation when select groups

---

25 *Papasan v. Allain*, 478 U.S. 265 (1986); *Papasan v. United States*, 756 F.2d 1087 (5th Cir. 1985).

26 *Plyler v. Doe*, 457 U.S. 202 (1982).

are denied the means to absorb the values and skills on which our social order rests.[27]

The third important federal case came in *Kadrmas*,[28] as plaintiffs in North Dakota alleged that fees for bus service denied equal protection because the plaintiff child could not afford to pay for transportation. The Supreme Court held for the state, but its 5–4 vote was a bare majority and indicated the unsettled nature of federal education claims. The Court warned that *Rodriguez* was not the last word, in that there are nuances that deeply interest the Court. The minority opinion expressed this well:

> The Court…does not address the question whether a state constitutionally could deny a child access to a minimally adequate education. In prior cases this court explicitly has left open the question whether such a deprivation of access would violate a fundamental constitutional right. That question remains open today.[29]

Although *Rodriguez* has been said to close off hope for a successful federal claim, the record disagrees. Federal courts are sympathetic to judicially unmanageable standards, and they are inclined to defer to legislative prerogative. Likewise, the nation's highest court is reluctant to declare education a fundamental right. But it is also clear the Court takes interest in education, as over time it revisits and refines earlier rulings. But in the end, it is clear that the case for school finance reform has had to turn to state courts to experience meaningful and systematic success.

State Origins

Development of the state case for equalizing money in schools parallels the federal path; in particular, there has been significant overlap of both time and nature of claims. In fact, lawsuits were often brought simultaneously in state and federal courts in the early days of reform. For example, *Burruss* and *Rodriguez* were both filed in federal court in the 1960s, but the California case of *Serrano*[30] actually ended at the state supreme court level in 1971 before the U.S. Supreme Court had ruled in *Rodriguez* in 1973. The nature of claims also overlapped, as state cases like *Serrano* made federal and state constitutional claims conjointly. But whereas success on the federal front was unlikely, state litigation occurred far more frequently and with significantly greater success.

Early State Cases

The first state school finance case to gain attention was *Serrano,* as the California Supreme Court ruled in what would become a model for state school finance litigation. Plaintiffs sought a ruling on issues of a fundamental right to education, wealth as a suspect class, and federal and state equal protection on these grounds. Plaintiffs

---

27 457 U.S. at 221.

28 *Kadrmas v. Dickinson Public Schools*, 487 U.S. 450, 108 S. Ct. 2481 (1988).

29 108 S. Ct. at 2491.

30 *Serrano v Priest,* 487 P.2d 1241 (Cal. 1971).

charged that the state aid plan created disparity and that these differences impacted the quality of schools. Plaintiffs also charged that some taxpayers paid higher tax rates and received poorer education. The net sum of such finance schemes, plaintiffs alleged, was to make the quality of education impermissibly dependent on local property wealth.

In a sweeping victory for plaintiffs, the state supreme court overturned the method of funding schools in California, finding that it violated both the federal Fourteenth Amendment and the state constitution's equal protection clause. This ruling ran counter to every trend. The California high court was harsh in its view of unequal opportunity, declaring:

> We have determined that this funding scheme invidiously discriminates against the poor because it makes the quality of a child's education a function of the wealth of his parents and neighbors. Recognizing, as we must, that the right to an education in our public schools is a fundamental interest that cannot be conditional on wealth, we can discern no compelling state purpose necessitating the present method of financing.[31]

That the federal claim was later overturned by *Rodriguez* did not deter the impact of *Serrano* at the state level because the lesson was that state courts might not adopt the same posture as federal courts; that is, state law may be more strict than federal law. *Serrano* provided a blueprint for continued litigation by its success on state-level fundamentality and equal protection claims, and it showed that state constitutions might be vulnerable in ways unavailable at the federal level. The impact of *Serrano* was to provide a blueprint for copycat litigation, and many state legislatures immediately saw *Serrano* as a harbinger of the future. As a result, an explosion of school finance reform litigation followed in other states, along with many legislatures voluntarily acting ahead of anticipated lawsuits.

Subsequent State Litigation

Bolstered by *Serrano*, dozens of state funding lawsuits followed, a fact of life that still rages. But while reformers' hopes were raised by early victories, results have been uneven. In fact, the outcome can be divided into successes and failures at the state level.

Failures

The case for state-level finance reform did not enjoy sudden and sustained success. Although a full accounting of the history of litigation is beyond this book, a few early cases illustrate that the state-level record included significant failures.

Shortly after *Serrano*, the Michigan Supreme Court handed down its decision in *Milliken*,[32] a ruling that flip-flopped in a dizzyingly short time. The original ruling was for plaintiffs and was modeled after *Serrano*, but the victory was short-lived

---

31   487 P.2d at 1244.

32   *Milliken v. Green*, vacated, 212 N.W.2d 711 (Mich. 1973); *Milliken v. Green*, 203 N.W.2d 457 (Mich. 1972).

because the Michigan supreme court experienced a change of sitting judges—a change that ended in reversal of the ruling. The new court vacated the prior decision on the basis that the evidence did not prove that equal protection of children in low-wealth districts was violated. Of particular importance to the court was the question of linkage between fiscal inputs and achievement, so that additional money could not be shown to provide greater and more equal outcomes.

The logic in *Milliken* would haunt reformers. The case for reform again went badly as, shortly after *Rodriguez*, the Arizona Supreme Court held for the defendant state in *Shofstall*.[33] The court had been asked to decide if that state's school funding law violated the state equal protection clause and the state constitution's *general and uniform* provision. The court interpreted general and uniform to mean that the state would provide a minimum school year, certify personnel, and set course requirements and standards. Although the court found a fundamental right to education, it saw legislative redress as the solution to political problems; that is, as the solution to school funding.

Still a third defeat came as the Illinois Supreme Court ruling in *Blase*[34] denied a narrow reading of the state constitution. Plaintiffs had based their claims on the constitution's strong wording, which said, "the State shall provide for an efficient system of high quality public educational institutions and services [and that] the State has the primary responsibility for financing the system of public education." Plaintiffs wanted the state to provide no less than 50% of costs, along with other strict equality provisions. The Illinois Supreme Court rejected this view, ruling that the language only expressed a goal rather than a specific command.

One final defeat shows how plaintiffs may fail, even when a state's constitution seems to strongly support equality. Plaintiffs' case failed in the state of Washington in *Northshore*,[35] despite all elements of victory seemingly in place. Plaintiffs' claims included the charge that the state had disobeyed a provision of the constitution, which read, "...it is the paramount duty of the state to make ample provision for the education of all children" and that the state had failed to provide a general and uniform system of public schools. Regarded as one of the states having the most forceful constitutional language, the Washington Supreme Court nonetheless denied these claims, noting that even if the state were only one school district, spending per child would still depend on geography, climate, terrain, social and economic conditions, transportation, special services, and local choices in curricula. The strength of language about ample provision for education was viewed unfavorably, as the court noted, "...constitutionally speaking, the duty or function is the same as any other major duty or function of state government."[36]

Although we have yet to discuss successes in state school finance litigation, it is important to emphasize the still unsettled condition of states' constitutional obligations. Although we will say later that litigation has moved school funding far ahead of

---

33 *Shofstall v. Hollins*, 515 P.2d 590 (Ariz. 1973).
34 *Blase v. Illinois*, 55 Ill. 2d 94, 302 N.E.2d 46 (Ill. 1973).
35 *Northshore v. Kinnear*, 530 P.2d 178 (Wash. 1974).
36 530 P.2d at 198.

where it would be had the force of law not been invoked, it is still true that plaintiffs risk defeat when raising what seems to them to be issues of fundamental justice in funding an equal education for every child. For example, of the 23 lawsuits active during mid-2007, plaintiffs fared poorly in the states of Arizona[37] and Oklahoma,[38] while plaintiffs in 21 other states hoped for different results in their respective litigations. In sum, although there have been numerous plaintiff victories in recent years, a realistic view recognizes that failure is very possible when engaging in high-stakes constitutional litigation.

Successes

Although plaintiffs lost many cases at the state level, especially in the early years of funding reform, a number of victories dramatically affected how schools are financed. A few important winning state cases following after the giddy win in *Serrano* illustrate the volatile context of school funding battles.

The blueprint for funding reform was aided by another victory soon after *Serrano*—the New Jersey Supreme Court's ruling in *Robinson*.[39] The high court reviewed a lower court's holding for plaintiffs wherein it was charged that the aid plan violated federal and state equal protections and denied students' fundamental right to education because tax revenue varied with district wealth and was unequalized. To reformers' dismay, the court denied fundamentality and wealth suspect class, stating that such findings would have the unintended consequence of changing our most basic political structures. But the court still overturned the school funding system by turning to the education article of the state constitution, which demanded a *thorough and efficient* system of schools—a requirement unmet due to lack of equalization in revenues, which violated the state's equal protection clause.

Other decisions for plaintiffs followed over the next few years. One of the more expansive state supreme court rulings came in the Wyoming case of *Washakie*[40] in 1980, as the court found that poor districts showed a pattern of less revenue as a result of low assessed valuation. The court accepted plaintiff arguments that the quality of education is related to money. The court cut to the core, stating, "...until equality of financing is achieved, there is no practicable method of achieving equality of quality."[41] The Wyoming court based its decision on the fact that certain provisions of the state constitution were more demanding than federal equal protections and because education was of such compelling value in that state that it was among the protected fundamental rights. Unlike most courts, the Wyoming high court embraced wealth as a suspect class, saying, "the state has the burden of demonstrating a compelling inter-

---

37 *Crane Elementary v. State of Arizona*, 1 CA-CV 04-0076 in the Court of Appeals State of Arizona (2006), app. den. Supreme Court of Arizona (April 2007).

38 *Oklahoma Education Association v. State ex rel. Oklahoma Legislature*, Case No. 103702. Decided May 8, 2007.

39 *Robinson v. Cahill*, 287 A.2d 187 (N.J. Super. 1972), *aff'd as modified*, 303 A.2d 273 (N.J. 1973).

40 *Washakie County School District v. Herschler*, 606 P.2d 310 (Wyo. 1980).

41 606 P.2d at 335.

est…served by the challenged legislation and which cannot be satisfied by any other convenient legal structure."[42]

The unsettled nature of state struggles is grandly typified by the battle over school funding that began in Texas with *Rodriguez* in federal court in 1973 and later moved to the state level. Failing in *Rodriguez*, plaintiffs turned to the Texas state supreme court, which ruled in *Edgewood*[43] in 1988 that education was a fundamental right in Texas and ordered the legislature to create a satisfactory remedy within a specific time period—a duty that the state legislature had difficulty meeting mostly for political reasons and consequently forcing the case to return repeatedly for judicial review. Suffering setbacks and gains, the Texas case moved through *Edgewood I*, *II*, and *III*, with the courts each time reviewing the legislature's efforts to improve equity and adequacy of school funding, in part by recapturing local revenues from the state's wealthier school districts for redistribution to poorer schools. Not surprisingly, such solutions were contentious, so that in 2001 high wealth school districts sued under *West Orange-Cove*,[44] claiming that a state-imposed property tax lid meant to limit funding disparities was unconstitutional. Plaintiff intervenors joined hundreds of school districts to the case and reshaped the basic nature of the suit, with a trial court in 2004 holding both the funding system *and* the property tax system unconstitutional,[45] with a subsequent state supreme court ruling enjoining state aid distribution pending legislative action on Texas' school finance woes.[46] Although a win for plaintiffs, the question in part became who actually had won? As a dissenting opinion filed by Justice Brister noted, "…though only five percent of the State's school districts claim a single statute is unconstitutional, the Court enjoins the State from distributing any money under the current Texas school financing system, an order that applies to every school district in Texas. Thus, because some districts get too little state money, all districts may get none. It is hard to see how this will help Texas school children."[47] And equally important, winning became an expensive prize when the timeline for "winning" was taken into consideration—that Texas school finance had improved since the days of *Rodriguez* seems certain, but the turmoil and unintended outcomes were sobering reminders that progress requires continued vigilance and a great deal of political messiness.

The drama and trauma of plaintiff victories is illustrated by two other important long-standing cases in Kentucky and New Jersey, both of which have provided insight on the nature of funding reform. One of the key plaintiff wins that propelled

---

42   606 P.2d at 335.

43   *Edgewood v. Kirby*, 761 S.W.2d 859 (Tex. 1988).

44   *West Orange-Cove Consolidated ISD v. Nelson*, 107 S.W.3d 558 (Tex. 2001).

45   *West Orange-Cove Consol. Indep. Sch. Dist. et al. v. Neeley et al.*, No. GV-100528 (250th Dist. Ct., Travis County, Tex., Nov. 30, 2004).

46   *Neeley v. W. Orange-Cove Consol. Indep. Sch. Dist.*, No. 04-1144 consolidated with No. 05-0145 consolidated with No. 05-0148, Supreme Court of Texas, 49 Tex. Sup. J. 119, 176 S.W.3d 746 (Tex. 2005). *Reh'g denied Neeley v. W. Orange-Cove Consol. Indep. Sch. Dist.*, 2005 Tex. LEXIS 966 (Tex., Dec. 16, 2005).

47   49 Tex. Sup. J. at 145.

legislatures to revise both their academic systems and their funding schemes was the Kentucky Supreme Court's 1989 ruling in *Rose*.[48] In a dramatic decision that shook the nation and spurred reform in many states, the Kentucky court held that the system of common schools was not efficient. Finding a fundamental right to education, the court concluded that this right was denied when the state's schools were underfunded and inadequate in educational programs—observations that caused the court to order a complete overhaul with massive new funds and total system redesign. Simultaneously, and much like the trauma seen in Texas, the 1990 New Jersey case of *Abbott*,[49] a multidecade continuation of the original *Robinson* case from 1973, stirred national consternation as that state's finance system was again overruled because the state aid formula did not meet the needs of poor urban districts and because the formula still violated the thorough and efficient clause. The court stated, "[f]rom this record we find that certain poorer urban districts do not provide a thorough and efficient education to their students....We find the constitutional failure clear, severe, and of long duration."[50] Although the court later found the level of fiscal resources to finally meet adequacy standards—a finding only after Abbott *I, II, III,* and *IV*—New Jersey's experience has stood as a monument to the war over fair funding. But it has been a struggle spanning decades in search of solutions and is not over yet, as in 2006 the governor of New Jersey proposed new measures and reforms linked to the court's long-ago original findings—changes that undoubtedly will experience legal challenge.

Winless in federal court, reformers have had to accept that the best available news is winning at the state supreme court level. Recent years have brought more wins than defeats (Fig. 2.8), and each year plaintiffs file new claims[51] and seek judicial review of established cases. The message is clear: To fully engage the nature of school finance litigation requires a willingness to fail and a tolerance for litigation as a campaign, rather than a battle or even a war—in other words, a long view is the only way to evaluate the impact of litigation on adequate and equitable levels of funding for schools. But at the end of the day, even bigger challenges exist: to prevent politics from creeping back into school funding once a court ends its monitoring, and to prevent citizens from resisting true school funding equalization through such avenues as

---

48 *Rose v. Council for Better Education*, 790 S.W.2d 186 (Ky. 1989).

49 *Abbott v. Burke*, 1990 N.J. Lexis 64, 575 A.2d 359 (N.J. 1990).

50 1990 N.J. Lexis at 168.

51 And the list is ever-encompassing and ever-expanding: For example, in 2006, several states and national organizations went on record in support of the National Education Association's NCLB-based lawsuit against the federal government, now on appeal from *Pontiac v. Spellings*, 2005 U.S. Dist. LEXIS 29253 (E.D. Mich., Nov. 23, 2005). The states of Connecticut, Delaware, Illinois, Maine, Oklahoma, and Wisconsin, along with the governor of Pennsylvania, the American Association of School Administrators, and officials in California expressed their displeasure over what they see as the unfunded mandate represented by NCLB. The argument is that because Congress, to date, had appropriated $31 billion less than the law actually authorized, states and school districts should not be obliged to spend more for NCLB's requirements than had been paid for by Congress.

political retribution and social withdrawal—perhaps to more exclusive school settings.[52]

Figure 2.8. Summary of Litigation Mid-2007

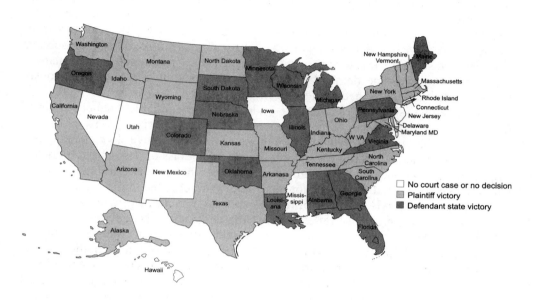

Source: National Access Network, Teachers College, Columbia University. Available at www.schoolfunding.info. Used with permission. Updated July 23, 2007.

52 For example, see David C. Thompson, *School Finance Litigation: Does It Make a Difference? A Review of Literature and Analysis of Selected Data in Four States* (internal document). This research was funded by The National Education Association, Washington, DC (1998). See also David C. Thompson and Faith E. Crampton, "The Impact of School Finance Litigation: A Long View," *Journal of Education Finance* 27, no. 3 (2002). More recently, see R. Craig Wood and David C. Thompson, "Politics of Plaintiffs and Defendants," in *Politics of Education Law: Effects on Education Finance,* 2004 American Education Finance Association Yearbook, ed. Karen DeMoss and Kenneth K. Wong (New York: Eye On Education, 2004), 37–45. Relatedly, see Faith E. Crampton and David C. Thompson, "When the Legislative Process Fails: The Politics of Litigation in School Infrastructure Funding Equity," in *Politics of Education Law: Effects on Education Finance,* 2004 American Education Finance Association Yearbook, ed. Karen DeMoss and Kenneth K. Wong (New York: Eye On Education, 2004), 69–88.

CAN SCHOOLS SERVE ECONOMICS, EQUALITY, PRODUCTIVITY, AND LIBERTY?

Our discussion in this chapter has pointed up the difficult situation that schools face when trying to satisfy all stakeholders equally well. Some parts of society pursue education for economic reasons, while others see schools as a forum for redressing social injustice. Still other groups view schools as a place where the principles of liberty should reign, though there is strong disagreement about whether liberty means freedom to achieve based on ability or whether freedom is only realized once schools have enabled society's less fortunate at the expense of the privileged. In all instances a common thread is the demand for educational productivity however variously defined, a demand that is becoming ever more strident.

Maintaining—or even establishing—adequate and equitable financial support for schools has become exceedingly complex. As costs have risen, taxpayer burden has grown at the same time that costs of other social services have skyrocketed. Attitudes about adequate funding for schools are a deep morass of desires, resentments, and mandates. On one hand, the numbers are so vast that it is hard to imagine revenues are inadequate and that to ask for more surely stretches the limits of reason, particularly as education is only one of many important government functions. On the other hand, the depth of need reflects increasing demands on schools from all quarters. And at the same time, the success of public education is being questioned relentlessly. The struggle comes not so much from whether or not people want the benefits of schooling, but rather from how to distribute education in ways that respect our heritage and our debt to society without losing our individual freedom to accept or reject educational benefits or to obtain them from nonpublic sources. It is exactly this tension that is reflected in schools: a tension among the forces of economics, equality, productivity, liberty, and democracy—a tension that may be irreconcilable within our present form of government because equality and productivity are always at odds, as are equality and liberty. But most importantly, it is in exactly this context that all school finance policy is made.

pointcounterpoint

Point

The protracted struggle in state legislatures and courts over school funding is divisive and wasteful. Common sense tells anyone that children have unequal needs, and common sense tells politicians to quit squabbling over school-aid plans because we have the technical knowledge to do what is right. The "controversy" is only a ruse to distract from the underlying fundamentals—those with money do not want to share it with those less fortunate, and to fund schools fairly is political suicide for elected officials. In sum, it is easier to outmaneuver court orders than to face political constituencies.

Counterpoint

The long history of school finance litigation has produced a dedicated set of reformers, all of whom seem to argue that no amount of funding will eliminate the perceived equality gap. The truly fundamental issue is that existing resources are poorly managed and any new money will be badly misused too. Plaintiffs in school finance regularly play on race and class and plead their case in the media ahead of entering the courtroom because their mission is to drive new money into schools regardless of demonstrable benefit. The only solution, if conceding that schools are in fact underfunded, is to combine existing/new funding with structural reforms in a high-stakes scenario.

Questions

♦ Which of these diametrically opposed perspectives on school funding best represents your own inclinations? Why?

♦ Do any arguments presented by either side fail to make sense? Why?

♦ How can states redress the legitimate issues in this discussion without surrendering their treasuries?

CASE STUDY

As the new assistant superintendent for management services in your school district, you sensed something was afoot at last night's school board meeting. Several board members seemed vitally interested in media reports that the state legislature might take renewed interest in school size/efficiency and that school district consolidation might be a hot topic in the next legislative session. You had seen the same reports and knew that questions were swirling in the state capital about keeping taxes down and avoiding tax increases at all costs, particularly as next year is an election year. You had worked in other states where lawmakers had taken similar interest, and you were savvy enough to realize that some issues take on a life of their own. In fact, you had mused silently, that there really was no difference between beliefs and reality, as reality simply was whatever people thought in large enough numbers to vote in that direction.

Your superintendent had mentioned the possibility of district consolidation in last week's administrative cabinet meeting. He had reviewed national trends and suggested that it appeared many states were jumping on the bandwagon. He had mentioned recent examples, including Arkansas' attempt in 2004 at massive consolidation; a proposal in Maine in 2007 to reduce districts to only 26 mega-districts; a South Carolina effort in 2007 to abolish the state's 86 school districts and instead to form 40 regional councils; and proposals in other states, generally at legislative behest and often with governors' backing. Consolidation proponents had cited savings such as reduced staff and fewer infrastructure demands, along with greater state flexibility in resources. Opponents, however, had vociferously countered, citing studies detailing hardships for students when schools close, reduced activity participation as a consequence of longer bus rides and loss of local school identity, and increased costs as administrative units would need to be expanded along with greater transportation costs and the need to construct new schools.

Following last night's meeting, your superintendent requested time to discuss with you what the district's position should be if consolidation were to become a local topic. Most important was to consider whether consolidation would help or harm your district as its enrollment size fell squarely in the middle of your state's profile. Although the superintendent thought your district was in no danger of being eliminated, real questions emerged about the impact of consolidation on staffing, facilities, curriculum, treatment by the state aid formula, and so forth. The point of the conversation came down to one question: What consolidation scenarios could be anticipated, and with what effect?

Not surprisingly, your superintendent asked you to prepare an analysis of likely scenarios. He indicated he would expect a background review of actions in other states and analysis of those situations that seemed most comparable to your own state. Your analysis should consider school districts surrounding your own and how those districts might be viewed through legislative eyes. Additionally, your study should consider the impact if your district needed to absorb enrollments from any closed districts. Your study, you learned, would be used in lobbying your local legislative representatives, the state school board association, and other power brokers in the state capital.

Below is a set of questions. As you respond, consider the context of this entire chapter and apply your new knowledge to the situation:

Questions

♦ What concerns do you believe will be immediately voiced by the community once this topic becomes public?

♦ How does this district's profile compare to your own place of residence?

♦ What would be the local reaction in your school district if consolidation were proposed?

FOLLOW-UP ACTIVITIES

♦ Obtain information on the history of education in your state (your state department of education is often a good source). Identify important issues such as the history of school district formation and reorganization, major legislative initiatives related to schools, and the relative autonomy (degree of centralization or decentralization) of educational decision making permitted by the legislature over time.

♦ Identify the major organizations in your state that have direct or indirect influence on educational policy making at state and local levels. State the nature of their influence and reflect on the degree of impact they have.

♦ Obtain a copy of the organizational chart in your school district, and trace the formal authority and power structure.

♦ Obtain a copy of your school district's most recent annual budget and identify the relative contribution of federal, state, intermediate, and local units of government. Interview your district's chief fiscal officer to learn the kinds and amounts of state aid your school district receives. Discuss any potential inequities in the state aid formula relative to your school district.

WEB RESOURCES

American Association of School Administrators, www.aasa.org
Education Commission of the States, www.ecs.org
National Center on Education and the Economy, www.ncee.org
National Center for Education Statistics, www.nces.ed.gov
National Conference of State Legislatures, www.ncsl.org
National School Boards Association, www.nsba.org
U.S. Department of Labor Bureau of Labor Statistics, www.bls.gov/
U.S. Census Bureau, www.census.gov/
U.S. Department of Education, www.ed.gov/

RECOMMENDED READINGS

Alperovitz, Gar. *America Beyond Capitalism: Reclaiming Our Wealth, Our Liberty, and Our Democracy*. Hoboken, NJ: John Wiley & Sons, 2005.

Anthony, Patricia, and Stephen L. Jacobson, eds. American Education Finance Association. Annual Yearbook. *Helping At-Risk Students: What Are the Educational and Financial Costs?* Newbury Park, CA: Corwin, 1992.

Berne, Robert, and Lawrence O. Picus, eds. American Education Finance Association. Annual Yearbook. *Outcome Equity in Education*. Thousand Oaks, CA: Corwin, 1994.

Chaikind, Stephen, and William J. Fowler, eds. American Education Finance Association. Annual Yearbook. *Education Finance in the New Millennium*. New York: Eye On Education, 2001.

Checci, Danielle. *The Economics of Education: Human Capital, Family Background and Inequality*. New York: Cambridge University Press, 2006.

Crampton, Faith E., and Terry N. Whitney. *Principles of a Sound State School Finance System*. A monograph of the Education Partners Project, Foundation for State Legislatures. Denver, CO: National Conference of State Legislatures, 1996.

DeMoss, Karen, and Kenneth K. Wong, eds. American Education Finance Association. Annual Yearbook. *Money, Politics, and Law: Intersections and Conflicts in the Provision of Educational Opportunity*. New York: Eye On Education, 2004.

Hanushek, Eric, and Finis Welch. *Handbook of the Economics of Education, Volumes 1–2*. Amsterdam, The Netherlands: North-Holland, 2006.

Jacobson, Stephen L., and Robert Berne, eds. American Education Finance Association. Annual Yearbook. *Reforming Education: The Emerging Systemic Approach.* Thousand Oaks, CA: Corwin, 1993.

Levin, Henry M., and Patrick J. McEwan, eds. American Education Finance Association. Annual Yearbook. *Cost-effectiveness and Educational Policy.* New York: Eye On Education, 2002.

Picus, Lawrence O., and James L. Wattenbarger, eds. American Education Finance Association. Annual Yearbook. *Where Does the Money Go? Resource Allocation in Elementary and Secondary Schools.* Thousand Oaks, CA: Corwin, 1995.

Stiefel, Leanna, Amy Ellen Schwartz, Ross Rubenstein, and Jeffrey Zabel, eds. American Education Finance Association. Annual Yearbook. *Measuring School Performance and Efficiency: Implications for Practice and Research.* New York: Eye On Education, 2005.

Theobald, Neil D., and Betty Malen, eds. American Education Finance Association. Annual Yearbook. *Balancing Local Control and State Responsibility for K-12 Education.* New York: Eye On Education, 2000.

Ward, James G., and Patricia Anthony, eds. American Education Finance Association. Annual Yearbook. *Who Pays for Student Diversity? Populations Changes and Educational Policy.* Newbury Park, CA: Corwin, 1991.

BASIC FUNDING STRUCTURES

THE CHALLENGE

Something that does not vary cannot be a function of anything else....However, it need not follow that this is the best approach for the state to pursue in its attempt to eliminate the positive relationship between fiscal capacity and educational opportunity.

Monk (1990)

CHAPTER DRIVERS

At the close of this chapter you will have reflected upon these questions:
- What is the context of funding schools in America?
- What is the overarching tax system at federal, state, and local levels?
- What are state-aid formulas?
- What is a fair funding formula?
- How do states fund schools?
- What funding improvements may be on the horizon?

THE CONTEXT OF FUNDING SCHOOLS

Our journey thus far has made the case that the context of funding public schools is highly complex, in large part due to the tense and confusing political environment in which education operates. The environment is tense because a multitude of governmental bodies vie for a limited pool of total tax dollars, and it is confusing because government does not function well in a resource competition scenario and because it has no way to engage a profit motive by which to stockpile spare resources. So while most organizations today are complex, by contrast people in business or industry have a much simpler task understanding their employer's funding needs. This is because, for most people, it is a simple matter to grasp that their employer's survival depends on offering products or services that consumers are willing to buy. Under such straightforward conditions, the business will die if the product or service is unpopular or is overpriced. In sharp contrast, most government will not die regardless of whether its services are popular, but it is placed in the position of demanding resources from a captive client base through the taxation process. Like it or not, schools fall under the government heading and thus compete for limited tax resources—and people do not like to pay taxes and frequently do not understand (or value) what their taxes buy. With that statement, we come to the crux of this chapter: Business stakeholders understand their sources of revenue in the form of products or services—education's stakeholders, however, have a much less market-driven product and a much fuzzier concept of revenue streams, so that many citizens never go beyond the general idea that too-high taxes somehow fund schools.

Although the topic of education's funding sources is very complex, we can obtain a working grasp of the issues by examining the sources and types of revenue used to fund schools. Relatedly, we can gain a deeper understanding of school funding context by considering the elements of school funding formula fairness as it has developed over the last century, largely in response to the legislative and litigative pressures that have enveloped schools for many years. And finally, we should consider the current and prospective status of school funding by exploring how states fund schools, along with an eye toward any improvements that may be on the horizon. In sum, now that we have a beginning grasp on the politics of schools, values, and money, it is time to expand our knowledge to include *revenue sources* and school funding *formula* plans.

REVENUE FOR SCHOOLS

A constant theme throughout this book is that revenue for schools is a source of tension in many states. The roots of this struggle fundamentally derive from disputes over what schools should do and the inescapable fact that school revenues are mostly derived from involuntary taxation. Although other revenue sources in fact exist, it is unrealistic to think that taxes are less than the lion's share *or* that taxes will be replaced soon by some magic pool of money.

WHAT IS THE OVERARCHING TAX SYSTEM?

The history of taxation is extensively covered in many locations, including our own books.[1] Everyone realizes taxes are necessary, and everyone enjoys the many benefits paid for by tax revenues. As we saw in the last chapter, a strong national defense, good highways, stable social benefits, and intergovernmental revenue sharing are among the services funded by federal taxation. City streets, police and fire protection, and safety codes are among the local tax benefits enjoyed by citizens. Roads, clean water, and community development often emanate from taxes paid to intermediate units of government such as counties. Of especial importance, local taxes provide many highly visible services, including a significant contribution toward meeting school costs.

The overarching tax system therefore has three principal players in the form of *federal, state,* and *intermediate/local* units of government. Each has a very different role, although overlap is meaningful. Each level of government also has a relationship to schools in some varying proportion.

What Is the Federal Tax System?

The federal tax system that exists today is far removed from the early awkward attempts to create a federal tax structure. Oddly, in a nation born of suspicion toward all central government, the federal tax system today has become a massive organization best perceived for rampant overspending and troublesome growth in national debt. The drama of overspending is reflected in efforts to balance the federal budget, a goal that ebbs and flows depending on the mood of Congress and White House administrations (Fig. 3.1, p. 74). That deficit reduction is important goes mostly unchallenged, as we saw earlier that federal spending has resulted in a deficit that amounted in 2006 to an unpaid liability of $28,423 against every man, woman, and child in this nation—a debt that increases daily.

At its most fundamental level, the debate over federal spending takes root in efforts to limit the role of central government. Historically a nation of tax protesters, Americans have fought heavy federal taxation until only recently. Numerous attempts at centralized taxation dating from the 1600s were bitterly opposed by the colonists and underlaid the Revolutionary War in 1776. Even the war itself was a target of tax protest, marking the first instance of a budget deficit as the new nation struggled with war debt. Early presidents and congressional leaders were themselves mostly antitax zealots, leading to a weak federal tax system that depended mostly on tariffs and customs for the first 125 years of nationhood. Repeated efforts to establish a federal income tax failed or were rescinded shortly after passage into law, including a lawsuit in which the U.S. Supreme Court declared invalid an 1894 income tax law

---

1   For a relatively brief history of taxation for public education illustrating contentiousness, see Chapter 3 in David C. Thompson, R. Craig Wood, and David Honeyman, *Fiscal Leadership for Schools: Concepts and Practices* (New York: Longman, 1994), 131–72.

Figure 3.1. Recent Historical Trend Line, National Debt: 1950–2010

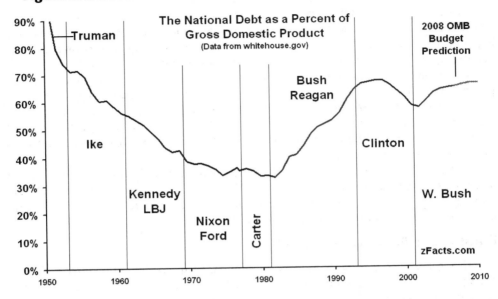

Source: http://zfacts.com/p/318.html. (The data are from the historical table 7.1 in the 2006 OMB Budget as downloaded from WhiteHouse.gov. It was plotted without modification.)

on the grounds that the federal Constitution did not expressly authorize Congress to collect such a tax.[2]

The needs of a growing nation, however, caused an impoverished Congress to propose the structure that eventually evolved into the tax system that exists today. In 1909, Congress proposed a Sixteenth Amendment to the Constitution, granting Congress the power to "lay and collect taxes on incomes, from whatever source derived, without apportionment among the States, and without regard to any census or enumeration." The amendment was finally ratified in 1913, whereupon Congress enacted a tax of 1% on personal incomes, which soon led to the now-familiar progressive tax system based on successively higher tax rates for higher incomes—a concept that has evolved into a massive arm of the federal government in the form of the Internal Revenue Service and yielding revenues that most people find incomprehensible. By 2005, individual income taxes hovered around the $1 trillion mark, corporate income tax around $278 billion, social insurance around $794 billion, excise taxes around $73 billion, and so on almost endlessly. These realities yielded about $2.2 trillion in federal revenue—numbers projected to jump sharply by 2010 (Fig. 3.2).

---

2   *Pollock v. Farmers Loan & Trust Co.*, 158 U.S. 601, 15 S. Ct. 912 (1895).

Figure 3.2. Federal Receipts by Source (in Millions of Dollars): 1935–2010

Fiscal Year	Individual Income Taxes	Corporation Income Taxes	Social Insurance & Retirement Receipts	Excise Taxes	Other	Total Receipts
1935	$ 527	$ 526	$ 31	$ 1,439	$ 1,084	$ 3,609
1940	$ 892	$ 1,197	$ 1,785	$ 1,977	$ 698	$ 6,548
1945	$ 18,372	$ 15,988	$ 3,451	$ 6,265	$ 1,083	$ 45,159
1950	$ 15,755	$ 10,449	$ 4,338	$ 7,550	$ 1,351	$ 39,443
1955	$ 28,747	$ 17,861	$ 7,862	$ 9,131	$ 1,850	$ 65,451
1960	$ 40,715	$ 21,494	$ 14,683	$ 11,676	$ 3,923	$ 92,492
1965	$ 48,792	$ 25,461	$ 22,242	$ 14,570	$ 5,753	$ 116,817
1970	$ 90,412	$ 32,829	$ 44,362	$ 15,705	$ 9,499	$ 192,807
1975	$ 122,386	$ 40,621	$ 84,534	$ 16,551	$ 14,998	$ 279,090
1980	$ 244,069	$ 64,600	$ 157,803	$ 24,329	$ 26,311	$ 517,112
1985	$ 334,531	$ 61,331	$ 265,163	$ 35,992	$ 37,072	$ 734,088
1990	$ 466,884	$ 93,507	$ 380,047	$ 35,345	$ 56,311	$ 1,032,094
1995	$ 590,244	$ 157,004	$ 484,473	$ 57,484	$ 62,727	$ 1,351,932
2000	$ 1,004,462	$ 207,289	$ 652,852	$ 68,865	$ 91,989	$ 2,025,457
2005	$ 927,222	$ 278,282	$ 794,125	$ 73,094	$ 81,136	$ 2,153,859
2010	$ 1,428,317	$ 325,459	$ 1,029,309	$ 63,600	$ 108,039	$ 2,945,724

Source: The U.S. Census Bureau. Available at: http://www.census.gov/govs/estimate /0500ussl_1.html

Although the federal tax system and its revenues have grown by leaps and bounds, the path has not been smooth. At the same time Congress has been under pressure to reduce debt and taxes, people have expected strong national defense, unemployment benefits, good retirement and highways, and so forth. Congress has always managed to spend more than it receives, and education has been one of its beneficiaries, although—as we now know—the federal role has been limited because the Tenth Amendment leaves education to the states. Nonetheless, federal revenues have been widely infused into schools. Ever since the Northwest Ordinance in 1787 first granted land to states for educational purposes, the federal government has tried to assist states in areas of federal interest. As we saw in the last chapter, the list of federally aided programs is long and includes special education, school lunch, vocational education, and many others. Although the role has been indirect, the dollars have not been trivial. Estimated federal on-budget funds in 2005 through the U.S. Department of Education totaled $71 billion—a sum excluding other federal programs indirectly benefiting schools, such as income security payments, social services grants, human development services, training and employment assistance, health services, and a wide scope of other federal aid to states that directly or indirectly assist education. Although there is a common perception of relatively minor involvement by the federal government in education, the data on federal regulations, requirements for services, and even the amounts of federal school aid meaningfully dispute the notion of a weak federal role.

What Is the State Tax System?

An important aspect of taxation in the United States has been the simultaneous development of multiple tax systems. As everyone knows, states have played a central role in the nation's history, so much so that even today we hear issues of states' rights debated vigorously in respected forums. People feel strongly about the relationship of government to its constituents, and the authority of states has been jealously guarded.

The pervasive tax nature now ascribed to the federal government is true of state tax systems too. The dissimilarity, of course, is the number of variations on tax themes, as there are 50 states but only one federal government. As a result, each state's tax system has been affected by unique economic and political factors within individual states and further affected by the relationship of states to the federal government.

As we saw earlier, colonial tax systems predated federal efforts to levy taxes. In fact, the system of elected representation to Congress guaranteed that states would closely guard their autonomy, as the U.S. Constitution granted to the states all powers not reserved to Congress itself. Differences in geography, climate, economy, and preferences further ensured that states would approach taxation differently. Many of the earliest colonial government structures were directly aimed at counteracting a strong federal seat of power, beginning with the Virginia legislature's defiance in 1619 against the Virginia Company's attempts to revoke certain freedoms. By 1700, all colonies had written charters guaranteeing liberties borne of conflict between the Crown and independent-minded colonialists.

Not surprisingly, colonial—and later state—systems of taxation were tightly linked to local politics and economics. As the need for revenue expanded with population growth, the New England colonies tended to tax personal property, land, and houses in the belief that every person's taxpaying ability was different and that everyone should pay. Concentrated wealth in the South meant only a few persons would pay big taxes, so a revenue system based on exports and imports was developed to shift taxes away from the wealthy few. Other taxes such as poll and faculty taxes were used as proxies for ability to pay. The middle colonies picked up this system and made refinements to these taxes. Colonies also ran lotteries or invented other special revenue sources.

As the nation developed, strong state curbs on federal power were deliberate from the outset. The Constitution gave the federal government only limited power to lay taxes for the purpose of paying debts and for the general welfare of the nation. States, however, were granted full powers, including control of local government, chartering of towns, building of roads and bridges, protection of civil liberties and, of course, care of the federal government via representation in Congress. Such responsibility was not free to states, however. By the end of the Civil War, colonial-style tax systems were no longer adequate given a growing population, and the answer seemed to be state authority to tax all property. Widespread tax evasion was rampant, however, in that homes and livestock were visible whereas other property, such as bonds, notes, and negotiable instruments, was easily concealed. The effect was to make states look bad, as the entire tax burden inadvertently fell to real property owners who could not hide their wealth.

Beginning about 1880, study commissions began exploring ways to improve state tax systems, especially administration of the property tax. This resulted in creation of tax equalization boards, efforts to improve property assessments, prosecuting tax evasion, and refining tax requirements on various property types. Efforts still met with limited success, as equalization proved politically distasteful and as evasion and resistance to taxes were impossible to eliminate. The numerous woes of property tax administration ultimately led to many recommendations that states should abandon the property tax in favor of other tax bases. Faced with such problems, states began to rely less on property, and by 1920 several states had adopted both individual and corporate income tax plans. Although the property tax at the state level has never been eliminated, states now have widely enacted income taxes, as well as many other taxes on commercial transactions such as sales and excise taxes.

Growth in state taxation has been phenomenal. In 1900, states were levying only small property taxes and other miscellaneous taxes, whereas states now regularly charge taxes against real estate and motor vehicles and reap huge sales and gross receipts taxes in addition to personal income taxes. States also long ago began withholding taxes for retirement and unemployment and many other social security-like programs. Federal revenue-sharing has entered the modern picture as well, so that by 2005, states were collecting more than $408 billion in intergovernmental aid, up from less than $200 million in 1900. The greatest growth has been in the individual income tax, which in 2005 produced more than $220 billion and in sales tax, which yielded another $213 billion to states. Although states depend on many sources for revenue, it is clearly sales and income that make up the lion's share of a total revenue scheme that yielded more than $1.6 trillion in 2005 (Fig. 3.3, p. 78).

Although state revenues have grown, states have found ways to spend most of their resources. The biggest state costs have been education, human services,[3] highways, health, and natural resources. In 2005, state education expenditures reached more than $427 billion. Human service costs reached nearly $317 billion in the same year, while highways received more than $76 billion. States generally have not engaged in deficit spending like the federal government, often because of individual states' balanced budget laws, which require balanced budgets. States also have found taxpayers more willing to support initiatives within state borders than has been true at the federal level, making state coffers relatively more flush with less resentment. But that is not to say that state resources have been ample, as the same Constitution that prevents the federal government from assuming a direct educational role has assigned that role to states—with the result that states have had to assume a massive share of education's costs, which has resulted in the complex state-aid formulas discussed later in this chapter.

---

3   This phrase may be more familiar to some readers as *welfare* or *ADC* (Aid to Dependent Children). In the postwelfare reform era, many states have renamed this *aid to children and families in poverty.*

Figure 3.3. State Government Finances: 2005

	(in thousands)		(in thousands)
Revenue	1,637,791,549	Direct expenditure by function	1,066,989,405
General revenue	1,282,318,490	Direct general expenditure	872,147,900
Intergovernmental revenue	408,449,375	Capital outlay	89,247,775
From Federal Government	386,027,090	Other direct general expenditure	782,900,125
From local governments	22,422,285	Education services:	
General revenue from own sources	873,869,115	Education	191,948,821
Taxes	64,811,258	Capital outlay	20,921,038
Property	11,349,052	Higher education	152,556,732
Sales and gross receipts	311,433,765	Capital outlay	19,809,592
General sales	212,906,626	Elementary & secondary	5,804,827
Selective sales	98,527,139	Capital outlay	629,605
Motor fuel	34,570,428	Other education	33,587,262
Alcoholic beverage	4,731,621	Libraries	476,094
Tobacco products	12,916,670		
Public utilities	11,022,793	Social services & income maintenance:	
Other selective sales	35,285,627	Public welfare	317,294,573
Individual income	220,254,617	Cash assistance payments	12,559,125
Corporate income	38,691,026	Vendor payments	264,786,985
Motor vehicle license	18,220,765	Other public welfare	39,948,463
Other taxes	48,162,033	Hospitals	42,324,183
		Capital outlay	2,251,684
Expenditure	1,470,456,615	Health	31,124,945
By character and object:		Employment security administration	4,377,732
Intergovernmental expenditure	403,467,210	Veterans' services	1,349,107
Direct expenditure	1,066,989,405	Transportation:	
Current Operations	738,063,183	Highways	75,787,718
Capital outlay	94,550,274	Capital outlay	50,768,213
Construction	77,219,745	Air transportation (airports)	1,380,795
Other capital outlay	17,330,429	Parking facilities	16,166
Assistance and subsidies	30,307,592	Sea and inland port facilities	1,173,179
Interest on debt	36,093,679	Public safety:	
Insurance benefits and repayments	167,974,677	Police protection	9,996,942
Exhibit: Salaries and wages	196,220,683	Correction	38,367,706
		Capital outlay	1,698,100
		Protective inspection and regulation	8,081,816

Source: The U.S. Census Bureau. Available at: http://www.census.gov/govs/estimate/0500ussl_1.html

What Is the Local Tax System?

From our discussion, it is clear that tax systems in the United States are interrelated and independent at the same time. The federal tax system is limited to those powers constitutionally allowed to Congress, and the federal branch by virtue of the Sixteenth Amendment has monopolized the individual income tax—a reality effectively limiting how far lower units of government can go to that same source without angering taxpayers. The state tax system is expected to pick up where federal responsibility leaves off, but with very broad state powers (and duties) implied. States have opted to tax income as well, although they have turned heavily to sales tax too, with additional reliance on the property tax. Yet states often have chosen to push tax-and-service obligations downward to local governments, in the perhaps convenient belief that people prefer government at the lowest common denominator. Schools have been impacted greatly by such shifts in power and obligation among levels of government, with strong implications for tax sources and school revenues.

Although federal and state governments have tended to be centrally structured, local government has been highly fragmented to include counties, cities, schools, and other very small units such as villages and townships. Despite proliferation of small units, local tax systems have been limited mostly to the property tax to address the many needs left to local government; that is, federal and state governments have dealt with broad issues, while local government has been assigned issues viewed as mostly local in scope. In many states, this has meant heavy local responsibility for schools, some kinds of welfare, local health, roads, police and fire protection, corrections, sanitation, and issues of economic development. In addition, local government is highly visible and accessible, so that patrons are more empowered and ready to invest energy in being heard, including complaining and forcing the outcome of controversial issues.

Because federal and state governments have first claim on tax sources, local units have had no choice but to tax the leftovers. This has meant that local government has come to depend on three main sources for funding. First, local units have turned to revenue sharing from the federal government, capturing more than $52 billion in 2005. A second source has been state revenue sharing, providing about $399 billion in the same year. The third source has been local taxation, yielding more than $448 billion, a burden borne in significant part by the local property tax. But like higher levels of government, local units have found ways to spend, as local units (primarily cities and counties) spent slightly more than the $1.3 trillion they collected in 2005 (Fig. 3.4, p. 80).

Although schools are local governmental units, they have not had the luxury of overspending, as most states keep education on a strict cash basis. In addition, revenue sharing has meant little to schools, as federal and state grants-in-aid to education do not participate directly in such sharing. Although states have tapped all their various revenue sources to fund their share of education's costs, we finally arrive at the observation that local districts have been limited almost entirely to property taxes for support of schools.

Figure 3.4. Local Government Finances: 2005

	(in thousands)		(in thousands)
Revenue	1,307,002,281	Education services:	
General revenue	1,160,395,873	Education	497,426,812
Intergovernmental revenue	451,494,652	Capital outlay	57,121,286
From Federal Government	52,128,887	Higher education	29,711,251
From State government	399,365,765	Capital outlay	3,082,480
General revenue from own sources	709,901,221	Elementary & secondary	467,715,561
Taxes	448,273,481	Capital outlay	54,038,806
Property	324,328,967	Libraries	9,394,832
Sales and gross receipts	71,830,490	Public welfare	44,712,587
General sales	50,048,343	Cash assistance payments	9,278,172
Selective sales	21,782,147	Vendor payments	4,539,917
Motor fuel	1,199,503	Other public welfare	30,894,498
Alcoholic beverage	413,499	Hospitals	60,989,787
Tobacco products	420,084	Capital outlay	3,789,141
Public utilities	11,528,580	Health	35,804,607
Other selective sales	8,220,481	Employment security administration	5,498
Individual income	20,675,556	Transportation:	
Corporate income	4,446,941	Highways	48,112,256
Motor vehicle license	1,433,269	Capital outlay	18,106,383
Other taxes	25,558,258	Air transportation (airports)	17,031,470
Expenditure	1,313,749,897	Parking facilities	1,387,197
By character and object:		Sea and inland port facilities	2,740,163
Intergovernmental expenditure	13,372,918	Public safety:	
Direct expenditure	1,300,376,979	Police protection	64,662,110
Current Operations	1,023,793,753	Fire protection	30,738,976
Capital outlay	183,989,519	Correction	20,885,203
Construction	141,946,530	Capital outlay	1,131,626
Other capital outlay	42,042,989	Protective inspection and regulation	4,790,941
Assistance and subsidies	9,278,172		
Interest on debt	55,748,463		
Insurance benefits and repayments	27,567,072		
Exhibit: Salaries and wages	498,049,641		

Source: The U.S. Census Bureau. Available at: http://www.census.gov/govs/estimate /0500ussl_1.html

Tax System Summary

For schools, the impact of multiple and overlapping tax systems has been complex and confining. First, federal aid to education has been sizable but limited in scope, with no expectation for change given federal Constitutional constraints. Second, state aid has become increasingly important, as states have responded to school finance reform and to aggressive litigation testing states' duties to schools. Third, local school districts have been heavily property tax dependent, so that in 2005, the mix of revenues to a typical district in the United States was 9.6% federal, 49.9% state, and 40.4% local—mostly from real property taxes (see Fig. 2.7, pp. 54–55). Fourth, the revenue mix has been highly varied on a state-by-state basis, with local support ranging from a low 27% in Nevada to a high of 87% in Hawaii in that same year. Fifth, schools usually have been prevented from tapping tax bases other than property, as most states do not allow schools to tax income or other kinds of personal wealth. The net sum is that schools are primarily supported by state and local taxes, with limited but meaningful federal assistance.

The tax system summary is a jumble of competing and complementary entities. The overarching tax system is made up of federal, state, and local tax structures, with the federal system relying on individual income taxes and with only a tertiary (although profound) relationship to schools. State systems are based mostly on individual income and retail sales taxes, with relationships to schools dependent on state preferences—a relationship consequently either primary or secondary. Local tax systems are based mostly on real property taxes—a reality that has caused the property tax to be seen as "the school tax" because schools seldom have any other taxing authority. Under these conditions, the local relationship to school funding is very strong. From this flows the observation that the kinds of revenue available to schools are fundamentally sales and income taxes through the state level and property taxes at the local level. And, finally, it is starkly clear that schools compete with all other government entities for tax revenue because there are practical limits on the amount of tax dollars that can be generated—and those same dollars must be apportioned among the many agencies sponsored and controlled by federal, state, and local governments.

FUNDING FOR SCHOOLS

With a basic—albeit brief—grasp of tax systems behind us, we turn to an overview of how school districts are funded. This is an issue that goes deeper than overarching tax systems, as it raises questions of distributional fairness and ultimately equality of educational opportunity. If we believe, as we said in the first chapter, that the amount of money available is important to the success or failure of schools, it follows that how money flows to local school districts is a critical question of fundamental sufficiency and fairness—that is, an adequacy/equity question.

In the last part of the chapter, we turn to exactly these issues. Our first priority is to gain an understanding of how states deal with school-aid distribution. From there, it becomes important to understand the principles of a fair formula for granting money to individual districts. And, finally, it is useful to consider whether there are innovations in school funding on the horizon. We tackle these issues now because all the chapters in this book fit together like a house of cards: that is, all the subsequent topics in this book will have no real world consequence if revenues are inadequately and inequitably distributed. In sum, *good tax systems must provide adequate revenue from multiple sources distributed to schools using equitable aid formulas*—only then can schools undertake the budgeting behaviors that comprise the remaining chapters of this book.

WHAT ARE STATE AID FORMULAS?

Almost everyone realizes that money for schools comes primarily from taxes. In most states, the real property tax is a major source of local revenue for schools. At the same time, almost everyone realizes that virtually no school district in the United States is completely at the mercy of local tax bases for funding education. Local *tax base* is simply too uneven to accept the revenue variability that would arise from *district wealth* alone, a fact recognized by even the most recalcitrant state policy maker who thinks the fairness debate has gone too far. Instead, most states have tried to develop state school-aid schemes that speak to some basic elements of adequacy and equity. School-aid formulas thus attract a great deal of attention at federal, state, and local levels, although states have been the primary player in designing and implementing aid formulas—both by choice and by force of litigation.

Under these conditions, state-aid formulas are legislative tools used to intervene into the disparities in educational opportunity that would be present if schools were entirely dependent on local tax base. It is not hard to imagine the size of such disparity absent intervention, as most states have wide extremes of local wealth, that is, *tax capacity*. A fairly common case, for example, is a public utility power plant in a small school district that creates vast *wealth per pupil* in the form of taxable property. Another district in the same state may be of similar geography and population size, but may have only marginal farmland as its tax base. Disparities in wealth per pupil in such cases can easily be 100:1 or greater, meaning that the wealthy district can raise $100 for every $1 raised in the poorer district—all at the same tax rate! The example in Fig. 3.5 is quite common, with the wealthiest district able to raise $25 million locally, five times more than the poorest district—all at a uniform tax rate of 100 mills (or $100 per $1,000 of assessed valuation)—ignoring the fact that a poor district almost never can tax itself at such a strenuous rate. The effect is vastly different tax rates to produce the same revenue per pupil, *or* vastly different expenditures per pupil if local patrons do not support the higher tax rate scenario. Any number of variations on this example can be created to fit any state's circumstance—states with huge cities, for example, face vast disparities in tax base because of suburban flight. *In sum, a state school-aid formula seeks to reduce or eliminate tax base differences by offsetting the effects of local wealth disparity on educational opportunity.*

WHERE DID AID FORMULAS COME FROM?

Americans have not been enthusiastic about paying taxes at any time in the nation's history. A big part of the reluctance to pay taxes was cultural, but real problems have existed in tax administration, aggravating an already bad situation. As we discussed earlier, tax evasion has plagued all levels of government, both as people sometimes have refused to pay taxes and—in the more modern case—as they have

Figure 3.5. Tax Capacity at 100 Mills Uniform Effort

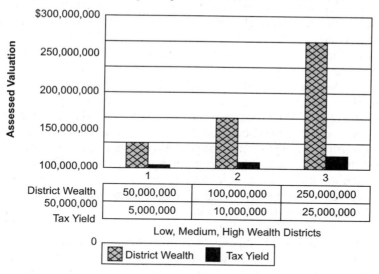

District Wealth	50,000,000	100,000,000	250,000,000
50,000,000 Tax Yield	5,000,000	10,000,000	25,000,000

Low, Medium, High Wealth Districts

District Wealth   Tax Yield

found ways to avoid taxes, both legally and illegally. The many tax problems faced by government led to the study of tax fairness and administration, so that knowledge about good tax systems, with implications for schools, grew rapidly during the first half of the twentieth century.

Growth of schools in the nation, accompanied by growth in state responsibility for education, also led to state interest in providing at least some fiscal aid to local schools. Although we are skipping much historical development here, it is the case that by 1890 states were providing nearly $34 million in aid to schools (approximately 24% of revenues). A goodly portion of such aid was stimulated by the fledgling concept of educational program equity that followed on the heels of the first studies within states revealing vast disparities arising from an exclusively local tax base reliance. Although state aid predates the work of Elwood P. Cubberley, he is credited with initiating the dramatic rise in interest in state aid, and in 1906 he published a monograph that set the tone for the future.[4] Cubberley's point was simple by today's standard, yet profound for his time, as he argued that all the children of the state are equal and entitled to equal advantages. In studying several states, Cubberley concluded that few, if any, had met this demand because educational quality varied greatly and generally rose or fell in close tandem with local property wealth.

---

4   Elwood P. Cubberley, *School Funds and Their Apportionment* (New York: Columbia Teachers College, 1906).

Cubberley's work sparked an entire growth industry, as other scholars undertook similar studies. Harlan Updegraff's work[5] in 1922 extended thinking another step. Studying rural schools in New York State, Updegraff argued that state aid should vary by local wealth and in correspondence to local tax effort. Where Cubberley had validated the need for aid and created the concept of equality, Updegraff introduced the ideas of *equalization* and *reward for tax effort*—that is, districts could receive more state aid by taxing themselves at higher rates. The next major advance came in 1923 with the work of George Strayer and Robert Haig.[6] Accepting all that had already been done, Strayer and Haig took another giant step forward by advocating that concepts of equality and equalization should also result in a degree of *minimum educational opportunity*. Their view essentially bound the state to go beyond just providing money to include some measure of program equality. They additionally argued that such a program should be available under *uniform tax effort*. The result was a *foundation program*, whereby the state would guarantee a financial/educational foundation on which local districts could then build.

Another significant step was taken in the work of Paul Mort in 1924.[7] Mort extended the minimum program concept by defining the *weighted* pupil, that is, arguing that educational programs will have different costs in order to be equal. For example, small schools cost more as a consequence of enrollment inefficiencies. His contribution was to critically press how states determine aid to districts, arguing that aid should vary along multiple criteria based in trying to estimate true educational costs, rather than just granting aid in a blindly neutral fashion.

The ideas of these early researchers were widely used when creating state-aid programs, as states struggled to conceptualize how they should aid schools. One last major breakthrough was less enthusiastically received, however. Henry Morrison, writing in 1930, was so disturbed by the extremes in quality of educational programs that he argued strongly for abolition of all school districts, favoring a complete state takeover.[8] This was not at all radical in his view because he believed that because states had the ultimate duty to control education, fiscal inequality would never be resolved until tax base and educational program control were entirely statewide affairs. Obviously, such thinking ran counter to local control and was not warmly embraced by most legislatures—a sentiment that endures today despite the obvious minimization of variability that comes with a uniform statewide funding system.

What Is a Fair Formula?

Development of state-aid plans clearly had basic fairness in mind, at least in terms of what theorists intended, by suggesting ways to make educational opportuni-

5   Harlan Updegraff, *Rural School Survey of New York State: Financial Support* (Ithaca, NY: Author, 1992).

6   George D. Strayer and Robert M. Haig, *The Financing of Education in the State of New York,* vol. 1 (New York: Macmillan, 1923).

7   Paul Mort, *The Measurement of Educational Need* (New York: Columbia Teachers College, 1924).

8   Henry C. Morrison, *School Revenue* (Chicago: University of Chicago Press, 1930).

ties more equal through the use of money. A state-aid formula, according to theorists' thinking, should fit the unique needs and features of school districts within each state, and the plan should apply universally within the state's borders. States worked at developing aid plans using these criteria, with each plan further reflecting certain educational and political philosophies and realities. For example, states taking an aggressive view of state responsibility for education developed school-aid plans that made the state a fuller funding partner. Conversely, states favoring a more local control perspective tended to devise aid plans that left considerable local freedom to exceed a set of educational minimums. These facts were the basis for a genre of state-aid plans that fall into several general types, based on what states believed to be fair. Over the years, grant-in-aid plans have become known as *flat grants, equalization grants, multitier grants*, and *full state funding grants*.

Flat Grants

The earliest form of state aid, a *flat* grant is a flat sum of money per unit, such as student or teacher, paid to districts without concern for a local share or local ability to pay. This plan was justified by its advocates as distributionally neutral. Critics, however, argued that wealth disparity remained unchanged and that aid amounts were often too low to make a real difference. Flat grants proved popular, however, so that in the early state-aid years as many as 38 states were using them to aid public schools. Indeed, popularity fell only as school finance litigation escalated in the 1970s. No state now relies solely on flat grants as the principal finance scheme, although they are still used for other purposes or in multitier combinations.

Figure 3.6 (p. 86) illustrates the operation and effect of a flat grant. The graph shows that while a $1,000 flat grant per-pupil surely would be welcomed in low-, medium-, and high-wealth districts alike, its impact is completely unrelated to local ability to pay for schools. It is likely most desperately needed in the low-wealth district, and it certainly represents a larger proportion of total expenditure per pupil in the poorer district.

However, introduction of a flat grant has absolutely no impact on equalization: that is, wealth-based inequalities are untouched while expenditures in all districts simply go up by exactly $1,000 (or alternatively, the local unit of government might choose to reduce local tax effort by an equivalent amount so that students are no better off dollar-wise or equalization-wise after the introduction of state aid). The net sum for poor districts was no change in equalization, *and* the net sum for wealthy districts was enrichment unrelated to educational need. Flat grants thus represented a significant step forward in terms of states participating in education's costs, but the flat grant represented no gain in reducing the inequalities related to unequal tax base.

Equalization Grant

Equalization plans include a wide variety of state-aid formulas seeking to grant aid *inversely* to local ability to pay for schools. Largely in response to the nonequalizing effect of earlier aid plans, equalization grants were designed to bring expenditure levels in rich and poor districts closer together, or at least to better equalize poorer districts' opportunity to spend at the same level as wealthier districts. Although many kinds of equalization grants exist, all such plans are based on the idea

Figure 3.6. Effect of a $1,000 Flat Grant

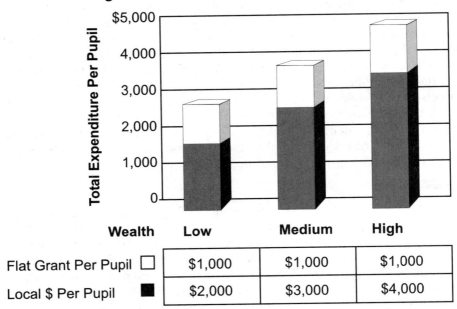

Wealth	Low	Medium	High
Flat Grant Per Pupil ☐	$1,000	$1,000	$1,000
Local $ Per Pupil ■	$2,000	$3,000	$4,000

of increasing state aid to those local districts with the least fiscal capacity. Differing political philosophies have driven actual formula designs in individual states, primarily by virtue of the decision that must be made: Should the state set expenditure levels and tax rates *or* should the state let districts set their own tax-and-spend limits? Major kinds of equalization plans flowing from this decision became known as *minimum foundation* plans and *resource accessibility* plans.

Foundation plans were based on a minimum concept. This meant several things. First, a foundation plan is politically and factually effective in that equality is "met" by requiring a uniform minimum expenditure level and uniform minimum tax rate in each school district throughout the state. Second, the state requires districts to provide a minimum standard educational program. Third, a foundation plan encourages higher local spending by authorizing additional local tax effort. Fourth, the minimum costs are better equalized because aid is inversely granted based on local ability to pay for schools. On the downside, minimum required expenditure levels must be meaningful, and the state cost-share must be high enough to encourage local effort above the minimum. The foundation has been the most popular equalization plan, and many states currently use some form of foundation plan as the primary means to distribute state aid. Several states also use a foundation in combination with other aid programs.

Resource accessibility plans also have sought to equalize school revenues by taking a different approach. While a foundation plan focuses on statewide minimum standards in tax rate and expenditure levels, resource equalization plans try to empower districts to make their own fiscal and program decisions unhindered by local wealth limitations. This means that variability in programs and expenditures are acceptable so long as availability of revenue is not the reason for such variability. So while foundation plans promote minimum equality, resource accessibility plans attempt to balance wealth, or ability to pay, in each district through formulas that adjust for tax base differences. The vehicles have been various *percentage equalizing* (PE) plans, and these plans have been further refined to include variations such as *guaranteed tax base* (GTB), *guaranteed tax yield* (GTY), and *district power equalization* (DPE). Each of these resource equalization plans approaches the problem of unequal resources uniquely. PE plans guarantee a constant percentage of budget from the state based on local ability to pay, with the local district setting costs and programs. GTB and GTY equalize revenues by assuring districts the same tax capacity as every other district. DPE carries the resource accessibility concept to its ultimate potential of *recapture of excess revenue* capacity by requiring that districts with wealth greater than the state's per-pupil guarantee must remit any excess revenue generated to the state for redistribution to poorer districts. Compared to the popularity of foundation plans, fewer states have adopted resource accessibility, and most states adopting some version of the latter plans have softened the most politically risky features. Almost no states have adopted a true power equalization formula, at least on a long-term basis. Equalization schemes have served a useful purpose, however, in that school finance reform in the 1970s gave impetus to self-scrutiny by states of their school aid formulas, with resultant improvement of equalization on a wide scale that has carried forward to the present day.

Figure 3.7 (p. 88) illustrates the operation and effect of a simple equalization plan. The graph shows a foundation plan, with a uniform tax rate and with an expected $5,000 per-pupil expenditure target. The poorest district raises only 20% of the target from local tax effort, and the state is obligated to provide the other 80%. Conversely, the wealthiest district raises 100% of the target at the uniform minimum tax rate. As we said earlier, countless variations on this scheme are possible. Some states provide local option leeway above the minimum expenditure, and the leeway may or may not qualify for state aid depending on the state's preferences. Recapture might be built in by setting the statewide tax rate high enough to produce more revenue than some districts can legally spend per pupil. The variations are too many to illustrate here, but the effect of aid inversely related to local ability to pay is clearly the aim of any equalization formula. Equalization plans are costly to states, both in terms of actual dollars when setting adequate resource levels and in political terms because concepts like low aid, zero aid, or recapture can take a toll over time if wealthy communities oppose sending their tax dollars to support other school districts (see the discussion in Chapter 2 on long-term political consequences of aggressive attempts at equalization).

Multitier Grants

Because all aid plans have politically objectionable features or inherent weaknesses, policy makers have sometimes created state-aid formulas that combine parts of several plans. For example, an astute legislature might enact a foundation program combined with local leeway. Variations might include capping local leeway, equalizing the local leeway portion at the same aid ratio as the foundation amount, or equalizing the local option only to a certain point after which no cap and no aid apply.

Figure 3.7. Effect of an Equalized Foundation Grant

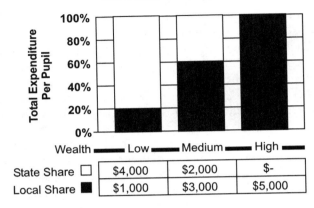

Foundation Plan Under Uniform Tax Rate
with a State Cost-Share Ratio 0-80%

	Low	Medium	High
State Share ☐	$4,000	$2,000	$-
Local Share ■	$1,000	$3,000	$5,000

Other pieces, such as flat grants or incentive aid, could also be attached to the basic formula structure. Such designs are known as *multitier* grants. Combinations of multitiering are limited only by good sense and money.

Several states use multitiering to set the state's share of education's costs. The most common mixture combines flat grants or foundations with some form of percentage equalization. As a general rule, one scheme provides base aid, while the other formula is added for political reasons. Figure 3.8 illustrates a very simple multitier aid formula by combining a base-mandated (foundation) per-pupil amount under uniform tax rate, with an additional 25% local option leeway added at the same aid ratio as the foundation amount. In this example, districts can choose to spend up to $6,250 per pupil, but they must tax themselves voluntarily for the portion identified as the local share of local option. The state's aid ratio, however, is guaranteed up to the maximum per-pupil expenditure level, so choosing to exert higher local tax effort means more aid in return for additional local spending on children's education. Of course, districts can choose to not exert the optional extra tax effort and forego the enticement of additional state aid. Many policy decisions are imbedded in these designs: for example, Fig. 3.8 contains a concession to wealthy districts, as it has been designed to provide an additional 25% spending window for any district opting for additional local tax effort—a disequalizing but politically smart move. In essence, multitiering has seemed to some states to be a palatable alternative in a world where politics and fairness must be carefully balanced.

Full State Funding Grants

We noted earlier that full state funding has never been accepted in the real-world policy arena. Regarded as radical and inimical to local control of schools, full state funding has received little support except in a couple of instances. The best defense of full state funding is its strict observance of education as the state's inescapable duty, but that has not been enough to offset the drawbacks associated with loss of local control and other broad policy objectives.

Figure 3.8. Effect of a Foundation Grant with Equalized Local 25% Option Leeway

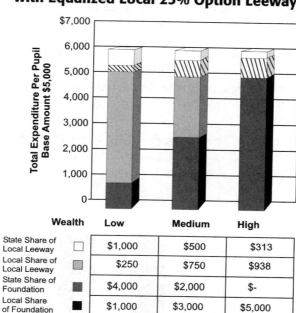

Wealth	Low	Medium	High
State Share of Local Leeway ☐	$1,000	$500	$313
Local Share of Local Leeway ▨	$250	$750	$938
State Share of Foundation ▩	$4,000	$2,000	$-
Local Share of Foundation ■	$1,000	$3,000	$5,000

Operationally, full state funding is extremely simple. It places all the resources of a state within reach of every child by requiring a statewide tax, apportioned equally without regard to location or wealth. The plan is different, however, in that there can be no local leeway because local tax-and-spend choices no longer factor into the plan. Furthermore, the tax is truly statewide and is not considered to be a local resource. Finally, recapture is inherently included because uniform statewide taxes will produce differing amounts from the various communities, with some communities generating excess revenue above permissible expenditure levels. These features are radically different from all other plans, particularly running contrary to local control—a feature confirmed in that all revenue collected locally is sent to the state for redistribution on a statewide basis—that is, local tax resources actually belong to the state.

With these stipulations, only a few states, under very rare conditions, have adopted full state funding. Hawaii's single-school-district structure has permitted full state funding, and the unusual nature of the District of Columbia's dependence on Congress for funding describes the only other true case. Some people would argue that their states are "nearly full state funded" because of high levels of state aid with only small local tax contribution. But for the most part, full state funding has been antithetical to the ideal of local control, despite the plan's ability to eradicate wealth-based differences.

Figure 3.9 depicts the ideal full state funding plan, although oversimplified here by a lack of vertical adjustments such as diseconomy of scale (discussed in the next section). Figure 3.9 shows a mandate that each district spend exactly $5,000 per pupil, with the local share financed by a uniform 20 mills tax effort. The poorest district can raise only $40 per pupil in local revenue, while the wealthiest district's tax yield per pupil exceeds the required uniform expenditure per pupil. The result is that the state must provide aid to all districts in the amount of $5,000 per pupil, but it does so in part by recapturing $1,000 ($6,000 - $1,000 = $5,000) per pupil from the wealthiest district and redistributing the recaptured amount to other districts that qualify for state aid—a balancing act involving state-level decisions on whether to set the statewide mill rate high enough to cover the total cost of education in all school districts, or whether to supplement educational expenditures by tapping other state sources such as sales and income taxes.

Figure 3.9. Full State Funding Per-Pupil Grant

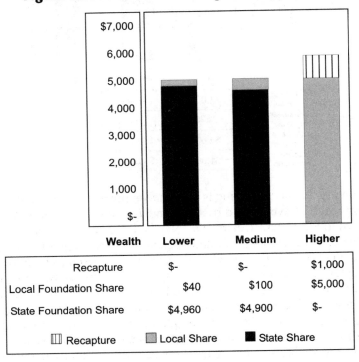

Wealth	Lower	Medium	Higher
Recapture	$-	$-	$1,000
Local Foundation Share	$40	$100	$5,000
State Foundation Share	$4,960	$4,900	$-

▦ Recapture   ▦ Local Share   ■ State Share

Adjustments to Basic Formulas

Our discussion to this point has only considered regular education programs, with no consideration for special adjustments to school aid formulas based on differences in the human condition. In its most basic form, this simply means that *horizontal* fairness requires all children to be funded as equals, but that children are not equally advantaged physically, economically, and so on. States have increasingly come to aid such differences, and a common vehicle is through *vertical* adjustments to the basic aid formulas we just described. As a generalization, vertical adjustments fall into categories of *need* equalization and *cost* equalization.

Need Equalization

The concept of need speaks directly to the differences among children relating to physical and economic disadvantage. Anyone who has spent time around children understands that they have complex needs that cannot be addressed simply by equality based in blind neutrality. Although there is much disagreement about how to address children's needs on physical, psychological, emotional, and many other dimensions, inequality of the human condition is undisputed. Need equalization has therefore become a critical player in state aid to schools. A huge outlay of programs has sprung up around the concept of special needs, most of which fall into categories relating to *compensatory education, bilingual education,* and *special education,* as well as *early childhood education.* It is a modern reality that most states provide some additional financial support to these areas in an effort to equalize fundamental differences.

Compensatory education primarily tries to redress social and economic inequality by targeted funding to low income students, a concept familiar in this book because the social context of education in Chapters 1 and 2 particularly spoke to these disadvantages. The federal government has long had an interest in compensatory education through many kinds of legislation, ranging from school breakfast/lunch to special reading programs. Additionally, many states provide aid to compensatory education, often added above the cost of regular education, either by a weighting scheme that adjusts for increased per-pupil costs, or by a flat grant added to regular education costs. Local districts are typically required to share in the extra costs. At the present time, about half of all states provides some kind of compensatory education services.

With growth in immigration, aid to *bilingual education* has become increasingly important to states and local school districts. Various court rulings have spurred the need for bilingual programs, in that civil rights legislation has been held to encompass language barriers. Court rulings and other federal legislation have caused states to provide bilingual programs or risk lawsuits or loss of federal funding for failure to meet bilingual mandates. The response has been varied, as states have taken very different approaches to aiding bilingual education. States with larger bilingual populations often spend the most and usually provide more extensive programs, while less-affected states spend less and sometimes provide more limited services. Most states now offer bilingual education in some form, with about half providing a formal weighting scheme. The most common methods use additional pupil weights or provide flat grants beyond regular education costs.

Aid to *early childhood education* recently took on new life. Various states have implemented new programs, both on the basis of preschool mandates and as a result of a belief that early intervention has a demonstrable investment return in later years of schooling. A large majority of states now provide some type of early childhood education services, although data are sparse on funding methods.

Special education has been the most visible vertical need program for many years. Although special purpose schools have been around for many decades, special education has taken on new meaning in the last four decades with enactment of federal special education legislation and an aggressive history of litigation surrounding the rights of special needs children (see Chap. 2). Although other vertical needs adjustments receive at least modest attention in most states, special education has been the center of intense activity, with every indication of continuing far into the future as a powerful political and legal force.

States generally fund special education in much the same way as other special needs programs, but the mandated nature of special education and the vast amount of money involved result in strict governmental monitoring, particularly because special education funding involves a mix of federal, state, and local monies. States typically fund special education by providing additional per-pupil or per-teacher weightings or by using *restricted* or *categorical* grants to reimburse districts for the excess costs of special education. Many states either weight pupils by handicapping condition or make other weighted provisions for instruction, such as funding special teacher costs or classroom units up to a capped amount. Other states pay all excess costs for special services or reimburse some percentage of total costs. A few states use flat grants or combinations of aid plans. An arena in which constant change prevents up-to-the-minute accuracy when reporting funding plans in a textbook, all states now provide some method of aiding special education.

Cost Equalization

The socioeconomic, political, and geographic uniqueness of states has encouraged other concerns for vertical equity as well. In particular, state responsibility for education has caused states to pay attention to other pupil inequities that may arise from a whole host of external conditions. Often these issues go to economy of scale, as districts may experience higher costs because of their very urban or very rural circumstances. Cost equalization in school funding usually takes two forms. One form recognizes that different costs may arise because of *economy* or *diseconomy* of scale. The other form considers the *marketplace*. For example, higher costs may stem from the price of urban life. But conversely, rural districts may face higher costs when trying to attract and retain personnel. Similarly, rural school districts may face higher costs related to distance education and transportation over long and sparsely populated distances.

States choosing to engage in school cost equalization do so based on political and educational ideologies. Politically it makes sense to take care of a state's constituents, and it is as educationally sound to care as much about unequal scale or market costs as it is to care about other kinds of special needs. Cost equalization is addressed most often through categorical aid or by pupil weightings attached to the regular aid plan. A majority of states now provides aid for extra cost factors such as enrollment density or sparsity, declining or increasing enrollment, grade level differences, and so forth. A few states have tried to create price indices based on market differences, although the complexity and political explosiveness have made it difficult to enact on a wide scale.

HOW DO STATES FUND SCHOOLS?

Our discussion throughout this entire chapter has illustrated that states have many goals when designing school-aid formulas.[9] At the most basic level, aid formulas are an attempt to redress tax base (local wealth) inequalities. Such inequality, if not abated, would result in unacceptable variations in educational program quality because money is linked to student achievement in a complex—although poorly understood—fashion. It is at least linked in that less money buys less instruction, and it is sufficient to say that less instruction is unacceptable to nearly everyone. The first goal of aid formulas, then, is to make more money available to all districts using state resources. Other goals are equally important. Among those goals are the need to address special human conditions, to reflect the unique problems of individual states, and to convince taxpayers that their voices are heard and that their resources are not wasted. At the same time, state aid formulas must satisfy external legal mandates based in constitutional equality. And certainly, states are attuned to political philosophies as they try to create aid plans that are neither overly intrusive on local control nor too benign to be effective.

Although it is impossible to publish absolutely current funding information in a textbook as a consequence of the constantly changing political arena, Fig. 3.10 (pp. 94–95) is excerpted from the most current authoritative compilation of state school aid features.[10] By far, foundation schemes remain the most popular type of aid formula, with only three states claiming to provide full or near-full state funding. Aid ranges widely across the 50 states, although how states accumulate and report these data leave much room for interpretation (e.g., a low dollar spending level receiving a high level of state aid is misleading). States also show a common concern for vertical adjustments, usually attaching these features to the basic state-aid plan in some fashion. Although schools in all states would opt for more money if offered, the data in this chapter indicate a legislative awareness of states' educational obligations, leaving only the details and amounts of aid open to serious debate.

ARE THERE INNOVATIONS ON THE HORIZON?

The issues in this chapter are complex from economic and sociopolitical perspectives and do not have simple solutions. Nor is there a very satisfying answer to the question of whether there will soon be new ways to fund schools. Consequently, it is essential to accumulate and weigh all the material in this chapter so that an understanding of the barriers to innovation can be comprehended.

---

9 See also *Principles of a Sound State School Finance System* (Denver, CO: National Conference of State Legislatures, 1996) where Crampton and Whitney enumerate five major policy goals state policy makers strive to incorporate in their education funding plans: equity, adequacy, efficiency, accountability, and stability.

10 Data years in Fig. 3.10 are the latest available. Each column represents the most recent available year. Note that reporting limitations prevent uniformity of years.

Figure 3.10. Major Features of State Aid Plans: 2002–2005

CRITERION LATEST YEAR	Formula Type 2005	Pupil Spending 2003	State Aid % 2002	LER Required 2005	Recapture 2005	Revenue Limit 2005	Lottery Earmark 2005	SPED Weight 2005	SES Weight 2005	ELL Weight 2005
Alabama	Foundation	$ 7,058	65.4	Yes	No	No	No	Yes	No	No
Alaska	Foundation	$ 7,791	68.7	Yes	No	Yes	No	Yes	No	Yes
Arizona	Foundation	$ 6,331	51.2	Yes	No	Yes	No	Yes	No	Yes
Arkansas	Foundation	$ 7,439	83.2	Yes	No	Yes	No	No	No	No
California	Foundation	$ 6,765	63.2	No	No	Yes	Yes	No	No	No
Colorado	Foundation	$ 7,490	44.9	Yes	No	Yes	Yes	No	Yes	No
Connecticut	Foundation	$ 9,605	38.8	Yes	No	No	No	No	Yes	Yes
Delaware	Flat grant + equalization	$ 9,472	70.5	No	No	No	No	Yes	No	No
District of Columbia	Foundation	$ 11,031	n/a	n/a	n/a	No	No	Yes	No	Yes
Florida	Foundation	$ 6,729	51.2	Yes	No	Yes	Yes	Yes	No	Yes
Georgia	Flat grant + equalization	$ 8,346	53.2	Yes	No	Yes	Yes	Yes	No	Yes
Hawaii	Full state funding	$ 8,123	98.0	n/a	n/a	No	No	No	No	No
Idaho	Foundation	$ 6,609	66.6	Yes	No	Yes	Yes	Yes	No	No
Illinois	Foundation/Flat grant	$ 8,030	40.1	Yes	No	Yes	Yes	No	No	No
Indiana	Foundation	$ 8,620	51.3	Yes	No	Yes	No	Yes	Yes	Yes
Iowa	Flat grant + equalization	$ 8,586	49.9	Yes	No	No	No	Yes	Yes	Yes
Kansas	Flat grant + equalization	$ 8,334	64.9	Yes	Yes	No	No	No	Yes	Yes
Kentucky	Flat grant + equalization	$ 7,451	66.9	Yes	No	Yes	Yes	Yes	Yes	No
Louisiana	Flat grant + equalization	$ 7,746	55.9	No	No	Yes	Yes	No	Yes	Yes
Maine	Foundation	$ 9,521	45.8	Yes	No	No	No	No	Yes	Yes
Maryland	Flat grant + equalization	$ 8,968	39.8	Yes	No	Yes	No	Yes	Yes	Yes
Massachusetts	Foundation	$ 8,921	43.7	Yes	No	Yes	No	Yes	Yes	Yes
Michigan	Foundation	$ 8,646	69.5	Yes	No	Yes	Yes	No	No	No
Minnesota	Flat grant + equalization	$ 8,270	64.9	No	No	Yes	No	No	Yes	No
Mississippi	Foundation	$ 6,646	63.5	Yes	No	Yes	No	No	Yes	No
Missouri	Foundation	$ 7,741	49.3	Yes	No	No	Yes	No	Yes	No
Montana	Foundation	$ 8,249	54.9	No	No	Yes	No	No	No	No
Nebraska	Foundation	$ 9,117	38.5	Yes	No	Yes	Yes	No	Yes	Yes
Nevada	Foundation	$ 6,394	64.9	Yes	No	Yes	No	Yes	No	No
New Hampshire	Flat grant + equalization	$ 8,186	52.4	No	No	No	Yes	No	Yes	No
New Jersey	Foundation	$ 10,908	43.4	Yes	No	No	No	No	Yes	No
New Mexico	Foundation	$ 7,668	83.9	Yes	No	Yes	No	Yes	Yes	Yes

CRITERION LATEST YEAR	Formula Type 2005	Pupil Spending 2003	State Aid % 2002	LER Required 2005	Recapture 2005	Revenue Limit 2005	Lottery Earmark 2005	SPED Weight 2005	SES Weight 2005	ELL Weight 2005
New York	General aid	$ 10,665	52.5	No	No	No	Yes	Yes	Yes	Yes
North Carolina	Foundation	$ 7,153	66.7	No	No	Yes	No	No	No	No
North Dakota	Foundation	$ 8,056	41.9	Yes	No	Yes	No	Yes	No	Yes
Ohio	Foundation	$ 8,735	47.7	Yes	No	Yes	Yes	Yes	No	No
Oklahoma	Foundation	$ 6,756	63.5	No	No	Yes	Yes	Yes	Yes	Yes
Oregon	Foundation	$ 7,753	61.3	Yes	No	Yes	Yes	Yes	Yes	Yes
Pennsylvania	Percentage equalizing	$ 8,777	39.5	No	No	No	No	No	Yes	Yes
Rhode Island	General aid	$ 9,386	43.5	No	No	Yes	No	No	Yes	Yes
South Carolina	Foundation	$ 7,776	56.0	Yes	No	No	Yes	Yes	Yes	No
South Dakota	Foundation	$ 7,663	43.6	Yes	No	Yes	Yes	No	No	No
Tennessee	Foundation	$ 6,704	49.1	Yes	No	No	Yes	Yes	Yes	Yes
Texas	Flat grant + equalization	$ 7,570	43.8	Yes	Yes	Yes	Yes	Yes	Yes	Yes
Utah	Foundation	$ 5,067	64.1	Yes	Yes	Yes	No	Yes	No	Yes
Vermont	Full state funding	$ 10,571	57.7	No	No	No	Yes	No	No	No
Virginia	Foundation	$ 8,071	44.0	Yes	No	No	Yes	Yes	No	Yes
Washington	Full state funding	$ 6,985	68.5	No	No	Yes	Yes	Yes	No	No
West Virginia	Foundation	$ 9,286	67.4	Yes	No	Yes	Yes	Yes	No	No
Wisconsin	Guaranteed tax base	$ 9,414	57.5	No	Yes	Yes	No	No	No	No
Wyoming	Foundation	$ 9,811	53.4	Yes	Yes	Yes	No	Yes	Yes	Yes

Legend:

LER Required = local tax effort is required before receiving state aid.

Recapture = state recaptures excess revenue capacity for formula redistribution.

Revenue Limit = state limits amount of revenue a district may raise.

SPED Weight = state uses a weighting factor or other adjustment to compensate special education excess costs.

SES Weight = state uses a weighting factor or other adjustment to compensate for socio- economic disadvantage (usually poverty).

ELL Weight = state uses a weighting factor or other adjustment to compensate for English language learner status.

The short answer to impending innovation in school funding is that there is little reason to expect major change. The reasons are simple, but profound. We already know how to build a good aid formula, at least on the surface, for inverse fairness purposes. We know far less about the impact of money on student outcomes, though, which leaves great uncertainty relating to how much money should be provided and how it should be directed. More specifically, we can build good revenue equalization schemes, but it is not that particular technology which holds us back—it is a forbidding combination of lack of knowledge about how to apply any given amount of money, coupled with the certainty that enough money still would not be available even if the first problem went away. In other words, our long-standing quip that any problem can be solved by throwing money at it is mostly true; we would be better able to do that, however, if only we knew how much to throw and where to aim. Our barriers, quite simply, are the dark holes in the science of teaching and learning, the vagaries of the human condition which seems to continually worsen, and the politics of competing for scarce tax dollars.

Under these conditions, dramatic innovation is highly unlikely. First, politics cannot be removed from state school aid plans because representative government reasonably requires legislators to represent their constituents' interests—meaning that any gains in aid plan features will disadvantage some constituents, leading to chipping away at gains through representative democracy. Second, no amount of formula refinement can offset underfunding. Third, a perpetually underfunded climate is likely far into the future because all governmental needs are increasing and because local and state governments are the most vulnerable to citizen pressure to reduce spending. We're reminded of a signboard near one of our universities that says, "Vote for responsible education: just say no to tax increases!" These conditions (and more) do not suggest that some new funding design is waiting to solve education's fiscal problems if only it could be "found." Rather, it suggests that educators, policy makers, and taxpayers have a hard road ahead if they are to resolve their political differences in ways that bring harmony instead of more shrill partisanship.

At the same time, we should celebrate the long way that school aid formula fairness has come, and we should give credit to educators, policy makers, and laypeople alike who have struggled to produce a system that works surprisingly well despite its evident problems. In fairness, the job faced by legislators is daunting as they try to appease vocal advocacy groups from all walks of life who compete for the same finite tax resources—a condition under which a win by one group always results in loss by another group because new revenue is rarely available. Educators deserve praise, too, as public schools have become vast social providers with broad missions far surpassing basic teaching and learning. Taxpayers also deserve understanding, as it must be conceded that government has grown by leaps and bounds with staggering monetary outlays. Society simply has not reconciled its insatiable appetite for entitlements with the cost of those conveniences. Accordingly, no magic school aid formula exists. Fairness, or the lack thereof, is both to the credit and discredit of the same players. The question becomes how to give all players everything they want—a difficult scenario when the human condition comes in conflict with simultaneously competing demands for excellence, equity, efficiency, and liberty.

pointcounterpoint

Point

Of all the many obligations faced by states, public schools should be the first priority—even at the expense of other social programs—given how lack of education always eventually translates into higher social service costs.

Counterpoint

When states experience revenue shortfalls, all state spending—including spending for public schools—must be reduced to a manageable level because states generally cannot engage in deficit spending. Failure to reduce costs is a tax increase in disguise, and living within the state's means is the only answer to uncontrolled spending increases.

Questions

- ◆ In your opinion, which state services are most important to fully fund? Why?
- ◆ How do states come to experience such budget shortfalls, and what should they do to correct such situations?

CASE STUDY

As one of the more established superintendents in your state, you have been asked to testify next month before a legislative interim committee studying school finance. You are no stranger to state politics, and it has long been your belief that your state's school funding formula is outdated and deficient in some important ways. More specifically, you have spoken out in the past in favor of increasing the formula base state aid and expenditure per-pupil amounts in the belief that the true costs of education are greater than current permissible levels, and you have lobbied for increased recognition of vertical adjustments to the state aid formula that would take into account an expanded definition of at-risk pupils. As you have considered the invitation to testify, it has occurred to you that you will be questioned closely because some members of the interim committee likely will represent school districts that would not benefit from your views.

As you began to prepare for your testimony, you ran through the "expectations" you will face. Certainly your own school board will want you to advocate positions favorable to your district—a fairly well-to-do community whose children perform well on state assessments and who go on to become businesspeople or college-educated professionals. Relatedly, the school finance formula in your state allows districts to levy a local option tax for program enhancements, and your district currently levies at the maximum, allowing you to fund exemplary programs that would have to be cut if the local option leeway were eliminated. Another set of expectations, you pondered, will come from rural districts, which you know have been under severe stress as a result of bad weather and depressed farm prices. Still another set of expectations will come from your state's urban districts, which have been hammered in the press over declining achievement scores, high transience, incidences of violence, and teacher union unrest. And, of course, there are the many districts throughout the state greatly resembling your own district's profile—that is, doing well and mostly wishing for new money to do more good things for children, but generally not wanting to rock the boat in the state capital.

The agenda for next month's legislative meeting devotes an hour to your testimony. You know the committee has already heard from experts on the elements of good school-aid formulas. Your testimony will conclude the information-gathering phase, after which public comments will be taken. The committee's goal is to recommend changes to the state-aid formula in the next legislative session.

Below is a set of questions. As you respond, consider your learning throughout this chapter and apply your knowledge and emerging beliefs/principles to the situation:

Questions

- ◆ In your opinion, what are the principles of a sound school finance system?
- ◆ What are the dangers and pitfalls in your upcoming legislative testimony?
- ◆ How will you go about satisfying the expectations of multiple constituents?
- ◆ Using your own state's school aid formula as a basis, what would you recommend to the legislative committee? How will you justify those changes, and what counterarguments could you expect from legislators, other school districts, and general critics of education spending?

FOLLOW-UP ACTIVITIES

- ◆ Obtain documents explaining the state-aid formula(s) in your state (these are often available through your state department of education). Identify the type of aid formula used in your state. Identify state revenue sources used to fund education (e.g., state general fund transfers, income tax, sales tax, lottery profits). Identify from these documents, if possible, your state's policy goals and priorities with regard to aid to local school districts.
- ◆ Identify how your state-aid formula addresses fairness to students and taxpayers. Consider how horizontal equity is addressed, and identify any vertical or other special adjustments related to need and/or cost equalization. Identify the amounts of money allocated to general aid, categorical aid, pupil weighting, and need or cost adjustments. Determine whether there has been any recent research on the equity or adequacy or your state's funding system and, if available, examine the results.

♦ Interview leaders of educational organizations (e.g., school board, teachers' union, administrators, state agencies, professional associations) to learn what they perceive as the strengths and weaknesses of your state's aid formula. Ask what needs to be done to improve adequate and equitable school funding in your state.

♦ Watch for meetings addressing school funding you can attend. These might include legislative committee meetings, legislative issues town meetings, teacher association meetings, local school board meetings, and so forth—any place where school funding will be discussed. Capture the issues and attitudes expressed, and try to identify the players who are most influential. Find out whether major changes may be on the horizon.

♦ Compare how your state funds education to other states in your region. Consider numbers of students to be educated, dollars legislatively appropriated, choice of state-aid formula design, and revenue (tax) sources for education. Assess which states provide the greatest degree of equity and adequacy in their funding systems, and justify your conclusions.

WEB RESOURCES

American Federation of Teachers, www.aft.org
Council of Chief State School Officers, www.ccsso.org/
Education Commission of the States, www.ecs.org
Education Week, www.edweek.com
National Access Network, www.schoolfunding.info
National Association of State Boards of Education, www.nasbe.org
National Center for Education Statistics, www.nces.ed.gov
National Conference of State Legislatures, www.ncsl.org
National Education Association, www.nea.org
National Governors Association, www.nga.org
National School Boards Association, www.nsba.org
U.S. Census Bureau, www.census.gov/govs/www/index.html
U.S. Department of Education, www.ed.gov

RECOMMENDED READINGS

Anthony, Patricia, and Stephen L. Jacobson, eds. American Education Finance Association. Annual Yearbook. *Helping At-Risk Students: What Are the Educational and Financial Costs?* Newbury Park, CA: Corwin, 1992.

Berne, Robert, and Lawrence O. Picus, eds. American Education Finance Association. Annual Yearbook. *Outcome Equity in Education.* Thousand Oaks, CA: Corwin, 1994.

Brimley, Vern and Garfield, Rulon R. *Financing Education in a Climate of Change.* 10th ed. Boston: Allyn & Bacon, 2008.

Chaikind, Stephen, and William J. Fowler, eds. American Education Finance Association. Annual Yearbook. *Education Finance in the New Millennium.* Larchmont, NY: Eye On Education, 2001.

DeMoss, Karen, and Kenneth K. Wong, eds. American Education Finance Association. Annual Yearbook. *Money, Politics, and Law: Intersections and Conflicts in the Provision of Educational Opportunity.* Larchmont, NY: Eye On Education, 2004.

Guthrie, James W., Matthew G Springer, R. Anthony Rolle, and Eric A. Houck. *Modern Education Finance and Policy.* Boston: Allyn & Bacon, 2007.

Hartman, William T., and William L. Boyd. *Resource Allocation and Productivity in Education: Theory and Practice.* Westport, CT: Greenwood, 1998.

Jacobson, Stephen L., and Robert Berne, eds. American Education Finance Association. Annual Yearbook. *Reforming Education: The Emerging Systemic Approach.* Thousand Oaks, CA: Corwin, 1993.

King, Richard A., Austin D. Swanson, and Scott R. Sweetland. *School Finance: Achieving High Standards with Equity and Efficiency.* 3rd ed. Boston: Allyn & Bacon, 2003.

Monk, David H. *Educational Finance: An Economic Approach.* New York: McGraw-Hill, 1990.

Mueller, Van D., and Mary P. McKeown, eds. American Education Finance Association. Annual Yearbook. *The Fiscal, Legal, and Political Aspects of Elementary and Secondary Education.* Cambridge, MA: Ballinger, 1986.

Odden, Allan R., and Lawrence O. Picus. *School Finance: A Policy Perspective.* Boston: McGraw-Hill, 2008.

Picus, Lawrence O., and James L. Wattenbarger, eds. American Education Finance Association. Annual Yearbook. *Where Does the Money Go? Resource Allocation in Elementary and Secondary Schools.* Thousand Oaks, CA: Corwin, 1995.

Stiefel, Leanna, Amy Ellen Schwartz, Ross Rubenstein, and Jeffrey Zabel, eds. American Education Finance Association. Annual Yearbook. *Measuring School Performance and Efficiency: Implications for Practice and Research.* Larchmont, NY: Eye On Education, 2005.

Theobald, Neil D., and Betty Malen, eds. American Education Finance Association. Annual Yearbook. *Balancing Local Control and State Responsibility for K-12 Education.* Larchmont, NY: Eye On Education, 2000.

Thompson, David C., R. Craig Wood, and David S. Honeyman. *Fiscal Leadership for Schools: Concepts and Practices.* New York: Longman, 1994.

Vesely, Randall S., and Faith E. Crampton. "An Assessment of Vertical Equity in Four States: Addressing Risk Factors in Education Funding Formulas." *Journal of Education Finance* 30 (Fall 2004): 2:111–22.

Wood, R. Craig, David C. Thompson, and Lawrence O. Picus. *Principles of School Business Management.* 3rd ed. Reston, VA: ASBO, 2008.

Operational-izing School Money

SCHOOL FUNDS: ACCOUNTABILITY AND PROFESSIONALISM

THE CHALLENGE

The demand of policy makers at the local, state, and federal levels for quality and useful data and outcome measures to evaluate fiscal and programmatic policy changes drives the need for data systems to become more and more comprehensive....Financial reports of state and local education agencies are used to compare actual financial results with legally adopted budgets; assess financial conditions and results of operations; assist in evaluating efficiency and effectiveness of processes; and plan for the future.

NCES, Core Data Finance Force (2003)

CHAPTER DRIVERS

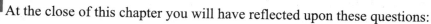

At the close of this chapter you will have reflected upon these questions:

- ♦ What is fiscal accountability?
- ♦ What are the fiduciary responsibilities of districts and administrators?
- ♦ How does the accounting process help establish accountability?
- ♦ What are the purposes of accounting?
- ♦ How are educational budgets allocated?
- ♦ How does school money get tracked?
- ♦ How do revenue and expenditure structures assist in tracking money?
- ♦ How do audits improve districts' ability to track money?
- ♦ What ethical standards should guide school leaders' professionalism in handling school money?

SETTING THE STAGE

The opening quotation to this chapter, along with the highly sensitive questions raised as chapter drivers, set a dramatic stage for an even deeper plunge into the world of school funding. As we said at the very outset, this textbook is a journey, and the interconnectedness of each chapter to the next is apparent as we begin an extended conversation about accountability for school money. Recall that we argued in Chapter 1 that citizens are increasingly involved in schools in ways best viewed as voting with their feet, and we followed in Chapter 2 by proposing that there are differing legitimate views on the value of education. We concluded in Chapter 3 that the problems faced by federal, state, and local governments are extraordinarily complex as they try to satisfy the demands of all constituencies. Our point was that schools are part of the fabric of the larger society, and citizens have the power to cause lasting change, either by forcing change or resisting it. Many school leaders have learned the hard way that the public is becoming bolder about voicing disagreement with what administrators have long regarded as routine policy in budgeting, curriculum, and so forth. In sum, the first three chapters sounded an alarm: school leaders must listen intently to their constituents, a warning that now leads to a discussion of fiscal accountability and the fiduciary trust because the best-laid educational plans mean nothing without a sound financial plan—a plan based on the highest ethical and professional accounting standards.

Until now, our discussion has focused on the broad principles of school funding. Starting in this chapter, however, we turn to the specific elements of implementing school budgets—the operational aspects of putting money to work in schools. We begin with money as an issue of accountability and trust because only a few people in a school system really understand the complex expectations to which administrators and others are held when handling public funds. Consequently, new and experienced school leaders alike must be thoroughly versed in the concepts of *fiscal accountability* and the *fiduciary trust*. Simultaneously, we must extend our knowledge of school funding by examining the *receipt of revenues* and the *restrictions on expenditures*. We should also gain a panoramic view of *how money flows* through a school system from beginning to end. Finally, we should internalize a *code of ethical standards* for handling public monies. Although complex, we tackle these topics because too many school leaders get in trouble in this arena—most frequently as a result of ignorance of good practice. In sum, the complexity of appropriate money handling is still less complex than facing the consequences of mishandling public funds.

SCHOOL FUNDS ACCOUNTABILITY

The concept of accountability for school funds is intimidating, and it deserves the fear and respect it invites. There is no defense for people who do not take time to fully grasp the weight of accountability for public money because all aspects of education suffer irreparable damage when proper accountability measures are not followed —that is, failure to establish good fiscal accountability results in pervasive distrust of everyone involved. As a consequence, we first examine the concept of accountability itself, followed by a deeper discussion of how money flows through schools.

WHAT IS FISCAL ACCOUNTABILITY?

Accountability is a term greatly overused in education these days. This does not mean that too much accountability exists, but rather that the word is applied too casually to a wide scope of activities ranging from curriculum to student achievement to mapping bus routes and winning ball games. In essence, this means that accountability is not always well defined, and its meaning is further elusive due to a lack of precise tools to measure what people hope to achieve when they think about accountability. In the fiscal world, however, accountability has a clear meaning. Fundamentally, accountability in fiscal terms means that people responsible for some activity involving money must provide evidence of appropriate care as conservators, which is now taken to include *wise use* of all resources. Importantly, the scope of accountability continues to expand so that wise use is being redefined constantly.

Accountability can be conceptualized on numerous levels. At its root, it describes the practice of sound business principles when handling money, regardless of whether the source of money is public or private. This definition can be traced back for centuries. Growth in schools in the United States has forced formal recognition of the importance of good business practice in education, with the first known business manager's position created in 1841, when the Cleveland, Ohio schools hired a manager to care for the accounting functions of the district. The ever-increasing complexities of managing the millions of dollars now characterizing virtually every modern school district have added greatly to needs for accountability awareness because the rising price of education continually increases the need for confidence that good business procedures are in place.

More broadly, accountability also has come to mean wise use of all resources in the care of the school district. This includes the accounting function, of course, but it also includes the decision-making process by which funds are spent and the outcomes linked to such expenditures. It is easy, for example, to know that spending resources on things that hold little chance for helping students is not a wise business practice; yet the issues in the first several chapters of this book suggest that wise resource use does not come easily. In other words, an increasingly sophisticated public is no longer satisfied with just good accounting procedures, choosing instead to ask more difficult questions about whether increasing teacher pay or creating new programs is wise educational and fiscal accountability. Struggles over which programs get funded or eliminated stand as proof of emerging applications of accountability, as do legislative and local debates on the relationship between funding and student achievement. This latter issue has reached historic proportions, as the *No Child Left Behind Act* of 2001 has caused states to require schools to increase minimum performance standards and as states have simultaneously enacted their own reforms that are often based in sanctions, loss of funding, and school district consolidation for either academic nonperformance or other efficiency reasons. Consequently, the topic of resource decision making and fiscal accountability is something we will return to frequently, particularly in later chapters when we address budgeting for educational programs.

What Are Fiduciary Responsibilities?

The easiest way to understand the weightiness of this chapter is to understand the definition of a *fiduciary*. As a noun, a fiduciary is a *trustee*. Trusteeship is itself a colorful word, having heavy weight attached by virtue of trust as its root. More specifically, fiduciary responsibility carries many pointed elements, with dictionaries all defining it as "...a trust, a thing held in trust, such as designating a person to hold something in trust for another ... and valuable only because of public confidence and support." The seriousness needs no development except to underscore the weighty language. For our purpose, a person with fiduciary responsibility is someone placed in charge of any kind of property and in whom others—the public, in schools' case—have placed trust, *so much so that one's personal reputation and professional livelihood are dependent on public confidence and support in wise use and conservatorship.* Under these sobering conditions, the level of trust is enormous—indeed, it is hard to conceive a more serious charge than that of a fiduciary, and the responsibility for millions of dollars entrusted to schools and their leaders is truly staggering.

As accountability has risen to a new level of public scrutiny, so have the duties and responsibilities of persons with fiduciary obligations. In other writings, we have detailed the duties of a fiduciary from the particular perspective of a school business manager. But it is easy to see that the fiduciary role also touches administrators, boards, teachers, policy makers, and laypersons to varying degrees because everyone comes in contact with school resources in some manner. We identified those duties as the following:

- ◆ *Planning:* the process of looking to the future, identifying resources and needs, and creating a master plan to follow.
- ◆ *Decision making:* the process of choosing among options, based on knowing that setting a course of action is not easy to reverse and that making choices precludes other options.
- ◆ *Organizing:* the process of preparing a plan for identifying needed human and fiscal resources and a sequence of events to reach a set of stated goals.
- ◆ *Directing:* the process of accepting responsibility to see that plans are implemented and carried out.
- ◆ *Controlling:* the process of monitoring progress against the original goals so that errors can be corrected during the implementation phase.
- ◆ *Evaluating:* the ultimate responsibility for determining if goals were met and whether resources were wisely used.[1]

These responsibilities have direct application to the business of schools. For example, administrators, teachers, and other staff have a shared responsibility for making schools successful so that only the level of direct involvement differs. As a

---

1   R. Craig Wood, David C. Thompson, and Lawrence O. Picus, *Principles of School Business Management,* 3rd ed. (Reston, VA: Association of School Business Officials, International, 2008).

rule, instructional staff carry out these duties in ways related to teaching and learning, although school site councils, decentralized budgeting, salary negotiations, and other aspects of participatory management have recently diffused formerly centralized fiduciary roles. Administrators and boards have more direct hands-on control of financial resources, although limited significantly by laws governing resource utilization and shared decision making. At the same time, policy makers are involved in setting financial guidelines and controls, in many instances providing primary leadership for increased accountability. Laypeople are increasingly involved, particularly by approving or rejecting budgets, serving on site councils, and either directly or tacitly controlling all planning activities through the democratic process. Indeed planning, organizing, directing, controlling, and evaluating are no longer discrete functions, as these critical duties increasingly involve interactions among multiple interest groups.

Although roles drive people's level of direct involvement in budget matters, interest in the fiduciary trust relating to schools and money always comes to the same end. Ultimately, the fiduciary interest relates to fulfilling the primary mission of schools—an accountability question—that is, *are schools doing what is expected?* The fiduciary path to answering this question also answers a second query: *What are the essential fiduciary duties associated with schools?* The bulleted list below indicates that meeting schools' primary mission is complex and—as we saw in earlier chapters—involved nearly $488 billion for schools in 2005, an issue of significant public trust:

- General management
- Office management
- Personnel management
- Staff development
- Collective negotiations
- Legal control
- Financial planning and budgeting
- Fiscal accounting and financial reporting
- Cash management
- Fiscal audits and reports
- Payroll management
- School activity and student body funds
- Purchasing and inventory
- School insurance and risk management
- Plant security and property protection
- School property management
- School plant maintenance
- School plant operations
- Educational facility planning

- School construction management
- Debt service and capital fund management
- Information management and technology
- School transportation services
- School food services
- Grants and contracts
- School-community relations
- Educational resource management.

How Does the Accounting Process Help?

Though not widely understood, the accounting process is *the* vehicle by which a substantial portion of accountability is carried out. Although not sufficient by itself to get at issues of school effectiveness under the meaning of broader accountability, *the accounting process serves a critical function by managing the single resource (money), which controls the purchase of all other human and material resources used to carry out the educational mission.* Importantly, emerging developments suggest that linkages will be increasingly established between the financial data examined in accounting and other forms of public calls for accountability.[2] In other words, tying school money to student outcomes continues to grow in importance.

What Are the Purposes of Accounting?

Broadly speaking, most people view accounting as a tool used in business to report profits and losses and to detect financial wrongdoing. That perception is correct, although it sells short the range of benefits gained from the accounting cycle and it misses that financial accounting also applies to nonprofit and governmental entities. In the case of schools, it also entirely misses a critical aspect of how accountability, funding, and student learning come together in a school district through the budget. We have held for many years that *a budget is the fiscal expression of the educational philosophy of a district and its schools*: that is, a budget is the implementation of the district's *educational plan*. By creating a budget, districts identify how money will be spent to achieve their stated educational goals. Only by accounting for how the budget is spent can it be known whether—in fiscal terms—the district is satisfying its programmatic expectations. These realities establish five key purposes of the accounting function, all of which are meant to keep the organization focused on its mission.

The first purpose of accounting is to set up a procedure by which all fiscal activities in a district can be accumulated, categorized, reported, and controlled. Each of these terms has specific meaning and value. Accumulating transactions sets up a

---

2   See, for example, the extensive and important revisions to fiscal reporting contained in the federal government's new accounting handbook *Financial Accounting for Local and State School Systems 2003 Edition* (Washington, DC: National Center for Education Statistics, 2003).

method of data collection in one location (a set of books) to view the district's fiscal activities. Categorizing transactions separates the various fiscal activities in terms of similarities, and it implies that grouping those transactions will provide useful analysis about where money is going. Reporting transactions makes the results of all activities known. Controlling transactions is essential because resources are finite, while needs are infinite.

The second purpose of accounting is to provide a means to judge progress toward goals. This is a cornerstone of the accountability issue, as schools increasingly must show wise use of resources beyond their traditional methods that have relied on standardized testing and other locally constructed achievement measures. The accounting function can provide a tool for assessing progress in several ways, and new directions are being sought constantly, particularly given public debates on school funding policy. One way in which the accounting function is able to help assess goal attainment is by tracking the financial condition of a district. For example, the accounting function monitors changes in balances of all funds and accounts held. To illustrate, if only 10% of instructional supply money remains by the end of the first month of the school year, the accounting function should flag a serious problem unless there has been a decision to spend money down to capture some other benefit such as bulk purchasing that offsets the otherwise alarming rate of spending. Similarly, at a later point we will discuss performance budgeting—an activity aided by the accounting function that can help judge progress on academic goals by tying fiscal information to student achievement data. The accounting function therefore helps assess whether expenditures and educational programs are in proper alignment.

The third purpose of accounting is complementary by providing hard evidence to the state that schools are meeting their educational responsibility. This purpose has an even more basic goal whereby accounting helps the state judge whether school districts, as legal arms of the state, are fulfilling the state's constitutional duty to educate. In other words, all states have inescapable duties to educate children, and accountability data—including financial data—are indicators by which states themselves may be judged. States' interest has increased as state aid to schools has grown, with states now demanding extensive reporting of school revenues and expenditures, from which many policy decisions are ultimately based. These realities have led to more uniform reporting requirements via standardized state budget documents and other reports in order to gather comparable data across districts. States themselves face upward accountability in the form of federal reporting to qualify for federal grants and federal revenue-sharing and to satisfy federal laws relating to educational equity.

The fourth purpose of accounting is to aid in budget preparation. As described in later chapters of this book, the task of building a budget at district and school levels requires historic data for baseline purposes. Indeed, budgeting is the act of placing money on line items in the total budget for the sole purpose of carrying out the district's educational plan. The process is bidirectional: The accounting function is satisfied in part by budgeting, and budget preparation requires accounting data. More specifically, accounting sets up both initial and end products by creating the funds and line items to which budget allocations are made, while the process of spending down a budget creates the data needed to carry out the accounting cycle *and* to establish a baseline for the next budget cycle.

The fifth purpose of accounting is to ensure proper handling of money and to guard against misuse of the fiduciary trust. This aspect of the accounting function is crucial to many issues discussed in earlier chapters given growing dislike among the public toward government. One direct outcome is suspicion aimed at public officials, making it critical for schools to observe the highest standards of transparency and integrity. All of us can relate cases of real or perceived abuse of public trust, and headlines speculating about misuse of public monies are commonplace. A critical aspect of the accounting function is to provide *proof* that public confidence is well placed. Accounting is thus a powerful tool for carrying out educational planning, control, and stewardship through budget structures and organization, while the budget itself is the accompanying vehicle on which all accountability rests. Accounting therefore provides a major accountability feature when it does the following:

- ◆ *Creates a complete record* of all financial transactions at district and school levels.
- ◆ *Summarizes financial activities* of the schools in reports required for proper, effective, and efficient administration.
- ◆ *Provides information* used in budget preparation, adoption, and execution.
- ◆ *Provides safeguards* on use of money and property, including protection against waste, inefficiency, fraud, and carelessness.
- ◆ *Creates a longitudinal record* to aid administrators, teachers, boards, and laypersons in program decision processes.

HOW ARE EDUCATIONAL BUDGETS ALLOCATED?

The last section introduced reasons and benefits of an accountability structure for tracking money, but it said nothing about what happens when money comes into a school district. This question of how educational budgets are allocated actually has several embedded questions that are discussed in greater detail in later chapters. For example, related questions arise regarding how to determine amounts of money to be assigned to budget lines during the budget-building process. Those are highly detailed questions that interweave the accounting and budgeting functions to make them work together—but we first need to understand the big picture of how money comes into a school district before becoming more specific about budgeting behaviors, either at district or school site levels.

Fund Structure

When we discussed educational revenue and aid plans in the previous chapter, we saw that school districts receive money from multiple sources, primarily federal, state and local governments. But regardless of how revenue sources are arranged in a given state, certain accounting principles apply that make it possible to permanently record revenues and, eventually, expenditures. For accounting and accountability purposes, we refer to the overarching record system as a *fund structure*.[3] Within the fund structure are the broad categories of *governmental* funds, *proprietary* funds, and *fiduciary* funds. Each of these must be clearly defined if we are to grasp the big picture of how money is allocated at any level.

As a preface to examining each operational fund's purpose, it is useful to underscore the fundamental point that schools operate under a system of *fund accounting*. Fund accounting is a term describing how the types of revenue and expenditure are organized and reported (in this case) for an educational organization. Fund accounting's primary value is based in the requirement that each fund may be used only for specific purposes and that the various separate funds in the fund accounting system must not be commingled. By way of specific example, schools must deposit state transportation aid only to the transportation fund for exclusive use in transportation-related expenditures. Analogously, special education money may not be commingled with other money. Thus the purpose of fund accounting is to recognize segregated fiscal operations, to track revenues and expenditures by function, and to provide accountability for these functions according to intended use.

Governmental Funds

The broad fund structure is actually comprised of individual funds. Governmental funds make up most of the various fund types in educational organizations, receiving most of the actual money receipted and spent by schools. Most districts operate four types of governmental funds. Although eventual fund structure is broken down further than these four funds suggest, the broad fund structure is comprised of:

♦ *General fund.* All money not reserved to other funds is placed in the general fund—hence its name, implying a general use fund. The general fund is the largest of all funds in a school district because most current annual instructional expenditures are paid from it, including teacher and administrator salaries, teaching supplies, insurance and utilities, and so forth.

♦ *Special revenue fund.* Money restricted to specific purposes, such as for compensatory education or special education programs, is placed in various special revenue funds. The purpose is to earmark monies to ensure they are spent only for specified purposes.

♦ *Capital projects fund.* A capital projects fund allows deposit and expenditure of money from a variety of sources (usually bond revenues) used to finance long-lived assets such as buildings, durable equipment, land, or other facilities. A capital projects fund is distinct from other operat-

---

3   From this point forward, a fund is an accounting entity for segregating types of money for receipt and expenditure purposes and no longer refers to money itself, as in "they lacked the funds to pay their bills." Careful examination of prior chapters will reveal that use of the word "fund" adhered to this definition, although readers may have not have been aware of the distinction at the time.

ing funds such as capital outlay and debt service funds which can also buy some long-lived assets.

♦ *Debt service fund.* A debt service fund allows receiving and expending money used to pay off long-term debts, including bond issues for school facility construction and upgrades or equipment purchases. Bond issues usually require establishment of debt service funds, with a separate fund established for each bond issue.

Proprietary Funds

Not all money received by school districts is governmental, requiring a separate accounting for such money. The convention for receiving and expending the most common types of nongovernmental monies is by creation of separate *proprietary* funds. Proprietary funds often involve fees for services and may be used to create a method of internal billing; as implied by its name, these are monies generated and "owned" differently than governmental money, which is the property of the state or other taxing unit. In contrast, proprietary funds are created to fit local needs and ways of doing business. They are further identified as either *enterprise* or *internal service* funds, a distinction made clearer as follows:

♦ *Enterprise funds.* These funds handle money from "local" activities such as athletics, school newspapers, student bookstore operations, and so forth. The idea is that these activities are like private enterprises, with services provided in exchange for fee. As a result, enterprise revenues and expenditures are maintained separately.

♦ *Internal service funds.* Larger school districts often produce goods or services within the organization that are purchased and consumed by other parts of the same organization. Examples include central printing or maintenance services. Such large districts may have an internal charge-back system, which also assists in tracking the cost and profitability of these various services.

Fiduciary Funds

Not all revenues fall neatly into either governmental or proprietary funds. One type of revenue of growing importance to school districts is money received from external nongovernmental organizations such as business partnerships, major gifts and endowments, donations, and other benevolent trusts. Although the vast majority of school districts do not have extensive fiduciary funds, a structure is available in case the opportunity arises. Such funds are known as *fiduciary* funds.

A district managing fiduciary funds is actually only a trustee, as the name implies. Appropriate revenue is deposited to a fiduciary fund, and expenditures are controlled by an agreement detailing the purpose of the fund, how the fund is to be managed, and the disposition of the proceeds if the agreement is ever dissolved. In general, fiduciary funds include two basic types:

♦ *Trust funds.* These may be of several different types. In all cases, however, the district has trusteeship and acts as the fund's manager. A pension trust fund is a common type and may exist when the district offers local pension benefits in addition to, or in lieu of, a state retirement system. An investment trust fund is another type and is used to account for the external portion (the part that does not belong to the school district) of investment pools operated by the district. Private-purpose trust funds are the final type: These may include nonexpendable trusts where the principal amount must remain intact, with the interest available for district benefit—similarly, an expendable trust fund may be set up, wherein both the principal and earned interest are available for district use.

♦ *Agency funds.* Agency funds are monies held in trusteeship by a school district for individuals, private organizations, or other governments. Examples include accounting for student activities or taxes collected for another unit of government. A historically common use of agency funds has included setting up a central payroll fund to reduce the number of accounts needed for payroll transactions to the various entities in a district—for example, teachers, administrators, support staff, and food service workers. Under one central fund, all data on wages, fringe benefits, tax withholding, and workers' compensation may be more efficiently monitored.

An Intermediate Overview

As we said at the outset, accounting is complex and exhaustive detail is not the main purpose of this textbook. Yet it is critical for everyone to grasp that there is a *structure* for school money that allows it to be *receipted, expended,* and *tracked* by its intended purpose. The picture is clearer if the total accounting system is viewed like a pyramid. From the broadest view, we see that the total *accounting system* is first made up of various *funds.* Districts in all states operate *governmental* funds made of up a *general* fund and *special revenue* funds, and most districts also have *capital project* and *debt service* funds. Similarly, all districts use *proprietary* funds to some extent, particularly for common operations such as *enterprise* funds, and many districts also have *internal service* funds. Far fewer districts will have extensive *fiduciary* funds. It is important to remember that the fund structure is the starting place for school district accounting and that everyone associated with schools is touched by fund accounting. More specifically, central administrators and boards of education are the *custodians* of all funds, and building administrators are often charged with administering *activity* funds. Similarly, teachers want adequate funding for salaries and instruction, and policy makers and higher units of government rely on fund accounting to direct the flow of school money, including state aids, and to judge the impact of educational and tax policy decisions. Of course, laypersons depend on fund accounting to assure educational experiences for children and to protect the fiduciary trust. In sum, accounting through the fund structure is truly part of overall accountability.

HOW DOES SCHOOL MONEY GET TRACKED?

Discussion to this point has illustrated how easy it is to become extremely complex when trying to provide an uncomplicated view of fiscal accountability in schools—and that is just the financial side without consideration for using money as a tool for educational decision making! However, one additional introductory step is needed: We should briefly explore how money is handled within the fund structure once it is received. To do this, we turn first to the twin concepts of *revenue* and *expenditure*. Second, we examine the *accounting cycle*. These concepts are foundational to the actual budget process discussed in later chapters because we need to understand the conceptual underpinnings if we are to learn how resources are assigned in the budget.

Revenue Structure

For accounting purposes, we need to consider a district's financial affairs on a two-dimensional plane—*revenue* and *expenditure*—even though we earlier moved beyond this when we conceptualized the budget as expressing the district's educational plan. The bigger picture argues that the budget is actually three-dimensional—that is, a budget triangle—when accountability for program planning is linked to revenue and expenditure. But for our present purpose, we first need to envision revenue simply as money going *into* schools, as contrasted to expenditure, which is that same money going back *out* in support of teaching and learning.

Revenue to education generally involves a three-tiered classification. The first tier is the *fund*, which we discussed earlier in this chapter. The second tier is the *source* of revenue. The third tier is the *type* of revenue. The concepts are interrelated.

Our earlier discussion about *fund* structure reenters the picture in that revenue received must be recorded in one of the funds operated by the district. For example, revenue earmarked for transportation must be deposited to the transportation fund, and revenue for any other restricted/categorical purpose must be placed in its appropriate special fund. Similarly, revenue not reserved to special funds is usually placed in the general fund, whereon it follows that expenditures must flow from that same fund.

When we examine actual budgeting behaviors in later chapters, it will be evident that the revenue side of a budget requires placing each revenue receipt on a line noting its source. Although each state has its own unique budget forms, the practice is universal. Placing money on a source line in the revenue side of the budget is required because it allows the district to report fiscal data to the state, to establish lobbying positions during legislative sessions, and so forth—that is, fund accounting is required by law, and accounting data tell many tales. Three revenue sources apply to school budgeting and accounting:[4]

 ♦ *Local and intermediate sources.* Local sources include money raised by the district, usually from local property taxes. Intermediate sources include money from governmental units that stand between the local district and the state, such as cities and counties.

---

4   U.S. Department of Education, Office of Educational Research and Improvement, *Financial Accounting for State and Local School Systems, 2003 Edition*. (Washington, DC: U.S. Government Printing Office, 2003).

◆ *State sources* include money raised within the state in which the district is located, generally state aid, but excluding funds passed through the state from the federal government.

◆ *Federal sources* include direct federal aid or state flow-through money, usually categorical aid.

Type of revenue refers to both source and use. Local revenues often include property tax, tuition, student transportation fees, investment earnings, student organization fees, revenue from textbook rentals, and so on. Intermediate and state revenues may include unrestricted grants-in-aid and revenue in lieu of taxes under tax exemptions or tax abatements granted by other taxing units. Types of revenue from federal sources include unrestricted grants-in-aid received either directly from the federal government or as restricted grants-in-aid from the federal level distributed through the state. Figure 4.1 illustrates how fund, source, and type of revenue come together in the revenue side of a school district's budget. In Fig. 4.1 (p. 116), the *fund* is the general fund. *Sources* include local, intermediate (county in this case), state, federal, and other. *Types* include ad valorem property, personal property in the form of recreational vehicles, and so forth.[5] Source codes are part of the system for reporting to the federal government.[6] Importantly, budget documents in the various states may look different from Fig. 4.1 because of differences in the underlying tax scheme, but the essential elements of fund accounting apply universally.

The system of revenue structure is important because it is used to allocate money to the different funds comprising a school district's total budget. Revenues are thus first classified by fund and source, and then broken into governmental, proprietary, and fiduciary groups for further distinction by fund, source, and type. Not all of this is apparent in Fig. 4.1, which only shows governmental general fund revenue, but it clearly illustrates that the very first step to creating an educational plan is receiving and depositing revenue so that an expenditure plan can be built—a plan in the case of Fig. 4.1 that takes into consideration the district's historical revenue trends when setting a new year's budget.

Expenditure Structure

Expenditure structure is significantly more complex than revenue for good reason. Revenue sources typically fit into only three categories, whereas expenditures

---

5   Describing each state's taxable property scheme is beyond the scope of this book. In Fig. 4.1, for school purposes, real property (real estate) is subject to taxation, as are the improvements on that land (ad valorem, or added value tax). The sample state in Fig. 4.1 also taxes personal property in the form of motor homes and other recreational vehicles, but exempts automobiles as a direct source of school tax revenue. The nuances among states are significant, as in Fig. 4.1 where automobiles are not taxable locally but where the state itself collects a motor vehicle tax, some of which finds its way into the state school aid distribution formula as state general fund revenues.

6   U.S. Department of Education, Office of Educational Research and Improvement, *Financial Acounting for State and Local School Systems, 2003 Edition*.

Figure 4.1. Revenue Side of a Sample Budget

01 GENERAL	12 mo 2007–2008 Actual (1)	12 mo. 2008–2009 Actual (2)	12 mo. 2009–2010 Budget (3)
Unencumbered Cash Balance July 1			
Unencumbered Cash Balance from Transportation, Bilingual Education and Vocational Education Funds			
Cancel of Prior Yr Enc			
Revenue: 1000 Local Sources 1110 Ad Valorem Tax Levied 2006 $			
2007 $			
2008 $			
2009 $			
1140 Delinquent Tax			
1300 Tuition 1312 Individuals (Out-District)			
1320 Other school district In-State			
1330 Other school district Out-State			
1410 Transportation Fees			
1700 Student Activities (Reimbursement)			
1900 Other Revenue From Local Source 1910 User Charges			
1980 Reimbursements			
1985 State Aid Reimbursement			
2000 County Sources 2450 Recreational Vehicle Tax			
2800 In Lieu of Taxes IRBs			
3000 State Sources 3110 General State Aid			
3130 Mineral Production Tax			
3205 Special Education Aid			
4000 Federal Sources 4590 Other Reserve Grants in Aid 4591 Title I (Formerly Chapter I)			
4592 Title (Math/Science)			
4599 Other			
4820 PL 382 (Exclude Extra Aid for Children on Indian Land and Low Rent Housing) (formerly PL 874)			
5000 Other 5208 Transfer From Supplemental General			
Resources Available			
Total Expenditures & Transfers			
Excess Revenue to State (recapture)			
Unencumbered Cash Balance June 30			

are broken into many different classifications. This means that districts have only a few sources of revenue, although they have many ways to spend money.

Budget documents in every state classify educational expenditures in a program budgeting format. Expenditures are classified by *fund, function,* and *object,* and may be further broken down by *project, instructional level, operational unit, subject matter,* and *job classification* if desired. States and local school districts vary greatly in amount of such detail, although each state's budget document specifies a minimum amount of coding that must occur. Such a classification schema permits accumulation of data that may be used for a wide variety of purposes, the first of which is tracking expenditures for program accountability. Each level in the expenditure classification scheme has discrete codes hierarchically arranged to track expenditures from broad to narrow. For example, the general fund is very broad, while the object breaks a function into various subcodes for detailed reporting and analysis.

Extensive detail of how far down expenditures can be broken is again beyond the scope of this discussion. For general purposes of understanding expenditure structure, however, consider the following statements that move from the broad to narrowly specific:

- ◆ *Fund.* Expenditures are first classified as an expenditure from a governmental fund, proprietary fund, or fiduciary fund. The purpose of starting with the fund should be clear: Revenue is first assigned to a fund on the basis of use in support of some educational activity and, consequently, expenditures must be assigned to the corresponding fund (e.g., Code 01 to designate general fund).

- ◆ *Function.* Expenditures can be classified by function, which refers to the general activity for which a purchased good or service is acquired. Function describes the areas of instruction, support services, operation of noninstructional services, facilities acquisition and construction, and debt service. These codes track expenditures more closely by identifying functions carried out (e.g., Code 2300 to designate an expenditure for general administration support services within the general fund).

- ◆ *Object.* Finally, expenditures are classified by object, or the item or service acquired. This includes nine major object categories, which can be further subdivided. The major categories include salaries, employee benefits, purchased professional and technical services, purchased property services, supplies, and so on (e.g., Code 310 to designate a board-level salary expense within the general fund).

Figure 4.2 (p. 119) helps illustrate this complex structure. Figure 4.2 is the expenditure side of one state's general fund budget document. Assume the district has received and deposited revenue to each of its operating funds. Assume also that the budget process is complete and that a legally adopted budget is in place—something we explore further in later chapters. Now the district has authority to spend money. More importantly, several other things are in place. In Fig. 4.2, we can see expenditure classification as follows: The *fund* is the general fund (Code 01). *Functions* in the general fund include instruction (Code 1000), support services (Code 2000), school administration (Code 2400), operations and maintenance (Code 2600), and so on.

These expenditure codes are broken down further by *object,* as with teacher salaries (Code 1000–110), teacher benefits (Code 1000–200), general administration salaries (Code 2300–100), and so on. The benefits are multiple. First, federal and state data-tracking is satisfied by uniform reporting methods. Second, the district may choose to analyze the minimum required data further by expanding it to include codes that report at progressively more incremental levels, wherein the purchase of teaching materials can be tracked to each school and each classroom—an activity that, *accumulated,* shows the cost (and potentially the impact) of instructional expenditures. In other words, accounting is not just an assurance against ineptitude, carelessness, or fraud, it is the other dimension of accountability in that costs of programs can be calculated, and those costs can be linked to student achievement data if the system is properly structured. For example, if low performance and underfunding simultaneously appear at an identifiable grade level, the data can call attention to both truths. At that point, good educational decision making must be engaged—perhaps more money for new textbooks is needed; teachers may need professional renewal; or additional teacher aides might be needed due to large class sizes that result in inadequate individualized attention—in other words, a host of options can be explored based on data available only through accounting and accountability, all of which can be derived by tracking revenue and expenditure in schools.

The Accounting Transaction

Although this textbook avoids becoming mired in the details of advanced school business management, a brief description of the accounting transaction is needed in order to have a complete overview of how money is tracked in schools. Administrators and school board members need such understanding because they are ultimately the responsible agents. Teachers rarely study accounting, yet they are negatively affected if someone engages in bad financial management—providing cash for school field trips or tossing athletic gate receipts into the car trunk over the weekend are two examples of poor business management and accounting practices. The list of bad examples can be very long, but the point is that virtually everyone is touched by the accounting transaction—and, frankly, it would be of little value to understand the big picture of accounting without the important detail of how money actually gets handled from beginning to end. Unfortunately, there is no easy way to explain the accounting transaction. A broad brush, however, can paint a useful description.

Earlier discussion in this chapter showed how the various funds provide a structure for grouping the financial activities of a school district by revenue and expenditure dimensions. This is an important first step in the accounting process because it segregates money according to its use. The next step, however, is to establish individual *accounts* within each fund wherein the actual money transactions occur. These accounts make up the record of assets, liabilities, revenues, and expenditures that occur in the broader fund context.

(Text continues on page 124.)

Figure 4.2. Expenditure Side of a Budget

01 GENERAL EXPENDITURES	12 mo. 2007–2008 Actual (1)	12 mo. 2008–2009 Actual (2)	12 mo. 2009–2010 Budget (3)
1000 Instruction 100 Salaries 110 Certified			
120 NonCertified			
200 Employee Benefits 210 Insurance (Employee)			
220 Social Security			
290 Other			
300 Purchased Professional and Technical Services			
500 Other Purchased Services 560 Tuition 561 Tuition/other State LEAs			
562 Tuition/other LEAs outsid the State			
563 Tuition/Priv Sources			
590 Other			
600 Supplies 610 General Supplemental (Teaching)			
644 Textbooks			
680 Miscellaneous Supplies			
700 Property (Equipment & Furnishings)			
800 Other			
2000 Support Services			
2100 Student Support Services 100 Salaries 110 Certified			
120 NonCertified			
200 Employee Benefits 210 Insurance (Employee)			
220 Social Security			
290 Other			
300 Purchased Professional and Technical Services			
500 Other Purchased Services			
600 Supplies			
700 Property (Equipment & Furnishings)			
800 Other			
2200 Instr Support Staff 100 Salaries 110 Certified			
120 NonCertified			
200 Employee Benefits 210 Insurance (Employee)			
220 Social Security			
290 Other			

01 GENERAL EXPENDITURES	2007–2008 Actual (1)	2008–2009 Actual (2)	2009–2010 Budget (3)
300 Purchased Professional and Technical Services			
500 Other Purchased Services			
600 Supplies 640 Books (not textbooks) and Periodicals			
650 Audiovisual and Instructional Software			
680 Miscellaneous Supplies			
700 Property (Equipment & Furnishings)			
800 Other			
2300 General Administration 100 Salaries 110 Certified			
120 NonCertified			
200 Employee Benefits 210 Insurance (Employee)			
220 Social Security			
290 Other			
300 Purchased Professional and Technical Services			
400 Purchased Property Services			
500 Other Purchased Services 520 Insurance			
530 Communications (Telephone, postage, etc.)			
590 Other			
600 Supplies			
700 Property (Equipment & Furnishings)			
800 Other			
2400 School Administration 100 Salaries 110 Certified			
120 NonCertified			
200 Employee Benefits 210 Insurance (Employee)			
220 Social Security			
290 Other			
300 Purchased Professional and Technical Services			
400 Purchased Property Services			
500 Other Purchased Services 530 Communications (Telephone, postage, etc.)			
590 Other			
600 Supplies			
700 Property (Equipment & Furnishings)			
800 Other			

01 GENERAL EXPENDITURES	2007–2008 Actual (1)	2008–2009 Actual (2)	2009–2010 Budget (3)

2500 Operations & Maintenance
  100 Salaries
    120 NonCertified			

200 Employee Benefits 210 Insurance (Employee)			
220 Social Security			
290 Other			
300 Purchased Professional and Technical Services			
400 Purchased Property Services 411 Water/Sewer			
420 Cleaning			
430 Repairs & Maintenance			
440 Rentals			
460 Repair of Buildings			
490 Other			
500 Other Purchased Services 520 Insurance			
590 Other			
600 Supplies 610 General Supplies			
620 Energy			
621 Heating			
622 Electricity			
626 Motor Fuel (not school bus)			
629 Other			
680 Miscellaneous Supplies			
700 Property (Equipment & Furnishings)			
800 Other			

2600 Operations & Maintenance
  (Transportation)
  100 Salaries
    120 NonCertified			

200 Employee Benefits 210 Insurance (Employee)			
220 Social Security			
290 Other			
300 Purchased and Professional Technical Services			
400 Purchased Property Services			
500 Other Purchased Services			
600 Supplies 610 General Supplies			
620 Energy			
621 Heating			
622 Electricity			
626 Motor Fuel (not school bus)			
629 Other			
680 Miscellaneous Supplies			

01 GENERAL EXPENDITURES	Code 06 Line	2007–2008 Actual (1)	2008–2009 Actual (2)	2009–2010 Budget (3)
700 Property (Equipment & Furnishings)				
800 Other				

2700 Student Transportation Services
  2710 Supervision
    100 Salaries
      120 NonCertified
	652			

200 Employee Benefits 210 Insurance	654			
220 Social Security	656			
290 Other	658			
600 Supplies	660			
730 Equipment	662			
800 Other	664			

2720 Vehicle Operating Services
    100 Salaries
      120 NonCertified
	666			

200 Employee Benefits 210 Insurance	668			
220 Social Security	670			
290 Other	672			
442 Rent of Vehicles (lease)	674			
500 Other Purchased Services 513 Contracting of Bus Services	676			
519 Mileage in Lieu of Trans	678			
520 Insurance	680			
626 Motor Fuel	682			
730 Equipment (Including Buses)	684			
800 Other	686			

2740 Vehicle Services & Maintenance
      Services
    100 Salaries
      120 NonCertified
	688			

200 Employee Benefits 210 Insurance	690			
220 Social Security	692			
290 Other	694			
300 Purchased Professional and Technical Services	696			
400 Purchased Property Services	698			
500 Other Purchased Services	700			
600 Supplies	702			
730 Equipment	704			
800 Other	706			

2790 Other Student Transportation Services
    100 Salaries
      120 NonCertified
	708			

200 Employee Benefits 210 Insurance	710			

01 GENERAL EXPENDITURES	Code 06 Line	2007–2008 Actual (1)	2008–2009 Actual (2)	2009–2010 Budget (3)
220 Social Security	712			
290 Other	714			
300 Purchased Professional and Technical Services	716			
400 Purchased Property Services	718			
500 Other Purchased Services	720			
600 Supplies	722			
730 Equipment	724			
800 Other	726			
2500, 2800, 2900 Other Supplemental Service 100 Salaries 110 Certified	730			
120 NonCertified	735			
200 Employee Benefits 210 Insurance	740			
220 Social Security	745			
290 Other	750			
300 Purchased Professional and Technical Services	755			
400 Purchased Property Services	760			
500 Other Purchased Services	765			
600 Supplies	770			
700 Property (Equipment & Furnishings)	775			
800 Other	780			
3300 Community Services Operations	785			
4300 Architectural & Engineering Services	790			
5200 TRANSFER TO: 932 Adult Education	795			
934 Adult Suppl Education	800			
936 Bilingual Education	805			
938 Capital Outlay	810			
940 Driver Training	815			
943 Extraordinary School Prog	823			
944 Food Service	825			
946 Professional Development	830			
948 Parent Education Program	835			
949 Summer School	837			
950 Special Education	840			
951 Technology Education	842			
952 Transportation	845			
954 Vocational Education	850			
955 Area Vocational School	852			
963 Special Liability Expense Fund	855			
972 Contingency Reserve	885			
974 Textbook & Student Materials Revolving Fund	889			
TOTAL EXPENDITURES & TRANSFERS				

Generally, five classifications of accounts are established within any given fund, such as the general fund. The five accounts are *expense, income, asset, liability,* and *net worth* or *fund balance* accounts. Their purpose is singular: All transactions involving revenue or expenditure or increases or decreases in the value of assets are entered (posted) to these accounts. Schools use the *double entry* method of posting transactions to the various accounts in a fund. Double entry involves entering both a *debit* (an entry on the left-hand side of the account ledger) to one account and a *credit* (entry on the right-hand side) to another account for each transaction. Asset and expenditure accounts (left-hand side accounts) are increased by debiting and decreased by crediting. Conversely, an income account (a right-hand side account) is decreased by a debit and increased by a credit.

An example of double entry posting of a transaction can be illustrated using a district that has just received a general fund tax distribution of $1,000,000. Using a double entry system, this payment involves two general fund account groups: the income account and the asset account (the cash account). The income account increases as the transaction is entered as a credit. The cash account also increases as the transaction is entered as a debit to its side of the ledger. If the district then hires a new teacher at a salary of $35,000, a new transaction in the general fund occurs. Categories affected are the cash account and the appropriate expenditure account containing teacher salaries. As a result, cash balance in the asset account is credited (decreased), and the expenditure account for salaries is debited (increased). The purpose of this complex process is important: Double entry is a tool that creates *a self-balancing set of books*, so that the assets of the district are not inflated. If this were not done, assets and liabilities would not balance, falsifying the actual cash position of the fund because appropriate additions and subtractions would not cross-balance revenue and expenditure activity—an error in financial position that would worsen if subsequent decisions were made on the basis of bad information.

The individual accounts in each fund are listed in the *general ledger,* a set of books that keeps all records in a single location. Each transaction is recorded in the general ledger by a complicated process. Before being entered in the general ledger, revenue and expenditure transactions are first recorded in a *general journal,* which is a chronological listing of transactions as they were initiated. Transactions are transferred from the general journal and posted to the appropriate accounts on the general ledger, again using double entry. This process brings together (summarizes) all similar accounts. Figure 4.3 is a sample journal entry for a given day showing the unpaid bills and charges to the appropriate expense and asset accounts. Figure 4.3 also shows how double entry creates a self-balancing set of books: That is, expenses are debited in the amount of $3,238.84, thus increasing the expense account, while assets are credited $3,238.84, thereby decreasing the district's assets. From this transaction, the district can know exactly how much it owes compared to its assets—a reflection of true cash position.

Figure 4.3. Typical Journal Entry

For the Journal Period Ending June 1, 2008

Expense Accounts			
Debit No.	1	Supplies	$3,175.63
	18	Miscellaneous	63.21
			$3,238.84
Asset Account			
Credit No.	20	Accts. Payable	$3,238.84

This process is repeated for each fund and transaction during the accounting cycle. Each accounting transaction is one part of ten steps:

1. Journalizing transactions;
2. Posting transactions;
3. Preparing a trial balance;
4. Preparing a work sheet;
5. Preparing financial statements;
6. Journalizing closing entries;
7. Posting closing entries;
8. Balancing, ruling, and bringing forward balances of balance sheet accounts;
9. Ruling temporary accounts; and
10. Preparing postclosing trial balance.[7]

The complexity of the accounting cycle underscores the need to account for all fiscal activity in a tax-based organization. Obviously, administrators and other school leaders and policy makers do not have the time or expertise to actually carry out these tasks, making it critical to secure qualified outside assistance and to provide good training for the employees who perform the daily entries in books of record—an assurance that makes it possible for school leaders to spend their time using financial data to make educational program decisions.

Auditing

Finally, we need to give attention to auditing to round out our discussion of tracking money in schools. Fortunately, auditing is easier to comprehend and absolutely vital to understanding schools and money because accounting and reporting would

---

7   Ronald E. Everett, Raymond L. Lows, and Donald R. Johnson, *Financial and Managerial Accounting for School Administrators* (Reston, VA: Association of School Business Officials, International, 1996), 17.

have no authority without the critical contribution of auditing. Auditing is the independent examination of accounting systems generally, and specific accounts in particular, to ensure the accuracy and completeness of the accounting records in a school district.

Most people are unfamiliar with audits, although the word strikes fear on a wide scale. Auditing conjures up images of fraud, embezzlement, or other fiscal wrongdoing. Although audits may reveal problems in accounting, including wrongdoing, they are actually the best protection for anyone in a fiduciary role because without auditing, innuendo and accusation gain very strong footholds—suspicion that may be unfounded but very difficult to dispel.

The purposes of audits are several. First, audits are meant to detect errors in accounting. With the enormity of financial data in a modern school district, errors can occur easily. Errors can be accidental or intentional. Auditing serves a second purpose of recommending changes to accounting procedures and improving fiscal operations. Finally, auditing demonstrates to states, the federal government, and local taxpayers that the educational mission is being financially supported according to law. Audits therefore are not to be feared unless wrongdoing is present; rather, audits advance the educational mission and serve to protect professional reputations.

Types of Audits

Several types of audits have been devised, each serving a different need. Audits fall into the two broad categories of *internal* and *external*. Audits are also known as *pre*audits, *post*audits, or *continuous* audits, based on their timing. Finally, all external audits are *general comprehensive* audits, *state* audits, or *special* audits. Each type has a unique purpose based on the data being sought.

Internal Audits

Internal financial auditing within a school organization is meant to provide a system of self-checks. Internal auditing ranges from basic monthly board reports to a full system of continuous internal monitoring, with accountants employed by a district to study and improve accounting systems. All systems engage in some amount of internal auditing. For example, budget reports on the financial status of the district sent to school board members prior to each meeting is a kind of internal audit. Internal auditing is required to produce monthly financial statements because journals and ledgers must be examined to generate income and expense statements. Mandatory state reports require internal auditing to produce and verify the data on which state aid requests are based. Internal auditing exists in all districts, although the extent varies by individual district.

Internal audits are usually either *pre*audits or *continuous* audits. A preaudit ensures proper accounting procedures in advance of a transaction. A continuous audit implies constant observation of the accounting system. Continuous auditing occurs through the system of checks and balances in place in most districts, whereby multiple approvals must be secured to spend money. The hierarchy from one actual district (Fig. 4.4, pp. 127–128) shows protections in place to guard against error or wrongdoing. Although internal auditing is never sufficient alone, it is an important tool of good management.

Figure 4.4. Accounting Checks and Balances

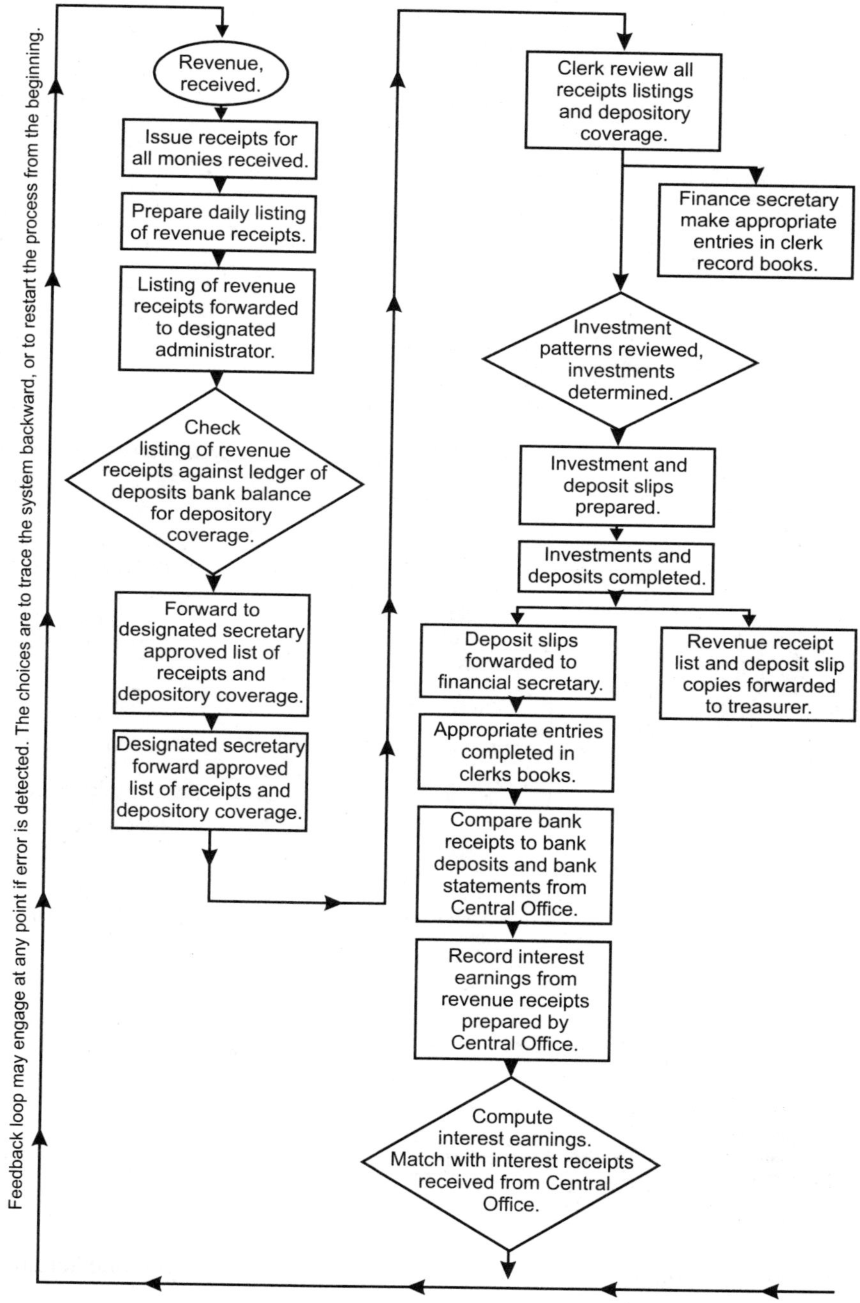

Feedback loop may engage at any point if error is detected. The choices are to trace the system backward, or to restart the process from the beginning.

Revenue, received.

Issue receipts for all monies received.

Prepare daily listing of revenue receipts.

Listing of revenue receipts forwarded to designated administrator.

Check listing of revenue receipts against ledger of deposits bank balance for depository coverage.

Forward to designated secretary approved list of receipts and depository coverage.

Designated secretary forward approved list of receipts and depository coverage.

Clerk review all receipts listings and depository coverage.

Finance secretary make appropriate entries in clerk record books.

Investment patterns reviewed, investments determined.

Investment and deposit slips prepared.

Investments and deposits completed.

Deposit slips forwarded to financial secretary.

Revenue receipt list and deposit slip copies forwarded to treasurer.

Appropriate entries completed in clerks books.

Compare bank receipts to bank deposits and bank statements from Central Office.

Record interest earnings from revenue receipts prepared by Central Office.

Compute interest earnings. Match with interest receipts received from Central Office.

(Figure 4.4 continues on next page.)

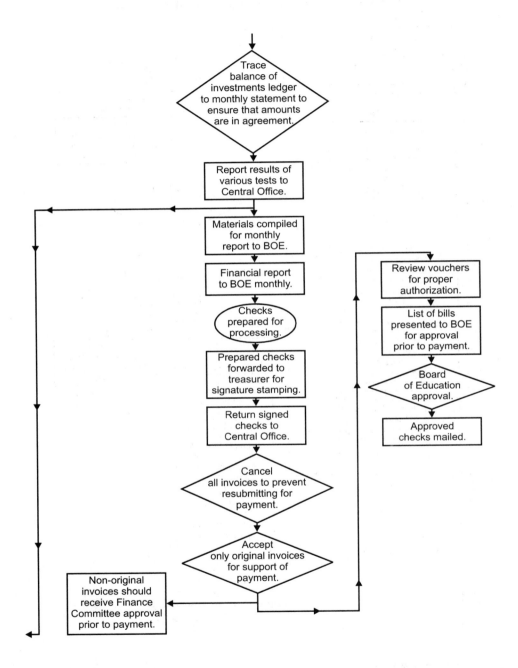

External Audits

Most people are more familiar with the *external* audit. External auditing is a formal examination of financial records in a school district by an outside expert to verify accuracy and legal compliance. External audits are always conducted by an independent auditing organization such as a certified public accounting firm or, in some instances, by state auditors checking for compliance with regulations.

External audits are exhaustive, yielding an audit report with recommendations on the audit findings. External audits are accompanied by a letter of transmittal stating the purpose of the audit, procedures followed, a statement of findings, and a list of recommendations. In most instances, the audit is conducted at the same time as preparation of the district's comprehensive annual financial report (CAFR). As a rule, most external audits are *general comprehensive audits* occurring at the close of an accounting period, usually an entire year. The report generally contains summaries of revenues and expenditures and compares cash balances against encumbrances to determine if statutory requirements were met. Governmental funds are examined separately under statements of budgetary accounts, and other funds such as fiduciary expendable trust funds and proprietary funds are also separately examined. If no problems are noted, the report is an *unqualified opinion* because its findings are not qualified by any *audit exceptions*. If concerns are present, the report is a *qualified opinion*. Audit reports are presented to the school board, with the board required to show receipt of the audit in its minutes and to show action to correct audit exceptions.

Although developed over many years, the audit process is not static and is subject to change. At the external audit level, perhaps the most significant change in many years occurred in 1999 when the Governmental Accounting Standards Board (GASB) adopted Statement No. 34, which changed how school districts issue financial statements in conformity with generally accepted accounting principles (GAAP). Statement 34, entitled *Basic Financial Statements—and Management's Discussion and Analysis—for State and Local Governments,* required that by year 2003 all school districts' presentation of financial information must meet new standards aimed at improved financial and operational accountability. According to the Association of School Business Officials International (ASBO), GASB Statement No. 34 was designed to require "...that a district demonstrate the extent to which it has met and can continue to meet its operating objectives in an efficient and effective manner into the future.[8] GASB Statement 34 moved schools closer to a business accounting model through its focus on cost data and through its efforts to make financial statements clearer to the taxpaying public by requiring, among other things, information about the cost of delivering services to students and information about general infrastructure assets of the school district. ASBO illustrated the major changes to district accounting and auditing procedures brought about by Statement 34, as seen in Fig. 4.5.

---

8 ASBO International, *GASB Statement No. 34 Implementation Recommendations for School Districts* (Reston, VA: ASBO, 2000), 5.

**Figure 4.5. Major Changes to Financial Statements
in School Districts Under GASB Statement 34**

Changes to Enhance Financial Accountability		Changes to Enhance Operational Accountability	
Previous Model	**New Model**	**Previous Model**	**New Model**
Information in basic financial statements aggregated by fund type	Information in basic financial statements presented separately for major governmental and enterprise funds	All reporting based on fund and fund types	Introduction of district-wide financial statements
Budgetary comparisons associated with the basic financial statements aggregated by fund type	Budgetary comparisons associated with the basic financial statements presented for general fund and each major special revenue fund with a legally adopted budget	Information on governmental activities limited to near-term inflows and outflow of spendable resources	District-wide financial statements provide additional long-term focus for governmental activities
Budgetary comparisons report only final amended budget	Budgetary comparisons report both original and final amended budget	Cost data available for business-type activities	Cost data provide for both governmental and business-type activities

Source: ASBO International. *GASB Statement No. 34 Implementation Recommendations for School Districts,* 2nd ed. (Reston, VA: Author, 2003), ix. By permission.

Accounting and auditing affect everyone connected to schools. Trouble-free audits are the ultimate affirmation of trust, in that administrators, boards, teachers, staff, children, and the community are well served by good financial management. On the other hand, everyone suffers if bad fiscal management goes undetected. The price paid for accounting and auditing is money wisely spent, although these tools still do not ensure accountability for wise educational decision making. Nonetheless, accounting and auditing play an important part in overall accountability by assuring educational stakeholders of absolute conformity with the law. In other words, it is much easier to closely monitor financial affairs than to explain errors that cast a pall on personal and professional reputations.

State Audits

In addition to internal audits and external general comprehensive audits, a variety of *state* audits may occur in school districts. State audits serve a different purpose and are designed to monitor compliance with statutes and regulations involving state or federal money.

The variety of individual state audit requirements makes it hard to generalize about details. Many differences rest primarily in how states choose to control education. In states emphasizing local control, state audits may serve to meet a minimum compliance standard. In states where education is strongly vested at the state level, state audits may be interested in more exhaustive review of finances and programs.

All state audits have a common goal of determining whether the state's financial stake in schools is protected. State audits thus focus particularly on those funds to which the state either supplies aid directly or to which the state acts as a channel for federal aid to local districts. In the case of federal funds, states are interested in maintenance of applications, expenditure reports, and transmittal documents. In the case of state funds, states are interested in all documentation relating to state aid claims. For example, transportation claims are often closely examined because many states invest large sums in student bus services. Likewise, states closely audit schools to ensure that federal monies are not commingled or improperly spent. State audits are state specific, although their goal is always to verify that the state's educational obligations and priorities are met.

Special Audits

Finally, school districts may be subject to *special* audits. Although fairly uncommon, the purpose of a special audit may relate to suspicion of serious error or fraud. One of the logical ways special audits occur is as an offshoot of a routine local or state audit. For example, a transportation audit might reveal that a district was claiming more children than were actually being transported. Likewise, internal auditing might cause a district to voluntarily seek a special audit; for example, inability to reconcile expense claims with receipts could result in a special audit. Other events such as inventory loss might result in special audit. Unfortunately, these examples are not entirely implausible as it is not possible to completely control individual behavior.

Accounting and accountability are constant companions for school administrators, board members, policy makers, teachers, and laypersons. The right way to do business requires at least:

- Strong internal accounting procedures, including segregation of duties based on checks and balances (see Fig. 4.4., pp. 127–128);
- Competent employees with sufficient time to do the work of accounting so that errors of haste are not made;
- Extensive documentation based on a system that includes the following:
  - Proof of school board approval of expenditures;
  - Statements showing receipts and disbursements;
  - Reconciled bank statements, including all canceled checks;
  - A system of purchase orders; and
  - A strict no-cash disbursement policy.

Figure 4.6. ASBO Code of Ethics and Standards of Conduct: Condensed and Paraphrased

- In relationships within the school district it is expected that the school business official will:
  - Support the goals and objectives of the employing school system.
  - Interpret policies and practices of the district to subordinates and to the community fairly.
  - Implement the policies and administrative regulations of the district.
  - Assist others as appropriate in fulfilling their obligations.
  - Build the best possible image of the school district.
  - Refrain from publicly criticizing board members, administrators, or employees.
  - Help subordinates achieve their maximum potential through fair and just treatment.

- In the conduct of business and the discharge of responsibilities, the school business official will:
  - Conduct business honestly, openly, and with integrity.
  - Avoid conflict of interest situations by not conducting business with a company or firm in which the official or any member of the official's family has a vested interest.
  - Avoid preferential treatment of outside interest groups, companies or individuals.
  - Uphold the dignity and decorum of the office in every way.
  - Avoid using the position for personal gain.
  - Never accept or offer illegal payment for services rendered.
  - Refrain from accepting gifts, free services, or anything of value.
  - Permit the use of school property only for officially authorized activities.
  - Refrain from soliciting contributions from subordinates or outside sources for gifts/donations to a superior.

- In relationships with other colleagues in other districts and professional associations, it is expected that the school business official will:
  - Support the actions of a colleague whenever possible, never publicly criticizing.
  - Offer assistance and/or guidance to a colleague when such help is requested or needed.
  - Actively support appropriate professional associations.
  - Accept leadership responsibilities, but refrain from "taking over" any association.
  - Refrain from using any organization or position of leadership in it for personal gain.

A FINAL WORD ABOUT PROFESSIONALISM

In this chapter, we have emphasized that the gravity of fiduciary trust cannot be overstated. This is the issue of *professionalism* in handling school money. Although we already addressed professionalism in the broad context of numerous warnings, we should take one further step by looking at published ethical standards that should be followed in every school district throughout the nation.

Codes of ethics exist for most professions. Administrators, teachers, and many community people belong to professional or trade organizations that have adopted ethical conduct codes. Standards are essential to the integrity of our entire social order, but we believe people with fiduciary capacity for public monies have an extraordinary duty to ethical conduct. The Association of School Business Officials (ASBO) International takes the same stance and has established a code of ethics that is fundamental to fiduciary relationships, a code applicable far beyond just those persons whose professions lead them to be ASBO members. Figure 4.6 excerpts key parts of the ASBO Code of Ethics. The preamble states:

> In this age of accountability, when the activities and conduct of school business officials are subject to greater scrutiny and more severe criticism than ever before, Standards of Conduct are in order. The Association cannot fully discharge its obligation of leadership and service to its members short of establishing appropriate standards of behavior.

The preamble captures the point of this chapter: that is, increasingly broad definitions of accountability, including accountability for student outcomes, are the defining feature of the future of education.

pointcounterpoint

Point

Educational leaders operate in a highly complex business environment in schools where they must balance the best interest of students with fiscal accountability to local, state, and federal entities. As administrators, they are responsible for the academic and fiscal success of schools, and they should be held strictly accountable for failures in either of these areas.

Counterpoint

Current and future school administrators are educators, not business executives. Their first priority is the education of students. Managing the "business" or finances of schools should be left to the district's school business manager or chief financial officer.

Questions

- ◆ Are there budget responsibilities in your school district that fall to middle-level administrators? If so, how can these school leaders be satisfied that their school budget/accounting knowledge is adequate to meet job demands?

♦ How can a school leader ensure that those performing the daily work of budgeting and accountancy are carrying out their duties accurately and ethically?

CASE STUDY

As the business manager in your school system, you were surprised to find three school board members waiting outside your office this morning. You quickly learned this was no social call. As the conversation unfolded, you began to be alarmed by what might well develop into a scandal involving the use of school district credit cards.

Although you were not new to the district, you had been in your position less than six months. As you had studied the district's business affairs, you had understood that credit cards were in wide use, although you were unaware that anyone might see those practices as a misuse of privilege. But because the board members' stories seemed plausible, your concerns grew as you listened. As the meeting progressed, you learned that a district employee had complained that the superintendent used his district credit card to make purchases at local restaurants, supply stores, nearby and distant hotels, and shops and casinos. The complaint also alleged that the brightly colored cards bearing your district's mascot had been a topic of conversation on the street, as citizens were said to have seen other employees using these cards "often and at strange times."

Given the severity of claims, your first reaction was to ask the board members if they had talked to the superintendent. They indicated the topic had come up before, but the superintendent had said imaginations were running wild. You knew the superintendent was at a national conference until the end of the week, so you promised the board members you would check into the situation and report back through proper channels.

Alone in your office, you scheduled a meeting with the superintendent for the next Monday. To prepare for your meeting, you met with your budget director to learn all about the district's credit card practices. As you listened, you grew more concerned. You learned that your district had an extensive outlay of credit cards across the district's 15 school buildings that were regularly checked out to employees for airline expenses, hotels, meals, supplies, and gasoline purchases. Central office staff had several cards available too, and the superintendent had a separate set of cards that he carried—in all, more than 50 credit cards were in play every day. When you questioned your budget director about this, she replied that the district had found that credit cards make it faster to obtain items; that many businesses no longer accept purchase orders; that a credit card is required to make travel arrangements by phone; and that bookkeeping is easier in many ways. When you quizzed her at length about requisitions and approvals and submitting itemized receipts, she revealed that principals did not follow a purchase preapproval process relating to credit cards; that staff were inconsistent about turning in receipts; and that the superintendent did not submit receipts and approved his own purchases. Finally, only the monthly credit totals were presented for board payment.

Although you still had much to learn, you knew that safeguards were not in place and that strong action was needed. The problem, though, was that you have to go about this in a manner that would garner support. Given the actual allegations and seemingly rampant suspicions, you knew this was going to be a difficult situation—and now, you mused, you needed a strategy by next Monday morning.

Below is a set of questions. As you respond, consider your learning throughout this entire chapter and apply your new knowledge and instincts to the situation:

- In your opinion, what are the pitfalls to be avoided when resolving this concern?
- What are your legal and ethical duties to this situation?
- What are the criteria and procedures that should be established for appropriate use of credit cards in school districts?
- How will you approach this matter with your superintendent?

FOLLOW-UP ACTIVITIES

- Obtain a copy of your school district's budget and identify the fund structure for revenues and expenditures. Identify which funds beyond the general fund your district operates. Identify special revenue funds, capital projects funds, and any debt service funds.
- Closely examine the general fund in your district. Interview your chief fiscal officer to determine what activities are paid from general fund. Discuss cash flow and fiscal resource management to determine how the district optimizes its assets. Ask about any problems the district encounters in this area.
- Obtain a copy of the monthly revenue and expenditure report for your school or program. Identify account codes and learn how the district accumulates and reports its revenues and expenditures, including any program planning uses. Interview a district accounting staff member to trace one or more receipts and disbursements through the entire accounting cycle. Ask how the district ensures the safe handling of money and disbursements, and compare these to the safeguards mentioned in this chapter.
- Obtain a copy of your school district's annual audit and identify the strengths and weaknesses of your district's accounting system. Interview your district's chief accountant to ask what audits are conducted in the district, how often, and for what purposes. Ask how the district's business office engages in regular training activities of administrators and staff to ensure they understand sound fiscal management.

WEB RESOURCES

Association of School Business Officials International, http://asbointl.org/
Education Commission of the States, www.ecs.org
Governmental Accounting Standards Board, www.gasb.org
National Business Officers Association, www.nboa.net
National Center for Education Statistics, www.nces.ed.gov
U.S. Department of Education, www.ed.gov

RECOMMENDED READINGS

Association of School Business Officials International. *The Job Description Handbook for the School Business Office.* Lanham, MD: Rowman & Littlefield Education, 1999.

Bolton, Denny G., and Gary W. Harmer. *Standards of Excellence in Budget Presentation.* Lanham, MD: Rowman & Littlefield Education, 2000.

Cuzzetto, Charles E. *Internal Auditing for School Districts.* Lanham, MD: Rowman & Littlefield Education, 1993.

Everett, Ronald E., Donald R. Johnson, and Bernard W. Madden. *Financial and Managerial Accounting for School Administrators: Tools for School.* 2nd ed. Lanham, MD: Rowman & Littlefield Education, 2007.

Everett, Ronald E., Raymond L. Lows, and Donald R. Johnson. *Financial and Managerial Accounting for School Administrators: Superintendents, School Business Administrators and Principals.* 4th ed. Lanham, MD: Rowman & Littlefield Education, 2003.

Granoff, Michael H. *Government and Not-for-Profit Accounting.* 4th ed. New York: John Wiley & Sons, 2007.

Hartman, William T. *School District Budgeting.* Lanham, MD: Rowman & Littlefield Education, 2002.

Hartman, William T., and Jacqueline A. Stefkovich. *Ethics for School Business Officials.* Lanham, MD: Rowman & Littlefield Education, 2005.

Meglis, Edward. *Let's Talk School Business.* Lanham, MD: Rowman & Littlefield Education, 1998.

National Center for Education Statistics. *Financial Accounting for Local and State School Systems 2003.* Washington, DC: Author, 2003.

Ray, John R., Walter G. Hack, and Carl I. Candoli. *School Business Administration: A Planning Approach.* 8th ed. Boston: Allyn & Bacon, 2005.

Stevenson, Kenneth R., and Don I. Tharpe. *The School Business Administrator.* Lanham, MD: Rowman & Littlefield Education, 1999.

Wood, R. Craig, David C. Thompson, and Lawrence O. Picus. *Principles of School Business Management.* 3rd ed. Lanham, MD: Rowman & Littlefield Education, 2008.

BUDGET PLANNING

THE CHALLENGE

Planning establishes the aims and objectives, how they are to be achieved, and the appropriate time lines. The functions for each area of responsibility within the business function should be clearly defined. These include providing machines, money, land, buildings, equipment, materials, services and other resources to schools; assisting personnel in attaining the goals and objectives of the district; hiring sufficient professional personnel to conduct the district's business successfully; controlling the operations of the district in the areas of administration, plants and budgets, and monitoring progress to assure good performance; engaging in long- and short-range planning to assure availability of adequate resources; and following good management so that the business division can realize the most from its people.

ASBO (1979)

CHAPTER DRIVERS

At the close of this chapter you will have reflected upon these questions:

- ◆ What is the primary purpose of a budget?
- ◆ What is a budget at its most basic level?
- ◆ What are the basic budget concepts?
- ◆ What are common approaches to budgeting?
- ◆ What is a good budget framework?
- ◆ What is the budget model?
- ◆ What is the general budget process?
- ◆ How are individual schools funded?
- ◆ What are the roles of stakeholders in budgeting?

BUDGETS AND SCHOOLS

The opening quotation to this chapter underscores that sound budgeting principles are comprehensive, wide-ranging, and enduring. Considered in context of how this book has sequentially linked each topic, it is predictable that we now turn attention to the specific elements of building educational budgets. In other words, we now have an understanding of the social context of schools, including recognition of a participatory and sometimes demanding constituent base. We have gained respect for the gravity of handling school money, and we have an initial grasp of how revenues and expenditures are accounted for via fund structures. Additionally, we have been introduced to the many decisions underlying the construction and operation of state aid formulas. In sum, we have built a foundation—a *framework*—for understanding money and schools. Consequently, we now start to address and apply the many individual elements of budgeting.

We begin by examining school district budgets from a broad perspective. Later chapters will explore additional aspects of budgeting in greater detail, but this chapter creates a foundation to which we will return often. In this chapter, we gain an overview of how budgets are built, with some attention to how money is directed to individual schools. To achieve these aims, we first define a budget at its most basic conceptual level. We then turn to a discussion of common approaches to budgeting, including appraisal of those approaches in terms of a good budget framework. The last half of the chapter is devoted to describing the general budget process and the roles of various stakeholders—school leaders, school staffs, and laypersons—the people who provide the money and those entrusted with its use. In this manner we become familiar with a very complicated process while staying true to our goal—to gain a better understanding of how district budgets and school budgets are operationalized.

CONCEPTUALIZING BUDGETS

Almost every idea in this book has been couched in terms of intense competition for financial resources. Earlier chapters revealed that public education is facing massive change, with powerful implications stemming from strident calls for excellence that stand in stark contrast to an environment suggesting ever-increasingly complex social and economic needs of children. Schools have been unable to fully meet these demands despite greater state assumption of education's costs because demand for government services at all levels has resulted in scarcity of money, at least in relation to the overall needs of society. At least one result of these tensions has been greater scrutiny of the financial operation of schools, so that everyone associated with educational policy making has needed to become better versed in the language of budgeting. As we just noted, that is our thesis in this chapter; that is, how budgets are envisioned and enacted is a topic of real importance because schools operate in a tense and competitive environment.

What Are the Basic Budget Concepts?

As we have built budgets and worked with educators and laypeople for many years, we have regularly encountered a lack of understanding attaching to the basic budget concepts underlying everything that goes into a financial plan for school districts and individual schools. This lack of understanding invariably involves *mistaken assumptions,* confusion about *budgetary purposes,* failure to understand the need for *strong leadership,* and uncertainty about the *uses of budgets.* When these elements are well understood, the district's mission and educational plan work well. Misunderstood, complication abounds.

The realities of today's complex environment frustrate many old but commonly held assumptions about school budgeting. Many people view school finance as a relatively low priority and are convinced that budgets can be managed by noneducators who only need accounting skills. We have forever resisted that premise, arguing that *everything* in education is driven by school finance and wise budget planning. This does not disrespect the view that teaching and learning are *the* critical acts of schooling, but it does strongly assert that no teaching and learning will occur without adequate funding and masterful budgeting because education simply is not free. Although it seems unnecessary to say that the foremost concept of school budgets is that programs cost money, it is a cold fact that escapes many educators who seem to want budget problems to just "go away" so that *their* role in education becomes most important. Reality does not respect idealism, however, so it is a basic fact that without good budgets there are no schools.

Although many people do grasp the power of budgets, others have missed a second fundamental concept—that the primary purpose of a budget is to translate educational priorities into programmatic and financial terms. Most people know the phrase "money talks," and money talks especially loudly in schools in that the budget is a statement of priorities. Seemingly unarguable, this concept goes much deeper and has a darker side: Because programs cost money, a budget is the execution of the individual and collective programs of a district or school so that top priorities are funded first. In other words, programs that are most valued are better funded, making it undeniable that *the budget is a fiscal expression of the educational philosophy of the district.*

A third fundamental concept is that budgets do not just "happen"; budgets are acts of leadership because budgeting is the *deliberate act of establishing priorities and describing and funding educational plans.* Budgets are created by people who are charged with carrying out the educational obligations of a school district. Although it is true that all districts must provide programs conforming to state law regarding days, hours, and minutes of instruction and various required and elective courses, the budget supporting any program is greatly affected by the attitudes of those in leadership positions. Leadership is quite broad and includes the community at large, which approves—or disapproves—total school operations; the board, which is legally charged with school operation; and school personnel who design and carry out approved educational programs. These persons play crucial roles: for example, administrators are hired to build the district's financial plan and to provide philosophical leadership and technical expertise—leadership that should be influenced by the teaching staff. Board members bring their views, which are often influenced by the community, and ultimately only the board can enact a fiscal plan. Consequently, it is critical to remember what enables educational programming—it is *money*, pure and simple—money taken from a public whose desire to support schools depends in great part on confidence in leadership. In sum, educational leaders should never underestimate the power of their expertise.

A fourth fundamental concept is similar in that budgets should be seen as a powerful political tool in schools. Again, money talks loudly, and the budget process is highly political. Anyone experienced in school affairs understands that the budget is a primary vehicle for expressing public approval or disapproval, that board attitudes about budgets are determined in the political arena, and that individual programs may rise or fall based on these earthy realities. Although politics are often viewed negatively by educators, in many instances these realities represent helpful opportunities. For example, failure to engage the public in the budget process is a serious mistake because ownership and enthusiastic approval of schools is vital to budget success—indeed, politics are very useful because a disengaged community is often apathetic or even hostile. The political side of budgets can be dysfunctional, of course, but politics can be valuable when remembering that budgets are the fiscal expression of an educational philosophy. The key is accepting and ethically using the political benefits of the budget process.

These concepts are the basis for many misperceptions about school budgets. It is unfortunate that so many people see budgets as dry documents interesting only to accountants and clerks because budgets are the tool that enable schools to function. It is also unfortunate that so few people realize that the budget is the fiscal expression of the educational philosophy of the district, so that it becomes even more critical to engage staff and patrons at every opportunity. It is further unfortunate that many school administrators fail to appreciate their own importance to the budget process, or, alternatively, refuse to use their power by instead keeping budgets at a level that discourages wide involvement and support. And it is also unfortunate that so many school leaders have viewed the politics of budgeting with distaste, instead of learning to take ethical advantage of political systems.

These concepts actually define a budget. First, a budget is a *description of a desirable educational program*. Second, a budget is an estimate of expenditures needed to carry out the program. Third, a budget is an estimate of revenues available to meet expenses. Our definition is thus three-sided. Although different from the accountant's view that sees only revenue and expenditure, the three-dimensional view best expresses our budget philosophy, which states that programs should drive both revenues and expenditures.

Figure 5.1 illustrates how we view the budgeting process, and it is intentional that the educational program is the base of the budget triangle. Although fiscal problems often cause the sides to reverse as programs are constrained by resources, it is important for community members, parents, boards, administrators, teachers, and others to not lose sight of the goal that budgets should be built on the basis of program needs. As the budget triangle illustrates, the definition of a budget is first based on quality programs and then well supported by revenue and expenditure plans that make envisioned outcomes possible.

Figure 5.1. Ideal Budget Triangle

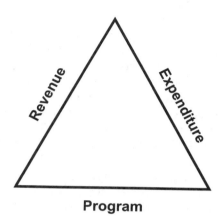

Program

ORGANIZING FOR BUDGETING

Our discussion to this point leads to one result: Budgeting is critical to the success of everything that happens in schools. Needless to say, something so important demands a high degree of organization, attention to detail, and fundamental accuracy.

Unfortunately, the importance of budgeting has gone largely unrecognized, at least until recently. This has coincided with the fact that school budgets have been an intensely local matter, with minimal state control relating to a few reporting procedures in order to qualify for state aid. Yet while state requirements have increased, the budget process has become only modestly more sophisticated in many school districts. Various efforts to devise budgeting systems have been made, however, whereby districts can adopt a budget framework consistent with their vision and operational philosophy. A brief look at the most common budget models helps to understand the various ways in which districts choose to organize their budgeting activities.

What Are the Common Approaches to Budgeting?

Efforts to improve budget practices have led to common approaches, particularly at the district level. These include *incremental* budgeting; *line-item* budgeting; *program planning budgeting and evaluation* systems; *zero-based* budgeting; *school site* budgeting; and emerging models of *outcomes-based* budgeting. The order relates to their chronological appearance and to the political processes that have increasingly impacted the school setting. The main purpose of any approach to budgeting is to detail where resources are targeted in response to children's needs, but there is a corresponding level of politics in each model that ultimately affects adoption and how resources ultimately are distributed. Consequently, each approach has benefits and drawbacks inherent to the model itself and to its political viability, so much so that adoption of a model should include consideration of both technical benefits *and* whether the model will fit local belief systems.

Incremental Budgeting

Incremental budgeting historically has been the most common way to build budgets. Incremental budgeting is a simplistic model that assumes the prior year's expenditures are an adequate base for creating the next budget. Incremental budgeting takes its name from the assumption that each budget line should receive the same increment (usually as a percent) increase or decrease during the next budget cycle.

Incremental budgeting strongly appeals to common sense. For example, there is sensibility to believing that next year's legislative allocation will be based on the prior year's funding. Legislatures themselves often couch new funding as overall percentage increases or decreases from the prior year. Additionally, there is common sense in thinking about budgets incrementally in terms of comparing multiple years to measure changes in revenue and costs. Many states' budget documents also require districts to show several prior years' data by line item to help the state assess fiscal health of school districts and to help districts track changes in budgeting behaviors over time. As a result, incremental budgeting has offered an alluring simplicity in a complex world.

Although incremental budgeting still forms the basis for some baseline decisions, there are drawbacks. Obviously, incremental budgeting focuses on aggregate trends and fails to analyze revenue and expenditure changes unless extra effort is made. Incremental budgeting also has ignored the targeted impact of money because it was developed at a time when there was low concern for measuring educational outcomes. Finally, it is obvious that incremental budgeting results in largely unquestioned equal increases to each budget line, potentially causing overfunding or underfunding of individual areas. In sum, this approach does little more than reveal gross trends while failing to speak to strategic allocation or returns on investment in educational programs. Still, some districts continue to believe that incremental budgeting is fair in that all areas of the budget are treated "neutrally."

Line-Item Budgeting

An improvement to incremental budgeting is development of *line-item budgeting*. This tool has been widely used for many years to assign different amounts to each line of the budget. In line-item budgeting, emphasis is placed on the specific objects for which funds are spent, wherein each line item in the budget is seen as the proper base for expenditure decisions. As a result, budgets are planned around each budget line, and the new budget is based on increases to each line's base, usually last year's spending level. For example, lines for instructional salaries, administrative and clerical salaries, repair, upkeep of grounds, supplies, and capital construction might be increased unequally.

Line-item budgeting has several advantages. The major benefit is that the budget is viewed as a sum of its parts. Additionally, each part is considered separately in terms of some measure of perceived need. Finally, line-item budgeting suggests consideration of actual program needs, although the concept is still unsophisticated. Because line-item budgeting has been in place for many years and because it is easily understood, it has survived despite the availability of newer budgeting tools.

Despite its popularity, line-item budgeting has drawbacks. One drawback is that it depends on the budget document almost entirely for complex decisions. Most state budget documents are not very informative because they are quite general, providing only broad lines such as instructional salaries, supplies, or miscellaneous "other" expenses. Too little information is given on how decisions are made; the process depends too much on experience; and little or no record of decision processes is evident—for example, it is impossible to determine what justification underlies adopted levels of expenditure for particular grades, programs, or projects. Such a method of allocating money allows secretiveness in budgets, vests power in only a few select persons, and does not encourage accountability. By far the most popular method until the 1960s, use of line-item budgeting has faded, although it is still more prevalent than it should be.

Program Planning Budgeting and Evaluation Systems

Program planning budgeting and evaluation systems (PPBES) arose from a realization that the budget should be more clearly tied to the educational program. This approach requires each unit in a district or school to establish goals through systematic planning that first reviews the program's goals before determining the object of expenditure. The process requires an educational plan where each unit seeks to meet its instructional objectives—a plan for spending, initially justified by needs. Money then follows the plan.

The benefits of PPBES are real. This model represents a major conceptual shift by deliberately linking programs and expenditures to a presumed cause-and-effect of money. PPBES contributes to accountability, both by its focus on programs and by its potential to use object-function codes to include productivity analysis. This conceptual framework includes projecting long-term costs of programs, so that advocates of PPBES believe that organizations are more likely to reach their stated goals and objectives when program is the first consideration in building a budget.

Not surprisingly, there are drawbacks to PPBES, particularly as both thinking and technology can outpace organizational readiness for change. Historically this was true of PPBES, as schools have had a hard time being prepared for the dramatic philosophical shift underlying program budgeting systems. This continues to plague PPBES, as it is difficult to smoothly connect budget goals, organizational patterns, and the many new structures needed by PPBES. Yet schools have had to consider program budgeting at increasingly greater levels, as newer accountability structures have forced this concept to a new intensity (see Outcome-Focused Budgeting later in this section).

Zero-Based Budgeting

As we said earlier, political realities overshadow school finance and budgeting. Politics clearly apply to *zero-based budgeting* (ZBB), as ZBB has been a case of external politics pressing change on schools during an era of fiscal austerity.

The advent of zero-based budgeting in schools coincided with fiscal problems that began to surface during the high inflation years of the 1970s. ZBB was first instituted in the federal government under President Jimmy Carter as an effort to control federal spending by enacting sunset laws to zero out unproductive government programs. Popular with antitax constituencies, ZBB was also implemented by many local governments in response to taxpayer discontent, and it was only a matter of time until schools experimented with the concept. The basic premise of ZBB is that budgets must be justified each year, with the central goal of cutting waste and improving efficiency.

Over the years, many school districts have adopted a modified ZBB model. A typical procedure is to build new budgets based on a percentage reduction from the prior year, with maintenance of prior year funding requiring extensive justification. The rationale is that greater efficiency can be injected into *any* district, and reductions as a matter of course help achieve that end. Another form of ZBB requires staff to prepare multiple scenarios and to justify each scenario (decrease, static, increase). The first scenario requires extensive description of the educational plan, with the new budget target set at a specified percentage below current funding. The second scenario requires maintenance of both the educational plan and the budget at the same level as the current year. The third scenario allows improvement and expects the budget to increase above the current year. In all instances, each scenario must detail differences between the current year and the next budget cycle, with full expenditure justification.

Benefits of ZBB are obvious. The product of an era of high inflation and perceived government waste, ZBB represents a chance to appease taxpayers by giving the impression of strong action to reduce waste and growth. Particularly sound is the idea that budget growth should not occur absent questions about actual contribution to the organization. The idea of multiple spending scenarios is sound, in that planning may improve if growth is restricted. Finally, common sense dictates that districts may be better prepared for reductions if systematic groundwork is laid ahead of actual need. On the other hand, drawbacks are real because the process of zeroing budgets is so complex. ZBB is a cost-reduction tool that can require more resources for effective strategizing than are saved in the end. The problem of internal strife also applies to ZBB, as elective and enrichment courses must make the same justification for existence as core areas. The notion of zeroing core courses is impossible, however, creating incredulity and requiring moderation that essentially becomes a modified zero-based budget model. Although most people still see ZBB as an intrinsically good idea, its problems are so great that many districts are wary of even using the language of ZBB. Vestiges linger, though, as many districts continue to use best/no-growth/worst-case scenarios in response to the uncertain revenue context commonly faced by schools today and when faced with the unavoidable cuts of recent years.

School Site Budgeting

In contrast to centralized budgeting methods, a recent popular trend is *school site budgeting*. School site budgeting is a school-based management tool following closely after the popularity of decentralized administration, with budget decisions pushed downward to the individual school level. It can be said that school site budgeting is a variant of program budgeting applied to each individual school within a district. Under this plan, each site is assigned resources based on some district-level redistribution formula that takes into account the number of students at each site in each grade level and program. Typically, the principal and a school site council comprised of patrons, parents, and staff are given responsibility for developing and managing a budget within limits of the total allocation. Depending on local preference, the council may be authorized to make decisions in such areas as salaries, supplies, activities, and so on—all within the requirement of not violating bargaining agreements, regulations of federally funded programs, any statutory requirements such as class size limits, or district policies such as school calendar or length of school day.

Advantages of school site budgeting are appealing because they complement the philosophical underpinnings of site-based management. In concept, site budgeting supports recent advances in learning theory because it values the impact of resources at the point of utilization—that is, resources are most meaningful at the individual classroom level under the care of the teacher as applied to student needs. Site budgeting is sound in that it involves all stakeholders, especially parents and teachers, in the education of children. The concept is especially attractive in an era when parent involvement is at an historic low, and it acknowledges the role of the home and community in each child's progress. The special value, then, is in providing a more holistic and inclusive view of education, making school site budgeting a viable option long into the foreseeable future.

Naturally, school site budgeting has some drawbacks. A primary disadvantage is its complexity, wherein school sites are once again asked to take on new roles and to accept new power brokers. Throughout history, schools have been semiclosed social systems, and the addition of community members and parents to complex decision making is stressful. Site-based budgeting requires real training for stakeholders, as administrators, teachers, and parents must learn about organizational and technical aspects of funding and must learn to work together cooperatively. And there are real dangers in the concept—that is, unless close attention is paid, equity among schools within a district may be upended through site based budgeting in that some schools will enjoy greater participation and advocacy. Similarly, some schools simply will do a better job at teaching and learning, making a child's education even more dependent on a given attendance site. Likewise, there is danger to site decisions in personnel matters, raising legal, ethical, and moral questions. But given current trends, school site budgeting is a likely companion for the foreseeable future—a fact borne out in that we return in a later chapter to take a more intensive look at implementing site-based budgeting.

Outcome-Focused Budgeting

Each of the various budget models examined so far has attractive features, as well as drawbacks. All models represent emerging thought and amalgamation, either as a result of progress or as a consequence of adaptation to individual school districts' needs. The political aspects of budgeting have been important too, and *outcome-focused budgeting* is a good representation of all such realities.

Outcome-focused budgeting has grown in popularity in governmental circles in recent years in direct response to interest in accountability. Fiscal austerity, along with competition for finite resources, has only served to increase the model's attractiveness. Outcome-focused budgeting is the practice of connecting the aims of the organization to the allocation of resources and finally to measurable outcomes such as test scores.

Although still in infancy, patterns in state aid allocations across the last decade have all headed in this direction. Likewise, the sanctions in the *No Child Left Behind Act* go directly to increased emphasis on outcome-focused budgeting. The advantages are clear: It is intuitive that an organization whose financial support depends on some performance measure will be much more attuned to fully meeting the standard, and it is unarguably legitimate to demand performance in exchange for continued financial support. The disadvantages are equally clear: Organizations facing severe threats to survival are likely to become victims of damaging stress, and the unintended consequence of slavish devotion to singular measures of outcomes is to slight or ignore the grander aims of developing the whole child. Notwithstanding, outcome-focused budgeting combined with site-level issues is the harbinger of the future.

What Is a Good Budget Framework?

Although budgeting approaches are increasingly mandated by federal and state governments, school districts still must approach the total budget process from a perspective that makes sense locally. The various choices in budgeting philosophies demand that school leaders individually develop a *framework for budgeting*; similarly, other stakeholders such as board members and laypersons serving on school site councils should understand the major issues affecting budgeting. Many questions about each type of budgeting philosophy must be asked, and leaders must ensure that both the district's temperament and their own values are served. As a consequence, there are several considerations to adopting a budget framework in order to ensure that districts and schools do not naively seize on a good idea that later proves unworkable.

The set of issues to be considered when choosing a budgeting philosophy warns against an uncritical attitude. Although one may ask why a personal philosophy about budgeting is important, it should be clear that participants' attitudes toward fiscal control must be congruent, or chaos and discontent—and even distrust—will follow. Because administrators, boards, staffs, and communities must work cooperatively to assure success in schools, it is essential to adopt a framework that meets the expectations of all stakeholders.

Hartman long ago proposed issues to be raised when adopting a financial structure at either district or individual school levels.[1] These issues relate to style, preference, and congruency of stakeholders in the budget process. Hartman proposed that consideration must be given to the district's history, in that rapid or abrupt changes in budget policies and operations may be met with indifference or resistance. For example, if the district has a history of constituent apathy in budget affairs, dramatically increased patron involvement is unlikely unless a long time is devoted to changing the district's culture. Likewise, budget decisions must be made in light of the historic role of the school board, in that districts with a history of strong board control will experience strife when trying to move quickly to decentralized models such as site based budgeting. Likewise, the fiscal condition of the district must be analyzed, as districts in poor

---

1   William T. Hartman, *School District Budgeting* (Englewood Cliffs, NJ: Prentice Hall, 1988), 28–29.

economic health should not decentralize due to the high costs and inefficiency of broad-based decision making. As Hartman cautioned, these and other issues should be considered before jumping on the bandwagon of any new innovation.

The inherent problems of each budgeting philosophy give rise to another option if carefully managed. As an alternative to strict adherence to any one philosophy, districts may choose to take the best aspects of each framework and meld them into a workable compromise. Although there is danger to assembling incompatible elements, there is value to applying the benefits each philosophy has offered to the field. The value of incremental budgeting is clear in working with legislatures, although leaders should encourage legislators to understand the value of looking at the various tasks of schools. Line-item budgeting has value in that every budget ends up with money assigned to each line. Program planning budgeting and evaluation systems is basic to the work of schools, and the focus on program in PPBES has brought budgeting into the modern era. Zero-based budgeting also helps by questioning protectionism. Site based budgeting is consistent with new designs of schools and is a likely companion of outcomes-focused budgeting, as accountability demands continue to escalate. Although inconsistency is always a risk, the best parts of each model are useful in the hands of skilled leaders. For example, regardless of whether a district is centralized or decentralized, the benefit of function-object code tracking for productivity analysis should not be ignored and ties neatly to the growing focus on measurable student achievement data (see discussion in Chapter 3 about accumulating expenditures by code).

Organizing for budgeting and developing a philosophy are essential parts of educational leadership. Organization and philosophy are consistent with the purpose of budgeting, which is to identify and prioritize needs, match resources with needs, and make educational goals operational. Although there is no way to become so skilled that there is no room to improve, leaders who operate from an informed framework are better positioned to see opportunities and problems during the actual building of budgets. With growing public interest in school funding, budgeting skills are a critical element of leadership.

CONSTRUCTING BUDGETS

Our discussion next leads to how school district budgets are actually built. Constructing budgets demands three kinds of knowledge. The first is a *general appreciation* for the critical impact of budgets on the educational process. This is crucial if leaders are to work effectively with legislators and local school boards and communities to provide good educational experiences. The second kind of knowledge is understanding of the *technical process* of budget-building on a general level. Although budgeting is state specific, a good grasp of procedures can be gained because there are common elements that apply irrespective of location. The third kind of knowledge is understanding of *specific state practices*. In the latter case, no textbook can cover the complexity of state-level budgets. But by establishing familiarity in the first two areas, all leaders can add state-specific details at the appropriate time. As a result, our study of budgets now moves to the process of budget construction in a general context.

What Is the Budget Model?

School budget construction follows a similar pattern in most states. Although states have specific forms and timelines to which budgets must conform, the process uses the format of the model displayed in Fig. 5.2. The model includes much of the information we learned in earlier chapters, where the interdependency of schools and external agencies such as federal, state, and local government is apparent. Because Fig. 5.2 includes both the political and technical dynamics of the budget process, the model frames our discussion throughout the remainder of this chapter.

Figure 5.2 The Budget Model

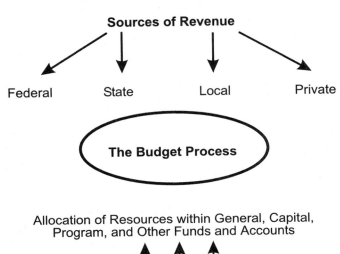

The model reflects the common belief that school budgets are built locally. Most people believe that the process is basically carried out as the local school board and administration work together to determine needs and set the budget. The budget model in Fig. 5.2, however, argues that the budget process is far more complex because it actually begins long before the amount of revenue available to a district is knowable. The model reaffirms our learning from prior chapters by showing that money flows to school districts from a variety of sources. Although districts receive the largest shares from state and local governments, school aid amounts vary greatly in individual states, so that the budget process is unique to each state and school district. Districts with high concentrations of federal land, for example, may receive a large proportion of revenue from federal sources. Similarly, the balance of state and local revenues varies widely among states. The mix of revenue sources has a powerful impact on the budget process, and mixtures are determined long before funding is ever known in any district.

The budget model also illustrates that revenue balance among sources is achieved entirely through the political process. We noted earlier that federal aid has been indirect and tied to special interests. Federal aid has also varied with changes in Congress and presidential administrations. Under President Lyndon Johnson, federal aid increased as a result of liberal social programs; under President Ronald Reagan, however, significant conservatism ruled the day. And today's version of the political process observes the powerful fiscal and programmatic impacts of *No Child Left Behind* and its subsequent reauthorization. Similarly, state budget processes depend heavily on the political will of state legislatures. States using a full state funding formula will differ greatly in type and amount of aid to districts, compared to states using minimum foundations. Economic health of individual states also determines revenue balance, as states with stagnant or depressed economies are more likely to shift costs of schools to local taxpayers. In all instances, balance is determined at political levels far above the local district, making local participation in politics a necessity.

The model particularly notes that federal and state aid is beyond local control *and* that this process is necessary in order for three other events to follow. The first event that follows is that the amount of federal and state revenue is the engine that drives local revenue requirements because the balance to fund programs must be raised by local taxes. The second event that follows is that local revenue drives many program decisions because there are both legal and practical limits on the amount of local taxes that can be raised. The third event that follows is that when federal, state, and local revenues are set, budgeting at the local level finally can be undertaken by assigning resources to the educational plan. Figure 5.2 shows that the process directly impacts classroom instruction. The model notes that although amounts of federal and state aid are beyond the control of local districts, in many states the local share varies by local taxpayer willingness to fund the balance. In other words, voter approval sets local spending priorities.

The budget model finally illustrates that, depending on the amount of local discretion, determination of the local share can be complex. The process is simplest in the few states using full or near-full state funding schemes. In states where a uniform local tax rate is required with no local option leeway, the process is also simpler in that federal, state, and local amounts are easily known, leaving discretion only in allocation to lines within a budget document. In states where local option leeway exists, determining local shares can be a sensitive political process. For example, some states require local budgets to be voted on by the public. Other states grant districts authority to increase budgets subject to a protest referendum. Other states permit boards to raise budgets without taxpayer recourse. The process is most difficult in states that allow tax rates to vary, mostly because taxpayers pay more attention to changes in tax rates than to total dollars in the budget.

Figure 5.2 effectively portrays the politics of school budgeting. Budgets are intensely complex creations, with multiple players having different interests and operating at different levels of power and influence. Budgets at the local level are externally driven in that revenues are determined in large part prior to local choices and limited by restrictions placed on districts by the state. Budgets also depend on the willingness of local patrons to support proposed spending levels because residents will make their satisfaction—or dissatisfaction—widely known. Except for the opportunity to politically influence appropriations at each of the three primary revenue source levels, district budget processes generally center on allocational issues meant to provide the best educational program possible under revenue constraints, leaving the impression that school budgets are a local affair.

What Is the General Budget Process?

At the local level, the budget process usually consists of four sequential interrelated activities. The first activity is *estimating revenue* for the new budget year. *Envisioning the educational program* is usually the second step. The third step is *estimating the expenditures* required to support the program. The fourth step is a set of decisions designed to *balance program needs against revenue and expenditure* realities. Consequently, the general budget process is the operationalization of the budget triangle. Ideally, programs should be determined first, but often revenues drive both expenditures and programs. Although this should be resisted to keep focus on a district's goals, leaders know that the budget process first calls for revenue estimation.

Estimating Revenues

Although states use their own budget documents and forms to calculate federal, state, and local funding, revenue is known to local districts in a common manner. Federal revenues are established at the national level and usually flow through a state agency, with notice of entitlement sent to qualifying districts. State revenues are determined through the legislative process, and districts are run through the state aid formula with entitlement notice sent to each district. Each district then calculates its local tax requirement, subject to state limits.[2] For example, states with aid formulas based on a classroom unit may permit total instructional costs of $30,500 per unit, with the state-aid formula supplying $20,000 per classroom. If federal aid were equal to $500 per classroom, then $10,000 must be raised locally. A variation achieving the same result might be through an aid plan requiring a uniform local tax rate of 20 mills paid to the state, with state aid returned to the district through a statewide staffing formula and salary schedule paying for 55 professional staff positions per 1,000 students. If local option tax leeway is permitted, any additional costs would be funded by local option levy. Likewise, in states funded on a per-pupil basis, the formula might determine the local tax requirement by providing aid in an equalized ratio between 0% and 100%, where the unfunded portion must be met by whatever local tax rate is required to raise the necessary funds. Many other highly state-specific configurations

---

2   As introduced earlier in Chapter 3, local tax effort is calculated in most states using mill rates. A mill is 1/1,000 of a dollar or $1 of tax yield for every $1,000 assessed valuation. A property valued at $100,000 market value and fractionally assessed at 12% for tax purposes and to which a 20 mill tax rate is applied would result in a tax bill of $240 (i.e., $100,000 × 12% = $12,000 × 0.020 = $240). A district's tax rate is found by dividing the local tax requirement by the sum of the district's total assessed valuation (e.g., $5,000,000 local share ÷ $250,000,000 assessed valuation = 0.020 mills).

exist, in that each state's funding mechanism determines how resources are raised. Figure 5.3 (p. 152) is an example of revenue estimation for a hypothetical school district, where $433,712 will be raised from local property tax in the new fiscal year, $4,005,159 from state aid, and so forth, to complete its general fund budget of $4,998,854.

In most states, revenues are estimated by each individual fund using state-approved worksheets and information from other agencies. As we saw in Chapter 4, fund accounting sets up multiple separate funds for revenue and expenditure purposes. For example, a state may require that all financial transactions be made from one of the following funds: *general, vocational education, special education, capital outlay, bond and interest, food service, transportation, adult education, bilingual,* or *inservice/staff development*. As we also saw earlier, fund-based budgets permit analysis of how money is spent and further permit states to categorically aid districts based on state educational philosophy. For example, rural states often place priority on aiding transportation for children in sparsely populated areas. Fund-based budgeting permits the state to choose to aid transportation at a high level, while aiding some other aspect, such as general fund, at a lower level. Similarly, urban states may provide greater aid to an adult education fund to improve adult literacy or to aid in dropout recovery. As a result, districts must carry out the revenue estimation process for each fund the district operates.

In many states, revenue estimation by fund may include the ability (or requirement) to levy different amounts of local tax for each individual fund. For example, the uniform tax rate common to many states usually refers only to the general fund from which the bulk of education's costs are paid. Many states that do not aid capital outlay or bond indebtedness therefore permit or require districts to levy a special tax for these funds. As a result, the series of funds operated by school districts can result in multiple revenue estimations and tax levies. Revenue estimation by fund is also political, in that it must be remembered that other governmental units also levy taxes for services and operate on fund-based budgets that also may require multiple tax levies. Aggregate tax rates assessed by all units of government may be lengthy, underscoring the importance of remembering that the school tax is only one of many types of taxes citizens pay. In other words, revenue estimation by fund can result in an aggregate tax rate for services including city, county, township, and special assessments two or three times higher (or more) than the school tax.

Revenue estimation is usually the first step in preparing a school district budget. This process is the simplest of the four budget steps because federal and state revenues cannot be altered except by the political process, and legislative decisions are usually complete before districts estimate revenues or calculate local tax requirements. Revenue estimation thus generally comprises estimating revenues by fund and entering amounts into the state budget document for comparison to program description and any necessary adjustments based on program expenditures.

Envisioning Educational Programs

The second activity in the budget process calls for review and establishment of the educational program. The process seeks to maintain the present program and to

Figure 5.3. Sample General Fund Revenue Structure

01 GENERAL	12 mo. 2007–2008 Actual (1)	12 mo. 2008–2009 Actual (2)	12 mo. 2009–2010 Budget (3)
UNENCUMBERED CASH BALANCE JULY 1	683,202	4,657	13,893
UNENCUMBERED CASH BALANCE FROM TRANSPORTATION, BILINGUAL Education AND VOCATIONAL Education FUNDS	2,368	12,368	0
Cancel of Prior Yr Enc			
REVENUE: 1000 LOCAL SOURCES 1110 Ad Valorem Tax Levied 2006 $	407,781		
2007 $	435,968	199,680	
2008 $		414,810	262,990
2009 $			433,712
1140 Delinquent Tax	14,897	16,648	6,779
1300 Tuition 1312 Individuals (Out District)			
1320 Other school district In-State			
1330 Other school district Out-State			
1700 Student Activities (Reimbursement)			
1900 Other Revenue From Local Source 1910 User Charges			
1980 Reimbursements			
1985 State Aid Reimbursement			
2000 COUNTY SOURCES 2400 Motor Vehicle Tax	276,484	258,224	252,155
2450 Recreational Vehicle Tax		6,642	14,166
2800 In Lieu of Taxes IRBs			
3000 STATE SOURCES 3110 General State Aid	2,298,537	3,620,788	4,005,159
3130 Mineral Production Tax			
4000 FEDERAL SOURCES 4590 Other Reserve Grants in Aid 4591 Title I (Formerly Chapter I)			
4592 Title (Math/Science)			
4599 Other	14,365	15,864	
4820 PL 382 (Exclude Extra Aid for Children on Indian Land and Low Rent Housing) (formerly PL 874)*	39,642	42,888	10,000
5000 OTHER 5208 Transfer From Local Option Tax	0	0	0
RESOURCES AVAILABLE	4,173,244	4,592,569	4,998,854
TOTAL EXPENDITURES & TRANSFERS	4,168,587	4,578,676	4,998,854
EXCESS REVENUE TO STATE			0
UNENCUMBERED CASH BALANCE JUNE 30	4,657	13,893	

consider new improvements. At times, fiscal issues may force program reductions, but districts should try to maintain or improve services.

Envisioning programs takes many forms. One method assumes the present program is adequate and that the budget should be built around the cost of program maintenance. A second method proposes improvements based on consultation with various constituencies. This method has gained popularity with the advent of school reform, so that many districts have school improvement plans linked to current research aimed at increasing excellence or targeting high-risk populations. Such designs may include school curriculum committees, task forces, site councils, community-school models, business or industry partnerships, and a host of other arrangements. Generally such efforts intend to look at the schools' program, with improvement and redesign as major goals. As a rule, envisioning programs is undertaken to better align curriculum and to specify outcomes in return for resources invested.

Regardless of how schools assess their programs, the underlying point is that programs cost money. The purpose of program description in budgeting is to identify the physical needs of programs in order to translate them into fiscal terms in the budget document. If program maintenance is the goal, the district can use prior year data as the basis, with allowance for increased costs in the new year. If improvements are being considered, the district generally turns to its proposed program description, which should include action statements about resources. A budget development calendar may be used to gather input and build the vision. The district's fiscal philosophy, such as site budgeting, will have a powerful impact on designing educational programs. The budget triangle seen earlier in Fig. 5.1 (p. 141) is a good illustration of how curriculum goals are translated into statements that can be quantified for budgetary purposes.

Envisioning the educational program is a complex process that—if done right—is time-consuming and expensive. But it should be the heart of budgeting because unless program vision is thoughtfully carried out, nothing more than maintenance will occur. In sum, envisioning the program is the critical link between estimating revenues and estimating expenditures.

Estimating Expenditures

Estimation of expenditures needed to support the educational program is the third activity in preparing a budget. Like revenue estimation, expenditure plans must follow state requirements for form and content. Although many unique features of expenditure estimation apply to different states, the process generally calls for placing revenue on the various proposed expenditure lines of each fund in the budget. Although it is difficult to say that any one step is most important, expenditure estimation is one of the most critical because underestimation of costs is disastrous. For example, failure to accurately calculate the costs of a new teacher salary schedule could result in unmet payroll, suit for breach of employment contract, and force school closures because revenues must equal or exceed all expenditures.

Expenditure estimation identifies the major cost determinants and makes best estimates of all changes for the new budget year. Estimating general fund expenditures, for example, requires negotiating salaries and benefits for employees, determining the number of positions required, determining movement of each staff member on the applicable salary schedule, determining quantities and costs of supplies, determining equipment costs, and finding costs of services such as professional inservice, legal fees, auditing, insurance, printing, security, data processing, and so forth. Figure 5.4, which shows the expenditure side of a hypothetical district's general fund budget document, illustrates the exhaustive nature of these activities. Importantly, these steps are repeated for each separate fund the district operates.

In most states, every item in the budget is driven by enrollment. Staff, supplies and equipment, size and number of buildings, and so forth are an absolute function of the number of children in school. As a result, estimating enrollment is the most important and difficult task in budgeting because no single method is always exactly accurate. Even with powerful population mapping tools, sudden in- and out-migrations due to human variables and economic shifts can affect accuracy. Enrollment projection techniques are remarkably useful, however, because they are all based on two important features. The first feature is an expectation that the conditions characterizing the past will continue. The second feature softens the apparent error of that assumption by requiring constant reevaluation and updating of the model's underlying assumptions. In essence, tracking shifts in population over time provides a smoothing effect to the data, a technique used in the most common methods of enrollment estimation—that is, trend analysis and cohort survival.

(Text continues on page 158.)

Figure 5.4. Sample General Fund Expenditure Structure

01 GENERAL EXPENDITURES	12 mo. 2007–2008 Actual (1)	12 mo. 2008–2009 Actual (2)	12 mo. 2009–2010 Budget (3)
1000 Instruction			
100 Salaries			
110 Certified	1,688,504	1,799,864	1,872,000
120 Noncertified	25,682	28,243	29,000
200 Employee Benefits			
210 Insurance (Employee)	28,949	33,640	34,000
220 Social Security	131,083	138,764	140,000
290 Other	3,039	3,642	3,800
300 Purchased Professional and Technical Services			
500 Other Purchased Services			
560 Tuition			
561 Tuition/other State LEAs			
562 Tuition/other LEAs outside the State			
563 Tuition/Private Sources			
590 Other	9,241	10,953	9,000
600 Supplies			
610 General Supplemental (Teaching)	85,984	102,760	104,000
644 Textbooks	52,486	62,384	65,000
680 Miscellaneous Supplies	4,685		3,960
700 Property (Equipment & Furnishings)	51,863	5,543	6,000
800 Other			62,000
2000 Support Services			
2100 Student Support Services			
100 Salaries			
110 Certified	60,504	64,164	65,500
120 Noncertified			
200 Employee Benefits			
210 Insurance (Employee)	562	699	750
220 Social Security	4,630	4,984	5,200
290 Other	59	100	100
300 Purchased Professional and Technical Services	7,982	9,641	10,000
500 Other Purchased Services			
600 Supplies			5,000
700 Property (Equipment & Furnishings)	4,291	5,007	
800 Other			
2200 Instructional Support Staff			
100 Salaries			
110 Certified	91,860	96,541	98,000
120 Noncertified			
200 Employee Benefits			
210 Insurance (Employee)	1,072	1,286	1,400

(Figure continues on next page.)

01 GENERAL EXPENDITURES	12 mo. 2007–2008 Actual (1)	12 mo. 2008–2009 Actual (2)	12 mo. 2009–2010 Budget (3)
220 Social Security	7,070	7,509	8,500
290 Other	112	148	200
3300 Community Services Operations	3,064	3,704	4,000
3400 Student Activities	28,564	34,296	35,000
4300 Architectural & Engineering Services			
300 Purchased Professional and Technical Services			
500 Other Purchased Services			
600 Supplies 640 Books (not textbooks) and Periodicals	14,389	16,841	18,000
650 Audiovisual and Instructional Software	12,684	15,092	17,000
680 Miscellaneous Supplies			
700 Property (Equipment & Furnishings)	4,066	4,905	5,000
800 Other			
2300 General Administration 100 Salaries 110 Certified	38,184	40,448	41,500
120 Noncertified	49,860	53,624	54,600
200 Employee Benefits 210 Insurance (Employee)	984	1,206	1,300
220 Social Security	7,115	8,492	9,000
290 Other	103	200	200
300 Purchased Professional and Technical Services	17,054	20,384	21,000
400 Purchased Property Services			
500 Other Purchased Services 520 Insurance			
530 Communications (Telephone, postage, etc.)	4,643	5,605	5,900
590 Other			
600 Supplies	8,106	9,653	10,000
700 Property (Equipment & Furnishings)	7,964	9,582	10,000
800 Other	13,165	16,769	16,000
2400 School Administration 100 Salaries 110 Certified	211,864	220,843	227,000
120 Noncertified	84,286	89,300	91,000
200 Employee Benefits 210 Insurance (Employee)	4,995	6,001	6,500
220 Social Security	2,505	26,984	28,000
290 Other	324	411	500
300 Purchased Professional and Technical Services			
400 Purchased Property Services			
500 Other Purchased Services 530 Communications (Telephone, postage, etc.)	1,793	2,174	2,200

01 GENERAL EXPENDITURES	12 mo. 2007–2008 Actual (1)	12 mo. 2008–2009 Actual (2)	12 mo. 2009–2010 Budget (3)
590 Other			
600 Supplies			
700 Property (Equipment & Furnishings)	4,001	4,624	5,000
800 Other			
2600 Operations & Maintenance 100 Salaries 120 Noncertified	192,386	200,784	205,000
200 Employee Benefits 210 Insurance (Employee)	1,995	2,396	2,500
220 Social Security	15,750	16,863	18,000
290 Other	209	255	500
300 Purchased Professional and Technical Services	1,248	1,498	1,500
400 Purchased Property Services 411 Water/Sewer	8,150	9,750	10,000
420 Cleaning			
430 Repairs & Maintenance	161,745	188,640	264,860
440 Rentals		61,980	42,840
460 Repair of Buildings	218,714	251,574	388,431
490 Other	37,984	45,472	55,000
500 Other Purchased Services 520 Insurance	32,345	36,542	37,000
590 Other		13,052	
600 Supplies 610 General Supplies	42,387	50,845	51,000
620 Energy 621 Heating	45,190	46,842	48,000
622 Electricity	67,810	69,742	71,000
626 Motor Fuel (not schoolbus)			
629 Other	22,196	32,482	26,000
680 Miscellaneous Supplies		12,052	4,000
700 Property (Equipment & Furnishings)	4,284	8,244	6,000
800 Other	2,361	2,876	3,000
2500, 2800, 2900 Other Supplemental Service 100 Salaries 110 Certified			
120 Noncertified			
200 Employee Benefits 210 Insurance			
220 Social Security			
290 Other			
300 Purchased Professional and Technical Services			
400 Purchased Property Services			

(Figure continues on next page.)

01 GENERAL EXPENDITURES	12 mo. 2007–2008 Actual (1)	12 mo. 2008–2009 Actual (2)	12 mo. 2009–2010 Budget (3)
500 Other Purchased Services			
600 Supplies			
700 Property (Equipment & Furnishings)			
800 Other			
5200 TRANSFER TO: 932 Adult Education			3,000
934 Adult Suppl Education			
936 Bilingual Education			
938 Capital Outlay	75,246	94,400	97,315
940 Driver Training	5,000	5,000	5,000
942 Education Excellence Grant Prog		10,000	5,000
943 Extraordinary School Prog			
944 Food Service			
946 In-service Education	5,136	4,533	11,798
948 Parent Education Program			
949 Summer School		10,000	10,000
950 Special Education	130,000	100,000	125,000
951 Technology Education			
952 Transportation	313,080	323,070	360,000
954 Vocational Education	6,000	12,864	15,000
955 Area Vocational School			
956 Disability Income Benefits Reserve			
958 Health Care Services Reserve			
959 Group Life Insurance Reserve			
960 Risk Management Reserve			
962 School Workers' Compensation Reserve			
968 Cooperative Elementary Guidance			
972 Contingency Reserve			
TOTAL EXPENDITURES & TRANSFERS	4,168,587	4,578,766	4,998,854

Trend analysis is the application of regression models to predicting enrollment based on previous years enrollment data. In its simplest form, trend analysis predicts future enrollments based on the manner in which previous enrollments deviate from a straight line. The formula for the regression line (fitted line) is $Y = Mx + b$ where Y is the future enrollment, M is a coefficient used in the model, x is a future year, and b is a constant showing the relationship between enrollment and year. Using multiyear historic data, a future year is entered, and the result is a predicted enrollment. Figure 5.5 shows a sample trend analysis. The regression formula casts a line of best fit, yielding projected enrollment for next year (Year 6). In the sample district's case, historic data indicate a steadily increasing enrollment trend, with Year 1 enrollment beginning at 1,990 students and increasing to 2,710 by Year 5. Figure 5.5 projects ahead one year, in this case, an enrollment of 2,900 students.

Figure 5.5. Trend Line Analysis of Enrollments

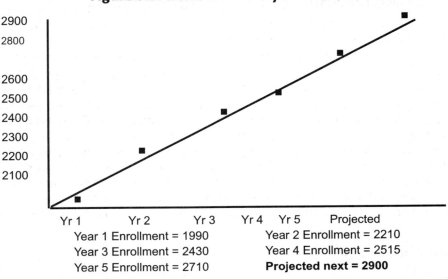

Year 1 Enrollment = 1990   Year 2 Enrollment = 2210
Year 3 Enrollment = 2430   Year 4 Enrollment = 2515
Year 5 Enrollment = 2710   **Projected next = 2900**

Trend analysis is most useful in larger districts because the averages in a regression line do not affect the district to the extent that would be true for smaller districts, where the loss of each student has a larger impact because each student is a greater proportion of the total budget. As a result, medium and smaller size districts often prefer other techniques that are more arithmetically straightforward, more intuitive, and more sensitive to changes in head count.

Cohort survival is an enrollment projection tool that groups students by grade level at entry to school and tracks them through each year they remain in the school district. In concept, cohort survival looks at entering kindergarten students in Year 1 and calculates how many enter first grade in Year 2, second grade in Year 3 and so on until graduation. Such a system more closely accounts for grade failures, dropouts, and migratory trends impacting student population.

Cohort survival requires enrollment data from the previous and present years for each grade. It calculates the percentage of change and survival as a percentage of the previous year's grade-level enrollment. For example, the middle part of Fig. 5.6 (pp. 161–162) shows that historically enrollments from first to second grade averaged only 94% of the prior year's grade-level population. This means that outmigrations or grade failure resulted in an approximate 6% average loss between first and second grades. This allows entry of the multiyear average into the bottom part of the analysis, where current first grade enrollment can be multiplied by 94% to project 376 students in second grade next year compared to 400 students in first grade in the present year. This process is repeated for each grade for several years into the future, whereupon enrollments are totaled by grade level. One additional point should be made. Kindergarten estimation is very unreliable and constitutes a special case in most school districts, requiring use of birth records, roundups, knowing local preschool numbers, and so on. Except for kindergarten, the data are generally smooth, and these numbers are used with relative confidence to assign staff, purchase supplies, plan facility use, and calculate other aspects of revenue and expenditure estimation. Because virtually all budgeting is based on enrollments, cohort survival a good tool as a result of its immediate sensitivity to changes in population.

The sheer volume of activities involved in estimating expenditures precludes their explanation in a single textbook chapter. For example, the next major activity following enrollment projection is projecting staffing needs. This is a complex set of events involving labor negotiations, salary schedules, and so on—topics that take up at least the same amount of space already used in this chapter! Enrollment and staff numbers also drive the purchase of teaching supplies, equipment, and facilities. As a result, we cover other aspects of estimating expenditures in future chapters; for example, Chapter 6 covers budgeting for personnel, Chapter 9 discusses budgeting for school facilities, and so on. For our purposes in this chapter, expenditure estimation is broadly detailed and begins with enrollment projection because accurate revenue and expenditure estimates must combine in the final budget and ultimately must be balanced.

Balancing the Budget

The fourth step in the budget process aligns estimated costs for each fund with anticipated revenues. Again, the process is easier in states that tightly control revenues by mechanisms such as allocating classroom units to each district. For instance, it takes little time to find salary costs if the state allocates 55 professional positions per 1,000 pupils—in such states, school districts will spend all their time deciding how to meet their instructional needs (given a set staff size) because no options exist for increased staffing. In states with more staffing flexibility, districts may spend much time playing with reallocation of money to various lines in the budget to achieve the best balance for their particular situation. In states where tax rates can vary through local option leeway, districts may also consider raising taxes to pay for a desired educational program. The process in all states, though, calls for *balancing* the revenue and expenditure sides of the budget because most states forbid deficit spending by schools.

Efforts to balance revenues and expenditures result in cause-and-effect scenarios, with nearly inescapable instructional impacts. For example, revenues may need careful review if program needs significantly exceed available funding. Alternatively, programs may have to be reduced if it is clear that revenues will continue to be inadequate. Although state-specific conditions sometimes limit available options, these activities—called budget adjustments—usually involve one of three common scenarios. The first scenario happens when new state legislation results in *increased revenue*, although other factors such as increased local property wealth can cause tax windfalls as well. The second scenario occurs when *revenues are static*. The third scenario appears when *revenue declines*. Each of these situations has been faced at some time by every school district, and the process for dealing with each one can be difficult and complex.

Figure 5.6. Cohort Survival Technique

Part I Historic Enrollments

Grade	2001–2002	2002–03	2003–04	2004–05	2005-06	2006–07	Average
Pre-K	500.0	500.0	499.0	502.0	500.0	503.0	500.7
One	490.0	501.0	498.0	499.0	501.0	400.0	481.5
Two	627.0	499.0	478.0	466.0	489.0	410.0	494.8
Three	590.0	611.0	497.0	477.0	477.0	488.0	523.3
Four	491.0	593.0	601.0	488.0	482.0	469.0	520.7
Five	399.0	478.0	578.0	615.0	479.0	489.0	506.3
Six	617.0	389.0	502.0	477.0	610.0	477.0	512.0
Seven	591.0	616.0	399.0	499.0	470.0	600.0	529.2
Eight	499.0	588.0	618.0	381.0	489.0	479.0	509.0
Nine	650.0	482.0	549.0	729.0	377.0	488.0	545.8
Ten	533.0	623.0	492.0	532.0	716.0	369.0	544.2
Eleven	811.0	540.0	622.0	499.0	415.0	616.0	583.8
Twelve	710.0	815.0	539.0	627.0	481.0	421.0	598.8
TOTAL	7508.0	7235.0	6872.0	6791.0	6486.0	6209.0	6850.2

Part II Survival Ratio

Grade	2001–2002	2002–03	2003–04	2004–05	2005-06	2006–07	Average
Pre-K		100%	100%	101%	100%	101%	100%
One		100%	100%	100%	100%	80%	96%
Two		102%	95%	94%	98%	82%	94%
Three		97%	100%	100%	102%	100%	100%
Four		101%	98%	98%	101%	98%	99%
Five		97%	97%	102%	98%	101%	99%
Six		97%	105%	83%	99%	100%	97%
Seven		100%	103%	99%	99%	98%	100%
Eight		99%	100%	95%	98%	102%	99%
Nine		97%	93%	118%	99%	100%	101%
Ten		96%	102%	97%	98%	98%	98%
Eleven		101%	100%	101%	78%	86%	93%
Twelve		100%	100%	101%	96%	101%	100%

(Figure continues on next page.)

Part III Enrollment Projection through 2012

Grade	Multi-year Average	2006–07 (actual)	2007–08	2008–09	2009-10	2010-11	2011–12
Pre-K	100%	503.0	503.6	504.2	504.8	505.8	506.4
One	96%	400.0	482.5	483.1	483.6	484.2	485.2
Two	94%	410.0	376.5	454.2	454.7	455.3	455.8
Three	100%	488.0	409.2	375.8	453.2	453.8	454.3
Four	99%	469.0	484.5	406.3	373.1	450.0	450.6
Five	99%	489.0	466.0	481.4	403.6	370.7	447.1
Six	97%	477.0	473.2	450.9	465.8	390.6	358.7
Seven	100%	600.0	475.8	471.9	449.7	464.6	389.5
Eight	99%	479.0	594.3	471.2	467.4	445.4	460.1
Nine	101%	488.0	485.4	602.2	477.5	473.7	451.3
Ten	98%	369.0	479.1	476.6	591.2	468.8	465.1
Eleven	93%	616.0	344.4	447.1	444.8	551.8	437.5
Twelve	100%	421.0	614.7	343.6	446.2	443.8	550.6
TOTAL		6209.0	6189.0	5968.4	6015.7	5958.4	5912.3

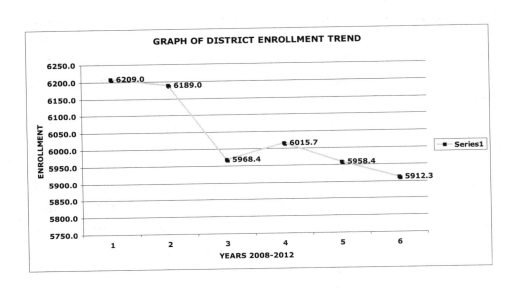

Increased Revenue

The problem of new revenue is a dilemma that schools often like. Although thought to be the least common scenario, the history of funding for schools suggests that revenue has grown over many years, both in real and adjusted dollars.[3] It must be remembered, though, that new revenue typically gets invested in expenditures that may be permanent *and* cumulative, as in the case of teacher salaries; that is, if salaries go up a modest 3% annually, the cumulative result is a 130% base increase over only a decade, an amount that is surely compounded by events such as additional college credits earned, experience step increases, and so forth that add to teacher salary schedule costs. In fact, the small 3% step increase is not just the 30% gain—it is more likely in the neighborhood of 50% or even more as a consequence of the accompanying experience and college credit aspects of salary schedules. It is no surprise, then, that school costs rise so rapidly because approximately 80% of budgets are dedicated to pay scales, of which teacher salaries are the vast bulk. Districts thus need a plan for dealing with revenue increases, especially because a revenue increase eventually results in an expenditure increase that is difficult to back away from later if the revenue pattern reverses.

Big revenue increases typically follow after unusual events. For example, in the 1950s and 1960s, the Cold War and social programs drove huge revenue spikes. In the 1980s and 1990s, revenue increases often accompanied legislative efforts aimed at school reform. Dealing with new revenue often meant spending in categories the state had targeted; for example, recently much money has been poured into at-risk programs and timely curricula such as special education, staff development, and parent education. Similarly, since 2001 hundreds of millions in new dollars have been earmarked for *No Child Left Behind*. Increased revenues have also stemmed from growth in tax base, as school tax rates often fail to drop despite rapid increases in property values. This phenomenon has had negative implications, however, as taxpayer protests have occurred throughout the nation and, in the worst cases, have resulted in tax limitation referenda. In states escaping tax protests, schools have sometimes profited by these tax windfalls. Often in such cases, schools have had the option of committing extra dollars to various funds in the budget or have chosen to shore up their capital and contingency funds.

The need for increased revenues actually is a far more common problem. Highly specific to state law, actually seeking to increase revenue can be difficult. Increasing revenue is easiest in states permitting local tax leeway options; even yet, choices are usually few due to state interest in equalization and because equalization is less expensive to the state if it caps local leeway at some ceiling, rather than providing open-ended aid to poor districts under cost-share or power equalization formulas. Absent local tax leeway, districts must turn to improved cash management; student fees; partnerships with businesses or other groups; and volunteers in lieu of pur-

---

3   Recent data suggest that education dollars per pupil have grown 3.5% annually over the last 100 years after adjusting for inflation. Consortium for Policy Research in Education. Feb. 2007. *Policy Briefs* (University of Pennsylvania, CEPRE), 1.

chased services.[4] Unless wide tax latitude exists, the most profitable option is improved cash management, with the goal of increasing investment income and underspending the budget to build cash reserves and offset tax increases for the next year. In hindsight, districts have experienced revenue increases mostly through inflation, state aid, and wise management—but they have generally had to spend any new money, rather than build cash reserves.

Static and Declining Revenue

The scenario of static revenue is not unlike the problems that occur when revenues actually decline. In fact, it may be argued that the difference is one of degree, as static revenue in a growing economy mimics decline. The problems are so similar that static and declining revenues can be discussed simultaneously.

Static or declining revenue is a dreaded event. Although history might suggest that the problem is uncommon, the reverse is actually true because effects on individual districts vary widely from the overall trends in a state or nation. In many states, districts have experienced static or declining revenues in response to poor state economies, enrollment losses, depressed land prices reducing tax bases, decreased sales and income taxes, and a host of other elements impacting school revenue. For example, energy-dependent states have had a particularly hard time in recent years because of volatile oil prices, and agricultural states have seen dramatic swings in property values as inflated land prices from the 1980s have collapsed and only partially rebounded. Similarly, more populous states have seen a massive influx of school enrollments outstripping revenue growth, while rural states simultaneously have experienced enrollment declines. Although revenues have grown rapidly overall, it is small comfort to individual districts because such growth is like the old saying that "a hand in the fire and a hand in the freezer on average is quite comfortable."

Regardless of cause, static or declining revenue forces a need to devise methods to balance the budget. There are few ideal solutions. From a practical perspective, often only two solutions are available: Districts must find replacement revenue from other sources *or* reduce expenditures. The best approach is to combine these strategies, but limits on revenue enhancement in many states often result only in expenditure reductions. The unfortunate reality is that personnel reduction-in-force (RIF) is the most effective tool, simply because salaries make up 80% to 85% of a typical district's budget. Such decisions are more than fiscal considerations because budget reductions cannot violate federal employment law, state employment statutes, district personnel and instructional policies, collective bargaining agreements, or other legal and moral obligations to the people who carry out the business of educating children. Such realities make it difficult to settle on any single reduction strategy. As a result, educational decision makers should involve as many staff and community members as possible because decisions made from a single point of view (e.g., the superintendent or the school board) can have severe legal and political repercussions.

---

4   See, for example, Faith E. Crampton and Paul Bauman, "A New Challenge to Fiscal Equity: Educational Entrepreneurship and Its Implications for Schools, Districts, and States." *Educational Considerations* 28 (Fall 2000): 53–61.

Although RIF is the major way to balance deep revenue and expenditure deficits, other efforts can provide real savings too. Under the best conditions, the preferred way is to cut costs by improving the efficiency of the district. Examples of strategies actually used by districts include:

- *Energy conservation:* adjusting thermostats in winter and summer, reducing the number of cooled or heated spaces, turning out lights, or making new energy-efficient expenditures such as thermal retrofitting to reduce costs in the long run. The latter is problematic in that the need to reduce budgets hardly places a district in a position to spend its way out of a budget deficit.

- *More efficient purchasing:* streamlining by not purchasing elective items, bulk discount buying, or "just-in-time" purchasing. Many districts claim significant savings from these strategies. Smaller school districts may realize cost-savings through cooperative purchasing with neighboring districts or municipalities.

- *Improved cash management:* investing idle funds wisely, underspending the budget to build cash reserves, reducing annual cash carryover, and so forth. Some strategies, however, have negative long-term impacts (e.g., reducing reserves) and—importantly—may actually starve instruction.

- *Improved risk management:* raising insurance deductible amounts, assessing the potential benefits and risks of self-insuring, bidding insurance coverage, and so forth.

- *Deferral or elimination:* delaying purchases of new equipment, supplies, and maintenance, although this strategy creates new problems—for example, delaying bus purchases results in old and possibly unsafe buses, raising liability questions and increasing maintenance, as well as higher replacement costs later. Similarly, undermaintained facilities are proof of what deferral can mean later. A variation on this strategy includes make-or-buy decisions, where the district keeps more tasks inhouse.

- *More efficient equipment and technology:* replacing buses with more economical units, using environmentally smart thermostats, automating some tasks to reduce personnel costs, and so forth. But care should be taken to calculate the cost-to-benefit ratio, including political ramifications.

- *Refinance long-term debt:* refunding bonds to cash in on lower interest rates can save many thousands of dollars if care is taken not to increase costs in the long run by extending bond payments over a longer period of time.

- *Implementing early retirement programs:* buying out high-cost teachers nearing retirement, replacing them with new faculty at lower salaries or alternatively leaving positions vacant.

- ◆ *Changes to bargaining agreements:* negotiating salaries and benefits downward, although difficult, is based on the theory that a job at a lower salary is better than a RIF.

- ◆ *Reduction-in-force:* reducing staff in the knowledge that the vast majority of costs are for personnel, leaving no other option if deep and permanent cuts must be made.

Although the list above moves from most desirable to least desirable options, even these measures may not be sufficient to balance a budget. In that case, the one remaining alternative is to cut programs. These include reductions in course offerings, changes in length of the school day, increased class size, and reduction of nonessential services not legally mandated in a given state, such as extended day programs or extracurricular activities. Care must be exercised, however, not to violate contracts or state laws. For example, in many states length of school day, hours of work, and class schedules are part of negotiated agreements, and many states have mandated preschool and extended day programs. Although cuts are never easy, reductions in staff and program are the most painful and the most destructive. As a result, such measures should be used only as a last resort.

Completing the Budget Process

Budget construction is nearly complete when *programs are envisioned, revenues and expenditures are estimated*, and a *balanced budget* is achieved. The budget still must be *approved*, however. Approval steps differ among states, but the process always results in legal adoption of the budget under statutory requirements. For example, in states where school districts are fiscally dependent on some other unit of government, approval usually means that the budget is forwarded to a higher authority, often a city or county board. In states where districts are fiscally independent, approval is more complex in that several events usually occur sequentially. Although highly state-specific, a general procedure calls for official publication of a budget summary, usually in a newspaper of general local circulation, followed by a waiting period, public hearing, formal adoption of the budget, and certification of the proposed or amended budget to some other governmental unit such as a county taxing authority. Publication is meant to give notice to the public of the budget hearing, with the waiting period to allow citizens a chance to prepare comments and to attend the hearing. Statutes usually call for the school board to vote in open session. The budget, if adopted, must be certified according to state statute. Because these laws are meant to guard against secrecy and impropriety, they must be rigidly observed or angry taxpayers could conceivably force school closures until a budget is properly adopted.

HOW ARE INDIVIDUAL SCHOOLS FUNDED?

The process discussed to this point details budgeting at the district level, but it says nothing about funding individual schools. As can be imagined, this is a difficult topic because states generally have not enacted true statewide school-level funding laws, leaving most of the nation's roughly 14,000 districts free to adopt their own school site budget philosophy. That is exactly the point of our earlier focus on adopting a local budget philosophy: that is, districts have great freedom to create internal budget structures, and those choices have a tremendous impact on individual schools. As a result, how individual schools are funded is as different as the number of districts that exist. Nonetheless, some common ways that districts fund schools can be reviewed.

Most school districts operate from a budget calendar such as the one in Fig. 5.7 (p. 168). Budget calendars range from very simple to highly complex. Figure 5.7 is fairly uncomplicated and is taken from an actual district of about 7,000 students. The calendar identifies all areas of the budget, assigns responsibility to an administrator, and lays out the budget process with deadlines. An important feature is that budgeting is a multimonth process that includes a flow chart of responsibility and (in this case) involves many people, including principals and other staff. The processes of estimating revenues, envisioning school programs, estimating expenditures, and balancing the budget are all evident in the sample budget calendar, as is the overall coordination of the budget process at the district level that brings these separate activities into a completed total budget prior to a new school year.

The budget calendar in Fig. 5.7 also notes another aspect of school budgeting, in that building principals are assigned a formal role. Although again dependent on local district preference, this budget calendar shows principals involved at almost all stages including the initial planning stage, program envisioning, preliminary budget review, requisition and purchase order preparation, and the daily administration of school budgets. Figure 5.7 might be used in a relatively central office-controlled district, but it could apply just as easily to a district using site based budgeting. In the first case, school principals would be asked about program needs, supplies, equipment, and facilities. In the latter case, principals would have significant control over daily resource use, including decisions about whether to buy teachers, aides, and so forth—in essence, the individual school would operate as a mini-district with ultimate accountability for productivity. We will explore these ideas later when we look at budgeting for instruction, and again when we look more closely at site based leadership and the future.

The process of budgeting at this point can be pictured as a pyramid turned upside down, flowing mostly from state to local. It begins with federal and state policies that make revenue available to school districts. Each district simultaneously determines its program requirements and matches revenues and needs, adjusting local revenue and programs to fill the deficit. Districts then apportion revenue to individual schools based on a preferred budget philosophy, using such concepts as fairness, horizontal and vertical equity, and preferences about decentralization and accountability. For example, a district may decide it wishes to assign block grants to each elementary school in exchange for the promise to increase student achievement on test scores by 5% next year. Principals and staffs may then consult with site councils and opt for more teacher aides instead of new playground equipment in hopes of meeting achievement goals. Another district, however, might take a different path by hiring a grant writer to seek additional funding and using the enhanced revenue to provide extra supplies, equipment, and instructional staff to meet some other set of learning

Figure 5.7. Sample Budget Calendar

Budget Area	Staff Responsible
General Fund	Board/central administration
Administration	Superintendent
School budgets	Principals
Travel: administrator and teacher	Director of Personnel
Special programs	Director of Special Services
Adult education	Coordinator Adult Education
Bilingual programs	ESL Coordinator
Capital outlay	Director of Maintenance
Driver education	Business Manager
Food service	Director of Food Service
Transportation	Transportation Director
Special education	Director of Special Education
Bond & interest budgets	Business Manager
In-service budget	Director of Curriculum
Vocational school budget	Director of Curriculum
Special projects and grants	Business Manager
Other budgets	As assigned

Preparation Calendar

Date	Description	Responsible
January	Distribute planning guide Meet with principals and program directors	Business Manager
March	Requests for new programs and personnel due	Superintendent, Business Manager, and Personnel Director
April	Seek board input on programs and new personnel	Superintendent, Curriculum, and Personnel Director
April	Building, program, and capital repair/improvements due	Directors and Principals
May	Bid capital outlay, instructional items and advise of bids	Principals and Business Manager
June	First draft of total budget	Superintendent and Business Manager
July	Board budget workshop	All administrators
July	Budget publication and hearings	Admin, Board, public
August	Adoption and certification	Business Manager

goals. The range of possibilities primarily depends on state laws and available revenues, in combination with local ingenuity.

WHAT IS THE ROLE OF STAKEHOLDERS?

Every chapter in this book has implied that school money is a legitimate place for multiple stakeholders to make their voices heard. This chapter is no different. We have underscored that there is a place in school budgeting for everyone—administrators, boards, teachers, policy makers, and laypersons. If the purpose of budgets is to identify the needs of schools, prioritize those needs, match resources with needs, and make educational goals operational, there is no good reason to exclude any of these persons, and there is much to be gained by their informed participation.

Although we believe everyone should take initiative and responsibility for school budgeting, we especially believe that good administrators should deliberately use the budget for specific stakeholder benefits. Administrators should use budgets to structure the educational plan, to read progress toward outcomes, to evaluate accomplishment of the plan, and to make adjustments when problems arise. However, budgeting is not only a central office function: increasingly, principals must account for program decisions, with greater responsibility for money under site based leadership. Boards are legally charged with responsibility for expending funds and must take responsibility for wise policy making. Teachers consume most of the budget, and their expertise in program planning should be used in creating the educational plan expressed by the budget. Policy makers need knowledge about educational programming, and feedback loops help them reach the decisions about funding schools that they are constitutionally required to make. And no audience is more crucial than laypersons, as these are the parents and community members whose taxes pay for schools and whose approval every district must have in order to keep its schools open. Figure 5.8 makes very clear the interaction of these constituent roles—it is not by accident that the link between strategic planning influences and school budget outcomes is the many decision makers who ultimately decide how well schools are funded.

The consequences of this chapter and our beliefs about budget construction have real implications. Carrying out the educational plan requires financial resources, forces value judgments, and requires linking inputs and outcomes in an integrated budget plan. Unfortunately, the budget triangle is too frequently turned on its side by economics in our imperfect world. Administrators must guard against losing sight of the purpose of budgets and stand as true leaders. As Ward avowed, education finance is not a "...technical and sterile area of study employing complex mathematics, arcane algebraic formulas [nor] a refuge for the methodologically minded to be avoided by those humanists in education who see their emphasis as being on children, instruction, and qualitative aspects of schooling.[5] Instead, a budget is the fiscal expression of the educational philosophy of a school district.

---

5   James G. Ward, "An Inquiry into the Normative Foundations of American Public School Finance," *Journal of Education Finance* 12, no. 4 (1987): 463.

Figure 5.8 School Budget Arena

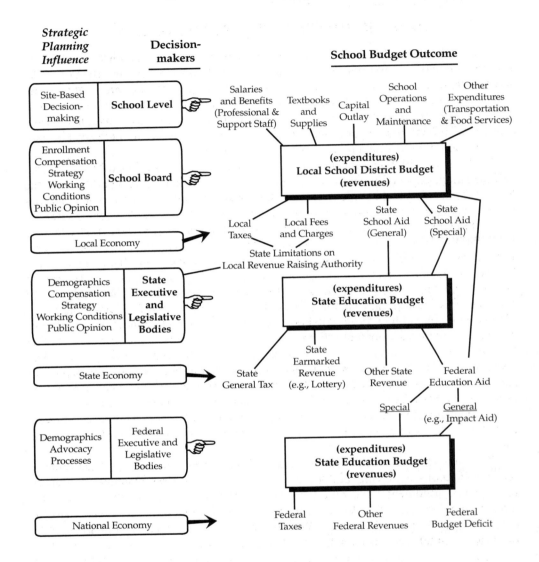

pointcounterpoint

Point

School leaders today, especially principals, are charged with the success of high-stakes educational programs and must be given responsibility for designing and expending site-level budgets if they are to meet their increased accountability expectations.

Counterpoint

School leaders today, especially principals, are so engulfed by instructional leadership duties, high-stakes accountability, and day-to-day operations that school districts should not require budget involvement by school site administrators—instead, districts should increase central support services to fulfill this "management" responsibility.

Questions

- ◆ Which view best represents your philosophy of budgeting? Explain why.
- ◆ How are principals, central office staff, teachers, and others involved in budget construction and daily budget administration in your own school district? If you were an administrator in your school district, how would you wish budgeting to be structured?

CASE STUDY

As a long-time principal in your school district, you were somewhat surprised at last week's administrative cabinet meeting when the new superintendent announced her desire to redesign the district's budgeting practices. As you listened, you learned she hoped to move many resource decisions to the school site level. As the discussion developed, you became both intrigued and worried when you realized that she was suggesting a wide range of constituent participation *and* increased site level accountability for the outcomes of expenditure decisions.

Inasmuch as all district and site-level administrators were in attendance at the weekly cabinet meeting, a vigorous discussion ensued. Several administrators, notably some of your fellow principals, seemed eager to seize the reins and accept responsibility for how money gets spent at the school site. Others seemed more reluctant, raising questions about how a new system would be structured, including concerns about individual school profiles, determination of each school's programmatic resource needs, and, of course, how evaluation of site-level resource decision making would be carried out. As the conversation progressed, it became clear that while the superintendent's idea was widely recognized as having merit, the district's administrative cabinet needed a blueprint for how such a plan would be constituted before everyone would unreservedly endorse such a dramatic change.

To move to the next level, the superintendent indicated that she would form a study group to consider and propose a redesign. She indicated that a workable proposal was due on her desk by the end of the school year—about eight months from now. As the most experienced principal in the school district, you were asked to cochair the study group along with the associate superintendent for management services. As the meeting broke up, your cochair asked you to step into his office, whereupon he requested that you take the lead in organizing the work to be undertaken at the committee's first meeting. Although you privately pondered that his job title might be better suited to the task at hand, you recognized that his motivation included the fact that you would have a better grasp on concerns likely to be held by the district's numerous school site administrators and that your insights might help avoid some pitfalls. In that you hope to move into a central office role shortly, you expressed willingness to accept the task and determined to yourself that you would be both careful and exhaustive in your approach.

Below is a set of questions. As you respond, consider your learning in this chapter and apply your knowledge and emerging beliefs/preferences to the situation:

Questions

- ♦ Based on your own organizational beliefs and preferences, do you believe the process this district is pursuing is wise? Why or why not? What advantages do you see? What problems might follow from this process?

- ♦ What steps should you take to begin this planning process? What factors need to be taken into account? What do you believe are the critical elements for such organizational changes to succeed? What pitfalls are immediately apparent? What hidden pitfalls may exist? How will you address the accountability aspect?

- ♦ How are your own school district's budgeting practices organized? What do you believe would happen if such a proposal were raised in your district? If such a practice is already in place in your district, how would you improve it?

- ♦ If you had been the superintendent in this case study, would you have embarked on this course? If yes, explain why. If no, what would you have done differently?

FOLLOW-UP ACTIVITIES

- ♦ Interview the appropriate central office leader to discuss the relationship between budgeting and strategic planning in your school district. Explore how the district conceptualizes its budget and the processes by which budgeting occurs. Discuss the overall process of estimating revenues and expenditures, including how the district involves employees and the school board in the process. Discuss the act of balancing the budget and the district's efforts to maintain and improve instructional programs.

♦ Obtain a copy of your district's most recent enrollment projections and interview the author as to how the projections were developed, e.g., methodology, data sources, etc. Discuss the assumptions that were used for the projections. Consider how different assumptions or different methodologies might affect the projections now being used. Explore how the projections affect budget planning in the district.

♦ Talk to one or more school site administrators in your district to determine how they are involved in the budgeting process. Ask how they involve their staffs and other stakeholders, and how they prioritize requests when expenditures exceed budget allocations. Ask how they would improve the budget planning process.

♦ If your state, district, or school uses school site councils, find out the extent to which councils are involved in budget planning activities. Review any state or school district policy documents and analyze the strengths and weaknesses of the decision-making roles these bodies play.

♦ Obtain a copy of your school district's budget calendar. Determine how and when your district obtains public input into the budget process at both formative and final stages. Interview your district's business manager or chief financial officer to determine how the district tries to ensure smooth passage of the final budget.

♦ Obtain a copy of your school and district budgets. Which budgeting approach described in this chapter is used in each? In your estimation, is this the optimal approach for your school or district? Explain your answer.

WEB RESOURCES

American Association of School Administrators, www.aasa.org
American Federation of Teachers, www.aft.org
Association of School Business Officials International, http://asbointl.org/
Council of Chief State School Officers, www.ccsso.org/
Education Commission of the States, www.ecs.org
National Association of State Boards of Education, www.nasbe.org
National Business Officers Association, www.nboa.net
National Center for Education Statistics, www.nces.ed.gov
National Conference of State Legislatures, www.ncsl.org
National Education Association, www.nea.org
National Governors Association, www.nga.org
National School Boards Association, www.nsba.org
U.S. Department of Education, www.ed.gov

RECOMMENDED READINGS

Crampton, Faith E., and Vesely, Randall S. "Resource Allocation Issues for Educational Leaders" in *Handbook for Excellence in School Leadership*, 4th ed., eds. Stuart C. Smith and Philip K. Piele. Thousand Oaks, CA: Corwin, 2006.

Goertz, Margaret, and Allan Odden, eds. *School-Based Financing.* Thousand Oaks, CA: Corwin, 1999.

Hartman, William T. *School District Budgeting.* Englewood Cliffs, NJ: Prentice Hall, 2002.

Jacobson, Stephen L., and Robert Berne, eds. American Education Finance Association. Annual Yearbook. *Reforming Education: The Emerging Systemic Approach.* Thousand Oaks, CA: Corwin, 1993.

King, Richard A, Austin D. Swanson, and Scott R. Sweetland. *School Finance: Achieving High Standards with Equity and Efficiency.* 3rd ed. Boston: Allyn & Bacon, 2003.

Mohrman, Susan, and Priscilla Wohlstetter. *School-Based Management: Organizing for High Performance.* San Francisco: Jossey-Bass, 1994.

Murphy, Joseph, and Karen Louis. *School Based Management as School Reform.* Thousand Oaks, CA: Corwin, 1995.

Picus, Lawrence O., and James L. Wattenbarger, eds. *Resource Allocation in Elementary and Secondary Schools.* Thousand Oaks, CA: Corwin, 1995.

Ray, John, I. Carl Candoli, and Walter G. Hack. *School Business Administration: A Planning Approach.* 8th ed. Boston: Allyn & Bacon, 2005.

Sorensen, Richard D., and Loyd M. Goldsmith. *The Principal's Guide to School Budgeting.* Thousand Oaks, CA: Corwin, 2006.

Stiefel, Leanna, Amy Ellen Schwartz, Ross Rubenstein, and Jeffrey Zabel, eds. American Education Finance Association. Annual Yearbook. *Measuring School Performance and Efficiency: Implications for Practice and Research.* Larchmont, NY: Eye On Education, 2005.

Wood, R. Craig, David C. Thompson, and Lawrence O. Picus. *Principles of School Business Management.* 3rd ed. Reston, VA: ASBO, 2008.

BUDGETING FOR PERSONNEL

THE CHALLENGE

For more than a decade, state after state has fashioned some version of an educational reform policy rooted in ambitious student learning standards that attempts to align higher expectations for all students with assessments, an accountability system, and other supporting policy features....These high expectations presume, at the very least, that a well-equipped and sustainable...workforce is available.

Plecki & Monk (2003)

CHAPTER DRIVERS

At the close of this chapter you will have reflected upon these questions:

- ♦ What is the scope of the personnel function in school districts?
- ♦ How are staffing needs determined?
- ♦ How do districts successfully recruit and select staff?
- ♦ What other personnel budget issues must districts consider?
- ♦ What are the issues in personnel compensation?
- ♦ What role do negotiations play in personnel and budget functions?
- ♦ What is current thinking about alternative reward systems?
- ♦ What are the fiscal and legal ramifications of reductions-in-force (RIFs) and dismissals?
- ♦ Why is due process important in RIFs and dismissals?
- ♦ What are the roles of various stakeholders in personnel matters?

THE GENERAL LANDSCAPE

The opening quotation to this chapter and the combined weight of all chapters thus far point to a highly complex relationship between the aims of schooling and the adults in schools charged with carrying out the educational mission. Our introduction to the budget process in the last chapter taught that the greatest proportion of education's costs is concentrated in the human resource function, in that compensation for personnel consumes approximately 80% of most school districts' budgets. A flavoring of these massive costs is seen in data on teacher salaries in public schools. In 1869, salaries averaged about $189 per year; by 1900, salaries had risen to $325. But by 1930, salaries had quadrupled to $1,420, and the number of teachers was growing rapidly. By 1950, salaries again more than doubled to $3,010 and nearly tripled to $8,840 by 1970. By 1990, salaries quadrupled again to $33,084 and had reached $41,807 (+26%) by 2000. By 2005, salaries had hit $47,750 (+14%) and were estimated to reach $52,446 (+10%) by 2010. These salaries paid 3.5 million public school teachers in 2005, with demand for new teachers rising by about 100,000 positions each year despite widely publicized candidate shortages.[1]

Sustained growth in both staffing and compensation suggests that school budgets may be under significant stress, especially given the considerable costs of reform as many states have recently enacted more stringent teacher license standards and have increased academic requirements for schools, and as federal education reforms such as NCLB have resulted in new costs for schools. Any change in these elements has repercussions throughout the entire budget, so that—for example—additional salaries for new positions have an effect on salaries of experienced teachers and simultaneously place stress on other operational areas of the budget. It is easy to understand that personnel costs are the single largest item in school budgets, a fact underscored by our discussion in the previous chapter when we emphasized that (after estimating enrollments and envisioning educational programs) costing out salaries, wages, and benefits is the next most important task in balancing revenues and expenditures. As a consequence, we turn now to the act of budgeting for personnel. We begin by considering the scope of the personnel function, followed by a discussion on determining staffing needs. We then turn to recruitment and selection and an examination of issues affecting compensation structures such as costing out traditional salary schedules and recent thinking about alternative reward systems. Finally, we consider the legal context of budgeting for personnel, inasmuch as the budget cannot be separated from a myriad set of risks and obligations that have implications for school district resources. In sum, the act of budgeting for personnel consumes nearly the entirety of a school district's finances—an act that in large measure determines the district's ability to accomplish its educational mission.

---

1   Data taken from U.S. Department of Education, National Center for Education Statistics, *Digest of Education Statistics 2005* (Washington, DC: NCES, 2006); U.S. Department of Education, National Center for Education Statistics, *Projections of Education Statistics to 2015* (Washington, DC: NCES 2006). Note that these figures are not adjusted for inflation—for example, when adjusted, average teacher salaries rose 2% between 1995 and 2005 (see Table 76).

THE PERSONNEL FUNCTION

We have already established that the majority of a school district's budget is taken up by salaries and related benefits. Most people probably classify these expenditures as costs, a view that cannot be fully dismissed. At the same time, however, many "costs" in education are actually purchased assets. In the case of the personnel function, the cost of salaries and fringe benefits actually can be regarded as having a positive impact on the total economy because teachers and other school personnel are active consumers whose salaries are returned to the local economy in exchange for housing, clothes, cars, food, and luxuries. An additional point often missed by education's critics is that school personnel also pay taxes to support schools. In a complex cycle, the personnel function represents a cost to the public only because money is taken from taxpayers and used for a public service; however, that same money represents an investment (rather than an expenditure) because most school dollars pay the salaries of people who buy within the same school district or trade area and may actually create more employment opportunity than they consume. As a result, the personnel function is both a human resource and a fiscal resource issue, combining to create human capital as a purchased commodity.

What Is the Scope of the Personnel Function?

The personnel function takes into account everyone who is employed by a school system. Yet when most people think of school staffs, they immediately think of the teaching faculty. Although teachers are at the core of what schools do, this view is inadequate because the personnel function embraces a much larger group that includes both certificated staff (teachers and other professionally licensed employees) and classified staff (custodians, bus drivers, teacher aides, cafeteria workers, and other noncertificated service personnel). All these persons have indispensable roles in operating a school district. As districts have become more organizationally complex and inclusive of the many elements that contribute to equal educational opportunity, the number of certificated and noncertificated staff has increased dramatically.

The size of the personnel function is exceeded only by its importance to successful school district operation. In fact, regardless of how well the fiscal operations of a district are managed, the true success of a school system ultimately depends on the people who work with children each day. Selection, employment, and retention of competent staff are the keys to cost-effective operation of schools. The critical role of the personnel function has led most districts to centralize this operation, with one person having line authority over all staffing matters. Although titles vary with local custom and even by school district size, an assistant superintendent for personnel, a director of human resources, or the superintendent may have direct responsibility for the personnel function. In large districts, responsibility often is further subdivided. For example, the chief fiscal officer may also serve as the personnel director for support staff, while a director of human relations may serve as personnel officer for certificated staff. In such cases, certain aspects may be coordinated between the two offices, while others remain separate. The purpose of a coordinated office, however, is to ensure appropriate linkages among all vital aspects of the district.

Regardless of how the personnel function is structured locally, good personnel administration expects certain characteristics that assist in furthering the work of the district and which links all operations under one umbrella. The umbrella and linkages should be provided in a policy manual that sets out all aspects of personnel policy. Good policies assure uniform communication and help monitor relationships between the goals of the district and the expectations of personnel. Policies must be clearly stated to avoid confusion for either the employer or employee and to form the basis for accurate interpretation and legal evaluation in the event of serious disagreement. An added benefit of policies is to provide a blueprint for action, which, in turn, has a greater opportunity for consistent action that will simultaneously enhance employee morale and productivity. Because program quality is a direct result of the skill of all certificated and classified staff working in unison, an effective and efficient school district wisely invests time and money in creating and maintaining sound personnel policies and operations.

When the personnel function is correctly assigned to an individual or office, governed by written policies and procedures, and organized efficiently, the benefit is evident in the form of strong leadership and good management. Leadership is apparent in that a district which merely maintains the status quo cannot consistently improve its programs. Alternatively, reliance on charismatic leadership to the neglect of proper management of the personnel function endangers the district in many ways, including liability for the many problems and conflicts that can arise in a highly peopled organization. The district's overall goals and objectives cannot be met except by proper control and management of all instructional and support staffs. Although it is sometimes hard to distinguish between the nuances of leadership versus management, the point here is that the organizational and directive functions of personnel must be carefully led and managed if the district is to function effectively because schools rely on competent personnel to fulfill their goals.

The scope of the personnel function is extremely broad, encompassing six major task areas:

1. Determining staffing needs;
2. Recruiting and retaining the most competent staff;
3. Assisting in individual development of competencies;
4. Assuring that staff are assigned and used efficiently;
5. Increasing and improving staff satisfaction;
6. Establishing clear expectations and ensuring competent performance evaluation.

The critical nature of these tasks underscores the need for both leadership and management. The personnel function requires good leadership for school improvement, and good management is needed to ensure useful performance assessment. The personnel function thus *assesses staffing needs* and *recruits, selects, inducts, compensates, evaluates,* and *retains* employees. The personnel function also embraces other duties, including *dismissal* of unsatisfactory staff. Although many of these duties are outside the scope of this book, the tasks of determining staffing needs, recruitment, selection, compensation, and dismissal are explored more fully here because of their close relationship to the act of creating a good budget.

Determining Staffing Needs

We noted in Chapter 5 that enrollment drives staffing. This concept requires further development because the basic budgeting task of estimating revenues and expenditures is based entirely on enrollment and staffing.

Ability to properly determine staffing needs is a function of organizing and using information about the district and its current and prospective staff. All districts maintain a database of employee information, if for no other reason than reporting for state aid purposes and information needed to calculate payroll. The database includes basic and descriptive information such as each individual's salary, insurance and other fringe benefit costs, record of leave days, and even projected retirement information that can be used to predict voluntary and induced staff changes. More detailed information is less likely to be well organized, however, because many districts believe they are too small to spend the time and money required to extensively forecast district needs. Although school districts must maintain basic information on employees, most districts still need to develop exhaustive staff data because the lack of comprehensive information inherently limits good decision making and because the uses for data nearly always rise to match its availability. Although later chapters in this book discuss the importance of data on other budget items such as transportation and school facilities, it is unfortunate that many school districts do not spend enough time setting up staffing files.

Information about the district and staffing is interrelated and should be designed to permit electronic linking because, in every instance, the district's profile drives staffing patterns. The database should contain much information, including population of the community, population of the schools, percentage of households with school-age children, ages of children in preschool through twelfth grade, in- and outmigration patterns, commercial and industrial characteristics of the district, major sources and types of employment, income and age of residents, and, of course, fiscal data on the district itself. This information is useful as a general backdrop to the actual population projections the district must make each year. In most states, enrollment is the basis for funding, and it is clear that the population of a community drives student enrollment. It should not be missed that demographic data are highly useful in predicting community attitudes toward school budgets.

Determining staffing needs is thus largely a function of predicting the profile of a community. But while many districts keep much employee information on file, it is often not preplanned or organized for projecting staffing needs. In thousands of small school districts, sizable amounts of data on employees are still kept on paper and accessed by hand only if needed. In larger districts, electronic databases are standard and contain information on staffs, including professional certification or other qualifications useful when considering noncertificated employees. As district size grows, these files typically contain information on prospective employees and may also contain projections of staff attrition by area and level.

Regardless of district size, an effort to create community profiles and employee databanks is essential because databases can be used to project whether staffing needs can be met internally, whether it will be necessary to look outside for new employees, or (under the worst conditions) whether it will be necessary to reduce staff at some future time. The employee database should be much broader than simple retrieval of areas of professional licensure and should permit other projections, such as calculating the cost of existing or proposed early retirement incentives. Such information intersects with the budget function, in that the cost of early retirement plans (compared to other scenarios such as savings accrued through hiring less experienced staff) must be available when making long-term policy and staffing decisions. Likewise, projections indicating a need for new staff also require budget input. The use of extensive databases makes it possible to descriptively assess present reality and to forecast future scenarios—an obviously critical function for the budget side of planning and organization. In most instances, the basic database is built and maintained in the personnel office and electronically linked to the budget office.

Although each district must develop databases to meet its unique needs, the goal is always the same. The personnel and budget functions in a school district must share information on many occasions, but the most frequent interaction is when staffing needs are reviewed. For current staff, the personnel function annually considers whether they will be rehired, and those decisions must be coordinated with the budget office, which must find money for salaries. There are times, of course, when the scenario is reversed, as the budget office finds that staffing is too expensive and the personnel side must find ways to deal with economic reality. But although these functions are codependent, the realities of the modern comprehensive school district cause the personnel function to most often drive the fiscal side by telling the business office what the staffing needs will be for the next school year.

Although a comprehensive community and staff database is essential, the technical side of determining staffing needs is different among states and individual districts. For example, some states calculate the number of pupils at each grade level and allocate staff positions to districts on a per-classroom basis. In this case, the school district has little meaningful control over the most basic personnel function of determining how many teachers it will hire because it can afford to hire only those teachers reimbursed through the state aid formula. In other states, districts are free to decide how many staff to hire by choosing among many competing expenditure categories within overall budgetary constraints; for example, a choice to reduce overall class size may be at the expense of expanding athletic or academic enrichment programs. An example of a centralized system is Washington's state aid plan, which converts full-time equivalency (FTE) students into staff units, which are then multiplied by a statewide salary and benefits schedule, with additional allocations for nonpersonnel-related costs. This formula, in response to legal battles over equitable funding, has had the practical effect of leveling expenditures (with staffing implications) downward in some districts in order to bring greater fiscal parity across all school districts. At the opposite extreme are states that have tried to reduce class size, as in Oklahoma, where state-initiated reform in the early 1990s mandated lower pupil-to-teacher ratios with the practical effect of driving up staffing requirements. A more middle-ground example of local decisions driving staffing is found in districts with school board policies limiting class size, with resultant staffing increases. A more complicated but common situation is when local boards have either been required by state law to negotiate class size or have voluntarily negotiated such agreements. In all these examples, it is clear that the personnel and budget functions are tightly linked.

Regardless of local circumstance, once a policy or law governing staffing is set, it is easy to apply the appropriate staffing formula to actual enrollments. After projecting enrollment, the process calls for applying some staffing formula, usually by dividing the number of students at each grade level by the approved ratio, yielding the required number of staff. The process is typically carried out at the district level, with input from individual schools. A simple illustration using a single high school might result in the following staffing pattern:

Formula: *Enrollment + Approved Ratio = Staffing Needs**

or

421 ninth graders + 20:1 ratio	= 21 ninth grade positions
373 tenth graders + 20:1	= 18.6 tenth grade positions
297 eleventh graders + 20:1	= 14.8 eleventh grade positions
<u>312</u> twelfth graders + 20:1	= <u>15.6</u> twelfth grade positions
1,403 pupil FTE	= 70.0 staff FTE

*This example considers only teaching staff; separate discussions about other staffing needs also must be carried out.

Of course, funding these positions is harder than simply calculating staffing needs, at times requiring adjustments to the staffing formula if funding is unavailable. This is especially true when enrollment fluctuates across years between grades or across individual school buildings. If the database reveals, for example, that other schools in the district are gaining enrollment and if our sample high school presently has 78 existing faculty (instead of the 70 needed next year), the district could reassign surplus teachers to other schools if their professional licensure matches vacancies. Obviously, this solution is more feasible as district size increases because small districts may have only one teacher per grade or only one high school. In many such districts, however, it is more likely that other enrollments will not offset the surplus, triggering other decisions about reassignment or even reduction-in-force.

Determining staffing is at once simple and complex. It is mathematically easy, but it is complex because such decisions affect real people and because layers of governmental policy may limit the options. Regardless, good decisions cannot be made without a comprehensive database that takes into account both community and employee profiles. For example, a district in the scenario just described might be able to lessen the impact of forced staff reductions if the database holds information on retirements or early contract buyouts. In a more positive vein, data can be used for targeted information-sharing such as inhouse mailings to employees when vacancies arise. For many reasons, an orderly plan for determining staffing needs is the next step after projecting enrollment.

Recruitment and Selection

When staffing needs are known, the next major task is recruitment, followed by selection of personnel. Regardless of the type of position, every employee classification should have a formal recruitment plan. The district needs to make decisions regarding number and type of positions, as well as minimum and preferred qualifications for each employee classification. The budget and personnel functions intersect here again, particularly regarding pay for current staff and whether the district must hire beginning teachers or whether it can afford more experienced staff.

Although in many states pay scales are largely a function of collective bargaining laws and how the negotiations process plays out in individual school districts, the goal is to attract and retain the most highly qualified people. This goal is difficult because the purpose is at odds with another competing goal of minimizing taxpayer costs. Although there are no good solutions, there are certain procedures in the recruiting and selection process that help soften the harshness of these realities.

At the outset of the recruiting process, the budget and personnel staffs should jointly produce a guidebook for the district. This guidebook is so important that it should be given to all current and prospective employees to familiarize them with the terms and benefits of employment. This document should contain a clear description of the hiring process, starting with application procedures and continuing through descriptions of how screening committees, interviews, contract offers, and pay periods and amounts will occur. Every current and prospective employee should be informed of training requirements and opportunities, and this information should convey a high level of standardization within each employee classification. These procedures should be closely tied to job advertising by the district and should be standardized with regard to internal and external search procedures consistent with equal opportunity selection of the best candidate for each vacancy.

When policies and procedures for recruitment have been set, the district is ready to recruit. For larger districts, this may mean hiring on the basis of anticipated vacancies. Large school systems visit teacher recruitment fairs across the nation every year, hiring candidates for vacancies that have not yet opened but that the district knows from experience will become available. In many instances, these districts are taking little risk because they know that they will not be able to hire staff for all openings. In other areas of the country, the process is simpler, as districts advertise via university placement offices and wait for applications to arrive. Even here, however, the personnel and budget functions continue to intersect, as success in recruiting is related to how well the salary schedule is designed and funded. Because many states do not have uniform or statewide teacher salary schedules or, in some cases, allow districts to exceed the statewide salary schedule, recruitment is the joint responsibility of wise personnel and budget planning.

When the district has successfully determined its staffing needs and has recruited as effectively as it can, the selection process begins. Because the success of district goals depends on the quality of personnel, selection is a critical responsibility. Even though the depth of the candidate pool and the marketplace affect who is hired, it must be recognized that the district's first obligation is to select employees on the basis of skills. Skills must be judged on the basis of documented training, relevant experience, and satisfactory performance. Additionally, many positions, whether certificated or not, require specific licensure from a state agency. Every position should be filled only after the appropriate person, often the superintendent, has made a final recommendation to the board. As we will see later in the chapter on legal liability, a valid employment offer usually cannot be made unless the board has approved the offer in a public meeting in a lawful manner.

The intersecting and conflicting goals of the personnel and budget functions are most apparent at the time of selection. The goal of the personnel function is to select the most qualified person to perform the duties of a specific position. This applies whether the person is being interviewed for a teaching position or a custodial position, and unqualified people should not be considered. The goal of the budget function is to hire that same person as well, but under impossible terms. The old adage, "…20 years old with 20 years experience and willing to work for $20,000…" accurately describes these terms. Of course, this is impossible, and some middle ground must be found that assures selection of quality staff within budget limits. Selection thus involves many steps, all aimed at hiring the best candidate at the least turnover. From the beginning of the process to its end, the relationship between the personnel and budget functions is apparent in that whatever job candidate is chosen, that person will have to be funded.

Other Personnel Budget Issues

Although it is beyond the scope of this textbook to delve deeply into the personnel side of district operations, it is important to note that there are other issues of budgeting for personnel that go beyond recruitment and selection. The most obvious issue is compensation policies and procedures, a topic we spend much time developing in the last half of this chapter. Other personnel tasks including induction, orientation, assignment, mentoring/ongoing support, evaluation, staff development, and so forth also intersect with the budget because these activities are costly to carry out and are further costly if poorly done because the result is lost opportunity, lowered job performance, and wasted financial resources. These issues are so important that although nothing is more central to the success of district mission than recruitment and selection, it is these other issues that consume most of the time of the personnel office.

The scope of the personnel function and its relationship to the budget function is thus highly complex. In general, the personnel function can be described as working closely with the budget office to determine staffing needs based on enrollment projections in the context of salaries and operating costs. Salaries take in a full range of certificated and classified employees. More specifically, the personnel function in tandem with the budget function is usually responsible for:

- ◆ Recruitment and selection
  - Describing role expectations for positions
  - Assessing qualifications needed to fit the role
  - Compiling appropriate information on candidates
  - Evaluating candidates on role and personal expectations
  - Rating eligible candidates on the criteria
  - Making the employment decision from among choices
- ◆ Compensation policies and procedures
  - Placing the employee in the most appropriate position

- Determining appropriate pay structures
♦ Personnel development
  - Inducting new staff to the district
  - Assigning staff to positions based on program needs
  - Orienting staff to the position and role
  - Providing mentoring and ongoing support
  - Evaluating staff on objective performance criteria
  - Developing staff through additional training

PERSONNEL COMPENSATION POLICIES AND PROCEDURES

As we have repeatedly emphasized in this book, enrollment drives revenue, which, in turn, drives expenditures. We have also noted that these realities may sometimes drive program decisions. But as we have further noted, expenditures primarily support personnel costs because for most schools approximately 80% of the budget goes to salaries and benefits. As a result, we turn now to compensation policies and procedures because this is the most critical budget activity that takes place—that is, inability to fund a good staffing plan invariably limits the quality of services available to children.

What Is the Role of Compensation?

The role of employee compensation is clear in the bulleted list above. Compensation is the reason people work—it provides their livelihoods and rewards their professional achievements. Compensation forms the basis for purchased services in schools and covers a range of work including administration, instruction and instructional support, transportation, food service, repair and maintenance, and so on. Compensation must be understood as more than just salaries and wages, however, because the money a school district pays employees is much larger than only earned income. For example, total compensation includes workers' compensation insurance, unemployment insurance, and social security benefits, to name just a few. Additionally, employee compensation typically includes other benefits such as various kinds of health insurance and leave pay. For example, there is paid time away from work including sick leave, bereavement leave, and personal leave. There are also many other kinds of direct and indirect compensation such as overtime pay, supplemental duty pay, and performance pay. Additionally, state retirement systems and local school district benefits add to a long list of compensation elements that people forget to include as income for public school employees. In sum, the strength of the total compensation package can be the basis for employee willingness to enter an employment contract.

General Issues

The longitudinal data on teacher salaries at the beginning of this chapter leave little doubt about the high cost of compensation, and growth in salaries will inevitably continue as new positions are needed to serve a growing population. At the same time, school staffs expect more pay as inflation takes its toll. The important missing observation, however, is that these amounts do not include the vast expenditures for nonteaching personnel or for fringe benefits, bringing the overall total to a very large sum. Yet, although the dollars are vast, on a personal level there is no great wealth gained by individual school employees. Figure 6.1 depicts trends in average teacher salaries for the last three decades, revealing that salaries have not changed much in constant dollars since 1970. Yet the total sum of education's costs makes staff compensation a critical problem in the face of finite resources.

Figure 6.1. Average Annual Salary for Public School Teachers 1970–2004 in Constant Dollars

YEAR	CONSTANT 2005 DOLLARS
1970	$43,773
1980	$39,433
1990	$47,354
2000	$47,339
2004	$48,159

Source: U.S. Department of Education, National Center for Education Statistics. (2006). *Digest of education statistics 2005*. Washington, DC: Author.

When the topic of public school pay is raised, most people think of direct salaries. All school districts pay salaries, and by far the majority reward staff, especially teachers, on a single-salary schedule. Historically, single-salary schedules were a means to correct pay inequities that discriminated unfairly along race, gender, and grade-level differences. Additionally, in many districts teachers were paid based on political party affiliation or other nonmeritorious bases. The practice was so prevalent that in 1918 the National Education Association noted that no single-salary schedule existed in a city school district anywhere in the nation. Although the single-salary schedule has many modern opponents who argue that lockstep schedules invite a flat organization and discourage individual merit, proponents have long held that it is superior to other choices because it fosters better working relationships, is less expensive to administer, and avoids serious problems such as favoritism, discrimination, and retaliation. The concept has spilled over into state government, as many states also use minimum salary schedules for state employees.

Administration of all forms of employee compensation begins with determination and formulation of a job description for each position in a school district. Complete and detailed written descriptions should be developed for every employee classification. If done properly, job descriptions are based on surveys, interviews, and assessments of what every job classification is expected to contribute to organizational goals. Job descriptions should be very clear so that all parties can agree on the nature, duties, and expectations. Each position should have a performance-based job description that includes statements about the method and amount of compensation.

Evaluation of performance based on goals can then follow, and performance should form the basis for an employee's location on the salary schedule. Obviously, descriptions vary by position. For example, the job description of a school principal is different and far more complex than the job description for a secretary. Examples of real job descriptions and their differences are shown in Figs. 6.2 and 6.3 (p. 188).

Although job descriptions should result in neutral salary decisions based on placement of employees according to district salary schedule policies, the actual salary structure is usually a function of two realities. In some states, collective bargaining applies to both certificated and classified employee groups. In other states, teachers bargain under collective negotiations, while classified employees and administrators are outside the negotiations law. In such instances, nonteaching staff salaries are often a function of prevailing wages obtained by informal comparisons between competing school districts. Once salaries are in place, however, annual adjustments across employee groups are likely to be a function of similar percentage increases. For example, it is unlikely that administrators will receive a much higher salary increase than teachers simply because of the negative aspect of public relations. In states where nonteaching staff have no legal bargaining status, it is likely that salaries will be decided after collective negotiations for teachers are complete, with percentage increases closely conforming.

Negotiations

The fiscal aspect of collective bargaining can be very time-intensive and complex. Because so much is at stake, both financially and in terms of future working relationships, it is important for all parties to develop trust and respect for each side's information and philosophical position. Many school districts hold informal contract discussions during the school year about employment concerns, including compensation. Discussions should always be with appropriate employee association or union leaders in order not to commit an unfair labor practice. Throughout the school year, as well as in multiyear contracts, dialogue with all groups eases the negotiations process by not allowing tensions to grow and silently fester.

The negotiations process is unique in each state because of different bargaining laws. In principle, however, the steps are similar depending on the extent to which outside arbitration is required. At whatever time of year salary and contract discussions begin, the budget office is called on by the personnel division to provide salary data for use in making fiscal projections and to provide cost analyses of any salary proposals. The reason is that short- and long-range costs must be known for all salary and contractual proposals before agreement can be reached regarding a new compensation plan. The budget office must include not only all direct costs of salary and fringe benefits, but it also must consider cash flow, cost of employee time, and any other items placed on the negotiations table by either side. Each of these issues must be analyzed for present and future costs and for the long-range impact on district financial health. The essence of all these activities is to conduct negotiations in good faith and to accurately anticipate all costs of compensation in order to balance revenues and expenditures in the final budget.

Figure 6.2. Sample Job Description for High School Principal

Position Title: High School Principal

Basic Function: Administers the school under the supervision of the Assistant Superintendent. Provides leadership to faculty and students; manages and directs all activities.

Performance Responsibilities:

- Demonstrates leadership through beliefs, skills, and personal characteristics.
- Ensures that teachers plan and provide effective instruction.
- Monitors, assesses, and supervises the approved district curriculum.
- Develops an effective staff development program.
- Promotes positive school climate by encouraging capabilities of all individuals.
- Uses a variety of data to improve the school's instructional program.
- Coordinates development of a written statement of the school's beliefs and goals.
- Determines whether the individual educational needs of pupils are being met.
- Evaluates the performance of the certified and classified staff members.
- Interprets, implements, and maintains Board policies and state school laws.
- Develops a program of public relations to further community support.
- Administers the school's budgeted allocations.
- Directs activities involving pupil/parent contacts concerning registrations, credits and transfers, suspensions, expulsions, pupil progress, placement, guidance and counseling matters, and other matters of a personal nature.
- Possesses a thorough understanding of child growth and development.
- Engages in a program of continuing professional development.
- Orients newly assigned staff members and ensures their familiarization with school policies/procedures, teaching materials, and school facilities.
- Creates a strong sense of togetherness through human relations techniques.
- Possesses skill in conflict resolution, decision-making, and consensus building.
- Performs other related duties as requested.
- Requirements: Valid certificate and 5 years teaching experience. Salary commensurate with experience.

Source: Adapted from the Denver Public Schools, Division of Personnel Services.

Figure 6.3. Sample Job Description for Secretary

Qualifications: Type, file, keep records, and take shorthand at 80 wpm

Reports to: Principal

Job Goal: Provide secretarial services to operate the school

Job Functions:

1. Assigns duties to and supervises work of clerical personnel in the school.
2. Provides input to the administrator on evaluations of clerical personnel.
3. Is responsible for typing and processing all confidential correspondence.
4. Provides the technical skills of typing, filing, record keeping and taking and transcribing shorthand and all other means of communication.
5. Maintains and updates reports, lists, inventories, attendance records, and other similar records that are modified frequently.
6. Serves as one of the school office receptionists and as the first-line public relations staff member when answering phone calls, responding personally to staff, students, parents, and community members, when greeting people in person.
7. Understands and is able to operate equipment including computers, typewriters, dictating equipment, duplicating machines, photocopiers, calculators, and other similar equipment.
8. Prepares certain administrative reports, communications, memoranda, legal notices, employment and vendor contracts, purchase orders, and work orders.
9. Coordinates the activities and schedule of the supervising administrator, permitting the administrator to perform as efficiently and effectively as possible.
10. Responds appropriately to all concerns and complaints from the public and staff and assists in providing an answer or remedy.
11. Conducts special activities in accordance with the specific job assignment, such as the annual school election and graduation.
12. Has a working knowledge of the business and budgeting procedures, as well as the legal obligations of the specific department.
13. Receives and distributes mail and other messages.
14. Provides other necessary secretarial services as requested by the supervising administrator.
15. Salary shall be paid according to years of experience and educational training in strict accordance with the district's board-approved secretarial salary schedule.

Source: Adapted from Galloway Township (NJ) Public Schools.

Basic Elements

After the relevant salary and contract data are collected and verified by both sides, the negotiations process is ready to begin. Agreement on the facts makes bargaining easier because the district's position at the table, the potential for favorable review at impasse or arbitration, and the union's receptiveness are all enhanced. Items on which initial agreement should be sought include cash projections, the impact of these data on the school district, historical data related to the issues, and data showing how the district compares to other districts of similar profile in the region and state. Careful preparation and presentation always increases the potential for success at the bargaining table, as well as aiding favorable treatment if fact-finding and arbitration are eventually required.

The principal goal of both sides in contract negotiations is to have a reasonable discussion about the facts in order to agree on a fair salary and benefits package. When agreement is struck, any changes are applied to the appropriate salary and benefit schedules. For example, for certificated teaching staff the first and most direct impact is adjustment to the single-salary schedule, both in dollars and in any changes to the structure of the schedule itself. For noncertificated staff, the impact occurs either in similar application to a separate salary/wage schedule or by adjustment to each individual's contracted salary/wage. The goal of fairness must be extended to the fringe benefit package as well. Thus, data reflecting the need to attract and retain high quality staff, as well as promoting professional growth for all employees, must be balanced with the ability of the district to fund the increased contractual obligations.

During the negotiations process, both management and labor come to the bargaining table with items they expressly want to negotiate. Preparation on the part of the school district focuses on collecting and examining financial data and any other current concerns of the district. The employee organization has interest in these same items, although for mostly different reasons. Items brought to the table by both sides are fairly common and include:

- *Strengths and weaknesses* of the entire contract;
- *Salary schedule,* including number and costs of each cell of the salary matrix over the life of the contract and a projection into the near future;
- *Basic data* on minimum, maximum, and actual average cost per employee over the life of the contract;
- *Comparative salaries* in competing school districts and industries;
- *Living standards* of the local community;
- *Personnel turnover,* as well as pending retirements;
- *Movement on the salary schedule* as a consequence of advanced training, as well as experience movement;
- *New programmatic needs and curtailments*; and
- *Future revenues and expenditures,* including tax levies and state aid projections.

In addition, the district and employee groups will need to gather and bring other nonfinancial data to the table. Generally this consists of such issues as:

♦ Are there parts of the contract that have not worked well?

♦ Is there a pattern of grievances over parts of the contract?

♦ Should parts of the contract be modified or dropped?

♦ What new issues may prove problematic?

These data are critical to the negotiations process and to compensation policies because, without good data, proposed costs are unobtainable and the ability to fund a future contract is unknown. Indeed, the district's fiscal integrity is at the mercy of accurate data.

Costing-Out Salary Proposals

Although terms and conditions of employment make up a large part of the total negotiations process, the most elemental aspect comes when salary is discussed. It is at salary time when the personnel and budget functions are most closely related because, if contract agreement is not reached, the district is likely to suffer low staff morale.

For certificated staff, discussion of salary is likely to center on improving the basic structure of the salary schedule and on increasing the dollar amount of the base salary. Figure 6.4 illustrates a single-salary schedule for a sample school district and provides an illustration of how contract negotiations occur in the majority of cases. Most of us are familiar with single-salary schedules like the one in Fig. 6.4, but three observations should be made before examining likely scenarios involving salary negotiations. First, the top portion of Fig. 6.4 shows the index that computes the dollars seen in the center portion. Second, Fig. 6.4 is actually two different versions of the same salary schedule; that is, the first (left-hand) half shows the current year, while the second (right-hand) half proposes a change in base salary. Third, the bottom portion of each half of Fig. 6.4 uses a few staff members from the sample district to show how a salary schedule is costed out. Figure 6.4 thus provides a basis for some extended discussion of the negotiations process and its impact on the school district's budget.

Although no two districts negotiate exactly alike, it is almost certain that teachers will propose three changes to the sample salary schedule in Fig. 6.4. The first proposal will be to increase the base salary. Both the teachers and the school district know this has the effect of increasing all other steps on the schedule because salary schedules are always step-dependent in some fashion. In other words, a change in base salary will nearly always increase all subsequent salaries. The second proposal will be to increase the number of columns. In districts without a doctorate degree column, the proposal will likely seek more columns beyond the master's degree (in Fig. 6.4, such a proposal would have to seek to insert new columns between existing columns or to add new columns beyond the doctorate). The third proposal will be to add steps at the bottom of some or all columns as a reward for longevity in the district. Board proposals, on the other hand, will almost certainly seek more restrictive language on non-salary items such as limiting or refining discretionary leaves and will

Figure 6.4. Sample Salary Schedule

BASE=$25,000

YEAR	BA + 0	BA + 15	BA + 30	Masters	MS + 15	MS + 30	Doctorate
1	100%	102%	104%	106%	108%	110%	112%
2	102%	104%	106%	108%	110%	112%	114%
3	104%	106%	108%	110%	112%	114%	116%
4	106%	108%	110%	112%	114%	116%	118%
5	108%	108%	112%	114%	116%	118%	120%
6	110%	112%	114%	116%	118%	120%	122%
7	112%	114%	116%	118%	120%	122%	124%
8	114%	116%	118%	120%	122%	124%	126%
9		118%	120%	122%	124%	126%	128%
10		120%	122%	124%	126%	128%	130%
11			124%	126%	128%	130%	132%
12			126%	128%	130%	132%	134%
13				130%	132%	134%	136%
14				132%	134%	136%	138%
15					136%	138%	140%
16					138%	140%	142%
17						142%	144%
18							146%

YEAR	BA + 0	BA + 15	BA + 30	Masters	MS + 15	MS + 30	Doctorate
1	$ 25,000	$ 25,500	$ 26,000	$ 26,500	$ 27,000	$ 27,500	$ 28,000
2	$ 25,500	$ 26,000	$ 26,500	$ 27,000	$ 27,500	$ 28,000	$ 28,500
3	$ 26,000	$ 26,500	$ 27,000	$ 27,500	$ 28,000	$ 28,500	$ 29,000
4	$ 26,500	$ 27,000	$ 27,500	$ 28,000	$ 28,500	$ 29,000	$ 29,500
5	$ 27,000	$ 27,000	$ 28,000	$ 28,500	$ 29,000	$ 29,500	$ 30,000
6	$ 27,500	$ 28,000	$ 28,500	$ 29,000	$ 29,500	$ 30,000	$ 30,500
7	$ 28,000	$ 28,500	$ 29,000	$ 29,500	$ 30,000	$ 30,500	$ 31,000
8		$ 29,000	$ 29,500	$ 30,000	$ 30,500	$ 31,000	$ 31,500
9		$ 29,500	$ 30,000	$ 30,500	$ 31,000	$ 31,500	$ 32,000
10		$ 30,000	$ 30,500	$ 31,000	$ 31,500	$ 32,000	$ 32,500
11			$ 31,000	$ 31,500	$ 32,000	$ 32,500	$ 33,000
12			$ 31,500	$ 32,000	$ 32,500	$ 33,000	$ 33,500
13				$ 32,500	$ 33,000	$ 33,500	$ 34,000
14				$ 33,000	$ 33,500	$ 34,000	$ 34,500
15					$ 34,000	$ 34,500	$ 35,000
16					$ 34,500	$ 35,000	$ 35,500
17						$ 35,000	$ 35,500
18						$ 35,500	$ 36,000
							$ 36,500

Projections based on zero dollar increase on base (see asterisk note below).

Name	Current salary	Current benefits	Current pkg.	New salary	New benefits	Proposed pkg.	% increase
Mary A.	$ 25,000	$ 3,000	$ 28,000	$ 25,500	$ 3,000	$ 28,500	1.8%
Bob B.	$ 29,500	$ 3,000	$ 32,500	$ 30,000	$ 3,000	$ 33,000	1.5%
Julie C. (frozen)	$ 31,500	$ 3,000	$ 34,500	$ 31,500	$ 3,000	$ 34,500	0.0%
James D.	$ 26,500	$ 3,000	$ 29,500	$ 27,000	$ 3,000	$ 30,000	1.7%
Janet E.	$ 33,500	$ 3,000	$ 36,500	$ 34,000	$ 3,000	$ 37,000	1.4%
Bill F. (frozen)	$ 36,500	$ 3,000	$ 39,500	$ 36,500	$ 3,000	$ 39,500	0.0%
Paula G.***	$ 35,500	$ 3,000	$ 38,500	$ 36,500	$ 3,000	$ 39,500	2.6%
and so on...							
TOTALS	$ 218,000	$ 21,000	$ 239,000	$ 221,000	$ 21,000	$ 242,000	1.28%

***will obtain doctorate by end of current school year.

COST TO FUND
$ 3,000

(Figure continues on next page.)

Base= $26,000

YEAR	BA + 0	BA + 15	BA + 30	Masters	MS + 15	MS + 30	Doctorate
1	100%	102%	104%	106%	108%	110%	112%
2	102%	104%	106%	108%	110%	112%	114%
3	104%	106%	108%	110%	112%	114%	116%
4	106%	108%	110%	112%	114%	116%	118%
5	108%	108%	112%	114%	116%	118%	120%
6	110%	112%	114%	116%	118%	120%	122%
7	112%	114%	116%	118%	120%	122%	124%
8	114%	116%	118%	120%	122%	124%	126%
9		118%	120%	122%	124%	126%	128%
10		120%	122%	124%	126%	128%	130%
11			124%	126%	128%	130%	132%
12			126%	128%	130%	132%	134%
13				130%	132%	134%	136%
14				132%	134%	136%	138%
15					136%	138%	140%
16					138%	140%	142%
17						142%	144%
18							146%

YEAR	BA + 0	BA + 15	BA + 30	Masters	MS + 15	MS + 30	Doctorate
1	$ 26,000	$ 26,520	$ 27,040	$ 27,560	$ 28,080	$ 28,600	$ 29,120
2	$ 26,520	$ 27,040	$ 27,560	$ 28,080	$ 28,600	$ 29,120	$ 29,640
3	$ 27,040	$ 27,560	$ 28,080	$ 28,600	$ 29,120	$ 29,640	$ 30,160
4	$ 27,560	$ 28,080	$ 28,600	$ 29,120	$ 29,640	$ 30,160	$ 30,680
5	$ 28,080	$ 28,080	$ 29,120	$ 29,640	$ 30,160	$ 30,680	$ 31,200
6	$ 28,600	$ 29,120	$ 29,640	$ 30,160	$ 30,680	$ 31,200	$ 31,720
7	$ 29,120	$ 29,640	$ 30,160	$ 30,680	$ 31,200	$ 31,720	$ 32,240
8	$ 29,640	$ 30,160	$ 30,680	$ 31,200	$ 31,720	$ 32,240	$ 32,760
9		$ 30,680	$ 31,200	$ 31,720	$ 32,240	$ 32,760	$ 33,280
10		$ 31,200	$ 31,720	$ 32,240	$ 32,760	$ 33,280	$ 33,800
11			$ 32,240	$ 32,760	$ 33,280	$ 33,800	$ 34,320
12			$ 32,760	$ 33,280	$ 33,800	$ 34,320	$ 34,840
13				$ 33,800	$ 34,320	$ 34,840	$ 35,360
14				$ 34,320	$ 34,840	$ 35,360	$ 35,880
15					$ 35,360	$ 35,880	$ 36,400
16					$ 35,880	$ 36,400	$ 36,920
17						$ 36,920	$ 37,440
18							$ 37,960

Projections based on $1,000 increase on base plus $300 fringe.

Name	Current salary	Current benefits	Current pkg.	New salary	New benefits	Proposed pkg.	% increase
Mary A.	$ 25,000	$ 3,000	$ 28,000	$ 26,520	$ 3,300	$ 29,820	6%
Bob B.	$ 29,500	$ 3,000	$ 32,500	$ 31,200	$ 3,300	$ 34,500	6%
Julie C.	$ 31,500	$ 3,000	$ 34,500	$ 32,760	$ 3,300	$ 36,060	5%
James D.	$ 26,500	$ 3,000	$ 29,500	$ 28,080	$ 3,300	$ 31,380	6%
Janet E.	$ 33,500	$ 3,000	$ 36,500	$ 35,360	$ 3,300	$ 38,660	6%
Bill F.	$ 36,500	$ 3,000	$ 39,500	$ 37,960	$ 3,300	$ 41,260	4%
Paula G.***	$ 35,500	$ 3,000	$ 38,500	$ 37,960	$ 3,300	$ 41,260	7%
and so on...							
TOTALS	$ 218,000	$ 21,000	$ 239,000	$ 229,840	$ 23,100	$ 252,940	5.87%

COST TO FUND

$ 13,940

***will obtain doctorate by end of current school year.

further seek to minimize hefty increases to the salary schedule. Almost everyone recognizes the futility of board efforts to negotiate most other items: For example, negotiating a salary decrease is highly unlikely except under conditions of severe fiscal exigency.

Some of the changes proposed by teachers have a chance for success because these changes seem reasonable to most people. But all changes must be considered carefully. The effect of increasing the base is seen in the right-hand side of Fig. 6.4 (pp. 191–192) where a $1,000 increase (+4%) raises the base salary to $26,000. But increasing the base by only a modest amount causes a ripple throughout the entire schedule, as all other salary steps take at least the same increase. This is because each step in Fig. 6.4 is indexed to the prior step. For example, a teacher on step one will get not only the 4% base increase, but also another 2% for a year's longevity. For just this one teacher, the cost of raising the base 4% is actually 6%. In many districts, step increments are often progressively greater with more years of experience, making this schedule's structure fairly conservative. Given the relative maturity of teaching staffs throughout the United States, care must be taken because, as salary schedules load on experience, they become very expensive. The first change proposed by teachers is thus far more costly than the modest $1,000 base increase might suggest, costing $13,940 to fund only seven teachers in our sample group (note that we added $300 to fringe benefits in recognition of rising health care costs).

The cost of the second proposal by teachers to increase the number of columns cannot be calculated quickly from the data in Fig. 6.4 because decisions would need to be made about how a new column should be structured. The general impact can be seen, however. For next year, only those teachers with college credits beyond the doctorate degree would qualify for movement to a new column. Assuming some teachers would be able to move, an expensive result follows. As expected, teachers who would qualify for extended columns are experienced and well educated—needless to say, salaries at the top end are much more expensive. And of course, the dollar effect becomes even larger when the base increases simultaneously, so that adding a post-doctoral column is a highly expensive proposition. In other words, although boards often want to increase the base, there are practical barriers.

The third proposal by teachers to add steps to existing columns is also costly. The purpose, of course, is to unfreeze teachers who have bottomed out on experience. Adding steps, however, multiplies against their salaries and the cost may be much higher than it first appears. Before a district can make such an agreement, it must be known how many teachers would qualify for vertical movement. Additionally, the district must know how many of those same persons also returned to a university during the past year and would further qualify to move horizontally. In other words, the district might have to pay newly unfrozen teachers twice—once by adding steps and again by moving to a new column—that is, the "down-and-over" effect is highly cumulative with returning staff members, and particularly so when considering structural changes proposed by employees who always stand to benefit from such change.

The data in this brief illustration have many benefits. One of the most important benefits is the ability to automate the salary schedule for instant "what-if" scenarios. Figure 6.4 (pp. 191–192) was indexed in a spreadsheet, so that as the base changes, all other cells update. Also, when data are agreed upon, both sides can immediately see the effect. Both sides also profit from the entire negotiations process in that, although the board will have to increase salaries next year at the budget's expense, it does so willingly in exchange for the least dollar amount possible at which it can hire satisfied employees. It is important for board members, administrators, teachers, and the public as a whole to understand that collective bargaining is a series of compromises and that one side rarely has complete success. By anticipating staffing needs, recruiting and selecting the best staff, and preparing and using budget data for good personnel compensation policies, both sides have a better chance of reaching an acceptable compromise.

Whatever proposals come to the table, several features must be understood and accepted. It must be understood that negotiations can be very confrontational, but the risk of bad relationships can be minimized through openness and trust. It also must be accepted that the personnel and budget functions must take negotiations seriously because the costs are pervasive throughout the district's budget—that is, a decision to meaningfully improve the salary schedule will come at a cost to other operations. However, failing to improve salaries is destructive to long-term district health at many levels. It further must be understood that an average 3% increase in teacher salaries, for example, will probably also result in a 3% increase for all nonteaching staff, including administrators. In sum, the multiplicative nature of a single decision can be surprisingly expensive when a simple 3% increase is costed across vertical and horizontal dimensions of the teachers' single-salary schedule, across noncertificated salaries, and across all administrators. In most cases, annual state aid increases are not sufficient to cover all new costs, making it necessary to either raise taxes or reduce other operations.

Instead of sitting on the sideline, the personnel and budget functions are directly involved in the negotiations process through production of data, costing out proposals, and working with both sides in search of agreement. In many instances, the board's negotiator may be an administrator. In some districts, the superintendent serves as chief negotiator, although the field and the professional literature caution that this may be risky. In other cases, an assistant superintendent for personnel and/or finance may serve in the lead board role. In other instances, the chief negotiator is an attorney, selected for adroitness or benefit of impartiality. Regardless of who serves as the board's spokesperson, the personnel and finance functions should be aware of the progress of negotiations and should be continuously consulted to determine the viability of any proposed actions.

No matter who serves in the lead role, there are skills and knowledge that must be exhibited. The chief negotiator must be knowledgeable of the state's collective bargaining statutes, be familiar with federal unfair labor practices, and have experience and prior success in such matters. Additionally, personal skills including emotional maturity, articulateness, flexibility, and the ability to reject ideas without alienating the opposing side are valuable.

In addition to the spokesperson, the board's team often consists of the chief fiscal officer for the district, a recorder, a board subcommittee, and others as appropriate. Team composition varies by local custom. Teachers are often represented by an attorney, a professional association or union official, or a suitable local faculty member; that is, each district differs in the culture of negotiations. As a generalization, most negotiating sessions follow custom whereby only spokespersons may speak, that written initial nonexpandable proposals must be exchanged in advance, and that each team keeps its own set of good notes. Generally, caucuses may be unlimited unless agreed otherwise. Again, it must be stressed that each state varies in statutory guidelines and local custom; for example, in some states bargaining sessions may be closed to the public. The scope of a sample state negotiations law is provided in Figure 6.5.

Figure 6.5. Sample Negotiations Law

Mandatorily Negotiable

1. Salary
2. Wages
3. Pay under supplemental contracts
4. Hours of work
5. Amounts of work
6. Vacation allowance
7. Holiday leave
8. Sick leave
9. Extended leave
10. Sabbatical leaves
11. "Other" leaves
12. Number of holidays
13. Retirement
14. Jury duty
15. Grievance procedure
16. Binding arbitration
17. Discipline procedure
18. Resignations
19. Contract termination
20. Contract non-renewal
21. Reemployment
22. Contract terms
23. Contract form
24. Probationary period
25. Evaluation
26. Insurance benefits
27. Overtime pay

Permissibly Negotiable

1. Academic and personal freedom (except constitutional)
2. Assignment and transfer of personnel
3. Association rights
4. Class size
5. Classroom management
6. School library hours
7. Teacher copyrights
8. Facilities, equipment, materials, supplies
9. Grading frequency
10. Security
11. Substitutes
12. Teacher aides

Nonnegotiable

1. Number of days or total hours of school
2. Nondiscrimination
3. Special education placement procedures
4. Teacher discipline if constitutional issue
5. First Amendment issues
6. Affirmative action
7. Student discipline if constitutional issue
8. Federal programs

Impasse Resolution

Despite best efforts, negotiations may fail and move to impasse. Under most states' laws, districts are required to recognize impasse and to engage in fact-finding, followed either by binding arbitration or by unilateral board contracts. Generally, impasse and fact-finding occur when the parties cannot reach agreement on terms and conditions of a new employment contract by some date specified in law. For both the personnel and budget functions, failure to successfully negotiate a new contract is a stressful event that introduces uncertainty and tension into employer–employee relations that are difficult to heal.

When negotiations reach impasse, most states' statutes invoke a timeline calling for a third party to examine the last best offers from both sides and to review the facts and issue a report. Depending on state law, this person may be a representative of the state's employment relations board or a person approved by some other state agency. Fact-finding in many states is not binding, but it is persuasive to the parties. In contrast, however, some states require mediation and/or binding arbitration if fact-finding does not produce a settlement. Mediation usually precedes arbitration, although in practice each state's statutes are unique. In several states, binding arbitration is immediately invoked wherein an impartial panel issues a report and both sides must accept the decision. Such a ruling cannot be challenged unless it can be successfully argued that the arbitrator exceeded his or her legal authority. In other states, the process only calls for impasse, fact-finding, mediation, and issuance of unilateral contracts if agreement is still not reached. In all instances, a statutory timeline like the one in Fig. 6.6 must be followed.

Figure 6.6. Sample Negotiations Timeline

Feb 1	Exchange of notices and proposals. A petition to the state to declare impasse may be filed.
Jun 1	Notice of impasse must be filed if applicable.
Jun 5	Five days set aside for consultation with state on impasse.
Jun 15	State issues findings. Arbitration process begun if needed.
Jun 20	Fact-finding board appointed with 5 days.
Jul 10	Fact-finding report issued within 20 days.
Immediate	Parties must meet to discuss fact-finding results.
Jul 20	Report made public after 10 days.
Jul 30	Board may issue unilateral contracts if no agreement.

In states where binding arbitration exists, the budget and personnel functions are unable to issue contracts, set budgets, or engage in most employment contract activities until negotiations are settled. This can be uncomfortable for both sides, which often must continue to work together, especially in states where public employee strikes are prohibited. Even more complex, however, is the total subjugation of the district to the will of an outside arbitrator who may make a decision that is financially difficult to fulfill. In states without binding arbitration, issues are tense, too, but the budget and personnel functions can resume operation earlier. At the opposite end of the spectrum, the issue of salary costs in unilateral contract states is obviously under far greater control.

Depending on the particular state's laws, negotiations are repeated with each employee group. But when contracts are finally settled, a major task of the budget and personnel functions is complete and these divisions can resume employer–employee relationships in which the new contract must be administered on a daily basis. In sum, at this point yet another budget-building block is in place.

OTHER ISSUES OF PERSONNEL BUDGETING

Although contract negotiations are the most critical element of budgets once projecting enrollment and estimating staff needs are complete, there are other important issues in budgeting for personnel. For legislators, school boards, administrators, staffs, and communities, three particular areas are important because they impact compensation structures and financial liability. These areas are proposals for *alternative reward systems, reductions-in-force and other dismissals*, and *due process* concerns.

What About Alternative Reward Systems?

A recurring theme related to compensation in schools is the concept of alternative reward systems. Most common among these themes has been the concept of merit pay. More recently, voices calling for total redesign of compensation systems have offered up a variety of schemes including salary incentives for knowledge-and-skills-based performance; differentiated duty pay; differentiated staffing; extra pay for national board certification; cash incentives such as signing bonuses, supplemental pay in fields where teacher supply is low or to attract high-performing teachers to low-achieving schools; and so forth. In all cases, the purpose is evident: to aggressively attract the most competent teachers to the field and to reward them along some discriminating performance dimension. And in virtually every instance, there is relatively little difference between the aims of traditional merit pay and the aims of other alternative reward systems in that these systems are not merely providing additional compensation for additional duties. In contrast, the aim is to reward superior performance on school or district goals by identifying a performance difference between people with similar jobs.

Although any differential reward system has long been subjected to strenuous criticism, there is evidence that school budgets increasingly will be expected to financially support some merit pay plan. Despite opponents' claims that merit systems discourage a collaborative environment, are highly subjective and often based on unproven evaluation methods, induce discord on goals, and generally fail to accurately measure performance, merit systems continue to make inroads into the hiring and compensating of school employees. Recent examples include an endorsement in 1999 of the concept of merit pay by the governors of 24 states; a requirement in 2002 in the state of Delaware that at least 20% of a teacher's performance evaluation must be tied to student improvement and that the salary system must include compensation for skills and knowledge; a law passed in 2004 in Arkansas establishing a knowledge-and-skills-based pay system for teachers and providing school-based performance awards; and announcements of new merit plans in Chicago in 2006 and New York in 2007 involving a total $38 million in new federal funds meant to reward high-performing teachers and administrators in hard-to-staff schools. Broadly, the list has also included differentiated pay plans that reward additional responsibilities and offer titles/duties involving mentoring, peer coaching, and serving as lead teachers; differentiated staffing plans recognizing advanced achievement and offering additional responsibilities and longer contract years along with titles such as career teacher or master teacher; knowledge-and-skill-based pay aimed at rewarding those persons who demonstrate named competencies at apprentice and mastery levels; and other state and local school-based performance award schemes tied to achieving pre-established performance goals. Whether merit pay strictly defined or whether some other performance-based plan is imminent seems not to be the major question—that is, school districts will continue to budget for single-salary schedules, but the ground is shifting whereby other alternative reward systems will increasingly join the compensation picture in a meaningful fashion.

As school districts build budgets, two key concerns about alternative pay systems should predominate. First and foremost is concern for how redesigned compensation systems will affect the district's internal working relationships. Most of the pressure for alternative pay systems has come from outside the profession, although it seems that there is no longer any wholesale rejection by educators of the concept of merit pay. In a recent national study, teachers were supportive of merit pay, although they simultaneously viewed it with serious reservations. The poll reported that 70% were willing to support incentives for teachers in low-performing and dangerous schools and that 67% supported more pay for teachers who work harder and work longer hours. Support stopped suddenly, however, when tying pay to student achievement, with only 38% favoring merit pay linked to test scores. Worries about merit pay implementation were strong as well, with 63% believing that merit pay would result in competition and harmful jealousy.[2] From these data, it makes no difference what merit pay is called: any plan that differentiates compensation on variables involving judgment leads to anxiety in schools; consquently, schools should plan carefully for the impact of alternative compensation plans.

Districts should secondly be concerned for how alternative pay systems will augment or supplant traditional pay structures and the resultant fiscal impact on the district. As we saw earlier, single-salary schedules are costly affairs, with only modest changes rippling nearly exponentially throughout the entire schedule. It is nearly inviolate that alternative compensation plans cost more, either by supplementing existing salary schedules or by substantially supplanting them. In either case, the costs will be at least additive, and it is rare when political entities driving such re-

---

2   The Public Agenda. *Stand by Me. America's Teachers—Don't Make Us Scapegoats* (New York: Author, 2003).

forms also fully fund those same reforms. In sum, school districts have reason to celebrate when compensation systems offer increased rewards, but the consequence and total cost of those systems need to be uppermost—at the legislative lobbying level, at contract negotiation time, and at budget management time.

What About RIF and Other Dismissals?

A second area of concern for the budget process involves reduction-in-force (RIF) and other dismissals. RIFs occur when districts have more staff than are needed, and other dismissals occur for cause such as unsatisfactory performance or uncooperative behavior. Although dismissals of all types are carried out through the personnel function, the budget is impacted because salary and benefits will be terminated, a new hire may be contemplated, and any dismissal always involves risk related to wrongful acts on the part of the district. In sum, the budget and personnel functions must minimize the damage and estimate the impact of these actions.

In contrast to merit pay which offers more money for desired behaviors, RIF reduces expenditure from a district's budget. In some instances, merit pay and RIF might be joined purposely, but the primary concept behind RIF is to reduce the budget, often in response to enrollment decline or other fiscal distress. RIF dismisses tenured or untenured staff for reasons unrelated to performance. Conversely, though, if an employee's performance led to enrollment decline, dismissal or nonrenewal may still be treated as RIF. The usual reason for RIF, however, is insolvency. It must be understood that when fiscal insolvency is claimed by a board, counterclaims by the teachers' association will center on validity of the board's data. Consequently, the school district must be able to substantiate its actions based on evidence. In this arena, the need for clear and precise data is paramount. When data are clear, dismissals will be supported by the courts.

When RIF is invoked, a series of important and complicated events is put in motion. Generally state law dominates this discussion, although federal employment law is important as well. For example, care must be taken to observe any federal protections such as free speech and to follow all state laws and local negotiated contract provisions such as employee rights to seniority and "bumping' and to make certain that no allegations of preferential treatment can be made during the dismissal process. Extreme care must be taken to avoid liability because some courts have liberally granted rights to both tenured and untenured staff. Other courts, however, have ruled that as long as constitutionally protected rights are respected, untenured teachers have no expectation of continued employment and possess none of the rights accorded to tenured employees. The concept of bumping is common in such situations, placing an extra burden on school districts to make certain that both laws and negotiated agreements affected by bumping are correctly followed; that is, in such situations teachers may bump other teachers with less seniority as long as other requirements are met such as professional licensure in teaching fields. Courts have also ruled that once RIF is declared, the district must complete the task and not create new positions. In other words, if asked, courts will watch to make certain that RIF is not a ruse for voluntary budget reduction or a diversionary scheme to avoid a difficult dismissal fight. As a consequence, school leaders must be familiar with every aspect of statutory requirements and local employment contract law.

In addition to RIF, other dismissals sometimes occur. Although it is often believed that a teaching job is a life appointment, reality is that tenured and untenured staff may be dismissed. There should be no underestimation of the local board's power in personnel matters. School boards and supervisors have authority to evaluate and dismiss, and these powers come by virtue of state legislatures granting both implied and delegated authority to operate the schools.

Even though school boards can dismiss staff, termination by RIF or for any other reason must not be undertaken lightly. This is true because in the vast majority of states significant differences exist between dismissal procedures for untenured versus tenured staff. Tenure grants expectation for a continuing contract and entitles the staff member to due process of law. In contrast, untenured teachers may expect only a term contract under whatever employment and dismissal rights are granted by constitutional and federal or state employment law. This does not mean untenured staff have no protection, because no one can be denied constitutional rights: that is, untenured staff may demand full due process if alleging that fundamental rights such as freedom of speech have been violated. In addition, statutes in each state govern other rights of untenured staff, making it mandatory to understand state law, the termination process, and terms of the employment contract.

Although our discussion gives the impression that it is easier to dismiss untenured staff and despite beliefs that tenure is a contract for life, there are many cases where tenured faculty have been successfully dismissed. The task is more difficult because state statutes generally provide specific reasons for termination of tenured employees, and by logic no dismissal can occur in tenured cases except for cause. Defensible cause includes incompetence, immorality, insubordination, felony conviction, unprofessional conduct, incapacity, and neglect of duty. Within limits of seniority and bumping, fiscal exigency also is a defensible cause for tenured dismissal. When any of these reasons is invoked, however, the right of termination falls to employers only if the claims can be substantiated. If challenged, failure to substantiate will likely result in a lawsuit along with liability for various types of restitution and compensation. As a result, great care should be taken when contemplating dismissal of any employee.

The most troublesome dismissal cases typically involve tenured staff. Courts have allowed a broad definition in matters of incompetence, requiring only reasonable evidence relating to lack of ability, lack of legal qualification, or failure to discharge required duties. Proof of incompetence is measured against others having similar duties. Incompetence may be shown by any one of the following criteria or some combination thereof:

- Lack of a proper teaching certificate;
- Lack of knowledge of subject matter;
- Lack of ability to establish reasonable discipline in class;
- Deficiency in teaching methods;
- Emotional instability demonstrating inability to effectively teach.

Both untenured and tenured staff may be dismissed for these reasons. In dismissing tenured staff, however, great care must be taken to document the charges in case litigation ensues. Additionally, in nearly all states there is a duty to remediate before moving to dismissal. Remediation must also be documented and should include a variety of activities designed to bring the employee up to at least an adequate level of performance. Remediation should help employees to be successful in the specific job, should define activities and duties of all parties, and should demonstrate good faith by the district to salvage the contractual interest of the employee. Documentation of failure by the employee to respond to remediation must be thorough because the first defense will be to say that the employee is not the worst case in the district and that the district did not perform in good faith. It is easy to see that serious liability, including award of monetary damages, accompanies improper dismissals.

Staff may also be dismissed for immorality. In the modern context, immorality is not confined to sexual misconduct. In a court, immorality is often based on prevailing community standards, in which the test is whether the act is detrimental to public welfare. Actions such as corruption or indecency constitute immorality, in that the standard may be defined as conduct that offends the morals of a community and that sets a bad example for the youth whose ideals a teacher is supposed to foster. Although immorality is broadly defined, care must be taken not to expose the district to liability for misapplication of the standard. For example, one of the touchy areas is unwed pregnant teachers. Generally, courts have not supported claims of immorality in such cases because of a lack of "proof" of immorality. This simply means that it is difficult to prove in the majority of communities that pregnancy results in harm to students in the learning process, or that the teacher's respect in the community has been affected. The issue is made more sensitive because in 1978 Congress passed the Pregnancy Discrimination Act, amending Title VII to include pregnancy under equal benefits coverage.

Dismissal is much easier in the case of insubordination. Willful disregard or refusal to obey reasonable directives always constitutes insubordination. Courts place the burden of proof on the district, however, particularly with tenured staff, given the property rights inherent to a continued employment expectation. A hasty decision to allege insubordination can be devastating, as insubordination as cause for dismissal has *not* been upheld when:

+ The alleged misconduct could not be proved;
+ Existence of a pertinent rule or verbal order was not proved;
+ The motive for violating a rule was admirable;
+ The rule or order was unreasonable;
+ The rule was invalid and beyond the authority of the maker;
+ The enforcement of a rule or order revealed possible bias or discrimination;
+ The enforcement of a rule violated constitutional rights.

If the employee can show that one of these reasons led to dismissal, courts will not support termination because directives must be reasonable. Insubordination and willful neglect must be proved and not merely assumed. It is wise to take care in dismissing for insubordination because, under an adverse ruling by a court, financial liability can follow.

Finally, employees may be discharged without liability for neglect of duty. In practice, neglect of duty may be part of a claim of incompetence. For example, neglect of duty might include failure to follow curriculum standards, failure to maintain discipline, failure to follow teaching lessons, and other similar actions or inactions. Neglect is distinct from insubordination, however, wherein an employee blatantly disregards directives. To withstand judicial challenge, charges of neglect of duty or insubordination must reflect prior notice and evidence of established policy or directives. Finally, other dismissals for acts such as felony conviction likely will be upheld because such offenses may have an impact on the performance and standing of the employee in the community. In many states, statutes declare that felony conviction is automatic evidence of unfitness. But as always, carelessness in substantiating dismissals for due process purposes may result in great harm to the district.

What About Due Process?

The seriousness of budgeting for personnel-related issues is clear when it is emphasized that districts are financially liable for any wrongful acts. Liability is broad and includes risk for improper dismissal given the near-certainty of forthcoming claims for reinstatement, back pay, and actual and punitive damages for violating the rights and reputation of the accused. These modern realities place a grave duty on school districts to discharge their obligations properly and to follow both procedural and substantive due process. Procedural due process ensures that parties are entitled to notice and hearing. Substantive due process is a constitutional guarantee that no one may be wrongfully deprived of their rights and must be protected from unreasonable action.

Although the personnel division has primary responsibility for developing due process guidelines conforming to the requirements of law, the financial implications of liability mean that the budget office is greatly affected and should be involved in development of such policies. A set of policies should be developed, approved by the board, and made known to staff. Due process consists of four elements that also apply to dismissal and should be considered any time there is reason to anticipate that a financial obligation might arise. In the case of contract termination, the tenured employee first must receive written notice giving specific reason(s) for nonrenewal—notification must conform to state statutes on timing and method of delivery. Second, an impartial hearing is required so that the employee can hear, examine, and refute any evidence. Third, the employee must be given opportunity to challenge these statements and to call witnesses. Fourth, hearings must occur at several levels in the district. The process begins with the immediate supervisor and administratively ends with the board. This ensures that the employee will have opportunity to be heard and to challenge actions at each level. Failure to provide these proceedings (or appropriate untenured process) will almost certainly result in severe consequences.

Determining whether due process has been accorded is a function of the external mechanics of proceedings and closer scrutiny of the total process. The administration and board must be careful to deal objectively with the facts and to procedurally follow each due process step. This is especially critical for tenured employees because these persons have property rights to continued employment, and procedural and substantive due process must be accorded in that property rights may not be removed arbitrarily. The duty of the school district is grave, as the U.S. Supreme Court has ruled that such interests of employees are "broad and majestic."[3] At the same time, appropriate dismissals should not be avoided because—notwithstanding the seriousness of violating rights and due process—failure to reverse poor employment decisions causes greater harm over time. All that is required is that dismissal be reasonable, that reasons for dismissal are not arbitrary or capricious, that defensible documentation exists, and that due process is properly observed.

WHAT IS THE ROLE OF STAKEHOLDERS?

Our discussion in this chapter has great consequence for everyone connected to schools. The most obvious consequence relates to the massive costs of educational personnel, driving 80% or more of every school district's budget. An equally important consequence is that personnel decisions represent the true resources and priorities of a school district so that human capital—that is, purchased human resources—is the most effective investment a district can make. In sum, a district's ability to reach its goals depends entirely on a highly competent and satisfied staff.

When viewed as a total process, the events delineated in this chapter (projecting enrollments, determining staffing needs, recruiting, selecting, compensating, and retaining high-quality personnel) constitute absolutely critical elements of budgeting. When these elements are properly addressed, the probability of success in providing a good education for all children is greatly enhanced. If done poorly or only adequately, the outcome is far less impressive. For school boards, a constitutional duty to appropriately carry out education rests in the relationship between the budget and staffing. For school administrators, the success of creating and balancing a wise budget is at stake, along with having to live daily with negative consequences if staffing and budgeting are poorly done. For teachers, professional success, employment stability, and personal happiness are at stake in the act of budgeting for personnel. For laypersons, the climate of the community and the economic and personal wellbeing of everyone, including children, hang in the balance. In essence, *budgeting for personnel drives revenue, expenditures, and programs at the most fundamental level.*

pointcounterpoint

Point

Traditional single-salary schedules based on education and experience do great harm to individual initiative by preventing the opportunity to be rewarded for improvements in teacher quality and student performance. Diversified pay plans offer the best opportunity for education to recruit and retain top talent and to address staff shortages through mechanisms like signing bonuses and pay for performance. Public schools should embrace these plans.

---

3   *Board of Regents v. Roth*, 408 U.S. 564 (1972).

Counterpoint

Traditional single-salary schedules were developed in nearly precise rejection of the kinds of things promoted today by advocates of diversified salary schemes. The history of discriminatory salary practices in public schools was overcome only through emergence of the single-salary schedule. It is ironic to suggest that advanced educational levels are an invalid basis for additional pay in schools, and it is nonsensical to argue that skills do not increase with experience. If merit pay systems are reintroduced in schools, the culture and productivity of education will change—but not for the better.

Questions

- ♦ Which of these starkly opposite views best represents your own beliefs and experience? Why?
- ♦ Would you be willing to accept new employment in a school system that had adopted an alternative compensation system? Why or why not?
- ♦ If your current school system announced it was considering a move to a diversified pay plan, would you be willing to participate in its development? Why or why not?

CASE STUDY

As an experienced successful principal, you recently completed your doctorate degree with an emphasis in human resource administration. In fact, your doctoral dissertation was a comparative analysis of collective bargaining laws in the 50 states. Upon completion of your degree, you accepted a position as personnel director for a school district in another state.

During your first week on the job, you learned several disturbing facts. You were greatly surprised to discover that the teaching staff had been working under an old contract for the past two years following a bitter and protracted negotiations war that had ended with issuance of unilateral contracts containing no salary increase. Your concern escalated when you learned that the school board president had been serving as the board's lead negotiator and that recently he had been quoted in the local press as saying that "…it was high time teachers in this district got with the program and got paid for good work instead of just showing up." You also discovered that the local teacher union president had fired back in the press, saying that the board president "…apparently planned to continue applying his finely honed skills in the meatpacking industry to the negotiations process where last year he dealt a death blow to any hope for good working relationships in the school district." And to make matters even worse, your secretary informed you later that same day that the district's building principals had requested a meeting with you to discuss the local teacher union's refusal to perform any extracurricular duties until a new master contract meeting their approval could be negotiated. Although you barely had time to realize that none of these issues had been made known to you during the interview process, it was clear that you had to respond quickly and effectively.

Below is a set of questions. As you respond, consider your learning in this chapter and apply your knowledge to the situation:

Questions

- Using your own experience in education and your formal learning here and in other settings about personnel practices, what do you identify as the major problems confronting you in this case study?

- As you contemplate the need for action in this situation, where should you begin? What needs to be done? Who should be involved? What can you do right away that will be positively perceived? What pitfalls should you anticipate?

- Could this situation occur in your own school district? Have there been instances in which similar tense moments have occurred? If so, what were the circumstances, and how was the problem resolved?

FOLLOW-UP ACTIVITIES

- Talk to your district's personnel director and outline the functions of his/her office. Make a list of duties, prioritizing from highest to lowest, including estimates of time spent on each of these functions. Explore the coordination between the personnel and budget offices.

- Obtain a copy of your school district's salary schedule(s) for employee groups and analyze the structure of each. Experiment with changes to the salary schedule structure, noting the impact of changes that likely would be popular in your district—for example, you might analyze changes proposed during last year's negotiations process (or the current year, depending on when you are carrying out this project).

- Talk to your local teacher union representative and a school district official to obtain a balanced view on the positive and negative aspects of personnel-related budget issues.

- Volunteer to serve on your school district's negotiations team.

- Obtain a copy of your district's personnel policy manual. Discuss its contents with a range of employees in your district, such as the personnel director, a site level administrator, a teacher, a noncertificated staff member, and a union president. Ask them to assess whether the manual is clear and comprehensive. Ask their suggestions for its improvement.

WEB RESOURCES

American Association of School Administrators, www.aasa.org
American Association of School Personnel Administrators, www.aaspa.org
American Federation of Teachers, www.aft.org
Association of School Business Officials International, www.asbointl.org

Education Commission of the States, www.ecs.org
National Association of State Boards of Education, www.nasbe.org
National Business Officers Association, www.nboa.net
National Education Association, www.nea.org
National School Boards Association, www.nsba.org
National School Public Relations Association, www.nspra.org
North American Association of Educational Negotiators, www.naen.org

RECOMMENDED READINGS

Azordegan, Jennifer, Patrick Byrnett, Kelsey Campbell, Josh Greenman, and Tricia Coulter. *Diversifying Teacher Compensation. Issue Paper.* Denver, CO: Education Commission of the States, 2005.

Dishman, Mike L., and Daniel Robert Murphy. *The Fair Labor Standards Act in American Schools: A Guide for School Officials.* Reston, VA: ASBO, 2007.

Jacobson, Stephen L., and Robert Berne, eds. American Education Finance Association. Annual Yearbook. *Reforming Education: The Emerging Systemic Approach.* Thousand Oaks, CA: Corwin, 1993.

Plecki, Margaret L., and David H. Monk, eds. American Education Finance Association. Annual Yearbook. *School finance and teacher quality: Exploring the connections.* Larchmont, NY: Eye On Education, 2003.

Stiefel, Leanna, Amy Ellen Schwartz, Ross Rubenstein, and Jeffrey Zabel, eds. American Education Finance Association. Annual Yearbook. *Measuring School Performance and Efficiency: Implications for Practice and Research.* Larchmont, NY: Eye On Education, 2005.

Webb, L. Dean, and Scott M. Norton. *Human resources administration: Personnel Issues and Needs in Education.* 4th ed. Upper Saddle River, NJ: Prentice Hall, 2002.

Wood, R. Craig, David C. Thompson, and Lawrence O. Picus. *Principles of School Business Management.* 3rd ed. Reston, VA: ASBO, 2008.

BUDGETING FOR INSTRUCTION

THE CHALLENGE

Today, about 61% of the education dollar is spent on instruction....Further, over the past 50 years the percent of expenditures spent on the classroom—or instruction—has remained consistent at about 60–61%. [But] there has been tremendous change in the composition of those classroom/instructional expenditures....[T]oday significant portions of such expenditures are spent on specialist teachers...and for extra services for struggling students.

Odden (2007)

CHAPTER DRIVERS

At the close of this chapter, you will have reflected upon these questions:
- ◆ What is instructional planning?
- ◆ What is the role of districts and schools in instructional planning?
- ◆ How do schools organize for instructional budgeting?
- ◆ What is the role and size of instructional budgets?
- ◆ What are the sources of revenue for instructional budgets?
- ◆ What are the elements of budgeting for instruction?
- ◆ What are the sources of instructional revenues?
- ◆ What does an instructional budget look like?

THE BIG PICTURE

Our journey thus far has offered an understanding of broad school funding concepts, with the ultimate goal of more closely examining the individual tasks of budgeting. A look back across the first six chapters underscores our progress: We have spent time considering the modern context of schools; the complex social milieu in which school funding policy is made; the sources of school funding; the seriousness of handling school money; the general process of budgeting; and the costs associated with personnel. This big picture has been steadily narrowing as we examine each specific element of budgeting. And so it is that we arrive at *budgeting for instruction* because it is sensible to turn next to a consideration of money and classrooms—a topic of intense interest to education's many stakeholders.

As always, we begin by moving from a general framework to increasingly specific elements. If school budgets and instruction are to be intelligently linked, the starting place is to define both instructional planning and the role of school districts and individual schools in that process. Underlying all this are issues of organizational structure—that is, how schools in a particular district are organized drives many other structures, including roles and responsibilities in budget decision making. Once these options are laid out, we consider how instructional budgets are created and implemented: for example, the role and size of instructional budgets, the sources of instructional revenues, and the specific elements of instructional budgeting. As a consequence, we move still deeper into the world of school money.

THE PLANNING FUNCTION

While the full range of instructional planning is not the focus of this book, our emphasis on strategizing for positive learning organizations makes it absolutely clear that building a budget based on the instructional goals of a district is an act of critical proportions. In fact, it has been our most fundamental premise that the whole purpose of budgeting is to build a revenue and expenditure plan to carry out the district's instructional mission.

What Is Instructional Planning?

Our experience as administrators has taught us many lessons about organizing and operating schools, with three overriding realities. The first reality is that successful instructional planning comes only as the result of hiring experts who envision and direct the teaching and learning process. The second reality is that a good instructional plan never gets carried out without the support of a strong financial plan. The third reality is that operationalizing good instruction requires something inseparable from the first two realities—that is, a deliberate plan based on a formal mission and a set of measurable goal statements. In sum, if the budget is the fiscal expression of the educational philosophy of a school district, the instructional plan brings together revenue sources in support of expenditures in order to effectuate the district's primary purpose.

District Mission and Goals

Mission and goal statements have become cornerstones of education in the last several years. Although everyone probably always knew or at least assumed value in publicly making guiding statements, much positive benefit has come from consciously focusing on mission and goals. The primary value has been that once such statements are made public, the performance burden increases noticeably. Although some people may question the wide sweep of mission and goal statements, suggesting that anybody knows them to be true, there is an increased duty to the district when it professes mission statements such as "All Children Can Learn." Although such beliefs should be unquestioned, history reveals that schools and society have not always believed that all children can learn, and the proof lies in the heated debates about the inherent value of special education and compensatory programs. Those debates are beyond the scope of this textbook too, but it is sufficient to say that a mission statement frames the attitude of schools so that the whole mindset of an organization can be driven by a mission that sounds simplistic but has the effect of focusing attitudes and performance on a promise made publicly.

The same is true of goal statements. In contrast to a mission statement, which is meant to be broadly exhortative, goal statements are specific and may be performance-based. For example, districts may adopt goal statements such as, "all children will reach at least the 60th percentile on grade-level standardized tests before passing to the next grade," or "all high school seniors will pass a criterion-referenced test with a state-approved minimum score permitting entry into the state's higher education system without remediation." The range of possibilities for goal statements is endless and ever-increasing as demonstrated by the difficult standard imbedded in *No Child Left Behind* legislation, but the purpose is simple: to focus the district on outcomes in the larger context of its overall mission and to state that focus in objective measurable terms. Both mission and goal statements have strong budget implications, so much so that budgeting for instruction becomes the centerpiece of all planning aimed at carrying out a focused mission and actionable/measurable goal statements.

School Mission and Goals

The critical act of mission and goal development also applies to individual schools within a district. Although seemingly redundant for individual schools to restate district goals, it is symbolic for schools to spend time and energy building commitment to the larger organization's aims. A simultaneous requirement, however, is that each school will also create its own mission and goals specific to each school's unique personality and needs. Although school mission and goal statements should complement district objectives, a school's own mission and goal statements should extensively reflect its programs' strengths and should extensively target the particular needs of its population.

If it is financially meaningful for a district to link mission and goals to the budget, there are equally significant budget implications for school mission and goal statements. As we will see later, districts often provide great latitude for individual schools to pursue their goals, and it is unquestioned that schools frequently have very different needs. Consequently, budget philosophy and fiscal operations at the school site level may differ based on those needs and preferences. In other words, mission and goals are not only district-level activities—they are essential budget-building blocks by focusing individual schools' planning on learning outcomes, which, in turn, should drive instructional spending.

For budgetary purposes, the planning function is the act of determining district and school mission and goals, coupled with an actionable expenditure plan to achieve those outcomes. As we saw in Chapter 6, personnel costs are a major cost center, but there remains a significant portion of every school district's budget that goes to nonsalary instructional expense. These latter costs are the focus of this chapter, together with how instructional budget decisions are made—decisions affected in significant part by how school systems are organized.

ORGANIZATIONAL OPTIONS

Instructional planning raises the issue of how schools are structured. We first alluded to organizational options earlier in Chapter 6 when we introduced budgeting strategies. It is clear, for example, that budgeting for schools involved in site-based leadership will be structured differently than in schools operating under a centralized hierarchy. Because instructional decisions are strongly influenced by organizational design, it is important to examine some options before considering how instructional budgeting might occur.

How Are Schools Organized?

Instructional budgeting is highly dependent on school district organizational design. Although there are many variations, districts are first driven by central administration's leadership style. As a result, the most common organizational designs include varying degrees of centralization, management teams, and site-based leadership. These designs drive most planning and decision making processes.

Centralized Structure

Not surprisingly, most decisions in highly centralized school districts are made in a tightly controlled central office environment, with budgets closely held at that same level. As a general rule, very centralized organizations are committed to line-item or program budgeting, and there is usually an attempt to make uniform allocations to schools as an expression of evenhandedness. Centralization usually is not absolute, however, in that it is often characterized by degrees of delegated responsibility. But ultimately, delegation of decision making in such districts is accompanied by strict central reporting and accountability.

Centralized control has noteworthy benefits and drawbacks. Among the benefits is the concept that the central office is ultimately responsible for everything that happens in the school district and that top leaders are expected to have the necessary expertise to make every important decision. An additional benefit is organizational efficiency, as there is no room for indecisiveness or disagreement if leaders are strong individuals. On the downside is the obvious fact that decision making and ownership are tightly held, so that endorsement of mission and goals and actions by subordinates are mandated. In such organizations, there is typically little staff involvement at any level in budgeting and only marginal involvement in instructional planning.

Management Teams

While relatively few highly centralized school districts still exist, use of management teams has grown rapidly. Management teams represent a middle ground between complete centralization and its opposite—decentralization. The management team concept argues that more heads are better than one, although many earmarks of centralization remain. The basic structure finds most big decisions made by central office staff who advise the superintendent from within a closely held cabinet. Central office staff, however, may offer such advice after having listened to interest groups within the district.

Management teams also offer benefits and drawbacks. A clear benefit comes from advice more broadly gathered, often by floating trial balloons among senior officials before any controversial decisions are made public. Benefits also include the checks and balances of other constituent consultation, and much efficiency inherent to central decision making is preserved. On the downside, people may complain that their input is not taken seriously, or that advisement is structured to elicit preferred answers. In such organizations, centralization is still evident, but budgets and instructional decisions likely are more widely delegated.

Site-Based Management

Although no data indicate how many of the nation's roughly 14,000 school districts are still highly centralized, many districts have tried to step away from that particular image. Indeed, it is difficult to imagine that such a design could continue to exist today given demands by employees and other stakeholders to have a voice in organizational decision making. Participatory expectations have given rise to site-based management (SBM) on a wide scale, including numerous instances where SBM has been written into law.

The modern impetus for SBM in schools largely began with the sweeping education reform enacted in 1990 in Kentucky, as that state's legislature responded to a state supreme court order to fix a constitutionally flawed education system. In responding to the court, the legislature ordered total restructuring of schools. The Kentucky Education Reform Act of 1990 was a monumental piece of legislation that required local school boards to implement school-based decision making vested in site councils comprised of parents, teachers, and principals. These persons were given substantial responsibility, including management of schools on a daily basis. For example, the Kentucky law charged site councils with the following:

- Setting school policy to provide an environment to enhance student achievement;
- Dividing the staff into committees by areas of interest for the purpose of making recommendations to the council;
- Determining the number of persons employed in each job and making personnel decisions on vacancies;
- Determining instructional materials and support services;

♦ Determining curriculum, including needs assessment, curriculum development, alignment with state standards, technology utilization, and program appraisal;

♦ Assigning use of staff time;

♦ Assigning students to classes and programs;

♦ Determining the schedule of the school day and week;

♦ Determining use of school space during the day;

♦ Planning and resolving issues of instructional practice;

♦ Implementing discipline and classroom management;

♦ Selecting extracurricular programs and determining policies relating to participation;

♦ Administering the school budget, including discretionary funds, activity funds and other school funds, maintenance, supplies, and equipment;

♦ Assessing student progress, including testing and reporting to parents, students, board, community, and the state;

♦ Creating school improvement and professional development plans; and

♦ Coordinating parent, citizen, and community participation.

The demands by the Kentucky legislature left no question about its intent. The rules had changed, and the purpose of putting stakeholders in charge of a decentralized system was clear. Similar legislation passed in Texas in 1990, and numerous other states copied the basic design in subsequent years, so that today SBM is pervasive in form and, in many cases, in genuine impact whereupon the underlying rationale is always the same: stakeholders want a strong voice in schools; expertise exists among educators and noneducators alike; and many decisions are believed to be best made at the school site.[1]

Predictably, site-based leadership designs have benefits and drawbacks. A clear benefit is that SBM stands as the epitome of the concept of shared decision making in which all stakeholders are extensively involved. Although no states mandating SBM nor all school districts voluntarily adopting it have likely gone to the lengths found in Kentucky, it is a real benefit that parents and communities have little ground to stand

---

1   In 2005, an analysis of SBM legislation revealed that 34 states and the Virgin Islands had relevant statutes on record. Among these were 17 states that had mandated SBM statewide in one form or another (Alabama, Arizona, Colorado, Florida, Georgia, Hawaii, Kansas, Kentucky, Massachusetts, Michigan, New Mexico, New York, North Carolina, South Carolina, Texas, Utah, West Virginia). Two states (Illinois and Ohio) had mandated SBM for specified districts: Illinois required SBM in all Chicago schools, and Ohio mandated that a site council be established in at least one building in districts with more than 5,000 students and that had not been identified as "effective" or "excellent" through the state accountability system. A third state, New York, both mandated SBM statewide and also placed additional SBM requirements on the New York City school district. Source: Education Commission of the States (Denver, CO, 2005). An update in mid-2007 by the authors of this text found 38 SBM-related bills passed in 16 states between 2000 and 2007.

on when complaining that schools are unresponsive. On the downside, efficiency of professional decision making is lost when laypeople become closely involved in complex decisions. Additionally, the many sensitive areas in SBM can be a source of legal and ethical concern as, for example, personnel decisions are made by site councils. Furthermore, the potential for inequality may increase as some schools inevitably perform better and strategize better financial and parental support structures.

Budget implications of SBM are self-evident and applicable regardless of how completely the SBM model is adopted. Although the model varies according to local preference or state law, SBM schools are required to accept far more responsibility for budget decisions—tasks formerly reserved to the central office. For example, individual schools may have to choose between buying supplies or hiring more personnel, or between maintaining facilities or funding student activities. As a consequence, latitude in decision making is gained, but a heavy burden falls on individual schools and a wide array of stakeholders (boards, central office administrators, principals, staffs, parents, and other school site council members) to agree on mission and goals, to gather and distribute available resources, and to produce measurable outcomes in response to such new latitude. The shift is fundamental at all levels: Under SBM the central office takes on a role of broad oversight, whereas, in sharp contrast, the individual school becomes the nucleus of authority, power, and direction.

In sum, many individual schools are taking on new powers, even under more centralized organizational designs because laws and the general public are seeking more control of public education's goals and outcomes. Accordingly it behooves all leaders to understand issues of organizational design in order to identify the parameters of appropriate and effective leadership, including determinations of the following:

♦ *Who has primary responsibility* for establishing the overall level of expenditure in a district and school?

♦ *Who has primary responsibility* for establishing expenditures for each major program or organizational unit?

♦ *Who has primary responsibility* for selecting specific resources within the allotted dollar amounts for each program?

♦ *Who has primary responsibility* for curriculum selection?

♦ *Who has primary responsibility* for new programs or for cutting current programs?

♦ *Who has primary responsibility* for establishing salaries and benefits?

♦ *Who has primary responsibility* for hiring personnel?

♦ *Who has primary responsibility* for establishing capital budgets and deciding how facilities and equipment are purchased and allocated?

INSTRUCTIONAL BUDGET CONCEPTS

As we have said repeatedly, all parts of a budget are sequentially linked so that the number of students drives revenues, which, in turn, drives staffing, thereby driving a huge proportion of total expenditures. But the instructional picture is not yet complete. The next step is to make certain our discussion has considered the non-salary portion of instructional costs.

What Are Instructional Budgets?

We can begin by asking, exactly what are instructional budgets? The question can be answered in several ways.

One reply is that the instructional budget is that portion of a budget remaining after excluding all noninstructional costs. By answering this way, the costs of food service, capital outlay, transportation, debt service, and most other separate funds are excluded. Under these limitations, the definition of an instructional budget defaults to the *entire* general fund as the best description of instructional expense. Although not entirely accurate, it is useful to picture instructional costs this way because direct instructional expense is what most people really mean in this instance. Using that logic, it is accurate to think of the general fund in this manner because the general fund truly does pay the vast majority of certificated and classified staff salaries, pays for instructional supplies, and pays for a large part of all other annual operating expenses associated with school buildings and instructional programs. By this definition, approximately 85% to 87% of a typical district's general fund budget goes to instruction (excluding business operations and maintenance; Fig. 7.1). Because everyone working in a school building or in central office either has a direct instructional role or an instructional support role, nearly all current expenditures can be viewed as instructional dollars.

Figure 7.1. How Does a District Spend Its Money?
Typical Sample School District

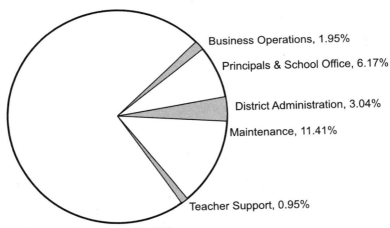

Business Operations, 1.95%

Principals & School Office, 6.17%

District Administration, 3.04%

Maintenance, 11.41%

Teacher Support, 0.95%

Teachers & Direct Student Services, 76.48%

A second answer is to say that the instructional budget is that portion of a total budget after subtracting all salary and nonteaching supply costs. By this definition, instructional budgets are not as large, but it nicely underscores the reality that the vast majority of education's costs lie in personnel and further illustrates that all other operations are funded by very low percentages of the budget.

A third answer is to say that the instructional budget includes all costs going directly to students. This would include teachers, supplies, equipment, special education services, and other support services such as librarians, counselors, and nurses, as well as transportation—all of which make up approximately 76% of the budget (Fig. 7.2). Including the professional and physical environment changes the mix and invites argument about "instruction" (Fig. 7.3, p. 216), but doing so has merit in that students in fact receive benefits greater than just direct instruction; that is, the cost of a good education is far more complex than thinking only about teacher salaries. In fact, the strongest argument for including all such costs is that all parts of the budget go together so tightly to create an educational plan that direct instruction would be far less effective if it were not for the contributions of warm classrooms, safe and clean buildings and grounds, nutrition and health services, and other system costs—i.e., the wide array of costs of running the system (Fig. 7.4, p. 216).

Figure 7.2. Direct Student Costs: Sample School District

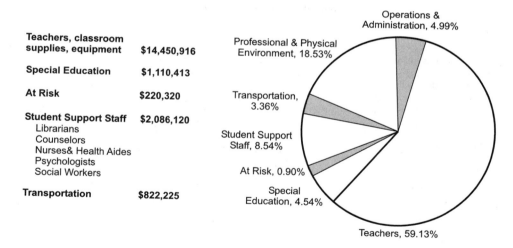

Teachers, classroom supplies, equipment	$14,450,916
Special Education	$1,110,413
At Risk	$220,320
Student Support Staff Librarians Counselors Nurses& Health Aides Psychologists Social Workers	$2,086,120
Transportation	$822,225

Operations & Administration, 4.99%

Professional & Physical Environment, 18.53%

Transportation, 3.36%

Student Support Staff, 8.54%

At Risk, 0.90%

Special Education, 4.54%

Teachers, 59.13%

Figure 7.3. Professional and Physical Environment:
Sample School District

Principal & School Office
   Principal
   Vice Principal
   Secretary & Clerks
   Office Supplies

Improving Teaching
   Staff Development Workshops
   Curriculum
   Inservice

Maintenance & Utilities
   Director of Plant Facilities
   Custodians
   Maintenance & Grounds Crew
   Utilities
   Water & Trash
   Security Officers
   Insurance

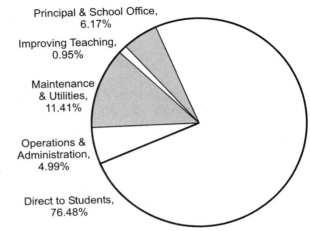

Figure 7.4. Running the System:
Sample School District

District Administration
   Board of Education
   Superintendent's Office
   Assoc. Supt., Site Support
   Assoc Supt., Central Support
   Research & Evaluation
   Election Expense
   Legal & Audit Services
   Special Education Director
   Transportation Director
   Human Resources
   Information Services

Business Operations
   Director of Accounting
   Director of Business Services
   Payroll
   Accounts Payable
   Data Processing
   Warehousing
   Purchasing

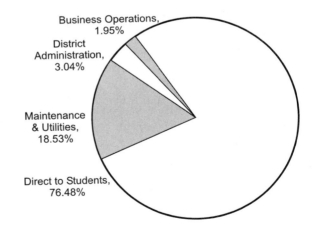

Although there are additional ways to look at instructional budgets, the most important features have been identified. Probably the most productive way to think of instructional budgets is to use the $\geq 80\%$ salary method, remembering that all remaining general fund money must cover all other general fund costs. This view is also helpful because it shows that the role and size of instructional budgets are all-consuming, in that instruction (broadly defined) is almost everything in the current operating budget and is supported by other segregated funds that carry out the "other" business of schools. Our view in this chapter is narrower because we are only concerned, for the moment, with that portion after salaries and after some general fund operating costs are known. In essence, instructional budgets are locally defined because how money is allocated to people in decision-making roles determines how any available funds get spent.

What Are the Sources of Revenue?

Our discussion in earlier chapters about revenue sources for public education deserves expansion now as we continue exploring the operational phase of budgeting. Our discussion laid out a revenue scheme made up of federal, state, and local monies. However, these sources only represented money coming into a school district from external sources in the macro view and did not develop the impact of such monies on individual schools. These and other sources actually make up a range of revenues that school districts receive and allocate using one of the budgeting philosophies discussed earlier.

External Sources

Most external revenue comes from three sources. Federal aid to education is mostly categorical, targeted at federal special interests such as compensatory education, special education, and so forth. At times federal aid has taken the form of unrestricted grants, in which Congress has determined that school districts should have fewer limitations on how money is spent as long as it can be shown that the money benefits children. General federal aid also exists, although the vast majority of federal funds is targeted to Congressional interests. Almost all federal money is "flow-through" funding, meaning that states are only intermediary recipients and are required to pass revenue on to school districts under federal regulations. Additionally, districts must be able to show that the money reached individual schools and students and was not commingled with money from other sources. The most distinguishing feature of federal aid, however, is its relatively minor status in the total revenue scheme, with a national average of approximately 9%.

State revenue comes to qualifying districts through a state-aid formula. As we saw in Chapter 3, state-aid formulas generally are meant to grant aid inversely to local ability to pay—that is, poor districts should receive greater state aid than wealthier districts. The entirety of Chapter 3 was devoted to describing variations on state-aid formulas, noting that most states rely on property, sales, and income taxes to fund the state's share of aid formulas. The distinguishing features of state aid are the growing dependence of school districts on such aid and the laws in some states on how districts must account for expenditures, either as discussed in Chapter 4 or as a consequence of site-based management as seen earlier in this current chapter. At the present time, state aid ranges from a low 27% to 87% of school districts' operating budgets, with an average of 49% across all states.

Local revenue comes to school districts primarily through property taxes.[2] As seen earlier, local revenue is frequently contentious because citizens are tempted to regard local taxes as the last chance to protest the cost of government. It has been a documented fact that permissive tax levies have been increasingly difficult to pass in the last few decades, with little sign of weakening resistance. In a few states, local districts have the authority to levy income, sales, or sumptuary taxes; such authority, however, is rare and only modestly productive as a result of statutory tax limitations and tax base overload. Obviously, the distinguishing feature of local revenue is its visibility to local patrons, a feature that can be a double-edged sword. At the present time, nationally approximately 40% of school district revenue is raised locally, although varying widely within states.

District Revenue Structures

The previous section was a short review of what we learned in earlier chapters. The unexplored features of revenue enter now, in that money coming into the school district must be distributed. Again, familiar concepts enter in play. In a centralized district, money is gathered in the central office and distributed using a philosophy such as line item budgeting or program planning/budgeting systems. In less-centralized districts, site-based budgeting may be used. But in all instances, care must be taken to provide an overarching budget structure to guard against inequitable distribution, to ensure that all programs are coherent, and to guarantee that all children's needs are served.

To meet this goal, districts exercise their available options. Highly centralized budgeting makes sense initially, as this structure allows the district to efficiently meet its obligations for neutrality and control. Under this plan, principals gather input from staff and forward purchase requests or work orders to the central office, where senior administrators prioritize requests, making sure that each school receives approximately the same overall budget treatment. This process then continues to spend down available money according to the prioritized master list. The benefit is clear: Control is present, efficiency is maximized, staff is not burdened by noninstructional financial duties, and all schools are treated equally. The drawbacks are equally clear: Control at individual sites is absent, decisions are made far from the point of need, neutrality may not be what actually is most equitable, and staff are completely uninvolved.

Another option is for central administration to establish grants to individual schools for selected purposes, while continuing to keep some items centrally funded. This scenario seeks middle ground between centralization and site-based budgeting by arguing that some tasks are best handled at the school level, while other costs are

---

2   It is important to note that while many people associate local property taxes with schools and that this perception is often reinforced by local media, the local property tax generally finances a wide range of local services, such as fire, police, and sanitation, and it is frequently an important source of revenue for local municipalities, counties, and states.

of no interest to individual schools; for example, maintenance of buildings and grounds, utility costs, transportation, personnel compensation, and the like are typical candidates for centralization. Under this plan, individual school grants tend to be solely for instructional budget purposes, as is also true of any other discretionary money sent to individual schools. The benefits are clear: Individual schools are not saddled with tasks that can be handled more efficiently at the district level, a degree of uniformity across the district is promoted, and individual schools have latitude within grants to fund school site priorities. The one drawback is significant: Because salaries consume most of a district's budget, instructional allocations may not entail big money, and schools still must queue up for capital projects and other large purchases such as textbooks and major equipment.

The third option, of course, is site-based budgeting. In its purest form, the district mostly acts as a funnel, flowing available dollars to schools. Under this plan, the board gives a formal charge to each school based on the district's mission and goals, and each school creates its own financial plan to achieve both district and school objectives. The benefits are clear: Moving money and freedom to the school site confers power on the people who have first-hand knowledge of needs and who have the skills to address local problems. The drawbacks are clear as well: If the district overdoes the concept, staff may rebel against noninstructional duties, some bad decision making is inevitable, and there is real danger that unequal resources and unequal outcomes will follow—after all, freedom is antithetical to uniformity.

Regardless of which instructional budgeting option districts choose, the flow of money is clear. Federal and state monies flow to local districts through distribution formulas, whereupon (within the limits of each state's laws) each school district decides whether to centralize or decentralize fiscal decision making. Resources at the district level are basically limited to tax dollars, although districts may benefit from private gifts, grants, foundations, and business partnerships, and fundraising efforts. As we noted early in this book, however, on the whole, revenue sources are few whereas expenditure opportunities are unending.

School Revenue Structures

It follows neatly from our discussion to expect that revenue at the school level is fundamentally dictated by district revenue amounts and by board policies on resource distribution. Other revenue that falls outside traditional thinking, however, also may be available at the school site. As a result, school revenues derive from two basic sources, one of which has not yet been discussed. These sources are the school district and the individual school site.

District revenues have been addressed already in this chapter. The issue, as we detailed, is how much revenue is allocated by the district to individual schools to be used at the discretion of the staff and administration and any specifics on how that revenue can be used. As we also discussed, this often takes the form of a uniform amount (e.g., a per-pupil dollar amount) upon which some district-controlled restrictions are placed. Figure 7.6 (pp. 226–231) at the end of this chapter develops this idea more fully.

School site revenue refers to money generated at the individual school level beyond what is normally distributed by the school district. Most schools generate some site-level revenue. For example, individual schools often apply for small state department grants, and states often participate in national grant legislation that may result in school site awards. Districts receiving larger grants might hold subgrant competitions within the district, with individual schools competing for funding. Schools can also apply directly to corporations, many of which have a record of funding innovative school projects. Numerous other grants are available to either school districts or school sites, such as those advertised in the *Federal Register*. In addition, private and charitable foundations are a source of school site revenue. Site revenue can also come from local businesses that agree to set up partnerships with individual schools, donating money, time, or materials for good causes. Schools and districts also raise money through their own foundations, booster clubs, and parent organizations. But although school-site revenue can be both a benefit by enhancing available revenue and a significant concern by inviting unequal resources between schools in a district, it nonetheless represents an important funding source.[3]

WHAT ARE THE ELEMENTS OF BUDGETING FOR INSTRUCTION?

Regardless of whether a school district chooses to centralize or decentralize instructional budgeting, there are elements common to the budget process. In fact, these elements are repeated to some extent at all levels in a district—again, something we will see later in this chapter when we showcase an instructional budget for a hypothetical school district. To launch this concept, let's assume in advance that our hypothetical district has chosen to engage in some decentralization and simultaneously to retain several efficiencies at the central office level. Our interest, therefore, is fourfold. First, a needs assessment is required to create the educational plan for both the district and each school. Second, the district must determine its total revenues and make decisions about allocations to each school based on the needs assessment. Third, individual schools must use the needs assessment and school-level allocations to establish their educational and expenditure plans. And fourth, the district must provide overall coordination of these activities.

Needs Assessment

Figure 7.5 identifies many of the important data elements required to build an instructional budget. Figure 7.5 depicts the environmental scan that should be prepared for both the district and each individual school. The scan seeks data targeting many of the conditions we discussed in Chapter 1 and strongly implies that available resources should be prioritized based on the scan's results. The scan paints a vivid portrait of the community, the school district, and each individual school so that people in leadership positions can see and understand the unique and shared needs of children. Assuming that our sample district has set a goal of raising student performance on

---

3   See, for example, Faith E. Crampton and Bauman, Paul, "A New Challenge to Fiscal Equity: Educational Entrepreneurship and Its Implications for Schools, Districts, and States," *Educational Considerations* 28 (Fall 2000): 53–61.

Figure 7.5. Environmental Scan

Indirect Influences on Student Performance	Student Descriptors	Student Cognitive Performance	Student Behavioral Performance	Direct Influences on Student Performance
Community Demographics	Gender	Criterion-Reference Tests	Graduation/Promotion Rates	Instructional Delivery Systems
Number and Types of Community Agencies	Student Perceptions of School	Norm-Referenced Tests	Discipline Referrals	Student Scheduling Patterns
Family Characteristics	Ethnicity	Grades	Attendance/Absentee Rates	Intervention Strategies
Community Crime Rate	Grade Level Enrollment	Student Portfolios	Pregnancies	Use of Technology
Youth Oriented Community Programs	Staff Perceptions of School	Teacher Anecdotal Records	Extra-Curricular Participation	General Purpose Classrooms
Community Employment Profile	Community Perceptions of School	Teacher-Developed Tests	Student Suspensions	Specialized Learning Labs
	Course Enrollment Patterns/Trends	District-Wide Content Area Tests	Dropout Rate	School Organizational Patterns
	Limited English Speaking Students			Mandated Programs

Source: Reproduced by permission of the publisher from M.S. Norton and L.K. Kelly, *Resource allocation: Managing Money and People* (Larchmont, NY: Eye On Education, 1997), 39.

standardized tests and increasing entry rates into colleges and universities, the environmental scan helps identify weaknesses that should become prime targets for increased spending. The political viability of the educational plan also can be tested through the demographic data in the scan. Results of all these activities will be used by our hypothetical school district at the central office level to establish the district's overall financial support for programs and by the individual schools in deciding how to spend site-level instructional monies to meet these goals.

Determining Revenues and Educational Plans

As noted earlier, revenues flow from federal, state, district, and school site sources. Chapter 5 identified the steps in creating school district budgets, and the present chapter points out additional decisions that may result in revenue for individual school sites. In our hypothetical school district, assume that the district has set uniform per-pupil allocations and further assume that individual school sites have taken initiative to secure some external funding for program enhancement purposes. At this point, the educational plan can be built and should address the priorities of the school district and each school site, as well as any concerns identified by the environmental scan. In effect, the process calls for setting short-term, intermediate, and long-range priorities for the school district, each school and grade level, programs, departments, and classrooms in such a way that resources are matched to children's needs by creating program-based budgets.

District Coordination

Regardless of the degree of budget decentralization, all school districts must accept responsibility for overall coordination of every aspect of the budget. Statutorily, only school boards may spend money, and the law assigns responsibility for all educational programs to the board. Additionally, efficiencies are gained by central coordination and management, and budgets are ultimately the district's inescapable responsibility. The budget calendar earlier in Chapter 5 (Fig. 5.7, p. 168) provided a clear understanding of the district's role in coordination. In our hypothetical school district, the board has centralized some district-wide activities but has chosen to grant substantial sums of instructional money to individual school sites.

What Does an Instructional Budget Look Like?

As we indicated at the outset of this chapter, the pieces of instructional budgeting cannot be carried out in discrete fashion. When conceptualized correctly, the individual elements of instructional budgeting are highly codependent—that is, demographics and student needs are revealed through scanning environments and other data collection mechanisms; fund accounting tracks and reveals how money is budgeted and spent; state aid formulas cause educational programs to flourish or starve; liability reduces discretionary spending; personnel costs and enrollments drive available resources; and school district budgeting philosophies determine how much money is available, how it is spent, and who makes spending (and consequently program) decisions. As we also noted, every aspect of the entire budget of a school district can be viewed as *the* instructional budget, although fund accounting conventions do not see the program side of budgets.

Figure 7.6 (pp. 226–231) presents data on our hypothetical school district and joins concepts from our earlier study of accounting with the concept of instructional budgeting. In fact, Fig. 7.6 is completely comprehensive by going to all issues in all chapters thus far—it even goes to future chapters by introducing capital outlay and transportation. Figure 7.6 focuses attention on the budgeting implications of the chosen organizational structure in our hypothetical school district, in that the district has decided to do the following:

♦ *Track* instructional budgets by accounting codes to permit accumulation of data by individual program;

♦ *Decentralize* many budget aspects while retaining central office oversight through the school board and central office directorships;

♦ *Allocate* uniform amounts per pupil for instructional program purposes;

♦ *Retain* overall transportation services at the central office level, while also allocating discretionary transportation budgets to schools;

♦ *Decentralize* some aspects of capital outlay and equipment purchases;

♦ *Link* expenditures to expected outcomes in a program budgeting model.

The result of this school district's budgeting philosophy is illustrated in Fig. 7.6 where it is clear that the district has acted to locate considerable budget and program authority at the individual school site. Great efficiency is gained by district oversight of functions like maintenance, repair, and construction of buildings while leaving school sites free to determine how programs are executed. The design results in individual schools accepting responsibility for large sums of money, along with the accompanying expectation for programmatic accountability. In our hypothetical district of about 7,700 pupils, total money assigned to all sites is $892,278—a sum meant to be spent on strategically targeted school needs. The fund accounting structure permits program and expenditure analysis, and proposed expenditures are justified by specifying expected outcomes. In Fig. 7.6 school staffs, administrators, and site councils have genuine authority to move money among funds.

Figure 7.6 (pp. 226–231) seems complex, and it is—in the sense that it carries out a very important task of creating the educational plan for the school district and multiple school sites. It makes good sense, however, when viewed first in terms of the overarching district plan and then in terms of what it means to each individual school site. A school principal receiving this document should understand it as an exhaustive planning tool to direct the educational process for the entire school district and each individual school. On the assumption that principals will work closely with their staffs and site councils to create planful instructional budgets for their schools, the following series of questions makes a very complex task and a lengthy planning document both purposeful and manageable:

♦ *General Background Questions*

• What is the district's overall mission?

• What are the district's goal statements?

• What is my school's overall mission?

• What are my school's goal statements?

- What were the results of the district's environmental scan?
- What were the results of my school's environmental scan?
- Does my school's educational plan address these needs?
- How can I spend my school's budget to meet these needs?

◆ *General Budget Questions (and Answers)*
- Where are the account codes I need to make purchases? (*see the beginning of Fig. 7.6, pp. 226*)
- Can I accumulate program costs? (*use the account codes*)
- What does my budget have to cover? (*see instructions in Fig. 7.6, p. 227*)
- How much money do I have for instructional programs? (*see remaining portions of Fig. 7.6, pp. 228–231*)
- What if I need more money? (*generate site revenue or seek more district funds*).
- How will I be accountable for outcomes? (*provide program outcomes for each purchase; account codes will accumulate costs over time; the district will help determine if outcomes are being met*)
- What do I do when I have a question? (*contact the central office*)

The budget structure in Fig. 7.6 is general in scope, but it clearly illustrates the underlying budgeting philosophy and operational elements that drive our hypothetical school district. From Fig. 7.6, the principal, staff, and school site council know to turn to school board documents to learn about the district's mission and goals. They also know they must be intimately familiar with the school's environmental scan, and they know to link the scan to student needs and to use these elements to construct the school's educational plan. They also know that many resource needs will be handled by the district such as textbook adoptions, and that each school site has been allotted money on a per-pupil basis—in fact, principals can find their schools listed, know the exact amount of available funds for instructional programs, transportation, and capital outlay, and understand that uniform per-pupil allocation is the basis for all funding in this district. Principals also know that program budgeting is fundamentally in their hands and that performance accountability—tied to mission, goals, and school profile—will follow for resource decisions made at the school site level.

WRAP-UP

Not all school districts are ready to follow the site-based organizational design set out in Fig. 7.6 (pp. 226–231). School district structure drives all resource decisions, and available revenue limits all decisions. The important thing is that instructional budgeting consumes most available resources, leaving only the details of how to divide the pieces—that is, district choices about local preference in resource allocation patterns.

Regardless of whether school districts opt to become more performance-accountable or whether they are forced to do so by legislation mandating constituent involvement in site councils or other similar structures, the budget will continue to be the focus of increased interest and accountability because the surest way to draw attention is to talk about public money. In the case of budgeting for instruction, it should not be otherwise—*money pays for schools, and schools provide opportunities for children*. In sum, instructional budgeting is the heart of education.

(Text continues on page 232.)

Figure 7.6. Hypothetical Instructional Budget

General Fund: School Program Codes

Line items can be refined or expanded in monitoring activities in your school or program. Contact the Director of Business for information.

ELEMENTARY	Year	Fund	Function	Object	Building	Program
Kindergarten	1	-00	-1000	-610	-xx	-01
Reading						-02
Math						-03
Language Arts						-04
Social Studies						-05
Science						-06
Textbooks						-07
Teaching supplies						-08
School office						-09
Postage						-10
Site council						-11
Grants (list)						-31
MIDDLE SCHOOL						
Physical Education	1	00	1000	610	xx	-01
Vocational Arts						-02
Home Economics						-03
Art						-04
Science						-05
Band						-06
Vocal music						-07
Languages						-08
Math						-09
Social Studies						-10
Publications						-11
Teaching supplies						-12
School office						-13
Postage						-14
Site council						-15
Grants (list)						-31
HIGH SCHOOL						
Physical Education	1	00	1000	610	xx	-01
Vocational Arts						-02
Home Economics						-03
Art						-04
Science						-05
Band						-06
Vocal music						-07
Languages						-08
Math						-09
Social Studies						-10
Publications						-11
Teaching supplies						-12
School office						-13
Postage						-14
Site council						-15
Grants (list)						-31

INSTRUCTIONS TO PRINCIPALS

You are responsible for all instructional money assigned to your school as outlined in this document. You should gather input from staff members and your site council. All budget requests and expenditures should be tied to the site plan for your school.

These instructions provide: (a) *account codes* used by central office to track cost of programs in schools—any purchase request needs to show the right codes; (b) *general notes* to guide you on how the district expects you to code your purchases; (c) a *list of instructional programs* that have separate budgets; (d) a *listing of all general fund budget allocations*—it is here that you know how much you have for your school for all accounts; and (e) sample *budget request forms*.

GENERAL NOTES

1. Teaching supplies includes general supplies, paper, folders, printer cartridges, etc.
2. School office includes general office expenditures, professional materials, printing, student assemblies, and reserve funds.
3. Materials should be purchased from program budgets: examples include magazine subscriptions, and other direct program expenses. Do not include textbook or equipment purchases here.
4. Remember to include shipping and handling when preparing purchase orders.
5. Transportation costs for program use will be charged to your school. This does not include transportation on regular routes before/after school.
6. Advance payment purchases are not allowed. Staff may not be reimbursed for out-of-pocket purchases.
7. No purchase will be approved without a purchase order in advance.
8. Repair of district-owned equipment will not be charged to schools. Routine expenses like reeds, pads, printer cartridges, etc. will be charged to programs.
9. Major purchases such as textbooks, curriculum adoptions, achievement tests and so forth are budgeted separately—see OTHER PROGRAMS below.

OTHER INSTRUCTIONAL PROGRAMS

CURRICULUM AND INSTRUCTION

Major purchases district-wide are budgeted separately, rather than charged to school budgets. The following categories are developed and administered by the Director of Curriculum and the Directors of Elementary and Secondary Education:

TEXTBOOKS   STAFF DEVELOPMENT   SPECIAL EDUCATION
CURRICULUM   GUIDANCE   TESTING

INSTRUCTIONAL MEDIA

The Director of Media Services coordinates all media services through school principals and librarians.

STUDENT ACTIVITIES

Athletics, debate, forensics, music contests, dramatics, and equipment purchases will be subsidized by the district. Separate line items will be set up for each activity. Submit all purchase requests according to the budget calendar.

GENERAL FUND INSTRUCTIONAL BUDGETS BY SCHOOL

The board of education annually sets the per-pupil allocation based on revenue availability and the recommendations of principals, staff and site councils. It must be understood that the board pays many other expenses centrally— amounts shown here should be considered discretionary in terms of how schools expend.

ELEMENTARY INSTRUCTIONAL PROGRAMS ($27.50 per pupil)

Washington School	(230 pupils)	$6,325
Adams School	(326 pupils)	$8,965
Jefferson School	(270 pupils)	$7,425
Madison School	(189 pupils)	$5,198
Monroe School	(276 pupils)	$7,590
J. Q. Adams School	(250 pupils)	$6,875
Jackson School	(479 pupils)	$13,172
Van Buren School	(159 pupils)	$4,372
Harrison School	(233 pupils)	$6,408
Tyler School	(362 pupils)	$9,955
Polk School	(198 pupils)	$5,445
Taylor School	(289 pupils)	$7,948
Fillmore School	(432 pupils)	$11,880
Pierce School	(459 pupils)	$12,622
Buchanan School	(316 pupils)	$8,690
Instruction-Elementary Totals:		$122,870

MIDDLE SCHOOL INSTRUCTIONAL PROGRAMS ($58 per pupil)

Lincoln School	(601 pupils)	$34,858
Johnson School	(598 pupils)	$34,684
Instruction-Middle School Totals:		$69,542

HIGH SCHOOL INSTRUCTIONAL PROGRAMS ($75.18 per pupil)

Hayes High	(1076 pupils)	$80,894
Garfield High	(986 pupils)	$74,127
Instruction-High School Totals:		$155,021
INSTRUCTION TOTAL	7,729 pupils	$347,433

INSTRUCTIONAL MEDIA ($19.25 per pupil)

Books, periodicals, AV supplies, teacher center, staff	$148,783

HIGH SCHOOL ACTIVITY PROGRAMS (each school)

Debate and forensics	$10,500
Dramatics	$1,000
Music contests	$3,250
Band uniform rotation (carries over budget years)	$5,000
ACTIVITY TOTAL 2 HIGH SCHOOLS (×2) =	$39,500

TECHNOLOGY REQUESTS

Instructional technology and computer services will be coordinated through the Instructional Media Center coordinator, in cooperation with the District Technology Committee.

FURNITURE AND OTHER EQUIPMENT

Direct all requests to central office for district-wide purchasing.

TRANSPORTATION BUDGETS BY SCHOOL

EDUCATIONAL FIELD TRIPS ($3.20 per pupil)

Washington School	(230 pupils)	$736
Adams School	(326 pupils)	$1,043
Jefferson School	(270 pupils)	$864
Madison School	(189 pupils)	$605
Monroe School	(276 pupils)	$883
J. Q. Adams School	(250 pupils)	$800
Jackson School	(479 pupils)	$1,533
Van Buren School	(159 pupils)	$509
Harrison School	(233 pupils)	$746
Tyler School	(362 pupils)	$1,158
Polk School	(198 pupils)	$634
Taylor School	(289 pupils)	$925
Fillmore School	(432 pupils)	$1,382
Pierce School	(459 pupils)	$1,469
Buchanan School	(316 pupils)	$1,011
	Field Trips-Elementary Total:	$14,298

MIDDLE SCHOOL FIELD TRIPS ($3.85 per pupil)

Lincoln School	(601 pupils)	$2,314
Johnson School	(598 pupils)	$2,302
	Field Trips-Middle School Total:	$4,616

HIGH SCHOOL FIELD TRIPS ($3.85 per pupil)

Hayes High	(1076 pupils)	$4,143
Garfield High	(986 pupils)	$3,796
	Field Trips-High School Total:	$7,939
FIELD TRIP TOTALS		$26,852

ATHLETICS

Lincoln School	$9,000
Johnson School	$9,000
Hayes High	$27,500
Garfield High	$27,500
ATHLETIC TOTALS	$73,000

ACTIVITIES ($1.90 mid-high, $5.65 sr. high)

Lincoln School	$1,142
Johnson School	$1,136
Hayes High	$6,079
Garfield High	$5,571
ACTIVITY TOTALS	$13,928

DEBATE and FORENSICS

Hayes High	$7,000
Garfield High	$7,000
DEBATE/FORENSIC TOTALS	$14,000

CAPITAL OUTLAY BUDGETS BY SCHOOL

Major capital projects are the district's responsibility. Schools have a small amount available for minor equipment needs. Money for copiers is available as shown here. Direct all items to central office that are not covered below.

MINOR EQUIPMENT ($4.50 per pupil)

Washington School	(230 pupils)	$1,035
Adams School	(326 pupils)	$1,467
Jefferson School	(270 pupils)	$1,215
Madison School	(189 pupils)	$850
Monroe School	(276 pupils)	$1,242
J. Q. Adams School	(250 pupils)	$1,125
Jackson School	(479 pupils)	$2,156
Van Buren School	(159 pupils)	$716
Harrison School	(233 pupils)	$1,048
Tyler School	(362 pupils)	$1,629
Polk School	(198 pupils)	$891
Taylor School	(289 pupils)	$1,301
Fillmore School	(432 pupils)	$1,944
Pierce School	(459 pupils)	$2,066
Buchanan School	(316 pupils)	$1,422
Lincoln School	(601 pupils)	$2,704
Johnson School	(598 pupils)	$2,691
Hayes High	(1076 pupils)	$4,842
Garfield High	(986 pupils)	$4,437
	MINOR EQUIPMENT TOTALS	$34,780

SCHOOL EQUIPMENT BUDGETS

Elementary total	$10,000
Lincoln Mid-High	$13,000
Johnson Mid-High	$13,000
Hayes High	$25,000
Garfield High	$25,000
Instructional Media Center	$16,000
SCHOOL EQUIPMENT TOTALS	$102,000

COPIER BUDGETS

Elementary total	$16,000
Lincoln Mid-High	$15,000
Johnson Mid-High	$15,000
Hayes High	$15,000
Garfield High	$15,000
Central office	$16,000
COPIER TOTALS	$92,000

GRAND TOTALS

Total Instructional Budgets	$535,716
Total Transportation Budgets	$26,852
Total Athletics, Activities, and Debate	$100,928
Total Capital Outlay Budgets	$228,780
TOTAL SCHOOL BUDGETS	**$892,278**

PROGRAM BUDGET REQUEST FORM BY SCHOOL

WASHINGTON ELEMENTARY
2008–09 Budget Year

Program Area: Reading

Code: 4-00-1000-610-80-01

Outcomes: Replaces 2001 copyright collection of storybooks. Children will increase reading time by 20 minutes per pupil.

Supplier: ABC Publishers, Inc.
12345 State Street
Uptown, NY 00000-0000

(See requisition for titles, grade levels, and numbers of books per grade.)

Cost per book:	$9.65
Quantity:	230
Freight:	$267.00
TOTAL:	$2,486.50

pointcounterpoint

Point

Legislatively mandated site-based management plans, while well-intentioned, have had the practical effect of requiring uninformed and sometimes uninterested people to become deeply involved in school operations. While some genuine level of lay involvement is important and even indispensable, this fundamentally political movement has gone too far and has resulted in meddling that—under certain circumstances—can become highly inappropriate.

Counterpoint

For far too long, school leaders operated closed educational systems that effectively made a monopoly of society's most important tax-funded enterprise. Site-based management models have been a welcome wake-up call to educators, but in true form, the "establishment" has in many cases managed to weaken citizen participation by assigning site councils unimportant busy work while claiming legal proscription against citizen involvement in the truly important operations of schools—namely, hiring, evaluating, and firing teachers and administrators. In sum, site-based systems have been a great start on school reform, but more is needed to truly accomplish the initial purpose.

Questions

- ♦ How are principals, central office staff, teachers, and others involved in budget construction and daily budget administration in your own school and district?
- ♦ What limits, if any, are imposed on site councils in your own school district?
- ♦ Based upon your readings so far, what do you consider to be the strengths and weaknesses of your school's and district's instructional budgeting practices? What recommendations would you make for improvements, if needed, and why?

CASE STUDY

As the newly hired curriculum director for your school district, you knew that you were in for a challenge. During your lengthy interview, the superintendent had spent considerable time laying out his desire to engage individual school sites more actively in the budget process and particularly to hold school principals and staffs accountable for the use of decentralized monies through aggressive academic performance targets. As the interview evolved, you learned that the state had recently placed two of the district's 12 elementary schools, one middle school, and one high school on academic probation for failure to meet state assessment standards and that several other schools in the district might be verging on a similar fate. The superintendent seemed convinced that a turnaround could be achieved if principals and staffs were given both the charge to increase performance and the promise of sufficient resources to meet standards. The superintendent made it clear that he expected you to spearhead this initiative and to put a well-founded action plan into place within a year's time. Upon conclusion of the interview, he noted that he would expect you to forward a proposed calendar of events within a matter of weeks after assuming your new position.

Shortly after accepting your new position, you attended a national conference on raising student performance levels. The many excellent sessions you attended convinced you that your district indeed could effectuate a turnaround by setting high goals, analyzing student data, investing in staff training for school improvement, reducing class sizes, increasing instructional time, implementing best-practice models in teaching and learning, providing extra help for struggling students, engaging parents in students' progress, and creating a community of shared leadership. The problem, you mused, was the typical one school leaders always face—where to begin, how to get others involved, how to build support, what tasks to engage and in what order, and, of course, high stakes with too little time.

Below is a set of questions. As you respond, consider your learning in this chapter and apply your knowledge and experiences to the situation:

Questions

- ◆ Based on your own beliefs and experiences, do you think this school district is headed in the right direction? Why or why not?
- ◆ Who should be involved in the initial planning stages of this transformation? Who are the most critical players? How will you garner their support? What barriers do you anticipate?
- ◆ What are the most pressing priorities in beginning this planning process? What do you believe are the critical elements for change of this magnitude to succeed?
- ◆ If you were one of the district's principals, would you greet this concept with enthusiasm or reservation? Why? What would be your most urgent questions?
- ◆ What will your proposed plan of action contain—that is, what calendar of events will you propose? In what areas do you anticipate the need for greater resources?

FOLLOW-UP ACTIVITIES

- ◆ Make an appointment with your district's curriculum director to discuss instructional budgeting in your school district. Prior to your meeting, request a copy of the district's instructional budget. Discuss with the curriculum director his or her perceptions as to how this budget interfaces with the district's mission and goal statements. Ask if or how the district goes about development of a curriculum-based, instructional budget.

♦ In your interview with the curriculum director, use the series of planning questions appearing in this chapter as a discussion guide. For example, ask questions about who has responsibility for establishing the overall level of instructional spending, who sets budgets for each major program or school, who selects the curriculum, who has responsibility for new programs or for eliminating current programs, and so on.

♦ If your district uses site-based budgeting, obtain a copy of your school's budget (e.g., see Fig. 7.6, pp. 226–231, which is a sample school-level instructional budget). Interview your school principal to determine how resource decisions are made at your school site. If your district does not use site-based budgeting, determine the level of funding available to each school site and discuss the decision-making process with your principal and the district's chief financial officer. Be sure to include discussion of resource/program accountability.

WEB RESOURCES

American Association of School Administrators, www.aasa.org
American Federation of Teachers, www.aft.org
Association of School Business Officials International, http://asbointl.org
Clearinghouse on Educational Policy and Management, www.cepm.uoregon.edu
Consortium for Policy Research in Education, www.cpre.org
Council of Chief State School Officers, www.ccsso.org
Education Commission of the States, www.ecs.org
Institute of Education Sciences, http://ies.ed.gov
National Association of State Boards of Education, www.nasbe.org
National Business Officers Association, www.nboa.net
National Center for Education Statistics, www.nces.ed.gov
National Conference of State Legislatures, www.ncsl.org
National Education Association, www.nea.org
National Governors Association, www.nga.org
National School Boards Association, www.nsba.org
U.S. Department of Education, www.ed.gov

RECOMMENDED READINGS

Anthony, Patricia, and Stephen L. Jacobson, eds. American Education Finance Association. Annual Yearbook. *Helping At-Risk Students: What Are the Educational and Financial Costs?* Newbury Park, CA: Corwin, 1992.

Berne, Robert, and Lawrence O. Picus, eds. American Education Finance Association. Annual Yearbook. *Outcome Equity in Education.* Thousand Oaks, CA: Corwin, 1994.

Goertz, Margaret, and Allan Odden, eds. *School-Based Financing.* Thousand Oaks, CA: Corwin, 1999.

Hadderman, Margaret. "School-Based Budgeting." *ERIC Digest* 131. Eugene, OR: ERIC Clearinghouse on Educational Management, 1999.

Hartman, William T., and William L. Boyd. *Resource Allocation and Productivity in Education: Theory and Practice.* Westport, CT: Greenwood, 1998.

Jacobson, Stephen L., and Robert Berne, eds. American Education Finance Association. Annual Yearbook. *Reforming Education: The Emerging Systemic Approach.* Thousand Oaks, CA: Corwin, 1993.

King, Richard A, Austin D. Swanson, and Scott R. Sweetland. *School Finance: Achieving High Standards with Equity and Efficiency.* 3rd ed. Boston: Allyn & Bacon, 2003.

Levin, Henry M., and Patrick J. McEwan, eds. American Education Finance Association. Annual Yearbook. *Cost-effectiveness and Educational Policy.* Larchmont, NY: Eye On Education, 2002.

Mohrman, Susan, and Priscilla Wohlstetter. *School-Based Management: Organizing for High Performance.* San Francisco: Jossey-Bass, 1994.

Murphy, Joseph, and Karen Louis. *School Based Management as School Reform.* Thousand Oaks, CA: Corwin, 1995.

Odden, Allan R. *How to Rethink School Budgets to Support School Transformation.* Vol. 3, Getting Better By Design Series. Arlington, VA: New American Schools, 1997.

Odden, Allan R., and Carolyn Busch. *Financing Schools for High Performance.* San Francisco: Jossey-Bass, 1998.

Odden, Allan R., and Lawrence O. Picus. *School Finance: A Policy Perspective.* Boston: McGraw-Hill, 2008.

Odden, Allan R., and Sarah Archibald. *Reallocating Resources: How to Boost Student Achievement Without Spending More.* Thousand Oaks, CA: Corwin, 2001.

Picus, Lawrence O., and James L. Wattenbarger, eds. American Education Finance Association. Annual Yearbook. *Where Does the Money Go? Resource Allocation in Elementary and Secondary Schools.* Thousand Oaks, CA: Corwin, 1995.

Plecki, Margaret L., and David H. Monk, eds. American Education Finance Association. Annual Yearbook. *School Finance and Teacher Quality: Exploring the Connections.* Larchmont, NY: Eye On Education, 2003.

Stiefel, Leanna, Amy Ellen Schwartz, Ross Rubenstein, and Jeffrey Zabel, eds. American Education Finance Association. Annual Yearbook. *Measuring School Performance and Efficiency: Implications for Practice and Research.* Larchmont, NY: Eye On Education, 2005.

Ward, James G., and Patricia Anthony, eds. American Education Finance Association. Annual Yearbook. *Who Pays for Student Diversity? Populations Changes and Educational Policy.* Newbury Park, CA: Corwin, 1991.

Wood, R. Craig, David C. Thompson, and Lawrence O. Picus. *Principles of School Business Management.* 3rd ed. Reston, VA: ASBO, 2008.

BUDGETING FOR STUDENT ACTIVITIES

THE CHALLENGE

The dispersed nature of student activity funds and the multiple site collections for some district activity fund revenues dictate a need for orderly controls on all activity funds. These controls include establishing lines of authority and a set of policies to guide the operation of all activity funds.

Thompson/NCES (2003)

CHAPTER DRIVERS

At the close of this chapter, you will have reflected upon these questions:

- What is the role of student activities in schools?
- What are student and district activity funds?
- What are the controls and lines of authority on activity funds?
- What policies are needed regarding segregation of duties, internal controls on handling cash, and disbursement procedures?
- What policies are needed for nonactivity funds such as fee receipts, sales tax, and petty cash?
- What cautions apply to the whole process of budgeting for student activities?

ACTIVITIES AND SCHOOLS

The opening quotation to this chapter suggests yet another highly complex aspect to funding equal educational opportunity because a total education includes providing learning experiences outside the formal classroom setting. A major aspect of the act of budgeting for schools thus involves providing a sound financial base for the many student activities supported by all school districts today.

There is no question that student activities demand very large amounts of time and money. In fact, activities are so central to the life of schools that many public attitudes about education are based almost entirely on the countless activities supported by the modern school district. Although it is unusual for books about school funding to contain much discussion of activity programs, the topic is so important to a comprehensive view of school money that we have devoted a chapter to ensuring that student activities are regarded as an essential aspect of equal educational opportunity.

As always, we begin by moving from general concepts to the more specific elements of budgeting—in this case, budgeting for student activities. To meet this goal, we first establish the role of activities in schools and then engage in a deeper examination of the operational aspects of activity funding. More specifically, we define activity funds and carefully distinguish between student activity funds and district activity funds, followed by an examination of controls on activity funds and relevant lines of authority for receiving and expending those same monies. Along the way we examine best practices relating to segregation of duties, internal controls on handling cash, and disbursement procedures, as well as offering advice on treatment of non-activity funds including fee receipts, sales tax, and petty cash. Finally, we end the chapter with strong words of caution because activity funds are one of the greatest sources of money problems in schools today.[1]

What Is the Role of Student Activities?

In truth, the role of student activities in the life of schools cannot be overemphasized. Although every school and district is different, an immediate sense of the importance of student activities is captured by simply glancing at the long list of activity programs supported by nearly every school district today. For example, a typical high school in modern America may support art clubs, auto clubs, camera clubs, cheerleader clubs, chorus clubs, computer clubs, speech and debate teams, drama and forensics teams, drill teams, modern language clubs, journalism clubs, math clubs, marching bands, pep clubs, student government, and athletic booster clubs. These are only a few of the student organizations that surround the really big activities such as football, basketball, volleyball, baseball, track, tennis, cross-country, wrestling, soccer, and other athletic and academic competitions—all of which require resources in the form of sponsors and coaching salaries, transportation, equipment, facilities, and so forth. To resurface a track typically costs well in excess of $100,000, and it must be

---

1   For a fuller development of student activity fund issues, see David C. Thompson, "Activity Fund Guidelines," in *Financial Accounting for Local and State School Systems 2003 Edition* (Washington, DC: U.S. Department of Education, NCES, 2004).

recognized that track is a sport that generates little in the way of offsetting revenues. The point is simply that student activities represent a huge financial outlay that is rarely self-funding, so that human energy, investment of time and money, and many other issues such as liability and the need for sound business practices quickly establish activities as a major school funding concern.

There is an additional reason why the role played by student activities cannot be overemphasized: that is, the importance of school activities in the lives of children. Starting with music and class programs at the elementary grades, small children enthusiastically perform for community audiences. Progressing into the high school years, young people form character and learn to work hard and stay in school as a result of athletic and other programs. In addition, activities encompass programs related to academics, so that activities represent an extension of the school day. Whether school leaders actually enjoy attending student activities or not, they generally learn to strongly support activity programs because they rightly come to understand that activities are not *extracurricular*—rather, they accurately view activities as part of the *cocurriculum* in ways deserving genuine support.

Finally, beyond the noble reasons for supporting student activity programs is a very practical justification for understanding the valuable role played by activities. School leaders sometimes joke that the quality of academic programs is judged by the shine on the floor of the school and by the success of athletic and academic competitions. Good school leaders, however, quickly grasp that success in activities *and* shiny floors boost pride in all school programs by broadcasting school achievements in highly visible ways. Because approximately 70% of all people in a typical district do not have children in school, it follows that approximately 70% of taxpayers see schools only from a spectator's view—as grandparents, sports fans, and so forth. Consequently, schools' physical appearance and student activity programs play an important role by elevating schools' visibility in yet another useful venue.

BUDGETING FOR ACTIVITIES

The sheer size of cocurricular and extracurricular programs today underscores the fact that a large amount of money is earmarked for student activities. As we will see, budgeting for activities is at once similar and dissimilar to other budget issues explored in this text. Similarities arise from the fact that many of the accounting principles seen earlier also apply to activity funds, so that revenue and expenditure dimensions and various account structures are mostly familiar. Differences arise, however, because (unlike other funds) activity funds typically are more loosely structured in the sense that fewer controls may exist and revenue and expenditure operations frequently are housed in multiple locations. Similarly, statutes controlling activity funds are more lax in many cases, so that numerous aspects of activity fund accounting are not strictly prescribed. In sum, the potential for error and fraud is highest in activity funding, making it essential to establish local student activity funding structures that not only amply support the contribution of activities to school learning, but which also defend against error and abuse.

What Are Activity Funds?

Activity funds are legal entities created in statute in most states for the sole purpose of segregating money in support of student activities. The unique nature of activity funds is evident in that statutes often define activities as cocurricular events, which may be further defined as student activities outside the classroom that complement the formal curriculum. Making such distinction has two key advantages. First, it creates the basis for expending district funds in support of activities by equating nonclassroom learning with the academic curriculum. Second, it sets up the mechanism for districts to separately support student activities and to account for money spent on activities. The first distinction is especially important because it is reasonable to believe that districts are not authorized to spend resources on programs unrelated to some curriculum goal. The second distinction is less profound, but it does set up useful controls and permits the existence of student-owned organizations, as will be seen later.

Activity funds are therefore accounting entities analogous to the general and special revenue funds and account structures seen in a school district's regular budget. Each activity fund is an independent accounting entity created to segregate its financial activities from that of all other funds, usually as a result of special restrictions on how money can be spent. Activity funds may only be spent for statutorily approved purposes, which are usually quite broad and limited only by the intent to spend activity funds for such purposes as athletics, music, special projects, and so forth—that is, activity funds may not be appropriated for any other use. Operation of activity funds, however, is very different from the district's regular budget. As we will see later, the collection, disbursement, and accounting for activity fund monies usually is housed at the school site level, with building principals designated as the activity fund supervisor. Furthermore, activity funds are distinguished by ownership: that is, whether the funds are owned by the district or by student organizations. In addition, the activity fund supervisor typically is responsible for accounting for all nonactivity fund monies, including many student fee collections, sales tax, and petty cash accounts. To make matters more complex, the ownership distinction creates special collection and disbursement issues. And to further complicate the mix is a vague (often wrong) perception among school organization sponsors and students regarding allowable uses of activity funds. Thus the school principal has a hard job by being multiply responsible for funds belonging to students, funds belonging to the district, administration of nonactivity funds belonging to the district, collecting and disbursing funds from a school base, transferring certain funds to the district for disbursement, and so forth. The potential for inadvertent error, misunderstanding, and even deliberate wrongdoing is self-evident.

Student Activity Funds

As we just noted, one unique feature of activity funds is the distinction of ownership. There is no analogous question of who owns the district's regular budget because the school board has total legal authority and control subject only to applicable statutes on permissible expenditures. In sharp contrast, activity funds are of two types. *Student* activity funds are owned by students—that is, students are the legal owners of certain activity funds and have the right to control how the money is spent, pursuant only to statutes, accounting guidelines, and applicable board policy.

Student activity funds consist of those student monies that involve a student-owned organization. Operationally, students in such organizations not only take part in the organization's activities but also are involved in the management of the organization. Examples include many of the clubs and organizations listed earlier. The definition is important for several reasons. Most obvious is that no one in the school district, other than students, can legally expend money from a student-owned activity fund account. In other words, money on deposit in a district-maintained activity fund is not always owned by the district. The other critical reason is subtler, in that districts must be very careful in subsidizing activities because district money could come under student control if not carefully directed.

The distinction of student ownership is not trivial and may be even more broadly construed. For example, on a broader scale many school districts have experienced legal problems trying to control organizations like booster clubs and religious groups that may organize around school-based activities, often with a request to be included in the district's chart of activity fund accounts. But issues of ownership and apparent sponsorship may arise, so that it is best to require groups not directly sponsored by the district to maintain separate bank accounts.

District Activity Funds

In contrast, *district* activity funds belong to the school district. District activity funds support cocurricular activities in which students participate but which are administered by the school district. Examples of district activities include the many district-sponsored organizations such as choir, band, orchestra, speech and debate, team sports, and so on. The definition is again important in that the distinguishing feature is that ownership and approval to expend these monies belongs to the board, rather than students. The accounting process is different too, in that district activity funds may be centralized in the district's books, rather than initially housed in the individual schools (as is the case with student activity funds). District activity fund structures escape the problems cited earlier, in that activities supported by the school district are accounted for at the district level, and all money is deposited through the district treasurer to the district's bank account.

Again, the distinction of district ownership is not trivial. Boards should maintain control of school district resources used to support student activities, and control would be lost by moving district funds into school-level student activity fund accounts.[2] Although parallel activity fund structures may seem redundant, the wise rule is that ownership determines who controls how money is spent.

---

2   The importance of ownership is apparent in the consequences of inattention. If, for example, a school board wished to subsidize a single student event it should do so by direct expenditure from its own funds. In contrast, if the board were to transfer district monies directly into a student-owned activity fund account (e.g., senior class), the transferred monies would immediately become the property of the senior class and the board could no longer require that the money be used for the targeted event.

What Are the Controls on Activity Funds?

The issues raised here suggest that large amounts of money are involved in student activity budgeting and that a complicated process governs what happens at both the district and individual school levels. This raises questions of controls on activity funds, which logically lead to further examination of issues such as lines of authority and wise policy development meant to make budgeting and administration easier. Almost nowhere in school budgeting is the word *control* more welcome than in activity funding—that is, controls are for the well-being of everyone involved. Our many years of experience tell us that more administrators risk dismissal for activity fund incompetence than for any other reason.

Lines of Authority

The need for clear lines of authority in handling activity budgets is underscored by our discussion to this point. Segregating activity funds from all other funds in the school district and the complications brought about by numerous school sites handling activity fund monies indicate a real need to maintain strict control; for example, gate receipts at an athletic event on a given night may easily exceed $10,000, assuring that activity budgeting and accounting is no small matter. In fact, it is not unusual for the activity fund chart of accounts at a typical high school to have a fund balance well in excess of $100,000. As we have emphasized repeatedly, there is almost no smear on a professional reputation as bad as violating a fiduciary trust, and one penny mismanaged will instantly lead to very damaging suspicion.

The general guideline for lines of authority for activity funds calls for the board of education to adopt sound policies governing establishment and operation of all activity funds. Of course, heat always rises, placing the superintendent in charge of properly administering board policies. The board treasurer, as the district's fiscal officer, should be appointed to implement and enforce a system of internal control procedures. These persons have first-line responsibility for all activity funds in the school district because both district *and* student activity funds are held on deposit by the district and must be reported in the district's financial statements. In sum, student-owned funds are agency (fiduciary) funds wherein the district acts as agent for these funds, while district-owned funds are classified as special revenue funds intended for support of student activities.

At the individual school level, each principal should be designated as the activity fund supervisor. Supervisory designation means the principal is responsible for overall operation of activity funds housed in that school, including collection and deposit of activity fund monies, approval of disbursements from the activity fund, and all bookkeeping responsibilities. The burden is a weighty one because, although custodial duties in fact may be delegated, final responsibility may not. It is precisely this point that gives rise to many of the policies we will note shortly regarding handling of money and multiple safeguards against misuse and embezzlement: that is, a principal may delegate duties, but responsibility may never be delegated away.

Multiple levels of activity fund ownership, responsibility, and sponsorship give rise to yet one more set of players in the line of authority. Organizational sponsors are often the first line of persons to initiate an activity fund transaction, and very often these people do not understand either the process or reasons for controls on activity funds. Sponsors need to understand the process of approved purchases, purchase orders, handling of cash, issuance of receipts, and so forth—items covered later in this chapter. The point here is that while sponsors have no direct line of authority in these matters, their presence places them in contact with lines of authority and represents still another opportunity for problems if proper procedures for receiving and expending activity funds are not followed.

Suggested Activity Fund Policies

In contrast to some earlier chapters where the issues at hand were more theoretical or sociopolitical, budgeting for activities invites a high level of prescriptiveness. In sum, the size of activity fund budgets and the risk of error or wrongdoing demand that stringent professional accounting and auditing standards be put in place in order to gain control over an arena that sees many players at many sites handling monies. As a result, a set of well-planned policies should be established and obeyed by everyone who deals with student activities and (consequently) school money. Although an exhaustive list is not feasible in a text of this nature,[3] useful insights can be given into policies on overall activity fund operation, segregation of duties, internal controls on handling cash, and disbursement of money because these are the areas representing daily operation and likely pitfalls.

General Policies

Establishment and operation of activity funds requires sound controls to ensure safe and effective management of district and student monies. Several of the following bulleted items have already been discussed, while others are added here to call attention to additional potential problems:

- *Professional accounting services should be obtained* to help set up the activity fund accounting system for the total school district. All staff and organization sponsors must be given proper training on activity funding.

- *The district treasurer should establish standardized forms and procedures.* Because the district accumulates and reports all student and dis-

---

3   Again, see David C. Thompson, "Activity Fund Guidelines." Additionally, individual states may have directive legislation and/or advisory guidelines regarding treatment of activity funds; see each state's statutory requirements for accounting for activity fund monies. More generally, useful references related to activity fund accounting include the following: Ronald E. Everett, Raymond L. Lows, and Donald R. Johnson, *Financial and Managerial Accounting for School Administrators* (Reston, VA: Association of School Business Officials International, 1996); Governmental Accounting Standards Board, *Guide to Implementation of GASB 34 on Basic Financial Statements—and Management's Discussion and Analysis—for State and Local Government* (Norwalk, CT: Author, 2000); Association of School Business Officials International, *GASB Statement No. 34: Implementation Recommendations for School Districts,* 2nd ed. (Reston, VA: Author, 2003); and, of course, *Financial Accounting for Local and State School Systems 2003 Edition* (Washington, DC: U.S. Department of Education, NCES, 2004).

trict activity fund transactions, the district should satisfy itself that standardized controls are in place.

♦ *All activity funds must be approved by the board.* Any request to create a student organization should include a statement of purpose and potential fundraising activity. To avoid confusion and to aid organizational goals, the name of the organization should be descriptive of its purpose. Organizations not directly sponsored by the district should be excluded from its financial activities.

♦ *The board should formally designate an activity fund supervisor.* Usually only one supervisor per school or attendance center should be appointed.

♦ *All fundraising should be approved in advance by the district.* Any group included in the district's activity fund chart of accounts should expect the district to approve its activities, including fundraising. It is well known that schools are assumed to have approved all activities, and unauthorized fundraising can create significant community relations problems.

♦ *Activity funds should be spent on students.* Although this seems obvious, problems frequently arise when organizations expire with unspent monies on deposit (e.g., senior class). Insofar as possible, money should be spent on those students who raised it.

♦ *Cash basis should strictly apply.* Cash basis requires that no money be spent or encumbered unless an equal or greater amount is already on deposit. This rule is frequently violated when sponsors or students place phone orders or seek reimbursement on good deals while shopping out of town. Strict adherence to advance purchase orders resolves this problem.

♦ *All activity funds must be audited* along with other funds in the district.

♦ *Activity funds should never be used for any purpose that results in a benefit, loan, or credit* to anyone.

Segregation of Duties

The importance of good policies on handling activity funds is underscored by sound business practices relating to segregation of financial duties. Bookkeeping errors can occur inadvertently, and the potential for intentional mishandling is always in the realm of possibilities. Risk of error and theft can be minimized by segregation of duties meant to reinforce general policies, tighten cash controls, and regulate all receipt and disbursement procedures.

Segregation of duties speaks to both intentional and unintentional error through the principle that no one person should be solely responsible for handling money. Daily instances of cash handling occur in all schools, and segregation of duties helps reduce many attendant problems. At the school level, the activity fund bookkeeper, appointed by the principal, should take the lead on most operations, including collecting activity fund money, preparing deposit slips, making deposits, preparing the fund accounting records, and preparing checks written on the activity fund account. These activities will be examined later during an audit and should be periodically reviewed internally as well. In addition, four particular duties need close attention. First, although a bookkeeper should prepare checks, a separate signatory should be required. Second, the principal as activity fund supervisor should be the primary signatory on checks—in some states, it is required by law that the principal sign all checks. Third, all checks should bear two signatures. Fourth, bank statements must be reconciled regularly with the fund accounting records, and someone other than the bookkeeper should prepare this reconciliation. These procedures, among others, protect against error and deliberate wrongdoing on the accounting side and serve to back up other internal controls on cash.

Internal Controls on Cash

The breadth and scope of student activities in schools today guarantees frequent handling of large cash amounts. Yearbook sales, event receipts, fundraisers, student photos, and student class projects such as vocational arts result in many thousands of dollars in cash transactions at the school site. Cash represents the greatest risk of loss, requiring additional internal controls.

The most important aspects of internal cash controls are well-trained employees and careful establishment of an audit trail to provide physical evidence for each step in cash transactions. In fact, the audit trail gives more insight to what might be missing rather than showing something was incorrectly done. Although professional accounting advice is required to properly handle cash, at least the following cash controls must be in place:

- *All fund supervisors and sponsors* must be trained and provided with written guidelines on handling cash.
- *All forms, receipts, and tickets* should be prenumbered.
- *Prenumbered items* should be safeguarded.
- *Prenumbered items* should not be printed inhouse.
- *Persons collecting cash* should be rotated regularly.
- *More than one person* should be present when cash is collected.
- *No cash collections* should be given to another person without a receipt.
- *The bookkeeper* must use prenumbered, bound receipts for all currency and checks received.
- *Cash receipts* should be kept intact and may not be used to make change or to make any kind of disbursement.
- *The bookkeeper* should make daily deposits. Any undeposited cash should be kept locked safely away.
- *Everyone* handling cash should be bonded.

These guidelines seem quite simple, but it is discouraging how frequently they are violated. Any experienced school leader has seen each of these rules badly abused. Actual examples include amazing stories: for example, principals and sponsors sticking school cash into their wallets or purses, ticket-takers at school events tearing off extra tickets to make the cash and tickets balance, blank prenumbered cash receipts lying carelessly on secretaries' desks, and clerks leaving cash unattended even for only a few moments. Especially appalling is the fairly common practice of tossing a bank bag stuffed with athletic gate receipts into a car trunk to be delivered to the school office the following Monday morning. Under these conditions, it is not difficult to see how people in schools get into big trouble when dealing with activity funds.

Disbursement Procedures

The final activity fund area we should consider is disbursement procedures. Disbursement refers to any financial transaction in which money leaves an account. This discussion can be short, because some of our other discussion involved disbursement as part of the total process. As a result, a bulleted list of guidelines makes these points quickly.

As we noted earlier, activity funds are either district-owned or student-owned. We also noted that student funds typically are handled at the school level, meaning most activity on these accounts occurs at various school sites. District funds are considerably more complicated, in that there can be an extra transaction involved because district funds are accounted for at the district level but may have flowed through a school first. An example makes this clearer. Assume the board has agreed to partially subsidize students' woodworking projects.[4] Materials are ordered, and the bill arrives. The district pays the entire bill and calculates how much each student owes. Students then make payment to the school office, which, in turn, makes a deposit to the revolving woodworking account within the activity fund. The school-site activity fund must then transfer these "district-owned" amounts to the district treasurer for deposit back to the district. It is not as difficult as it seems, but this relatively simple example underscores the meticulous nature of activity fund budgeting and accounting.

A more typical daily activity fund transaction finds a club or organization wanting to buy something. In that case, advance approval is obtained, a purchase order is written, goods are received, and the bookkeeper makes payment. The opposite is true if money is received, however—that is, cash is received, receipted, and deposited. Our interest here, however, runs toward how to disburse money properly. Accordingly, disbursement procedures for student activity funds are:

♦ *Disbursement requires approval* of the student group's sponsor and the activity fund supervisor (usually the school principal).

♦ *Disbursements should be backed up by a voucher* signed by the sponsor and principal.

---

4   Discussion in the next section of the text will reveal that this transaction actually involves a nonactivity fund account, although it is carried in the activity fund chart of accounts at the school-site level. The activity described here is a student-fee-type transaction. However, it is a common transaction easily recognized by the reader and serves the purpose of demonstrating a disbursement activity.

+ *Disbursements should be made by prenumbered check* with multiple signatures.

+ *Documentation must show* who requested the purchase, what was purchased, which activity fund account should be charged, the amount, and the check number.

Additionally, it may be wise to establish a dollar limit for student activity fund disbursements that requires higher approval if exceeded.

The elements of activity fund budgeting discussed up to this point are, in many ways, simply common sense. Yet at the same time, it is easy to see how administrators, staff, and others can get into deep trouble or become confused about the nature of activity funds. Consequently, the three big rules to observe are:

+ Be very careful when handling money.

+ Spend money only for what it is intended.

+ Use fund accounting (the tool for segregating money) so that the first two rules can be efficiently met.

It is also wise to remember that activity funds may be the greatest source of financial problems for school people today.

What About Nonactivity Funds?

In addition to true activity funds, school districts and individual school sites collect other kinds of money that must be handled just as securely. This task falls to the same people who are in charge of activity funds although, in a strict sense, we are now talking about nonactivity fund monies. The money in question here often relates to curricular programs and does not definitionally belong in the activity fund structure (see footnote 4 in the previous section). Examples of this type of money include fees related to various programs such as class materials, laboratories, physical education, and so forth. Still other kinds of nonactivity fund monies are handled at district and school levels, such as sales tax and petty cash. Our interest here has less to do with the intricacies of these monies and more to do with making sure that school leaders know that these monies exist and must be handled differently because—once again—the area is fraught with pitfalls.

The following descriptions are meant to introduce different kinds of nonactivity fund monies that are typically received by most schools. For our purpose, the most important thing to focus on is that these are generally monies that will be transferred to the district because they are almost always district-owned or received on a fiduciary basis. A more detailed examination is not appropriate for this text because these monies are merely tools to satisfy certain accounting principles and do not represent educational planning devices—although they do represent opportunities for mishandling.

Fee Funds

As noted earlier, schools usually have several fee fund accounts. For example, schools collect fees for instructional supplies and materials, enrollment fees, food service fees, lab fees, shop and towel fees, home economics fees, musical instrument rental fees, and so forth. These monies represent user charges and are owned by the district, which will, in turn, replenish the appropriate district fund when the school site activity fund bookkeeper remits collections to the district treasurer. The district then uses fee receipts to continue providing services.

Fee funds do not represent usable revenue at the school level. Fee funds are "receipt-only" funds, and no disbursements can be made from fee funds. The school merely acts to collect fees on behalf of the district for convenience reasons.

Sales Tax

Another type of nonactivity fund money often collected at the school level is sales tax. The concept itself needs little explanation, although at times it becomes confusing about whether schools should be charging sales tax. The universal rule is that when schools do collect sales tax, the school is merely the collection point and acts as the remitter to another level. School districts usually have the freedom to choose whether to let individual school sites directly remit sales tax collections or whether to centralize tax collection for a single remittance to the state. The confusing aspect is usually related to individual states' laws because it is not always clear whether sales tax should be charged. That issue is answerable only in the context of each state, with the general guiding principle that items for resale are usually subject to sales tax collection in most states.

Petty Cash

The last area of nonactivity funds common to individual school sites is petty cash. Every school in America likely has a petty cash account, but it is often misunderstood and misused. Petty cash is a source of cash used for making small disbursements without writing checks or, alternatively, making payment more quickly than could be done by going through the district's normal bill-paying channels. Petty cash accounts do not involve much money as a general rule, although—as we have repeatedly said—even the smallest sum of money must be handled properly. Examples of uses for petty cash might include paying game referees with a check drawn on the petty cash fund on game night, buying postage stamps, and other small cash purchases.

Because petty cash accounts represent more opportunity for trouble than may be the case for other kinds of money, petty cash is often statutorily limited in amount. In addition, districts should establish clear policies on uses of petty cash because of the ease with which these accounts can be defrauded because it is possible (unlike other district funds) to make actual cash payments from petty cash. Board policy should include at least the following:

- The board should set an amount for petty cash accounts and state the intended uses. A maximum disbursement amount should be set, above which board approval is required.

- The activity fund bookkeeper should act as the petty cash custodian. Access to petty cash should be strictly regulated.

- The petty cash custodian should require signed receipts from all persons receiving cash to create an audit trail. Receipts should document the purpose of the disbursement and which fund should be charged when petty cash is replenished at month's end.

What Does an Activity Fund Report Look Like?

Although the different requirements of state laws and wide range of student groups recognized by school districts prevent a universal format for activity fund reporting, the complex picture and set of responsibilities involved in activity funding is best conceptualized visually. Figure 8.1 (p. 250) presents a month-end activity fund balance report for a hypothetical high school in a district of about 7,000 students. As we continually say throughout this book, numbers tell great stories, and Fig. 8.1 speaks in telling fashion. First, it can be easily seen that this high school has a wide range of student activities—almost every conceivable organization has a place in this school's programs. Second, it can be seen that some accounts are district-owned (e.g., athletics), while others are student-owned (e.g., choir fundraising). Third, it can be seen that fee funds are reported in the school's activity fund (e.g., parking permits), although the revenue will be transferred to the district at a later time. And fourth, our point about handling large sums of money is dramatically highlighted here, as this single high school in a medium-size district has a month-end cash balance of $69,442.08—no insignificant amount of money for which the school's leader must take responsibility.

A FINAL WORD OF CAUTION

School activity programs have long been accepted as a critical contributor to the total gestalt of educational opportunity. Fiscal outlays for support of student activities are much larger than people often realize in that district cash subsidies, student-owned deposits, and the value of land, buildings, and personnel required to carry out a successful activity program are enormous. But as we argued at the outset of this chapter, there is a high payoff for everyone involved.

The high profile of student activity programs raises the stakes of budgeting in many ways, however, and memories can be unpleasant. Two such cases illustrate this point. The first case involves a school principal, respected in his state, who lost his job and his professional licensure as a result of cash receipts that were "stolen" from his unlocked car. The second case underscores the latent power that can be aroused when activity programs are threatened. In that case, a district facing a $5 million shortfall because of state-aid rescissions decided to cut several athletic programs—a decision that cost several school board members and administrators their elected positions and professional employment. Nearly everyone has similar stories, but the point is simply that the prominence and size of student activity programs make them a poor place to engage in lax fiscal practices or bad decision making. The critical feature always ties back to wise leadership in the context of fiduciary trust. In the case of activity funds, it is particularly school-level leaders who are on the firing line.

Figure 8.1. Sample Cash Balance Report
for Activity Fund Accounts

ACCOUNT NUMBER/TITLE		BEGINNING CASH BALANCE	CURRENT MONTH TRANSACTIONS	ENDING CASH BALANCE
109 .XXXXX.XXX.XX.XXX.X	SEASON TICKETS	$ 1,362.03	$ -	$ 1,362.03
110 .XXXXX.XXX.XX.XXX.X	ACTIVITY TICKETS	$ 11,235.09	$ -	$ 11,235.09
111 .XXXXX.XXX.XX.XXX.X	CONCESSIONS	$ -	$ -	$ -
112 .XXXXX.XXX.XX.XXX.X	PARKING PERMITS	$ 8,739.84	$ 565.00	$ 9,304.84
114 .XXXXX.XXX.XX.XXX.X	FOOTBALL	$ 4,114.05	$ 1,871.20 -	$ 2,242.85
116 .XXXXX.XXX.XX.XXX.X	BOYS BASKETBALL	$ 10,131.35	$ 3,182.17 -	$ 6,949.18
117 .XXXXX.XXX.XX.XXX.X	BASEBALL	$ 161.84	$ 187.10	$ 348.94
118 .XXXXX.XXX.XX.XXX.X	BOYS TRACK	$ 140.00	$ 490.00	$ 630.00
119 .XXXXX.XXX.XX.XXX.X	SOCCER	$ -	$ -	$ -
120 .XXXXX.XXX.XX.XXX.X	WRESTLING	$ 8.42	$ -	$ 8.42
122 .XXXXX.XXX.XX.XXX.X	CROSS COUNTRY	$ -	$ -	$ -
124 .XXXXX.XXX.XX.XXX.X	BOYS TENNIS	$ 308.86	$ 120.00	$ 428.86
126 .XXXXX.XXX.XX.XXX.X	GOLF	$ 17.50	$ -	$ 17.50
128 .XXXXX.XXX.XX.XXX.X	BOYS SWIMMING	$ 2,788.38	$ 109.03	$ 2,897.41
130 .XXXXX.XXX.XX.XXX.X	GIRLS TENNIS	$ 469.02	$ -	$ 469.02
131 .XXXXX.XXX.XX.XXX.X	GIRLS SOCCER	$ 33.68	$ 426.10	$ 459.78
132 .XXXXX.XXX.XX.XXX.X	GIRLS VOLLEYBALL	$ -	$ -	$ -
134 .XXXXX.XXX.XX.XXX.X	GIRLS BASKETBALL	$ 6,745.51	$ 1,282.03 -	$ 5,463.48
135 .XXXXX.XXX.XX.XXX.X	SOFTBALL	$ 32.97	$ 111.32	$ 144.29
136 .XXXXX.XXX.XX.XXX.X	GIRLS SWIMMING	$ 1,603.06	$ 129.45	$ 1,732.51
138 .XXXXX.XXX.XX.XXX.X	GIRLS GYMNASTICS	$ -	$ -	$ -
140 .XXXXX.XXX.XX.XXX.X	GIRLS GOLF	$ -	$ -	$ -
141 .XXXXX.XXX.XX.XXX.X	WEIGHT TRAINING	$ 7,035.23	$ 4,076.40 -	$ 2,958.83
142 .XXXXX.XXX.XX.XXX.X	TOURNAMENT ACCOUNT	$ 925.26	$ 1,008.58	$ 1,933.84
143 .XXXXX.XXX.XX.XXX.X	WRITERS CLUB	$ 1.64	$ -	$ 1.64
144 .XXXXX.XXX.XX.XXX.X	STUDENT SUPPORT GROUP	$ 16,602.31	$ 11,040.44 -	$ 5,561.87
145 .XXXXX.XXX.XX.XXX.X	CITY BASKETBALL	$ 3,551.84	$ 110.00 -	$ 3,441.84
146 .XXXXX.XXX.XX.XXX.X	DRAMATICS	$ 1,834.92	$ 41.00	$ 1,875.92
147 .XXXXX.XXX.XX.XXX.X	DRAMA TRIP	$ 19,998.54	$ 14,780.01 -	$ 5,218.53
148 .XXXXX.XXX.XX.XXX.X	THESPIANS	$ 656.88	$ 16,008.06 -	$ (15,351.18)
150 .XXXXX.XXX.XX.XXX.X	DEBATE	$ 920.35	$ -	$ 920.35
151 .XXXXX.XXX.XX.XXX.X	SCHOLARSHIP BOWL	$ 825.00	$ -	$ 825.00
152 .XXXXX.XXX.XX.XXX.X	CAP AND GOWN	$ -	$ -	$ -
154 .XXXXX.XXX.XX.XXX.X	NEEDY STUDENT	$ 355.42	$ 5.00	$ 360.42
156 .XXXXX.XXX.XX.XXX.X	NEWSPAPER	$ 1,400.00	$ 848.00 -	$ 552.00
158 .XXXXX.XXX.XX.XXX.X	MUSIC CONTEST ACCOUNT	$ 216.12	$ 195.19 -	$ 20.93
160 .XXXXX.XXX.XX.XXX.X	MUSIC SUPPORT GROUP	$ 1,517.89	$ -	$ 1,517.89
161 .XXXXX.XXX.XX.XXX.X	VARIETY SHOWS	$ -	$ 1,347.05	$ 1,347.05
162 .XXXXX.XXX.XX.XXX.X	SPECIAL MUSIC	$ 1,916.19	$ 100.00	$ 2,016.19
164 .XXXXX.XXX.XX.XXX.X	CHORALE	$ 4,817.36	$ 4,817.36 -	$ -
166 .XXXXX.XXX.XX.XXX.X	SCHOOLWIDE TALENT	$ 134.92	$ -	$ 134.92
168 .XXXXX.XXX.XX.XXX.X	JAZZ GROUP	$ -	$ -	$ -
170 .XXXXX.XXX.XX.XXX.X	ORCHESTRA	$ 263.00	$ 50.00	$ 313.00
172 .XXXXX.XXX.XX.XXX.X	CHOIR FUNDRAISING	$ 9,679.28	$ 10,530.00 -	$ (850.72)
173 .XXXXX.XXX.XX.XXX.X	PEP CLUB	$ 1,924.66	$ 192.24	$ 2,116.90
174 .XXXXX.XXX.XX.XXX.X	CHEERLEADERS	$ 598.73	$ -	$ 598.73
178 .XXXXX.XXX.XX.XXX.X	STUDENT COUNCIL	$ 12,338.69	$ 2,104.76 -	$ 10,233.93
			FUND BALANCE= $	69,442.08

pointcounterpoint

Point

School leaders today, hard-pressed to find funding for both academic and extra-curricular programs, have been dealt an unnecessary blow through recent actions in many states to ban or restrict vending machine food and beverage sales in schools. These vending contracts, some of which paid as much as $100,000 per year to individual schools, were critically important because those funds were typically used to pay for computers, sports program, and numerous after-school activities.

Counterpoint

Given the growing concern about childhood and adolescent health in this country and the role of proper nutrition, school leaders' first responsibility is to ensure that the school environment is one where healthy eating choices are reinforced. School leaders should welcome federal and state initiatives that discourage if not bar the sale of "junk food" in schools. Furthermore, funding student programs and activities with such money is unethical, similar to using taxes on tobacco sales to fund smoking cessation programs.

Questions

- ♦ Which of these two diametrically opposing views best represents your beliefs and experiences? Why?

- ♦ How are student activities funded in your school and district? What role do vending machine revenues play; for example, how much profit do they generate and what kinds of products are sold? If your school does use vending machine proceeds for this purpose, how would you replace these revenues if they were no longer available?

- ♦ Does your school have a wellness policy in place as required by federal law? Has this policy affected your school's choices with regard to the sale of food and beverages outside the food service program? If so, how?

CASE STUDY

Upon assuming your new position as principal of a large high school, you undertook a review of your building's activity fund operations with your business clerk.

As you educated yourself about local activity fund practices, you became very concerned about lax financial procedures. Among your growing list of anxieties were the fact that last year's comprehensive audit had noted problems in activity fund cash receipts and disbursements, wherein auditors had noted 42 instances of cash entries to the student yearbook account for which no prenumbered receipts were found; had noted that nearly $90,000 in athletic equipment purchases were made for which corresponding requisitions/purchase orders were signed and dated after the vendor's invoice had already been paid; had noted that several activity fund accounts showed negative balances; and had noted that monies received were not always deposited timely because on multiple occasions cash deposits were not made for several days after receipt. Your clerk was apologetic but indicated that the district had had difficulty keeping good office help and had regularly used student office aides to carry out tasks such as selling yearbooks. The clerk also indicated that it had been the prior principal's long-standing practice to allow the athletic department to order equipment on the spot from sales calls and to complete the purchasing paperwork later.

As you worked late into the evening, you considered other findings from your inquiry into activity fund practices wherein, independent of your conversations with the business clerk, you had made other disturbing discoveries. You knew from your own observations over the last several days that office staff kept the petty cash box in an unlocked desk drawer, and you had personally seen an office worker make a quick run to the supply closet at the back of the office complex while leaving uncounted cash lying on top of a desk. You also reflected that you had seen cash register drawers at athletic concession stands left open momentarily while the attendant was distracted by serving multiple customers simultaneously. So far there had been no reports of missing cash, you reflected silently, but on the other hand you had only been on the job for a few short weeks. With nearly a half-million dollars total activity fund budget in your care, you knew something had to change—very quickly.

Below is a set of questions. As you respond, consider your learning in this chapter and apply your knowledge and instincts to the situation:

Questions

- ◆ Using your own experience and formal learning to this point, what elements of this case study are genuinely serious issues of concern? Why? What steps should the principal take immediately to address the most pressing concerns?

- ◆ As these issues seem to have developed over time, what barriers do you anticipate in correcting the situation? How will you go about it?

- ◆ What can a school leader do to protect against shoddy activity fund practices?

- ◆ Using your own experience as an educator, what examples of poor activity fund management accounting have you encountered? How could these have been avoided?

FOLLOW-UP ACTIVITIES

- ◆ Make a list of all student activities in your district and explore how they are funded. Distinguish which activities are student funded and which are district owned.

- ◆ Make an appointment with your district's treasurer to discuss handling of student activity funding. Obtain a copy of your district's board poli-

cies and guidelines on activity funding. Discuss the district's procedures for receipting and disbursing activity fund monies.

♦ Obtain a copy of an activity fund report from one of the high schools in
your district. Analyze it for number of dollars, number of student
groups, and so on. Talk to the principal about how the activity fund is
supervised and the lines of authority and control that are in place. Identify strengths and weaknesses in the system, and address how the weaknesses might be approached.

WEB RESOURCES

American Association of School Administrators, www.aasa.org
Association of Certified Fraud Examiners, www.acfe.com
Association of School Business Officials International, http://asbointl.org
Education Commission of the States, www.ecs.org
Governmental Accounting Standards Board, www.gasb.org
Institute of Internal Auditors, www.theiia.org
National Business Officers Association, www.nboa.net
National Center for Education Statistics, www.nces.ed.gov
National Conference of State Legislatures, www.ncsl.org
U.S. Department of Education, www.ed.gov

RECOMMENDED READINGS

Cuzzetto, Charles E. *Internal Auditing for School Districts.* Lanham, MD: Rowman
& Littlefield Education, 1993.

Cuzzetto, Charles E. *Student Activity Funds: Procedures & Controls.* Lanham, MD:
Rowman & Littlefield Education, 1999.

Everett, Ronald E., Donald R. Johnson, and Bernard W. Madden. *Financial and Managerial Accounting for School Administrators: Tools for School.* 2nd ed.
Lanham, MD: Rowman & Littlefield Education, 2007.

Everett, Ronald E., Raymond L. Lows, and Donald R. Johnson. *Financial and Managerial Accounting for School Administrators: Superintendents, School Business
Administrators and Principals.* 4th ed. Lanham, MD: Rowman & Littlefield Education, 2003.

Granoff, Michael H. *Government and Not-for-Profit Accounting.* 4th ed. New York:
John Wiley & Sons, 2007.

National Center for Education Statistics. *Financial Accounting for Local and State
School Systems 2003.* Washington, DC: Author, 2003.

Wood, R. Craig, David C. Thompson, and Lawrence O. Picus. *Principles of School
Business Management.* 3rd ed. Reston, VA: ASBO, 2008.

9 BUDGETING FOR SCHOOL INFRASTRUCTURE

THE CHALLENGE

A sound school finance system is fair in distributing resources to all children, provides adequate money to carry out the full range of services assigned, does so at a high level of efficiency…and relies on stable and predictable revenue sources—all in the context of meeting the full slate of modern educational needs. To reach this end, school infrastructure funding must be included at full parity if children are to be equally advantaged and none left to the miserable physical conditions that existed in some schools in the United States at the start of the new millennium.

Crampton & Thompson (2003)

CHAPTER DRIVERS

At the close of this chapter, you will have reflected upon these questions:

- What is the role of infrastructure in public schools?
- How is school infrastructure defined?
- What is the current condition of school infrastructure?
- What is included in a comprehensive definition of school infrastructure?
- How much money do schools need for infrastructure?
- How is school infrastructure currently funded at state and local levels?
- What are the goals of and activities involved in infrastructure planning?
- What is the role and nature of maintenance and operations?
- How do schools organize for maintenance and operations?
- What is the role of the school site leader in maintenance and operations?

PHYSICAL NEEDS IN PERSPECTIVE

As indicated in the opening quotation to this chapter, no study of school funding is complete without a deep concern for the role of physical infrastructure in schools. The high cost of capital outlay, debt service, maintenance and operations, and other large physical outlays such as technology and general facility modernization have subtly but relentlessly lurked beneath the big picture as we have worked our way through the maze of school funding topics. By underlying our discussion we mean that some costs may go unnoticed in the rush to adequately fund instruction (e.g., teacher costs), but that less visible costs can be more powerful than the most obvious ones. In other words, while the role of funding school facilities is critically important, other costs consume the vast majority of education's resources. As a consequence, we need to deliberately spend time articulating education's physical infrastructure needs and consider how the budgeting process addresses this aspect of equal opportunity.

We begin by first exploring the role of school infrastructure, focusing our discussion on its nature and size. We then turn attention to the current condition of school facilities in the United States and offer estimates of costs to redress deficiencies. We follow with an extended discussion of how schools' infrastructure needs are funded, with a strong assertion that infrastructure funding lags far behind progress in funding other areas of education's needs. With that general framework in place, we are ready to consider how school infrastructure planning and maintenance and operations are carried out—that is, a different, but related, set of issues. More specifically, we turn attention to how infrastructure planning occurs, the effect of demographics and programs on school facility planning, the role of maintenance and operations, and how schools organize their maintenance activities. In sum, although school infrastructure has never enjoyed the high profile of topics like school reform, budgeting for physical infrastructure plays a crucial role in funding education due to the high cost of facilities and relationships between infrastructure quality and educational program success.

NATURE AND SIZE OF SCHOOL INFRASTRUCTURE

Although it is popular to overdramatize issues to capture headlines, it does not overstate the case to say that public education's physical infrastructure needs are a serious—even dire—problem far into the foreseeable future. This "safe" prediction derives from the many stressors on school budgets described in this textbook, combined with the fact that while much concerted effort has been exerted in recent years to reform schools, far less attention has been given to the need for effective physical learning environments. As the American Association of School Administrators (AASA) noted long ago, "[F]rom every corner have come reports, articles, speeches and goal statements about student achievement, unmet needs and education reform… but all these pronouncements have been strangely silent about one essential ingredient…that affects every child's health, safety and ability to learn: *the classroom.*[1]

1　American Association of School Administrators, *Schoolhouse in the Red. A National Study of School Facilities and Energy Use* (Arlington, VA: Author, 1991), 1.

Pronouncements of this nature are not insignificant in a time when reform of failing schools has widely captured headlines. The source of alarm rests in evidence that education's physical infrastructure is also failing in ways that surely impede general reform. Numerous reports have warned about the condition of school facilities, and school leaders and policy makers have been told of the cost for repair and replacement. As we will see shortly, estimates run into billions of dollars, mostly because schools have funded other current needs by delaying maintenance and repair to school buildings. Although our discussion in this book has been overshadowed by unlimited needs and finite resources, forced choice is most evident when funding infrastructure because schools have had to choose between spending for instruction and spending for bricks and mortar in which to house those programs. In sum, it is an ever-spiraling crisis that underscores the crucial role of planning for capital needs, particularly since infrastructure is the single largest investment a school district ever makes at any one time.

What Is the Role of Infrastructure in Public Schools?

Different language has been used over the years to describe the physical environment of education. School plant and facilities have been the common terms describing school buildings, and capital outlay usually has referred to all aspects of paying for the permanent facility and equipment needs of schools. In a broader and more recent context, the term *infrastructure* has been used frequently because it captures the whole range of capital needs in a single word. All these terms have been useful in describing the role of physical environments by implying that planning for instructional programs alone is not enough to meet the educational needs of children. The role of infrastructure was captured by AASA when it stated:

> The most exciting curriculum innovations in the world have trouble succeeding in cold, dank, deteriorating classrooms. If the work environment is unattractive, uncomfortable, or unsafe, school districts have difficulty competing with other sectors of the economy to woo talented teachers....Students know the difference too! When *USA Today* polled 72,000 students as to what they would do with more school funds, their no. 1 priority was school maintenance and construction. Teens responding to the survey called their buildings "filthy and a disgrace."[2]

Although we do not suggest that poor conditions describe a majority of schools in the United States, we do argue that needs far outstrip resources and that the data point to ever-mounting infrastructure needs in most school districts. Other chapters in this text suggest good reasons for this crisis, as competition for tax dollars continues to rise. The crisis has worsened as pressure has been placed on school facilities through the expanding scope of education mandates and reforms, and stress has followed from the complex and sometimes arcane ways in which schools are financed and maintained. The role of infrastructure is to support good instructional programs by providing a safe, appropriate, and inviting physical environment for learning—a role

---

2   AASA, *Schoolhouse in the Red*, 11.

that often has taken a backseat to the costs of demographic realities, curriculum reform, salaries, and other school services. Yet it is clear that the best reforms will fail if the physical environment impedes learning. In sum, deferring construction and maintenance may represent a short-term solution, but such decisions ultimately represent false economy by impeding the work of schools.

The Condition of Schools[3]

The headlines heralding school infrastructure decay make it easy to believe that the poor condition of schools in the nation is a newly discovered reality. In fact, problems of school facilities and capital needs have long been noted by education critics. In 1831, William A. Alcott graphically described the problems of school facilities when he stated:

> Few, indeed, of the numerous schoolhouses in this country are well lighted. Fewer still are painted, even on the outside. Playgrounds for the common schools are scarcely known. There is much suffering from the alternation of heat and cold and from smoke. The feet of children have even sometimes been frozen. Too many pupils are confined to a single desk or bench where they jostle or otherwise disturb each other....Hundreds of rooms are so small that the pupils have not on average more than five or six square feet each; here they are obliged to sit, breathing impure air, on benches often not more than six or eight inches wide, and without backs.[4]

Fortunately, almost no schools today suffer the full force of Alcott's criticisms. Students no longer sit on benches, health standards regulate ventilation, and most schools provide tolerable light and thermal environments. Rigorous construction standards apply to all new schools, and many existing schools have been retrofitted to meet these standards.[5] No public school facility has escaped some regulation because schools must comply with fire and boiler inspection and standards of the Environ-

---

3   The following section draws substantially on Faith E. Crampton and David C. Thompson, eds., *Saving America's School Infrastructure.* (Greenwich, CT: Information Age Publishing, 2003).

4   William A. Alcott, "Essay on the Construction of School-Houses," August 1831, quoted in David C. Thompson, *Educational Facility Equity and Adequacy: A Report on Behalf of the Plaintiffs in Roosevelt v. Bishop* (Manhattan, KS: Wood, Thompson & Associates, 1991), 1.

5   A partial listing of such organizations that publish standards includes the American Concrete Institute (ACI), American Institute of Architects (AIA), American Institute of Steel Construction (AISC), Architectural Woodwork Industry (AWI), American Welding Society Code (AWSC), National Building Code (NBC), National Electric Code (NEC), National Fire Protection Association (NFPA), National Illuminating Engineering Society (NIES), National Plumbing Code (NPC), Uniform Building Code (UBC), Underwriters Laboratories, Inc. (UL), American Association for Health, Physical Education, and Recreation (AAHPER), American Association of School Administrators (AASA), American Institute of Electrical Engineers (AIEE), Association of Physical Plant Administrators (APPA), Association of School Business Officials (ASBO), American Society of Mechanical Engineers (ASME), American Society for Testing and Materials (ASTM), Council of

mental Protection Agency (EPA) for hazards such as asbestos, radon, and lead; standards of the Occupational Safety and Health Administration (OSHA); and accessibility under the Americans with Disabilities Act (ADA). As a result of efforts to provide a better learning environment, modern schools are largely relieved of the very worst conditions of earlier times.

Simply enacting building codes, however, has not led to excellent school facilities across the nation, as regulations have focused on crises such as asbestos or other life-threatening hazards. Furthermore, although many aspects of the physical environment in new schools are legislated, existing facilities generally have not been fully upgraded to the same standard. The result has been that existing schools remain an object of concern because numerous national reports have concluded that their infrastructure still is in a state of emergency. Although many good schools do exist, reports have argued that others are badly deteriorated, with many too old to safely function or too outdated to meet the demands of a modern education and equality of opportunity.

Although Alcott's description may be a relic in many ways, in other aspects it lingers today. Recent research on the quality of school environments has exposed substandard school facilities, painting scenes of unsafe and unhealthy classrooms described by critics as resembling conditions in poverty-stricken third world countries.[6] In addition, research describes health hazards associated with air quality in portable classrooms, a widely used alternative to new construction, often in response to legislation mandating class size reduction or as a stopgap solution to growing student enrollments.[7] These conditions, not unlike Alcott's day, are juxtaposed with new research linking student achievement and the physical environment.[8]

As awareness and sophistication of research into school infrastructure have grown, new understanding of the depth of need indicates that physical deficits are larger than previously believed—and are still growing.[9] Previous best estimates of deferred maintenance in U.S. schools dated from the 1980s[10] and were estimated in

---

Educational Facility Planners, International (CEFPI), National Board of Fire Underwriters (NBFU), and the National Bureau of Standards (NBS).

6   See, for example, Jonathan Kozol, *Savage Inequalities: Children in America's Schools* (New York: Harper Perennial, 1992); and U.S. General Accounting Office, *School Facilities: The Condition of America's Schools* (Washington, DC: U.S. Government Printing Office, 1995).

7   See, e.g., Zachary Ross and Betsy Walker, *Reading, Writing, and Risk: Air Pollution Inside California's Portable Classrooms* (Washington, DC: Environmental Working Group, 1999).

8   See Faith E. Crampton, *Investment in School Infrastructure as a Critical Educational Capacity Issue: A National Study* (Scottsdale, AZ: Council of Educational Facilities Planners International, 2007).

9   See, generally, Faith E. Crampton and David C. Thompson, eds., *Saving America's School Infrastructure* (Greenwich, CT: Information Age Publishing, 2003). See also National Education Association, *Modernizing Our Schools: What Will It Cost?* (Washington, DC: Author, 2000).

10   American Association of School Administrators, Council of Great City Schools, and National School Boards Association, *The Maintenance Gap: Deferred Repair and Renova-*

1995 at $112 billion.[11] Recent research, however, shows this deficit is still unfunded and that true infrastructure needs were underestimated because the U.S. General Accounting Office (GAO) only inquired about deferred maintenance, safety, and accessibility. In contrast, the newest data argue that if unmet needs are vast in only the context of general upkeep and repair, they are staggering in the context of a fuller definition of total infrastructure and equal educational opportunity. Figure 9.1 illustrates the modern definition of infrastructure and endorses costs of improvements associated with educational program adequacy.

Results from the most recent comprehensive national study of infrastructure deficits (Fig. 9.2, pp. 262–263) show that states' unmet funding needs in 2000 exceeded $266 billion,[12] more than double the estimate provided by GAO only five years earlier. Total unmet funding need varied dramatically across states, from $220 million in Vermont to nearly $48 billion in New York. When expressed in per-pupil terms, states and local school districts needed to spend an additional $1,100 per student on average each year for a five-year period to address unmet needs, an increase of 100% over actual spending rates. Consequently, it is not surprising that the American Society of Civil Engineers, who biennially rate the quality of America's infrastructure, gave schools a "D" in 2005.[13]

These data join with other reports of troubled school facilities in that population shifts, issues of economic health, and adequacy of infrastructure are closely interwoven. Although population in some areas of the nation has grown, schools have continued to age without new money to meet the demand for construction, renovation, and modernization. In contrast, population in other locations has steadily declined, raising questions about the future of individual schools and districts. In all instances, fully 50% of schools were built 35 to 45 years ago, and it is not surprising that many buildings are now in poor condition because the typical school was built with a life

(Text continues on page 264.)

---

tion in the Nation's Elementary and Secondary Schools (Arlington, VA: Author, January 1983); Ann Lewis, *Wolves at the Schoolhouse Door: An Investigation of the Condition of Public School Buildings* (Washington, DC: Education Writers Association, 1989); and Sharon J. Hansen, *Schoolhouse in the Red: A Guidebook for Cutting Our Losses* (Arlington, VA: American Association of School Administrators, 1992). See also two special issues of the *Journal of Education Finance* on the status of state and local funding of capital outlay: David S. Honeyman, R. Craig Wood, and David C. Thompson, eds., *Journal of Education Finance* 13, no. 3 (Winter 1988), and David S. Honeyman, R. Craig Wood, and David C. Thompson, eds., *Journal of Education Finance,* no. 4 (Spring 1989).

11   U.S. General Accounting Office, *School Facilities*, and Laurie Lewis, Kyle Snow, Elizabeth Faris, Becky Smerdon, Stephanie Cronen, and Jessica Kaplan, *Condition of America's Public School Facilities: 1999* (Washington, DC: U.S. Department of Education, National Center for Education Statistics, June 2000), a recent update of the General Accounting Office (GAO) study placing the total at $127 billion.

12   Crampton, F.E., & Thompson, D.C. (Eds.). (2003). *Saving America's school infrastructure* (p. 17). Greenwich, CT: Information Age Publishing.

13   American Society of Civil Engineers, "Report for America's Infrastructure: 2005 Grades," www.asce.org/reportcard/2005/page.cfm?id=103.

Figure 9.1. Comprehensive Definition of Infrastructure

♦ *Deferred maintenance.* Refers to maintenance necessary to bring a school facility up to good condition, that is, a condition where only routine maintenance is needed. If a facility is in such poor condition that it cannot be brought to good condition or if it would cost more than to construct a new facility, deferred maintenance can refer to replacement of an existing facility.

♦ *New construction.* May be a response to pupil overcrowding; to federal, state, or local mandates requiring additional facilities such as class size reduction measures, or to projected enrollment growth. Construction of a new facility includes the building(s); grounds (purchase, landscaping, and paving); and fixtures, major equipment, and furniture necessary to furnish it.

♦ *Renovation.* Includes renovations to an existing facility for health, safety, and accessibility for the disabled. Renovation may include work needed to accommodate mandated educational programs.

♦ *Retrofitting.* Applies to areas such as energy conservation (e.g., installation of insulation or energy-efficient windows) and technology readiness (e.g., electrical wiring, phone lines, and fiberoptic cables).

♦ *Additions to existing facilities.* May be necessary to relieve overcrowding; to meet federal, state, or local mandates such as class size reduction; or to accommodate projected enrollment growth. Cost of additions usually includes fixtures, major equipment, and furniture necessary to furnish them.

♦ *Major improvements.* Refers to grounds, such as landscaping and paving.

Note: Some states use the term *capital outlay* rather than school infrastructure. In some states, the definition of capital outlay may be broader —e.g., in some states, capital outlay includes major equipment and/or equipment over a specific dollar amount.

Source: Faith E. Crampton, David C. Thompson, and Janice M. Hagey, "Creating and Sustaining School Capacity in the Twenty-First Century: Funding a Physical Environment Conducive to Student Learning." *Journal of Education Finance* 27 (Fall 2001) 633–52.

Figure 9.2. Infrastructure Funding Need by State

State	Total Need ($)	Per Pupil ($)/5 yrs	Per Pupil ($)/10 yrs
Alabama	1,519,210,061	398	221
Alaska	727,014,291	1,074	588
Arizona	4,748,568,494	983	536
Arkansas	1,761,701,495	758	422
California	22,000,000,000	704	386
Colorado	3,805,239,627	1,045	574
Connecticut	5,000,000,000	1,828	1,033
Delaware	1,046,354,648	1,836	1,022
Florida	3,300,000,000	271	151
Georgia	7,061,967,931	942	517
Hawaii	752,533,936	713	386
Idaho	699,469,537	517	278
Illinois	9,213,000,000	824	458
Indiana	2,477,797,613	486	269
Iowa	3,359,129,953	1,386	776
Kansas	1,793,241,845	774	430
Kentucky	2,441,607,196	749	418
Louisiana	3,104,098,619	812	454
Maine	452,064,540	448	253
Maryland	3,891,926,876	905	504
Massachusetts	8,919,014,500	1,822	1,025
Michigan	8,071,127,040	963	541
Minnesota	4,517,232,516	1,068	597
Mississippi	1,038,890,864	406	226
Missouri	3,475,160,989	759	423
Montana	901,492,663	1,101	607
Nebraska	1,608,849,896	1,119	622
Nevada	5,256,000,000	2,888	1,568
New Hampshire	409,511,478	403	226

State	Total Need ($)	Per Pupil ($)/5 yrs	Per Pupil ($)/10 yrs
New Jersey	20,709,650,065	3,247	1,810
New Mexico	1,410,624,747	778	422
New York	47,640,000,000	3,214	1,802
North Carolina	6,210,938,727	902	502
North Dakota	420,000,000	749	420
Ohio	20,900,000,000	2,302	1,291
Oklahoma	2,204,070,041	732	410
Oregon	2,407,425,974	859	475
Pennsylvania	8,465,134,387	927	521
Rhode Island	1,420,952,603	1,882	1,060
South Carolina	2,574,018,400	803	451
South Dakota	498,604,766	706	390
Tennessee	2,273,702,904	466	257
Texas	9,467,620,774	453	248
Utah	8,490,336,757	3,385	1,841
Vermont	220,090,007	425	239
Virginia	5,701,313,528	986	548
Washington	5,478,902,777	1,067	589
West Virginia	1,000,000,000	686	384
Wisconsin	4,762,337,059	1,087	608
Wyoming	530,888,665	1,125	614
Total	266,138,818,788		

Source: Faith E. Crampton, "Unmet School Infrastructure Funding Need as a Critical Educational Capacity Issue: Setting the Context," in *Saving America's School Infrastructure*, eds. Faith E. Crampton and David C. Thompson (Greenwich, CT: IAP, 2003), 3–26.

expectancy of 50 years. The general rule is that maintenance costs increase rapidly when a school reaches 30 to 40 years of age, with accelerated deterioration between 40 and 50 years of age. Although disturbing to taxpayers, costs of upkeep on older buildings and technological obsolescence are important factors that underlie the expert view that most schools more than 50 years old should be replaced unless they hold worth as historical landmarks or are put to alternative uses. Additionally, fully 25% of schools now in use were built between 1900 and 1950—that is, under these combined conditions, half of all schools have marginal future utility, and another 25% are overdue for replacement.

Although it is easy to understand that the ultimate impact of infrastructure deficits is deterioration of the learning environment, it is difficult to meaningfully address the issue due to limited tax resources and the tremendous expense represented by bricks and mortar. One of the more aggressive solutions is litigation to force states to absorb the unfunded need, and some success has been experienced by plaintiffs in a small number of states.[14] To date, plaintiffs in 37 states have cited funding for infrastructure in school finance lawsuits, with six focusing claims exclusively on inequitable and inadequate infrastructure funding.[15]

Other proposals have advocated for special state-level legislation to provide one-time infusions of money for school infrastructure, such as during the 1990s when a large number of states enjoyed economic prosperity, often with substantial state budget surpluses.[16] But despite favorable times, most proposals focused on partial or short-term solutions to the problem of infrastructure deficits because the cost to address the backlog of needs seemed so overwhelming and because other constituent groups were also lobbying for the use of state surpluses for other aims like tax relief. In most instances, states have genuinely lacked the fiscal capacity to deal fully with these enormous costs, largely because they have never developed infrastructure funding plans and revenue sources having the specific goal of aiding infrastructure at the same level given to general fund operating costs. Figure 9.3 (pp. 265–269) reveals the

(Text continues on page 270.)

---

14 See Faith E. Crampton and David C. Thompson, "When the Legislative Process Fails: The Politics of Litigation in School Infrastructure Funding Equity," in *Politics of Education Law: Effects on Education Finance. 2004 American Education Finance Association Yearbook*, eds. Karen DeMoss and Kenneth Wong (New York: Eye On Education, 2004), 69–88. See also David C. Thompson and Faith E. Crampton, "School Finance Litigation: One Strategy to Address Inequities in School Infrastructure Funding," in *Saving America's School Infrastructure*, eds. Faith E. Crampton and David C. Thompson (Greenwich, CT: Information Age Publishing, 2003), 163–90.

15 Molly A. Hunter, "Facilities in School Funding Cases," *www.schoolfunding.info*.

16 National Conference of State Legislatures, *State Budget Actions 1998* (Denver, CO, 1999) and National Conference of State Legislatures, *State Tax Actions 1998* (Denver, CO, 1999). The National Governors Association and the National Association of State Budget Officers estimated the average state surplus for fiscal year 1999 at $31 billion (7.1%) of state budgets. See National Governors Association and the National Association of State Budget Officers, *The Fiscal Survey of States* (Washington, DC, December 1998).

Figure 9.3. State School Infrastructure Funding Programs

State	State Funding Program	Flat Grant	Equal-ized	Basic Support	Full Fund-ing	Cate-gorical Grant	None
Alabama	Guaranteed tax yield for capital improvements.		X				
Alaska	Grants with required local contribution ranging from 5% to 35%. Reimburses debt up to 70%. Debt must be preauthorized.		X				
Arizona	Full state funding within required state standards. Per-pupil amount for "soft," short-term capital needs.		X		X		
Arkansas	Provided within basic state aid: Average daily membership (ADM) × wealth index × $39.	X	X				
California	State provides approximately 55% to 66% of costs.						
Colorado	Included in Basic Support Program: $223–$800 per pupil.			X		X	
Connecticut	Equalized funding for 20% to 80% of eligible costs. Magnet schools receive 100%. Additional funding for initiatives such as early childhood, reduced class size, full-day kindergarten.		X			X	
Delaware	State pays 60% to 80% of costs. Equalized based on taxing ability.		X				
Florida	Public Education and Capital Outlay (PECO) funds projects based on need.					X	
Georgia	Equalized funding based on assessed valuation per pupil, ranging from 75% to 90 %. Special local sales tax (SPLOST) funds are also included in the formula. Grants for new classrooms, reduced class size initiatives. Additional incentives available for low wealth district districts.		X			X X	
Hawaii	Full state funding				X		

(Figure continues on next page.)

State	State Funding Program	Flat Grant	Equalized	Basic Support	Full Funding	Categorical Grant	None
Idaho	Subsidies for debt retirement based on mill rate, health, & safety issues.					X	
Illinois	Equalized grants based on equalized assessed valuation (EAV) per pupil at the 90th percentile. Grants for debt service equaling 10% of principal × grant index.		X				
Indiana	Flat grant of $40 per pupil in average daily attendance (ADA) in grades 1–12. Purpose is debt service.	X					
Iowa	Grants based on enrollment size and inverse relationship with sales tax proceeds. Required local equalized match based on district fiscal capacity. Minimum match is 20%.		X				
Kansas	Weighting per pupil in basic aid of 0.25 for costs of new facility. Grants for debt service equalized inversely to assessed valuation (AV) per pupil.	X	X				
Kentucky	Flat grant of $100 per pupil. District levy of $0.05 per $100 of assessed valuation (AV) equalized if property wealth is less than 150% of state average. Grants for debt service based on percentage of district unmet needs compared to state unmet needs.	X	X				
Louisiana	No state funding.						X
Maine	Funding for debt service based on local share for approved projects.		X				
Maryland	Funding based on state share of minimum foundation per pupil. Minimum is 50% of costs.		X				
Massachusetts	Reimbursement of 50% to 90% for approved projects. Funding based on calculation of property value, average income, district poverty level, and incentive points (type of construction, project manager, efficiency, maintenance history).		X				

State	State Funding Program	Flat Grant	Equalized	Basic Support	Full Funding	Categorical Grant	None
Michigan	No state funding.						X
Minnesota	Funding by weighted average daily membership (ADM) × ($173 + district average building age). Equalized debt service aid. Incentive grants such as $30 per year round pupil served, health, & safety issues.		X			X X	
Mississippi	Flat grant of $24 per average daily attendance (ADA). Other grants based on specific needs.	X				X	
Missouri	No state aid.						X
Montana	Funding for debt service only. Based on ratio of district mill value per pupil enrollment and the state mill value per pupil.		X				
Nebraska	Funding for accessibility and environmental issues: $0.052 per $100 assessed valuation (AV).					X	
Nevada	No state funding with the exception of special appropriations for two districts due to extreme need.						X
New Hampshire	State funds 30% to 55% of building costs depending on number of towns. Funding is not equalized.	X					
New Jersey	*Abbott* districts receive 100% funding. Non-*Abbott* districts receive equalized funding (minimum of 40%) based on district wealth (personal income and property tax base). Some districts may be eligible debt service aid.		X				
New Mexico	Equalized funding for voter-approved 2-mill levy. Grants for critical needs if district is bonded to 65% of capacity.					X	

(Figure continues on next page.)

State	State Funding Program	Flat Grant	Equalized	Basic Support	Full Funding	Categorical Grant	None
New York	Equalized funding based on Building Aid Ratio and Approved Building Expense.		X				
North Carolina	Funding provided based on average daily membership (ADM), growth, and low wealth. Additional flat grant from proceeds of corporate income tax.	X	X				
North Dakota	No state funding.						X
Ohio	Funds Ohio School Facilities Commission. Equity list developed based on 3-year average property wealth; local district must pass levies. State design manual requirements.		X				
Oklahoma	No state funding.						X
Oregon	No state funding.						X
Pennsylvania	Funding (reimbursement) based on the greater of district's market value aid ratio, capital account reimbursement fraction, or density.		X				
Rhode Island	Funding for debt service. State share ratio = 1- ((district wealth per pupil/state wealth per pupil) × 62%). Minimum funding 30% of cost.		X				
South Carolina	Funding allocated per pupil based on available funding divided by K–12 average daily membership (ADM).	X					
South Dakota	No sate funding.						X
Tennessee	Funing through the Basic Education Program. Based on cost per square foot per average daily membership (ADM) + 10%for equipment + 5% for architect fees + debt service at state bond rate.					X	

State	State Funding Program	Flat Grant	Equalized	Basic Support	Full Funding	Categorical Grant	None
Texas	Guaranteed yield funding through the Instructional Facility Allotment which is based on size of district, property value, averge daily attendance (ADA), and amount of annual debt service.						
Utah	Equlized funding based on local effort tax rate of $0.0024 per dollar of taxable value and need.		X				
Vermont	Funds about 30% of cost of project based on prioritized needs. Debt service reimbursed based on the guaranteed yield provisions of the general aid formula.		X			X	
Virginia	Flat grant of $200,000 per district. Remaining amount prorated based on enrollment and ability to pay. Per pupil supplement for maintenance and debt service.	X	X				
Washington	Funding is based on eligible area, area cost allowance, and matching ratio. Required local effort (matching ratio) is determined by comparing district assessed valuation (AV) per pupil to state assessed valuation (AV) per pupil.	X	X				
West Virginia	State funding is based on need: efficiency, adequate space, educational improvement, educational innovations, health and safety, and changing demographics. Lottery money is dedicated to debt service.					X X	
Wisconsin	Funding is included in the basic support program.			X			
Wyoming	State supplements mill levy if assessed valuation per average daily membership (AV/ADM) is below 150% of state average.		X				

Source: Catherine C. Sielke, "Financing School Infrastructure Needs: An Overview Across the 50 States," 33–37.

patchwork approach many states have taken toward funding school infrastructure, with several states providing no funding whatsoever and only a handful of states funding school infrastructure in any meaningful manner—either in total dollars or in a progressive cost-share ratio.[17]

Although health and safety and construction standards have greatly advanced school environments, these improvements have required great sums of money. The vastness of infrastructure needs, growth in deferred maintenance, the reluctance of legislatures to include infrastructure as an important element of equal educational opportunity, and inequities in local fiscal capacity have all resulted in school facility planning that has not been sufficient to offer uniformly adequate physical environments to every child. As a result, many school districts have had to divert instructional funds to pay for infrastructure-related emergencies or, alternatively, have had to watch their deferred needs grow and their facilities deteriorate.

How Is School Infrastructure Funded?

The modern condition of public education's physical infrastructure is a cumulative image of how thoroughly states have chosen to aid school facilities.[18] As we will see, there is a sharp difference in how general education is aided compared to how facilities and related capital needs are funded. In contrast to the complex formulas developed to provide state aid to general fund, special education, transportation, and several other school services, infrastructure has been neglected at state and local levels.

An important reason for infrastructure underfunding has been reluctance to forsake tradition. School facilities have long been considered a local expense, dating from an era when far fewer children attended school and facility costs and programs were simpler. Schools stood as symbols of local cooperation, often raised by hand with volunteer labor and donated materials and land. Technological obsolescence did not exist, and demands on local tax bases for other services were minimal in a mostly rural nation. Communities were fiercely protective of their schools and rejected outside help. The dawn of the twentieth century, however, marked the end of local tax base adequacy, as movement from an agrarian to an industrial economy led to rapid

---

17 See Catherine C. Sielke, "Financing School Infrastructure Needs: An Overview Across the 50 States," in *Saving America's School Infrastructure,* eds. Faith E. Crampton and David C. Thompson, 27–52.

18 This section does not specifically address federal funding of school infrastructure given its limited role. At present, only one small federal program exists, Qualified Academy Zone Bonds (QZABs). Enacted in 1997, this is a tax credit for bondholders rather than an aid program for states and school districts. See Qualified Zone Academy Bonds, *www.ed.gov/programs/qualifiedzone/index.html.* Qualifying QZAB school districts do not pay interest on these bonds, but are responsible for paying the principal from their own resources. See Letter from Margaret Spellings to Chief State School Officers (March 1, 2007), *www.ed.gov/policy/elsec/guid/secletter/070301.html.* The annual federal allocation ($400 million divided among the 50 states) is modest given the total infrastructure need of school districts nationwide. For more information on QZABs, see Qualified Zone Academy Bonds: Frequently Asked Questions, *www.ed.gov/programs/qualifiedzone/faq.html.*

growth in cities and schools. Yet despite growing needs for more school revenue and broader tax bases, many states continued to follow a tradition of local responsibility for funding school facilities. Although other state aids appeared in rapid succession, infrastructure needs continued to depend on local property wealth and were often hindered by restrictive statutory debt limitations and tax rate caps.

Pressure on local tax bases gave rise to a second major cause for school facility neglect. As education's importance grew, students stayed in school longer and were joined by populations needing more instruction and other aspects of compulsory education. Early in the twentieth century, educational growth was accompanied by economic prosperity, but the stock market crash in 1929 caused school revenue to falter. The Great Depression nearly halted growth in education spending, and school construction was nonexistent for nearly a decade. After World War II the backlog of facility needs was recognized, but it was "resolved" by rapid construction of cheap school buildings that were never meant to last. The result was a backlog of unmet needs, followed by hasty construction and emerging educational technology that quickly made facilities obsolete.

A third source of neglect was that all these problems were worsened by slowness on the part of states to become involved in funding school facilities. Although increased costs and demand for new programs severely strained local resources, states were still reluctant to become involved, citing deference to local control issues. As needs grew, however, a few states began providing aid, but most often aid was conditioned on other outcomes. For example, in 1901, Alabama began to aid capital outlay; the purpose, though, was to help rural schools and did not imply a broader state duty to education. Other states followed suit, with each plan varying in reasons, amounts, and methods. For instance, Delaware and South Carolina began offering capital aid to schools in 1903 for African-American children. Likewise, between 1898 and 1927 aid plans were enacted in Arkansas, Delaware, Maine, Minnesota, Missouri, New York, Oklahoma, Pennsylvania, Rhode Island, Tennessee, and Wisconsin—facility aid primarily offered to encourage consolidation of countless tiny school districts. The result of such selective aid schemes was that as late as World War II, only 12 states provided general aid to capital outlay and debt service for local schools.

Economics, politics, and local control thus have been the major causes of underfunded school facilities. Yet recently states have become more aware of school infrastructure concerns, especially as some courts have begun to link capital needs and other areas of school finance fairness. As seen earlier in Fig. 9.3 (pp. 265–269), a large majority of states now provides some type of aid to school infrastructure, although not necessarily adequate or uniform aid. Some states have assumed a majority of costs, whereas others provide a smaller share. States actively attempting to aid facilities do so using full state funding or equalization grants or provide aid through the general fund mechanism, while states making less aggressive efforts have traditionally used matching grants, flat grants, state loans programs, building authorities or similar devices, or by allowing school districts to incur bonded indebtedness. Although operation of each plan depends on the goals of each state, these plans usually resemble the general fund aid schemes from which they derive their names.

Full State Funding

As the name implies, full state funding plans assign total responsibility to the state for the cost of building programs. Under these conditions, the state pays for school facility construction—and in some instances, maintenance—and in return may expect to control many of the decisions that would otherwise be made at the local level if facilities were locally funded. For example, under a full state funding scheme the process of acquiring new facilities may involve various levels of bureaucracy wherein state resources are allocated first to those districts in greatest need. Although the plan satisfies principles of equity, full state funding of facilities is rare in that most states have chosen to embrace traditional facility funding practices. Even in those states where full state funding has been adopted in name, practice may resemble a modified approach that still uses a local property tax levy rather than a single statewide tax.

Full state funding of school infrastructure has the same advantages found in fully funded general aid formulas (see Chapter 3). Full state support conceptually represents the most equitable system, in that facilities are funded based on the wealth of the entire state. But as expected, disadvantages follow. The difficulty of identifying the full extent of needs typically results in unexpected costs to the state. Similarly, concerns about loss of local control arise when centralized authority is imposed. Furthermore, there is a basis for concern about extravagance when districts no longer need to be frugal in assessing their needs. Conversely, there is basis for fears about declining local taxpayer support when schools are not locally financed. Although several states have experimented with forms of full state support for facilities, only a few states have actually adopted this funding plan for the long-term.

Equalization Grants

Equalization plans for funding school facilities closely resemble the equalization aid formulas found in general fund financing. Equalization usually involves grants to local school districts, wherein state facility aid increases as local ability to pay declines. Variations on equalized grants have been devised in several states. For example, if power equalization principles (see Chapter 3) are adopted, a feature may be that a district can choose to increase its cost share and qualify for more aid. Alternatively, equalization grants, although possibly limited by state definition of an approved facility, may aid districts up to a maximum amount based on district wealth. Unlimited variations exist, as states set aid criteria based on policy preferences and fiscal realities.

Regardless of how states structure equalization aid plans, the critical feature is the cost-share based on ability to pay. This feature is the greatest strength of such schemes, in that aid flows inversely to local wealth. Another advantage may be a greater degree of local control wherein a district can manipulate its tax rate, either to purchase better facilities or to provide tax relief. Disadvantages are few and relate more to political problems, such as the difficulty of achieving meaningful equalization. Similarly, financial constraints and political pressures to aid all districts may serve to restrict total amounts of aid available. Although many states have adopted forms of facility equalization grants, most have capped funding at some level that lets the state keep control of its resource outlays.

General Fund Aid

Only a few states have chosen to build infrastructure aid into their general fund aid programs. Separate from maintenance and operations, which have often been considered current operating expenses and thereby housed in the general fund, general fund aid on a broad scale only recently has been used to channel money to school facilities. By default, such programs distribute aid according to whatever equalization principles are included in the general fund. The logic of such schemes is simply that facilities are part of the total educational program of the district and equally deserving of support at the same level of aid received by all other general fund expenses. Although highly laudable, the cost of such plans has prevented widespread adoption.

Matching Grants

Likewise, only a few states have chosen to aid facilities using matching grants. First designed to aid the general fund, matching grants are an effort to acknowledge facility needs and to neutrally aid school districts. In its basic form, matching provides aid to all districts by granting a legislatively determined share of costs regardless of local fiscal capacity. For example, the state might share costs on a 50:50 ratio based on legislative preferences and state treasury limitations. Matching plans satisfy three goals. First, matching is acknowledgement of needs. Second, matching is an effort to provide neutral aid, either from the perspective of not discriminating among districts or recognizing the politics of aiding all districts regardless of need. Third, matching permits the state to limit its fiscal exposure by controlling the percentage required at the local level.

The major advantage to matching grants is political, and the negative aspect of uncritically providing aid to wealthy districts is obvious. The latter issue has frustrated widespread adoption, so that no state currently offers true matching grants, although at times some states may offer equalized grants with minimum aid provisions to all districts regardless of equalized tax capacity.

Flat Grants

Flat grants have long been used to provide general aid to schools based on beliefs about politics and about the general benefit of state participation. States using flat grants offer districts a set sum of money per unit of need based on legislative policy decisions and the state's fiscal condition. The formula is simple by granting a flat sum, irrespective of local wealth, on some basis such as pupil count or number of classroom units. The result is that local costs are lowered as a consequence of the state's participation, leaving districts free to reduce taxes or to use the additional state funds to enhance programs.

The principle of flat grants has been used to fund school facilities. Under this plan, all districts receive aid, and dependence on local wealth is reduced. Political realities are aided too, at least in those wealthy districts that otherwise would not qualify for aid. Disadvantages follow, however, in that flat grants have been woefully inadequate to fully meet infrastructure needs. Although better than no aid, it is well established that flat grants do not intervene in wealth variations.

State Loans

State loan programs represent one of only two unique inventions involving school infrastructure. Although other facility aid plans are an acknowledgement by the state of the inadequacy of local tax base to satisfy districts' needs, state loans are a special recognition of the high cost and intergenerational benefits of school facilities. A state loan program fundamentally concedes that current local tax revenues are inadequate to provide facilities and consequently allows districts to incur debt in order to provide housing for educational purposes. Loan programs are exactly what the name implies, in that the state loans money to districts for school facility needs. As a general rule, these loans carry expectation of repayment.

State loan programs have advantages and disadvantages inherent to their nature and design. Advantages may include lower interest rates based on strong security ratings for investors because the state itself either makes the loan or guarantees it. Districts can either borrow money at lower cost or buy more facilities for the same cost that would be experienced under traditional debt mechanisms bearing private market interest rates. A second advantage is that some states have structured school construction loans to permit forgiveness if the district cannot fully repay. The disadvantages, however, are meaningful in that local wealth and ability to pay are still negative elements, as districts in the greatest need may be the least able to afford the higher cost of borrowing. Historically this method has been frequently used, but its use has declined with growing awareness of the depth of school infrastructure needs.

State or Local Building Authorities

The only other unique facility funding invention works much like state loans except that private funds are frequently involved. Typically, state or local building authorities are legislative creations allowing school districts to borrow for infrastructure projects, but without actually bonding against the wealth of the local district (see later bond mechanism discussion). School building authorities encourage the use of private capital to construct and lease or lease-purchase schools for several reasons. First, building authorities do not generally involve an outlay of state monies. Second, the state reaps the political benefit of liberalizing facility acquisition at virtually no cost to itself. Third, local debt limits usually do not apply, making it easier for poorer districts to obtain new facilities. Fourth, no local bond election is required, avoiding a major obstacle of voter resistance. Under these conditions, school building authorities have been used in some states to assist local districts in redressing their infrastructure needs.

Advantages to state or local building authorities lie in their unique ability to tap resources without restrictive legal debt limitations and in the ability to obtain needed facilities in a shorter time given no local referendum requirement—a huge benefit because school bond elections frequently have failed throughout the nation. Opponents, however, have seen such authorities as a subterfuge, citing avoidance of the intent of referendum and the cost of higher interest rates inherent to using private capital. Although criticism has been significant, school districts in some states have made considerable use of such mechanisms, with noticeable dependence on lease-rent or lease-purchase of school facilities.

Intermediate Summary

Although all states now acknowledge the impracticality of funding infrastructure needs entirely on the local tax base, several states still provide no aid to school facilities and many others offer only relatively low amounts of aid. Among those states aiding local infrastructure costs, classification of aid schemes is challenging because states do not use comparable language, and the numerous hybrid funding plans are difficult to categorize succinctly. Figure 9.4 (pp. 276–278) provides additional information from the various states about bond programs and state aid for debt service, and Fig. 9.5 (pp. 279–280) offers still a third layer in the form of "other" school infrastructure programs. Taken conjointly, a wide array of aid programs is in place, although again it must be emphasized that almost no states support school infrastructure at the same level seen for general operating aid. As is demonstrated in the next section, the local community remains heavily impacted by infrastructure costs.

How Is the Local Cost Share Funded?

By every measure, the cost of school facilities is truly enormous. In 2006, taxpayers in the 50 states spent more than $25.3 billion on school construction. Of this amount, $13.7 billion was spent on new construction, while $3.3 billion went for additions along with another $8.3 billion for modernization.[19] These figures, however, do not take into account school district debt on construction projects, which the U.S. Department of Education estimated at $11.5 billion for 2002–2003.[20] Although state aid undoubtedly paid some portion of these long-term costs, the vast majority of school districts throughout the nation have had to finance a large share of infrastructure projects using revenue derived from local property taxes. Generally, the local share is paid from some combination of three funding sources: *current revenues, sinking funds,* and *bonded indebtedness.*

Current Revenues

We know from our earlier discussion that local school districts generally must supplement state aid to satisfy their facility needs, and obviously total responsibility for infrastructure costs rests entirely with the local district in no-aid states. Although several methods for raising local monies exist, financing capital needs through current revenues is the oldest. As implied, local revenue is derived on an annual basis from taxes levied during the current year. For example, if a district has an assessed valuation of $500 million and a statutorily permissible tax rate for capital outlay of four mills, the district can generate $2 million in current revenues for facility purposes. Similarly, if a district has a valuation of only $7 million and the same maxi-

(Text continues on page 281.)

---

19 33rd Annual Official Education Construction Report. *American School & University* 30 (New York: Penton Media, May 2007).

20 U.S. Department of Education, National Center for Education Statistics, *Digest of Education Statistics 2002*, Table 156, *http://nces.ed.gov/programs/digest/d05/tables/dt05_156. asp*

Figure 9.4. Bond Programs and State Aid for Debt Service

State	Bonds	Conditions	Debt Limits	State Aid for Debt
Alabama	X	Municipality may issue bonds; districts may issue revenue warrants	None reported	None
Alaska	X	State approval	None reported	Reimburses up to 70%
Arizona	X	Voter-approved for projects that exceed state standards	10% for unified districts	None
Arkansas	X	Voter-approved second lien bonds	30% of assessed valuation (AV)	None
California	X	Voter-approved	None reported	None
Colorado	X	Voter-approved	None	Part of basic program
Connecticut	X	Issued by municipality, not school district	None reported	Limited
Delaware	X	Voter-approved	10% of assessed valuation (AV)	None
Florida	X	Voter-approved	None reported	None
Georgia	X	Voter-approved	10% of assessed valuation (AV)	Yes
Hawaii		Full state funding		
Idaho	X	Voter-approved with super majority	10–20 years	Partial subsidy for interest
Illinois	X	Voter-approved	None reported	10% of principal × grant index
Indiana	X	No approval but subject to remonstration	2%	Flat grant: $40 per average daily attendance (ADA) in grades 1–12
Iowa	X	Voter-approved with 60% majority	5% of assessed valuation (AV); 20 years	None
Kansas	X	Voter-approved	None reported	Equalized grants based on assessed valuation (AV) per pupil
Kentucky	X	Districts sell bonds with state oversight	20 years	Yes

State	Bonds	Conditions	Debt Limits	State Aid for Debt
Louisiana	X	Voter-approved	10–20% of assessed valuation (AV); 40 years	None
Maine	X	Voter-approved	State approval	Yes
Maryland		Only state-issued bonds		
Massachusetts	X	Voter-approved	25% of assessed valuation (AV)	None reported
Michigan	X	Voter-approved	15% of assessed valuation (AV); 30 years	None
Minnesota	X	Voter-approved	15% of market value	Equalized
Mississippi	X	Voter-approved with 60% majority	15% of assessed valuation (AV)	Included in flat grant; $24 per average daily attendance (ADA)
Missouri	X	Voter-approved	15% of tax base; 20 years	None
Montana	X	Voter-approved	45% of assessed valuation (AV)	Yes
Nebraska	X	Voter-approved with 55% majority	None	None
Nevada	X	Voter-approved	15% of assessed valuation (AV)	None
New Hampshire	X	Voter-approved with 60% majority	None reported	None
New Jersey	X	Voter-approved	None reported	Formula considers debt service, district basic aid percentage, eligible costs, and school district fulfillment of maintenance requirements
New Mexico	X	Voter-approved	6% of assessed valuation (AV)	None
New York	X	Voter-approved	None reported	Equalized funding available
North Carolina	X	Voter-approved	None reported	Yes
North Dakota	X	Voter-approved with 60% majority	10% of assessed valuation (AV)	None
Ohio	X	Not reported	None reported	None

(Figure continues on next page.)

State	Bonds	Conditions	Debt Limits	State Aid for Debt
Oklahoma	X	Voter-approved with 60% majority	10% of assessed valuation (AV)	None
Oregon	X	Voter-approved with a 50% majority of 50% of voters	Based on assessed valuation (AV) and school grade level	None
Pennsylvania	X	Voter-approved	No limit	Reimbursement based on approved payment schedule
Rhode Island	X	Not reported	None reported	State share calculated; minimum state funding is 30%
South Carolina	X	Voter-approved	8% of assessed valuation (AV)	None reported
South Dakota	X	Voter-approved	10% of assessed valuation (AV)	None
Tennessee	X	Voter-approved Issued by local municipalities, counties, etc.	None reported	Part of basic state aid
Texas	X	Voter-approved	None reported	Part of instructional facility allotment
Utah	X	Voter-approved	40% of market value	Included in facility funding
Vermont	X	Voter-approved	None reported	Based on guaranteed yield provisions of basic aid formula
Virginia	X	Voter-approved for county schools	None	Lottery allocation & maintenance supplement program
Washington	X	Voter-approved	None reported	
Wisconsin	X	Voter-approved	10% of assessed valuation (AV); 20 years	None*
Wyoming	X	Voter-approved	10% of assessed valuation (AV)	Supplements mill levy if assessed valuation (AV) per average daily membership (ADM) is less than 150% of state average

*Updated by authors of this text, 2007.

Source: Catherine C. Sielke, "Financing School Infrastructure Needs: An Overview Across the 50 States," 40–43.

Figure 9.5. Other School Infrastructure Programs

State	Additional Funding Availability
Alabama	Revenue warrants that do not exceed 80% of pledged revenue
Alaska	None
Arizona	None
Arkansas	State loan program
California	Developer fees
Colorado	Voter-approved mill levies up to 10 mills for 3 years
Connecticut	State loan program
Delaware	May assess a tax rate without referenda for state match requirements
Florida	Up to 2 mill levy without voter approval; voter-approved .005 sales tax
Georgia	Grants; voter approved .001 local option sales tax up to 5 years
Hawaii	None
Idaho	2/3 majority approved tax levies
Illinois	None
Indiana	Leases, rentals
Iowa	County local option sales tax, .005 up to 10 years
Kansas	Additional mill levies with approval of State Board of Tax Appeals
Kentucky	None
Louisiana	None
Maine	State revolving loan fund
Maryland	None
Massachusetts	None
Michigan	State loan fund, sinking funds of 5 mills up to 20 years
Minnesota	State loans
Mississippi	3 mill levy up to 20 years without voter approval; state loan fund
Missouri	Lease purchase up to 20 years
Montana	Building reserves
Nebraska	Voter-approved mill levies

State	Additional Funding Availability
Nevada	Voter-approved mill levies, developer's fees
New Hampshire	None
New Jersey	Lease purchase
New Mexico	None
New York	None
North Carolina	Local option sales tax
North Dakota	Voter-approved building funds up to 20 mills annually
Ohio	None
Oklahoma	Mill levy up to 5 mills annually
Oregon	None
Pennsylvania	Some nonelected debt allowed
Rhode Island	Leases, reserve funds
South Carolina	Children's education endowment fund; funding based on total revenue available, basic aid formula, weighted pupils, and need
South Dakota	None
Tennessee	Lease purchase, capital outlay notes
Texas	Lease purchase
Utah	Revolving loan fund
Vermont	Sinking funds
Virginia	Revolving loan fund; pooled bond issues
Washington	Fund reserves; special levies
West Virginia	None
Wisconsin	State loan fund; sinking funds
Wyoming	None

Source: Catherine C. Sielke, "Financing School Infrastructure Needs: An Overview Across the 50 States," 45–46.

mum tax rate, current revenues for capital projects will raise only $28,000. If in the same example the state were to have no limit on tax rates in local districts, the poorer district would have to levy about 286 mills to generate the same revenue available to the wealthy district.

The benefits and limitations of local financing via current revenues are evident in the illustration. The major advantage is that current revenue is a cash basis method that avoids interest costs incurred if borrowing money for infrastructure projects. Additionally, districts are unlikely to be extravagant if revenue must be on deposit prior to expenditure. At the same time, very serious drawbacks exist. The most important disadvantage results from disparate property wealth among school districts, in that high wealth districts will have access to outstanding school facilities while low wealth districts will not be able to afford equal access.

Few districts are able to effectively use the current revenue or pay-as-you-go method because most local tax bases are far too low to raise enough money to fund all facility needs. In addition, most states limit the maximum millage that can be levied for local infrastructure projects. But even if states allowed unlimited local tax leeway, it would be impractical to try levying the millage needed to raise adequate funds in poorer districts. As a result, the usefulness of current revenues is mostly confined to small projects.

Sinking Funds

Because current revenues are mostly insufficient, sinking funds have been permitted in many states. A sinking fund is like a savings account that accumulates until it is large enough to pay cash for a project. In this scenario, districts are allowed to levy general or special taxes to be placed in a reserve fund for a specified project or for undesignated purposes. Assuming an adequate tax base, sinking funds have the ability to grow rapidly because the money is invested in interest-bearing accounts. For example, a tax levy of $1 million per year invested at 5% interest grows to $5.8 million after only five years.

Sinking funds have advantages for both school districts and taxpayers. The obvious benefit is that it encourages saving for public projects. Additionally, a sinking fund is efficient because interest costs are avoided as no money is borrowed. Finally, a sinking fund is prudent in that districts can engage long-range planning without the haste of caring only about daily survival. Predictably, these benefits are rarely realized for several reasons. First, sinking funds still depend on the wealth of the district—as a result, only wealthier districts generally have additional resources to set aside. Second, inflation will reduce the future value of a sinking fund; even a low inflation rate of 2% reduces the value of $1 to only 67¢ after 20 years. Third, gathering large sums not earmarked for specific projects is inadvisable because voters who originally approved a tax levy might disfavor eventual uses of the sinking fund. Finally, even if sinking funds are earmarked, needs may change by the time enough money is gathered. As a result, relatively few states allow true sinking funds in the modern tax watchdog environment.

Bonded Indebtedness

Because neither current revenues nor sinking funds are feasible solutions to larger infrastructure problems, school districts frequently turn to bonded indebtedness. Bonding is a device by which districts are statutorily permitted to incur long-term debt for the purpose of acquiring fixed assets such as facilities. Although debt is prohibited under cash basis laws for schools' current operations in most states, an exception is regularly made for acquisition of facilities. Methods by which districts may incur bond debt depend entirely on the laws of each state. In most states, school districts are authorized to bond for infrastructure needs, subject only to statutes on referendum and debt limitations. In other states, differences relate primarily to whether districts are fiscally independent or dependent, and on whether the state controls bonding through a central state authority.

In most states, bonding for school facilities is a local affair. Although bonding is a form of borrowing money, it is different from traditional private borrowing in several ways. When individuals or businesses want to borrow money for construction, they typically approach a lending institution to request a mortgage or its commercial equivalent—that is, a debt instrument is devised that uses the purchased property to secure the loan in case of default. In contrast, governmental units do not operate by these same rules. Although bonds create a legal debt, the private paper is replaced by the bond mechanism, which has two key features. The first feature is that bonds are sold at open market and purchased by many investors instead of a traditional lender. The second feature is that public properties purchased through bond sales cannot be foreclosed. Thus a bond sale for school facility purposes creates neither a mortgage nor collateral. Collateral is theoretical in that the full faith and credit of government —that is, the school district or other governmental unit such as the state—is pledged to secure the debt.

Bonding has many benefits. Investors see bonds as attractive investments because the chance of default is low. Investors are further attracted to bonds because the interest paid is generally tax-exempt. Although bond interest rates are generally lower than private market rates, bonds are attractive investments because lower untaxed earnings may still net more income than higher yield investments after taxes—a win-win situation as schools pay less interest and as investors invest safely under favorable tax conditions. The only drawbacks to bonding are, of course, the added cost of interest which is added to the life of each bond issued and the whimsicality of referendum.

The Bonding Process

The process of bonding follows similar steps in all states. Most states require a referendum (bond election) whenever a school district wants to pursue a facility project that exceeds current revenues or cash reserves. A referendum is a request for approval of infrastructure debt by placing the question on the ballot at a general or special election so that voters in the district can approve or reject the proposed project. The purpose of referendum is to assure that voters are willing to pay the extra taxes needed to retire the debt. Although horror stories of bond election failures abound and the poor condition of many schools testifies to voter unwillingness to approve new taxes, the referendum is basic to the democratic process.

When voters approve a bond issue, they are agreeing to higher taxes over time to repay the many investors who emerge as buyers for the bonds. Bonds are like promissory notes in that an investor buys one or more bonds at open sale, often in denominations of $1,000 or $5,000. The investor then expects to be repaid in the form of principal and interest over a set period of time. To amortize the bond schedule, the district levies taxes that are deposited to a special fund from which it makes semiannual or annual bond payments.

When a district decides to initiate a bond sale, a series of steps is involved. Determination of the project is usually the first step. As is discussed later under facility planning, this includes determining needs at school board and community levels and working with architects to describe needs and estimate costs. When the project is envisioned and costs are known, the next step requires the district to decide if it can afford to undertake the project. This step is critical because every state places debt limits on public agencies, including schools. Generally, the debt limitation is expressed as a percentage of the assessed valuation of the school district. For example, if a district were to have an assessed valuation of $500 million with a 10% debt ceiling, total debt in terms of borrowed principal could not exceed $50 million. The third step is to schedule a bond election. State statutes are very specific in these matters. Although the local district usually has little involvement in actually conducting an election, the district typically makes all decisions about election timing and carries sole responsibility for any campaigning to enhance the likelihood of voters approving the bond issue. If the referendum fails, the district must regroup to determine cause and decide whether to resubmit the question to voters. Generally, any new election is accompanied by escalated public relations and may include a scaled-down project at lesser cost. If the referendum is successful, the district can proceed to the fourth step of preparing the bond sale. Specialized legal counsel is required because of the complexity of bond laws, and financial counsel is required because the bond market is complex and competitive. When counsel have prepared for the bond issue, an official advertisement is issued to investors, usually through widely read financial publications and by bond prospectus.

Although the bonding process is normally completed by following these four steps, the infrastructure project is only beginning. The planned work must be performed, and the project actually extends beyond construction completion and first occupancy because the district has committed to long-term debt repayment. Obviously this requires revisiting the financial plan on an annual basis, levying taxes and depositing proceeds into special debt service funds in preparation for disbursement, and maintaining and protecting the new physical assets. As seen in earlier chapters on budgeting, accounting and taxation, all these processes are important to the successful operation of a school district. Because so much money is at stake, facilities and bonding are areas of special care because a district's infrastructure makes it possible to carry out the instructional mission of schools.

INFRASTRUCTURE PLANNING
AND FACILITY MAINTENANCE

Until now our discussion has centered on how schools raise money for infrastructure projects, primarily from the perspective of building new facilities or major remodeling and renovation or acquisition and integration of technology—projects requiring large sums of money. Although big projects can involve current revenues either in the form of local dollars or state aid, there are two other facets to budgeting for infrastructure that must be discussed—that is, facility planning, and maintenance and operations. Although complementary to all infrastructure issues, a separate examination of these topics is useful in making some additional points.

What Is the Role of Infrastructure Planning?

Although school districts engage long-range planning in many areas, in some ways infrastructure planning predicts the success or failure of all other plans. An excellent curriculum built on the latest technology will be weakened if facilities are poorly designed or maintained; likewise, the most highly skilled teachers will be frustrated if classrooms are cramped or unsuited to the content to be taught. For example, old buildings with inadequate electrical service often cannot support the technology expected in today's classrooms and media centers. Similarly, old buildings with poor ventilation systems are dangerous places for chemistry programs. Even new buildings may be problematic if overcrowded or built with insufficient attention to the learning environment. Although sparkling facilities will not overcome bad teaching, planning for infrastructure is more than just architectural design—it is the total integration of space with the instructional and support functions of a modern school system.

The value of infrastructure planning has long been recognized. Wise leaders know that poor planning is costly through wasted money, lack of long-range flexibility, and underuse of facilities. As a result, good planning requires organization to oversee all aspects of facility planning and operations. Larger districts often hire an assistant superintendent who is charged with all facility-related tasks. Very often this person has subordinates who perform more specialized functions. In smaller districts, these duties may fall to the superintendent or business manager, with greater reliance on outsourcing for needed services. Although district size may drive how the school system organizes its planning activities, all districts need a staff person who is knowledgeable about both education and facility management.

In larger districts, an office of facility planning may be established. This office has as its major task the ongoing study and analysis of facility needs according to five goals. The first goal is to prepare and maintain a comprehensive analysis of all facilities in the district. The second goal is to assure a well-designed physical environment to enhance teaching and learning. The third goal is to assure that all facilities remain useful over the life of each building because outmoded facilities hurt teaching and learning and are often very costly to maintain. The fourth goal is to evaluate facilities for future educational programs in ways that assist decisions to reconstruct or retire buildings. The fifth goal is to preserve maximum flexibility in all buildings so that future generations are served. Plant planning should thus reflect careful thought about the following:

- School-age population to be served;
- Location and transportation of school-age population;
- Programmatic offerings of the district and each school;
- Overall long-range facility needs of the district;
- Fiscal ability of taxpayers in the district;
- Overall organizational structure of the school system; and
- Overall economic and demographic future of the district.

These areas make up planning for infrastructure—that is, demographic planning, capital program planning, facility planning, educational program planning, architectural review, site selection and acquisition, and construction.[21] These factors deserve a brief discussion because they are the elements districts use to justify many decisions about the total educational program.

Demographic Planning

One of the biggest mistakes in planning for infrastructure is failure to adequately account for the demographics of the school district. For example, even the best facilities would be compromised if schools were inconvenient to the location of children. Demographic planning is thus the study of a district's profile, including social, economic, and population issues. Demographics drive infrastructure planning because the goal is to serve the needs of the school community.

Demographic planning varies greatly based on the unique characteristics of each school district. For example, districts with growing populations must anticipate housing patterns so that land can be bought ahead of rising market trends. Other districts engage in demographic planning to predict future facility needs in relation to stable or declining enrollments. A major task of demographic planning is to conduct accurate facility surveys that research the district's profile, analyze findings and propose alternative solutions, and recommend a plan of action. A comprehensive educational survey describes the community's characteristics and educational needs, determines pupil population characteristics, describes the educational program, appraises existing facilities in relation to needs, develops a master plan, assesses resources, and makes recommendations. Because it is comprehensive, the survey forms the basis for careful long-range infrastructure planning.

Description of community characteristics and educational needs is the starting point. The survey should inquire into population characteristics, density, and changes over time. It should examine changes in land use, including zoning and changes that have occurred because of population trends. Analysis should examine traffic and assess development and land use under growth conditions to predict likely locations for new schools as well as continued viability of existing facilities. Socioeconomic

---

21 R. Craig Wood, David C. Thompson, and Lawrence O. Picus, *Principles of School Business Management,* 4th ed. (Reston, VA: ASBO, 2008).

status must be studied, in that economics may limit choices. Inversely, rapid population growth in professional communities may result in constant upward mobility requiring new state-of-the-art schools. Other community characteristics should be examined, including vocational opportunities, parental expectations, and public attitudes toward schools and taxes.

The critical element in demographic planning, however, is enrollment projection because quality space must be provided for all students. As discussed in Chapter 5, population projections entail seeing community trends, birth rates, historic and present enrollments, and calculating retention in the district and each attendance center. The most common enrollment projection tools include cohort survival and trend line analysis, although large districts may use other methods such as population mapping or saturation analysis to estimate the effect of housing developments. Obviously, accurate data are critical to long-range infrastructure planning, as well as many other aspects of budgeting.

Capital Program Planning

A second activity, often known as capital program planning, is closely related to demographic analysis. Capital program planning is the anticipation of a district's capital needs in relation to its demographic profile. The purpose is to analyze the district's financial characteristics and status to estimate both the limitations and ability of the district to pay for current and future infrastructure needs. Capital program planning usually involves bonding, sometimes aided by federal impact funds or state aids.

The normal result of capital program planning is creation of a capital improvement plan (CIP) that projects all capital needs for the future, usually over a period of five to 20 years. The CIP prioritizes projects, primarily because resources are seldom sufficient to address all needs at one time, especially if current revenues are expected to provide a significant part of the money. For example, roof replacement on all buildings more than ten years old might be the highest priority, with the CIP first targeting buildings with immediate needs. Another example might find the district trying to replace computers in all classrooms according to a priority schedule. Obviously, more aggressive CIPs can occur if bonding is used; for instance, a district might replace all roofs and HVAC (heating, ventilation, air conditioning) systems in a single bond issue, or it might retrofit all buildings with wireless technology to support new school-based technology centers that were built with bond money under the long-range infrastructure plan. When renovation, retrofitting, new construction, or major equipment purchases are contemplated, the CIP must provide an analysis of revenues over the full period of debt retirement. A feature of a CIP is that its adoption is often considered authorization to proceed with projects. Finally, the CIP should be reviewed and updated as projects are completed and as needs and financial conditions change.

Facility Planning and Programming

The nature of planning for infrastructure does not allow totally discrete operations in a capital improvement plan. For example, although the sequence calls first for establishing the population base to determine facility needs, it is necessary to overlap demographic planning with capital program planning. Likewise, to envision facilities and educational programs requires knowledge of the financial options and demographic needs of a district. Thus facility planning and programming makes up another task for the district's facilities office, along with other activities described in this section.

The purpose of facility planning and programming is to identify the desires and constraints under which any educational facility will have to function. Generally this activity involves consideration of the goals and objectives of the district and each individual school, and it also usually defines instructional and organizational plans. Many constituencies should be involved in facility planning and programming, including the community and staff along with professional planners such as architects and educational consultants. Although facility programming and planning is complex, the overall goals should include the following:

- Is the facility structurally sound?
- Is it healthful and safe?
- Is it efficient to operate?
- Does it support the program?
- Is it attractive and comfortable?
- Is its location convenient for the users?
- Is its space optimally used?
- Is it the right size?
- Can it be modified?

Answers to these questions, together with demographic and capital program data, are the basis of the CIP. If all answers are affirmative, the district should keep its course by maintaining its investment and regularly reviewing the CIP. If, on the other hand, answers are negative, the district must undertake corrections.

Architectural Planning

Districts that have identified demographic, capital, and programmatic needs must recognize when they have reached the limits of district staff expertise, in that all modern facility projects require professional architectural planning. This has become especially true as concerns about health, safety, and accessibility have surfaced in both litigation and legislation. Consequently, architectural planning represents a fourth activity in school infrastructure planning.

Although architects or engineers must design new or reconstructed schools, it is less well known that many states require architectural services when an educational facility is modified. For example, adding an elevator can invoke other codes on fire protection, electrical service, and other laws that force the entire facility to be brought up to the most current building codes. Similarly, even the removal or addition of an interior wall may require an entire facility to be made fully accessible under the *Americans with Disabilities Act* (ADA). The point is that very few projects can be done in-house or by phoning a local construction company due to the modern complexity of local, state, and federal regulations.

Selection of an architect is a critical element of facility planning. Most districts use the services of one architect for smaller jobs, but engage in design competition if larger projects are involved. Remodeling jobs, like a new HVAC system or divider walls to reshape interior spaces, are sometimes noncompetitive. Big projects such as renovation, expansion, or new school buildings typically require competition. Because competition is complex and costly, the process is usually reduced to asking architects to submit portfolios on their experience, qualifications, previous examples of similar projects, and rough cost estimates. The board, administrative staff, and consultants make a judgment based on such items as experience of the firm, budget, and overall reputation. As emphasized in earlier chapters, care must be taken to follow all statutory requirements in awarding contracts, including contracts for professional services.

Construction Planning

The value of good architectural services is evident in two critical aspects of facility planning. The first aspect involves planning the project and working to develop project specifications. The role of architects is to work within the physical and fiscal realities of the district and to work with staff to be sure the facility will function well. The second aspect involves actual oversight of the project through completion. These two features are part of the architect's overall responsibility in construction planning, and it should be apparent that the legal liability and technical competence involved in these tasks make architectural services an absolute necessity.

Construction planning thus represents a fifth task in infrastructure planning by joining the services of architects, educational consultants, and school staffs to design a facility project. Because architects are not educators, districts need the services of a consultant to create educational specifications that communicate the district's vision to the architect. Educational specifications are first stated in generalities by local staff and communicated to the consultant. The consultant reviews the statements and examines existing facilities. Depending on the nature and size of the project, the consultant may work with a committee to define needs and expectations. The goal is for the consultant to use the district's broad vision to create a highly specific document that leads the architect to develop an appropriate design. For example, the educational specifications define the school program by classroom and by instructional facility, including requirements for all special areas (e.g., media center, cafeteria, auditorium, physical education, vocational facilities, etc.). The importance of these activities is underscored by the Council for Educational Facility Planners International (CEFPI), which has described educational specifications as the blueprint for the future.

If new construction is required, activities may result in preliminary designs and drawings presented to the school board. Once preliminary plans are approved, actual working drawings and specifications are developed. Plans must be examined to ensure that the design is integrated with curricular and instructional goals, and the facility should embrace other needs of the larger community. Input from instructional leaders is essential during the design phase to avoid inefficiency and waste.

When the design is complete, actual physical improvements begin. The major task of schools during the work phase is to be certain that the district keeps close contact with the project. One important reason is that lack of supervision over the project could result in legal problems if it is later found that the district should have kept itself better informed of any problems. A second reason is that the district must state in writing any concerns or changes to the project. A third reason is that payments for work will be made during the construction phase, and the district must be satisfied before any funds are released.

The work phase requires scheduled payments from the district's cash reserves or from bond proceeds. These payments satisfy material and labor claims. Architectural fees are usually a percentage of the project; in contrast, contractor fees are set by competitive bidding. When the project is finished, a percentage is typically held back pending final acceptance and proof that bills, payrolls, and mechanics' liens by all contractors, subcontractors, and vendors have been satisfied. Additionally, the board's attorney must assure that the district will have clear title.

The role of planning for infrastructure is broad and includes demographic plans, capital program plans, educational program plans, and architectural and construction plans, all of which apply to both alteration and expansion of facilities and to new construction. All infrastructure projects must be financed by legally permissible methods using cash or debt, and expert counsel ranging from legal and financial services to architectural and construction services must be used. The role of the district is to acquire and coordinate these services—a role that demands sound educational and fiscal planning.

What Is the Role and Nature of Maintenance and Operations?

We have stressed the value of planning because the cost of physical infrastructure and the dependence of educational programs on good facilities are enormous. As we noted earlier, a fine educational program is damaged by poor school facilities. As a result, a sound program of maintenance and operations (M&O) is critical in order to keep buildings, equipment, and grounds in good condition and ready for use.

Organizing for M&O

The maintenance and operations function is often organized under a central office administrator with line authority over all physical plant activities and related staff. Obviously, actual organizational structure depends on district size, with larger districts employing hundreds of plant service workers. A medium-size school district might resemble the organizational chart in Fig. 9.6 (p. 290) where both diversification of work and efficiency of scale are evident. In Fig. 9.6, final responsibility rests with the school board, which delegates to the superintendent, who delegates to a general director (the point at which Fig. 9.6 begins). As a result, plant planning and operations and maintenance are joined, with a key person coordinating their performance.

Figure 9.6 develops a central maintenance division that provides services to all schools in the district. These services are often provided on an in-house basis if the district has decided it is more cost-efficient to employ permanent staff with specific skills, rather than to outsource these functions to private firms. Figure 9.6 illustrates a school district of approximately 16,000 students and provides an example wherein the district has decided that it has enough work to justify the cost of operating its own

Figure 9.6. Sample Facilities Organizational Chart

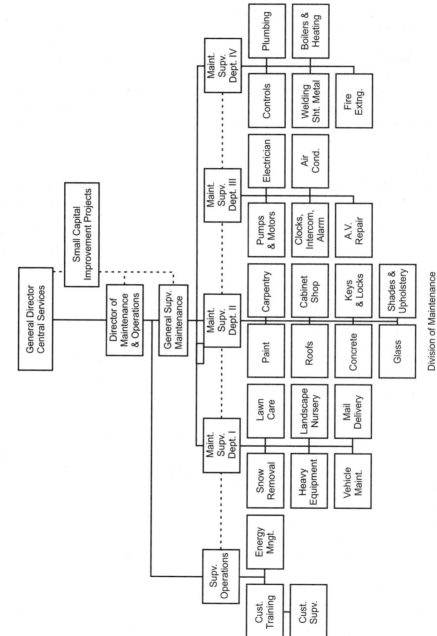

maintenance division to perform many specialized tasks. The plan appoints an assistant superintendent for plant planning to oversee a director of plant services, who oversees a director of maintenance and operations, a general supervisor of maintenance, and so on. Obviously, as district size decreases, the chart becomes organizationally simpler, even though the same tasks still need to be performed.

Organizing for maintenance and operations demands assessing facility needs on the basis of cleaning, repairing, and replacing the district's capital investments. The overarching organizational task therefore includes determining maintenance and operations needs, prioritizing into short-term and long-term plans, and staffing competent and efficient M&O programs. Organizing for these tasks forms the basis of determining maintenance needs and conducting the many facility operations of a modern school district.

Determining Maintenance Needs

As a rule, maintenance of old and new buildings requires skilled evaluation of all component systems. Component systems include footings, foundations, and basements; interior and exterior walls; roofs and flashings; doors, windows, and frames; floors and ceilings; mechanical systems; electrical systems; aesthetics, equipment, and furniture; grounds; and energy conservation. This list points out the need for skilled employees and specialized contracted maintenance. Foundations, footings, and basements should be regularly inspected by staff for visible problems, and regular evaluation by engineers or architects should be scheduled. Walls and roofs should be inspected regularly, with repairs like sealing cosmetic cracks and light masonry repointing done in-house. Mechanical and electrical systems should be inspected, with problems reported promptly. Painting, refastening trim, cleaning traps, replacing washers in valves, adjusting doors and windows, replacing shades and lighting, and so on can be done in-house. A maintenance plan should include energy conservation, including a formal energy audit and energy-saving steps.

The goal of determining maintenance needs is to identify concerns and to prevent new problems. Once needs are known, the district must schedule and fund repair or replacement. As a general rule, districts should spend a minimum 4% to 6% of the general operating budget for maintenance. Unfortunately, much of the facility dilemma today results from failure to follow a program of preventive maintenance. Another contributor is the failure of society to provide sufficient money to protect the enormous investment represented by education's infrastructure. It is a simple fact that no amount of excellent facility operations can overcome the failure to engage in maintenance of basic systems.

Conducting Facility Operations

Although long-term maintenance is key to the financial and instructional health of schools, smooth day-to-day operation of facilities is equally important to the safety and welfare of everyone at school. As we said at the outset of this chapter, there are data showing that the physical condition of facilities has an impact on learning—dirty or badly maintained schools send a message that education is not valued. In other words, quality of the educational program *is* judged by the shine on the floor, and students attending well-maintained schools feel pride. Routine maintenance is essential, and the contribution of polished floors to student achievement should not be devalued.

The maintenance function comprises the tasks of keeping a school open for use. As a rule, the most important skill is organization. Maintenance staff must be organized for efficiency within the limits of cost, labor, and time. Every aspect of maintenance must be organized by a timetable, so that staff know what must be done. Generally, tasks can be broken down into routines of vacuuming, sweeping, mopping, dusting, cleaning glass, and emptying trash; steam-cleaning, buffing, or waxing floors; cleaning whiteboards or chalkboards; cleaning halls, including walls, water fountains, and waste containers; and noting damage needing repair. Daily activities include both routine tasks and repairs, although component system evaluation by staff can occur on a monthly or quarterly basis. Minor repairs like fixing trim or changing light bulbs can be scheduled on an as-needed basis, while other tasks, such as painting, should be done during nonschool times. Daily tasks should be performed on staggered schedules using a square-foot–acreage formula or by enrollment size of the school. Various formulas for custodial tasks exist, such as the following:

Acreage [1 person per 10-acre site] plus

Square feet [1 person per 15,000 sf of building]

or

Enrollment: [1 person per ~275 elementary students]

[1 person per ~200 secondary students]

Although many additional activities not described here are needed to ensure a clean, safe, and healthful school, no aspect is more important than proper initial and ongoing training for custodial and maintenance staff. Training may result in overall improvements including higher standards of service, lower employee costs stemming from greater efficiencies, less waste, fewer hazards, less deterioration of school plant and equipment, more flexibility in shifting employees among buildings, and greater respect for custodial workers on the part of the public. Facility operations and maintenance are critical to the good work of schools and depend on highly competent staff to create the best possible conditions for equal educational opportunity.

The Role of the School Leader in Maintenance and Operations

The research described in this chapter points to the critical importance of physical environments in schools. Research provides strong evidence that educational leaders must ensure that facilities and grounds are well-maintained, as their condition plays an important part in students' academic success. Site-level school leaders are ultimately responsible for the appearance and condition of their schools; as a consequence, they should become familiar with district maintenance and operations policies and procedures because it is their duty to ensure that the total school environment is conducive to student learning.[22]

Depending on school district size and the presence or absence of strong collective bargaining agreements, the responsibilities of a school leader for maintenance and operations can vary greatly. In smaller districts, they may be directly involved in hiring, supervising, and evaluating maintenance staffs. In larger school districts where custodial staffs are more likely to be covered by a collective bargaining agreement, hiring, supervision, and evaluation may be centralized. Alternatively, in larger school systems custodial and maintenance operations may be outsourced to a private contractor. The role of the school leader varies greatly in these circumstances, so that school leaders need to become very familiar with the content of collectively bargained contracts and any other outsource agreements. By doing so, the school leader will avoid many problems and will be better prepared to engage all staff—including teachers—in maintenance and repair issues. Only when all stakeholders are actively involved will it become ingrained that the school's physical condition is an important factor in the learning environment.

Although the size and cost and complexity of maintenance and operations—indeed, the entirety of infrastructure—causes primary responsibility to be located in the school district's central office, the opportunity to enhance the safety and security of school facilities and grounds through sound maintenance and operations occurs first at each school site. Some measures are straightforward—for example, requesting and maintaining sufficient exterior lighting of buildings, parking lots, and other areas including athletic fields is an effective low-cost deterrent to crime. Other commonsense maintenance issues fall to school site leaders such as ensuring that exterior and interior door locks are in good working order and cannot be easily bypassed. Likewise, if the school's grounds have shrubbery near doors and windows, the school leader should insist on pruning in order to prevent their use as cover by vandals and criminals. Likewise, school leaders should insist on repair of cracked or uneven sidewalks and parking lot potholes that place students and adults at risk of injury. Similarly, prompt removal of graffiti discourages gang activity and vandalism. In other words, risk management and maintenance/operations are districtwide and schoolwide obligations, and close attention to commonsense issues can greatly reduce barriers to the effectiveness and enjoyment of the learning environment.[23]

---

22 See Faith E. Crampton, David C. Thompson, and Randall S. Vesely, "The Forgotten Side of School Finance Equity: The Role of School Infrastructure Funding in Student Success," *NASSP Bulletin* 88 (September 2004): 29–56.

23 Some school districts have proactive policies in place for use by school site leaders. Additional assessment tools are available; see, e.g., Tod Schneider, Hill Walker, and Jeffrey Sprague, *Safe School Design: A Handbook for Educational Leaders* (Eugene, OR: ERIC Clearinghouse on Educational Management, College of Education, University of Oregon, 2000), 40-41.

WRAP-UP

Planning for infrastructure is a highly complex operation. But as we noted at the outset of this chapter, it is false economy to underspend for facilities. Unfortunately, infrastructure neglect now spans generations, and it is reality that the age of cheap construction and high maintenance will continue to plague schools because the nation has a long history of underinvesting in school infrastructure. But as we also said early in this chapter, facilities are the single largest investment school districts make at any one time—an investment that must be protected to provide excellence and equality for children.

pointcounterpoint

Point

With research telling us that school infrastructure plays a critical role in students' academic success, states have a responsibility to ensure that all children attend safe, clean, and modern schools. As such, states must take a lead role in funding school infrastructure to compensate for inequities in local fiscal capacity.

Counterpoint

From the beginning of the common school movement, construction and maintenance of school facilities has been a local responsibility. The tradition of local control has allowed school districts to decide for themselves the kinds of facilities they want. Because greater state funding almost always leads to more state control, states should not take a lead funding role in order to respect local autonomy.

Questions

♦ With which of these viewpoints are you most in agreement? Why?

♦ In your estimation, would your school district benefit from a larger or smaller state role in funding school infrastructure than is currently state law? How so and why?

CASE STUDY

As the newly hired vice principal at a PreK–8 school, you were brimming with enthusiasm at the thought of working closely with colleagues, parents, and students. You were especially eager to impress the principal, who had already earned your esteem by informing you that she saw you as an equal partner in leading the school, even though this was your first formal administrative position. She had indicated she wanted you to become involved immediately and that one of your many responsibilities was oversight of the day-to-day operations of the school, including maintenance and grounds. You knew this was an important role because you had already noticed the cleanliness and attractiveness of the school and because the principal had repeatedly emphasized that the appearance and condition of the building were symbolically important to staff and students and to this community. She had also noted that this was accomplished on a very limited budget. The principal had then introduced you to the head custodian, who had been with the school 20 years. When the principal left the two of you to get acquainted, the head custodian's pleasant demeanor immediately vanished. Wasting no time, he curtly informed you that he obviously knew his job well and that he would not welcome any interference in his maintenance of the building and grounds. You had thanked him for his candor and assured him that you wanted to work cooperatively, but inwardly you had a sinking feeling.

At the initial all-school meeting, the principal introduced you to the faculty and mentioned that one of your responsibilities was ensuring the smooth daily operation of the school. She encouraged faculty and staff to come to you with any maintenance or repair issues. The next day was the first day of classes, and early that morning three veteran teachers marched into your office to angrily report that their classroom windows would not open and that it would be impossible to teach or learn as the temperature was predicted to be very hot that day. One teacher added that they had completed work orders to fix the windows last spring. Soon thereafter, a teaching assistant appeared in your doorway to report that a student restroom toilet was overflowing and that water and waste were seeping into the hallway. In character with your emerging day, the assistant added that this particular toilet had overflowed several times last year. At exactly that point, a distraught parent stormed into your office to complain that her asthmatic daughter had been once again been placed in one of the portable classrooms and had had an attack a few minutes ago. As she ended her story, she emphasized that she had made numerous complaints last year about how something was triggering her child's asthma and had requested that her daughter not be asked to travel between buildings—but, as she put it, her request obviously had been ignored.

Faced with multiple problems, you immediately contacted the head custodian and outlined the problems. "We'll get on them," he responded crisply, "but you'll need to pay overtime for my staff and myself. We can't attend to emergencies and get our regular work done too."

Below is a set of questions. As you respond, consider your learning in this chapter and apply your knowledge to the situation:

Questions

♦ How will you address the head custodian's request for overtime? Explain your rationale.

♦ In hindsight, is there anything you could have done prior to the first day of school to prevent these problems (or similar ones) from occurring?

♦ As you look toward the rest of the school year, how will you ensure the smooth day-to-day operations of the school?

FOLLOW-UP ACTIVITIES

♦ Identify how school infrastructure is financed in your state. This may include obtaining state department documents or examining relevant statutes. If your state uses an aid formula to assist in debt service, determine the type of aid, the size of the allocation, how districts qualify for aid, and the impact of the formula on your district. If your state does not provide aid to facilities, determine whether any surrounding states do.

♦ Interview your director of facility planning (or the central office administrator with this responsibility) to determine how current infrastructure projects are funded in your school district. Identify how much debt your district currently carries for school infrastructure, the nature of the debt, and the amortization schedule.

♦ Obtain a copy of your district's capital improvement plan (CIP). Interview your director of facility planning to determine how planning for school infrastructure occurs in your district. Ask how your district assesses its short, intermediate, and long-term needs. Determine the total cost of the CIP and its impact on local taxes.

♦ Interview the appropriate central office person with regard to daily and scheduled maintenance and operations. Learn how these functions are organized at the district level and the amount and percentage of the school district's annual operating budget devoted to M&O. Ask about the role of site-based leaders, like principals, in school maintenance and operations.

WEB RESOURCES

American Society of Civil Engineers, www.asce.org/asce.cfm
Association of School Business Officials International, www.asbointl.org
Clearinghouse on Educational Policy and Management, www.cepm.uoregon.edu
Council of Educational Facilities Planners International, www.cefpi.org
National ACCESS Network (Litigation), www.schoolfunding.info
National Business Officers Association, www.nboa.net
National Center for Education Statistics, www.nces.ed.gov
National Clearinghouse for Educational Facilities, www.ncef.org
National School Boards Association, www.nsba.org
U.S. Department of Education, www.ed.gov

RECOMMENDED READINGS

Chan, Tak Cheung, and Michael D. Richardson. *Ins and Outs of School Facility Management: More than bricks and mortar.* Reston, VA: ASBO, 2005.

Council of Educational Facilities Planners International. *Schools as Centers of Community.* Scottsdale, AZ: Author, 2003.

Council of Educational Facilities Planners International. *Creating Connections: CEFPI Guide for Educational Facility Planning.* Scottsdale, AZ: Author, 2004.

Council of Educational Facilities Planners International. *Schools as Successful Communities: An Element of Smart Growth.* Scottsdale, AZ: Author, 2004.

Crampton, Faith E. "State School Finance Legislation: A 50-State Overview and Analysis." *Journal of Education Finance* 32 (2007):470–87.

Crampton, Faith E., and Terry N. Whitney. *Principles of a Sound State School Finance System.* A monograph of the Education Partners Project, Foundation for State Legislatures. Denver, CO: National Conference of State Legislatures, 1996.

Earthman, Glen I. *Planning Educational Facilities for the Next Century.* Reston, VA: ASBO, 2000.

Ray, John R., Walter G. Hack, and I. Carl. Candoli. *School Business Administration: A Planning Approach.* 8th ed. Boston: Allyn & Bacon, 2005.

Smith, Timothy, Rebecca Porch, Elizabeth Farris, and William Fowler. *Effects of Energy Needs and Expenditures on U.S. Public Schools.* Washington, DC: U.S. Department of Education, National Center for Education Statistics, 2003.

Strickland, Jessie Shields, and T.C. Chan. "Curbside Critique: A Technique to Maintain a Positive School Yard Image. *School Business Affairs* 68 (May 2002):24–7.

Szuba, T., and R. Young. *Planning Guide for Maintaining School Facilities.* Washington, DC: School Facilities Maintenance Task Force, National Center for Education Statistics, U.S. Department of Education, 2003.

Wood, R. Craig, David C. Thompson, and Lawrence O. Picus. *Principles of School Business Management.* 3rd ed. Reston, VA: ASBO, 2008.

BUDGETING FOR TRANSPORTATION AND FOOD SERVICE

THE CHALLENGE

Every day approximately 475,000 yellow school buses provide transportation services throughout the nation, transporting about 25 million school-children to and from school and amounting to more than 50 million student trips daily—a number that does not include an additional estimated five million daily roundtrips for extracurricular activities! The net sum results in an annual total of 4.3 billion road miles traveled each year. Similarly, vast participation numbers are generated for school food service operations, as annually over five million school lunches are served along with nearly 1.7 million school breakfasts.

Compiled from School Transportation News
and USDA Food and Nutrition Service
Program Data (2007)

CHAPTER DRIVERS

At the close of this chapter, you will have reflected upon these questions:

♦ What are the definition, role, and scope of auxiliary services?

♦ What are the origins and purposes of transportation systems?

♦ How is school transportation funded?

♦ How does the law relate to transportation funding?

♦ What other school transportation issues are relevant to budgeting?

♦ What are the origins and purposes of food service systems?

♦ How is food service funded?

♦ What other food service issues are relevant to budgeting?

SETTING THE STAGE

As we draw closer to the end of our study of how public schools are funded, we should devote time to examining the area of auxiliary support services. We have at least two goals. The first goal stems from a belief on our part that there is a tendency in society to see the mission and work of schools as almost entirely instructional, which then leads to other areas of school district operations being undervalued when, in fact, they should be highly prized for their role in providing equal educational opportunity. Our second goal follows closely, in that a book examining the many aspects of schools and money would be incomplete if it failed to address transportation and food services because schools would be very negatively impacted absent these essential operations. Our belief about such matters is simple but unshakable: We believe every child has a right to an equal education without regard for socioeconomic status, and that every child should be able to get to school without hardship and should be able to attend classes free of hunger. In sum, it is our belief that equal opportunity is mocked when schools are physically inaccessible or when children are underfed—a belief arguing that all stakeholders in public schools should be very concerned with organizing and operating efficient systems for transporting and feeding children.

As in earlier chapters, we open our discussion by defining the role and scope of auxiliary support services. Our interest then turns to the origins and purposes of transportation systems, along with a discussion of the intersection of law with the transportation function. We round out the transportation section with an examination of how transportation is funded in the 50 states, concluding with a brief consideration of other relevant transportation issues, such as bus purchasing, bus maintenance and safety, and so on. In similar fashion, we turn next to food service systems, examining the issues and funding methods used throughout the nation. Of importance to this discussion is consideration for the organization and fiscal management of food services, inasmuch as food service—unlike most school district operations—is initially viewed as a revenue-generating enterprise, but complicated by also having serious educational and ethical implications attaching to equal opportunity. In sum, then, our discussion in this chapter considers a key element of a total educational experience by exploring and appreciating the role of auxiliary support services in the teaching and learning mission of schools.

The Role of Auxiliary Services

Although auxiliary services can be more broadly defined, we use the term here to refer to selected noninstructional support services, usually funded under segregated fund accounting systems. This definition typically limits auxiliary services to the areas of pupil transportation and school food services. These two auxiliary operations are large and complex regardless of school district size, as urban districts use many buses to transport thousands of pupils over relatively short distances and as rural districts may operate many buses in order to traverse countless open and sparsely populated miles. Actual operating costs may be proportionally similar, as large and small school systems alike face issues of staffing, bus safety, vehicle maintenance and replacement, liability insurance, and so on. Similarly, food service operations in both rural and urban school districts employ many staff, as urban schools hire hundreds of food service workers and as rural districts also employ large staffs relative to lower numbers of students and small school sites. Transportation costs in 2003 reached $16.0 billion nationally, a sum just slightly greater than the $14.6 billion spent for food service.[1] Under these complex conditions, it is clear that transportation has become a major cost center for schools as issues of liability, safety, and equal access have arisen—a scenario closely replicated by food service, which has become its own major cost consideration as a result of wide-ranging services that include lunch, breakfast, and after-school snack programs, free and reduced price meals for economically disadvantaged children, commodity support programs that aid schools and bolster agricultural markets, federal and state subsidies meant to make school meals more affordable, and many other aspects of improving learning through health and nutrition.

The role of auxiliary services is thus great and demands efficient organization and close management because these essential noninstructional support services contribute meaningfully to the social and educational mission of schools.

THE TRANSPORTATION FUNCTION

There is no doubt that pupil transportation is one of the most visible services provided by school systems today. Bright yellow school buses arrive in front of the homes of more than half of all schoolchildren in the United States each morning, and the bus is often the last school contact of the day. The transportation function is even larger, however, ferrying students on field trips and to athletic and academic events, and assisting other services such as special education so that recent data indicate an approximate total 475,000 school buses traveling over 4.3 billion miles per year.[2] With an average annual expenditure of $520 per regular education child and another average $2,400 per special needs child, school transportation is indeed a major cost factor in school district budgets. But like other arguments posited in this textbook (e.g., the importance of shiny floors), schools are viewed more favorably when the transportation function operates smoothly. But when buses are late or when other problems arise, everything about schools seems suspect. As a consequence, the transportation system is one of the most critical and visible noninstructional activities of any school system.

What Are the Origins and Purpose?

Widespread transporting of students to and from school has largely developed as a result of school district consolidation dating from the early days of the twentieth century. Although assumed to have arisen as a result of the invention of motor vehicles, school transportation and state financial support actually have been in existence since 1869, when Massachusetts became the first state to spend public funds for pupil

---

1   U.S. Department of Education, National Center for Education Statistics. *Digest of Education Statistics 2005* (Washington, DC: Author, 2006), 183.

2   *School Transportation News.* (Updated February 2007). *http://www.stnonline.com.*

transportation. While the Massachusetts law was the first of its kind, pupil transportation has had no choice but to grow rapidly as compulsory attendance laws, school district consolidation, and the advent of motor vehicles have dramatically altered society. Not surprisingly, consolidation alone has led to huge change, as between 1917 and 1922 nearly 20,000 small schools disappeared and 4,500 one-room schools were closed every year until 1960.

Unlike some aspects of fiscal support for schools, from the earliest days the American public has seemed willing to spend for transporting students. Support was likely a result of a common recognition that what individuals could do only poorly could be done far more efficiently by an entire community. A spurring factor was geographic isolation in a largely agricultural nation, a demographic that persisted until only a short time ago. In recent years, however, public school transportation has taken on even more importance because of a host of court rulings on issues affecting equal educational opportunity, including questions about transporting private school pupils and the special needs of disabled students. A major transportation role has additionally arisen from court-ordered desegregation plans involving mandatory busing, which for many years added to the size and challenges of school transportation systems. Even more recently, charter schools and flexible-year attendance plans have added to the complexity of pupil transportation services. With the sheer magnitude of transportation systems added to ever-burgeoning regulation and rising insurance costs, the transportation function has experienced enormous change in size, complexity, and importance since its humble origins.

While the purpose of pupil transportation is simple, its full application is more complex. As we stated earlier, in our view no student has equal educational opportunity if schooling is inaccessible as a consequence of inadequate transportation, and states and local districts have long worked to make schools available to students who live beyond reasonable distances. Providing such service, however, has evolved into a multibillion dollar industry ranging from employment for bus drivers to insurance against a myriad set of risks. Greatly complicating these costs are issues of efficiency and accountability—concepts that are themselves made more complicated by competing public goals. For example, parents often have one set of expectations for a transportation system while the state and school district might operate from a different set of purposes. Similarly, pupil transportation may require new facilities, and movement of populations in a community may create new transportation demands. Likewise, racial integration may require new school attendance boundaries and so on—concepts that are sometimes in conflict over both limited resources and differences of opinion. Additionally each state, as well as each school district, has unique needs that may further feed the complexity of transportation designs. For instance, no two states or school districts are identical on variables such as population density, number of pupils to be transported, topography, road conditions, and length of routes affecting the size of buses placed on routes. To make such matters even more difficult, there are many other decisions that fall to the local level, such as whether a school district should operate its own bus system or outsource the transportation function to private for-profit companies. And local decisions are even affected by state-aid formulas, making transportation a very complex function—at least in contrast to its basic intent.

Although the origins of school transportation are traceable to a simple concept, implementation is so complex that districts have had to create extensive transportation organizations. The result is often a decision to devote a salary line to a transportation director who is charged with setting and carrying out bus management policies, establishing controls, arranging training programs, and coordinating maintenance services. Often the transportation director also has responsibility for planning bus routes and preparing regular and special route schedules for students and transportation staff.

The job of director of transportation services requires a range of talents and specific skills. The relevant knowledge base includes ability to efficiently organize a large transportation fleet and to possess effective human relations skills in working through human resource problems. Additionally, the transportation director must be skilled in decision making in order to lead people and manage problems effectively. The director also must have deep knowledge of very diverse topics, including computer bus routing, budgeting, and labor laws, as well as competence relating to other legal requirements such as drug testing and handling of hazardous materials, to name only a few. Because of potential liability involved in all aspects of the transportation function, the director must demand strict accountability—that is, the transportation director, in cooperation with administrative supervisors, is ultimately responsible for all transportation issues.

Although many people are involved in carrying out the total transportation function, the transportation director is the first-line person responsible for overseeing all school district transportation goals and operations. These goals and accompanying procedures and responsibilities should be placed into a comprehensive transportation manual. The manual should be a well-written public document, and training for all transportation staff must be carried out in order to serve the objectives and policies of the school district. All transportation regulations, as well as employee evaluation policies, should be included in the manual. Recruitment plans, job descriptions, training information, and the requirements for each job should be included, and special emphasis should be given to driver training, pupil discipline, energy conservation, disability issues, public relations, bus routes, and bus schedules. While these elaborate procedures and responsibilities seem only distantly akin to the origins of transporting children at taxpayer expense, the basic purpose has not changed—that is, making education available to every child on an equal basis still remains the first goal.

What Is Transportation Law?

Although all transportation issues are complex, none is more serious than the area of transportation law. Many court cases have focused on liability in transporting students, and a large body of case law has centered on the issue of authorization to provide transportation at public expense.[3] Several cases have addressed the use of public funds to transport private school students,[4] and other cases have addressed who can be transported,[5] as well as whether districts have authority to deny transportation.[6] Of course, transportation for desegregation has been heavily litigated and continues to be of very recent court interest.[7] While it is not the purpose of a school finance textbook to review all transportation case law, a brief overview serves to underscore the weightiness of the law's relationship to school transportation and, consequently, the potential impact on the budget process.

Access to education via transportation services has been the focus of lawsuits at the U.S. Supreme Court level on many occasions. In a case seemingly unrelated to transportation, the U.S. Supreme Court ruled in *Cochran v. Louisiana State Board of Education*[8] in 1930 that public funds could be used to buy textbooks for children attending private schools because it applied a test that became known as the child-benefit theory. According to *Cochran*, courts could relax the church–state entanglement prohibition of the U.S. Constitution[9] by deciding whether the child is the prime beneficiary of a public expenditure involving private schools. If children

---

3   See, e.g., *Raymond v. Paradise Unified School Dist.*, 31 Cal. Rptr. 847 (Cal. 1963); *Woodland Hills School Dist. v. Pennsylvania Dept. of Educ.*, 516 A.2d 875 (Pa. 1986).

4   See, e.g., *Board of Educ. v. Antone*, 384 P.2d 911 (Okla. 1963); *Cumberland School Comm. v. Harnois*, 499 A.2d 752 (R.I. 1985).

5   See, e.g., *Madison County Board of Educ. v. Brantham*, 168 So.2d 515 (Miss. 1964); *People ex rel. Schuldt v. Schimanski*, 266 N.E.2d 409 (Ill. 1971).

6   See, e.g., *Shaffer v. Board of School Dir.*, 522 F. Supp. 1138 (Pa. 1981); *Kansas v. Board of Educ.*, 647 P.2d 329 (Kan. 1982).

7   See, e.g., *U.S. v. Jefferson County Board of Educ.*, 372 F.2d 836 (11th Cir. 1967); *Swann v. Charlotte-Mecklenburg Board of Educ.*, 312 F. Supp. 503 (N.C.1970), *aff'd*, 402 U.S. 43 (1971); *Monroe v. Jackson-Madison County Sch. Sys. Bd. of Educ.*, No. 72–1327, U.S.D.C. (W.D. Tenn.), 2007 U.S. Dist. Lexis 39789 (decided May 18, 2007); *Parents Involved in Community Schools v. Seattle School Dist. No. 1*, Nos. 05–908 and 05–915, U.S. S. Ct., 2007 U.S. Lexis 8670 (Dec. 4, 2006), decided together with No. 05–915, *Meredith, Custodial Parent and Next Friend of McDonald v. Jefferson County Bd. of Ed et al.*, on certiorari to the U.S. Court of Appeals for the Sixth Circuit (June 28, 2007).

8   281 U.S. 370, 50 S. Ct. 335 (1930).

9   The First Amendment to the U.S. Constitution reads: "Congress shall make no law respecting an establishment of religion, or prohibiting the free exercise thereof; or abridging the freedom of speech, or of the press; or the right of the people peaceably to assemble, and to petition the Government for redress." This has been interpreted to mean that "entanglement" of church and state could follow from involving public funds and private schools, and resulted in the so-called Lemon test of *Lemon v. Kurtzman* (403 U.S. 602, 91 S. Ct. 2105 [1971] *rehg. denied*), which applies a tripartite test to determine if a law has the effect of (a) advancing the cause of religion, (b) resulting in excessive entanglement, or (c) has a secular

received the benefit, the Court reasoned, the expenditure would not violate separation of church and state if other care was taken. *Cochran* became the basis for a 1947 ruling affecting transportation in *Everson v. Board of Education*[10] when the Court ruled that reimbursing bus fare to parochial and private school children was permissible in that public and private interests were not crossed with the establishment of religion when the child-benefit theory is applied to busing. The Court observed that transportation is like police, fire, and other protections available to churches and other private organizations, saying that to deny a benefit would make the state an adversary of the church. But despite the Court's long-ago rulings in *Cochran* and *Everson,* issues of commingling public funds with private and religious interests have returned many times for further judicial rulings.[11]

The arena of transportation law continues to be unsettled, as illustrated by a more recent case involving questions of violating equal opportunity when children must pay bus fees to get to school. This issue was taken up by the U.S. Supreme Court in *Kadrmas v. Dickinson Public Schools.*[12] Underlying the dispute was an attempt by the state of North Dakota to encourage school consolidation, which included financial incentives for districts that voluntarily participated. A school district chose not to consolidate and simultaneously decided to begin charging fees for bus service. Plaintiff parents brought suit, claiming a constitutional right to a free public education. The Supreme Court ruled for the defendant state, holding that the fee was rational and that equal protection was unharmed. The Court held that the state's financial problems were a rational basis for instituting fees, that transportation services need not be provided at all, and that purely economic legislation must be upheld unless it is patently arbitrary. The Court left several issues unsettled, such as whether education is a constitutional right, but it settled generally that schools may charge user fees. In an unfolding world, the right to a free public education presently includes allowing charges for transportation—a practice permitted in some states despite protests by state court litigants because those states have determined that transportation is not part of a free system of public schools.[13]

A large body of other transportation litigation also financially impacts schools, particularly as transportation is a risk activity fraught with potential liability. Although extremely safe, the transportation function does experience bus-related accidents and injuries. Current data from the National Safety Council indicate that the

---

purpose. Opponents of "parochiaid" object on the grounds of these three prongs of the *Lemon* test.

10 330 U.S. 1, 67 S. Ct. 504 (1947), *rehg. denied.*

11 The net effect of *Everson* was to allow each state to opt whether to offer transportation services to nonpublic school students. As expected, states have not issued identical rulings: e.g., denying transportation as in *Luetkemeyer v. Kaufmann,* 364 F. Supp. 376 (W.D. Mo. 1973), *aff'd,* 419 U.S. 888, 95 S. Ct. 167 (1974) and permitting transportation as in *Pequea Valley School Dist. v. Commonwealth of Pennsylvania, Dept. of Educ.,* 397 A.2d 1154 (Pa. 1979), *appeal dismissed* 443 U.S. 901, 99 S. Ct. 3091 (1979).

12 487 U.S. 450, 108 S. Ct. 2481 (1988).

13 See, e.g., *Sutton v. Cadillac Area Pub. Schs.,* 323 N.W.2d 583 (Mich. Ct. App. 1982); *Salazar v. Eastin,* 890 P.2d 43 (Cal. 1995).

national school bus accident rate is 0.01 per 100 million miles traveled compared to 0.96 for other passenger vehicles, and that each year about 6 children are fatally injured inside school buses and another 16 children are fatally injured in bus loading zones. Significantly, though, the National Highway Traffic Safety Administration indicates that 96% of the 8,500 to 12,000 children injured in bus accidents each year experience only minor scrapes and bruises, leading the federal government to consider school buses about nine times safer than other passenger vehicles during the school commute.[14] But the risk element is heightened for school districts because they serve as a common carrier rather than a private carrier and consequently have the utmost duty to ensure student safety. As a generalization, districts accept many forms of liability when transporting pupils.

Liability is controlled by various state tort concepts and is further affected by individual states' statutes regarding pupil transportation. As we discuss in greater detail in Chapter 11, a tort claim may arise when a school district or an employee is charged with negligence. To establish negligence, someone must have been injured and it must be shown that a reasonable person similarly situated could have foreseen and prevented the injury. Because school employees control and operate the transportation function, opportunity is present for an injured party to allege negligence and to attempt a liability claim against the school district's resources. For example, the transportation director is usually the person who sets bus stops—if an accident occurs, liability may arise if hazards were ignored.

Although exhaustive legal analysis is beyond the scope of this text, it is important to emphasize that liability suits raising transportation questions have had varying results. For example, in *Vogt v. Johnson*,[15] a seven-year-old child waiting for a school bus at the designated stop tried to cross the highway and was killed. The Supreme Court of Minnesota ruled that the driver of the bus, acting as agent of the district, was not liable at the time of the accident because custodial responsibility for the child had not yet arisen and because no amount of precaution on the part of the district would have prevented the accident. But significantly, while some cases have upheld this logic there are other cases to the contrary, as in the Oklahoma decision in *Brooks v. Woods*,[16] which stands in sharp contrast. In *Brooks,* the district was held negligent because of the location of a school bus stop and the subsequent resulting injury to a student. The bus stop had been established adjacent to a five-lane highway with a 45-mile-per-hour speed limit, and the scheduled arrival of the bus fell directly within rush hour traffic. While waiting for the bus, a child was hurt. Key to the ruling was that the child was known by the school to have physical and mental limitations. The appeals court ruled that the district's duty to exercise responsible care extends to any activity of bus transportation that rests outside the control of parents.

No completely exhaustive set of guidelines can be created for every situation a school district and its employees may face. However, in a negligence case, the defendant must show that all actions were those of a reasonable and prudent person under

---

14 *School Transportation News.* (Updated February 2007). *http://www.stnonline.com.*

15 153 N.W.2d 247 (Minn. 1967).

16 640 P.2d 1000 (Okla. Ct. App. 1981).

the circumstances. A few more cases illustrate how such liability may turn. In *Mitchell*,[17] a North Carolina school district was held liable when a child fell on an icy sidewalk and was crushed under the bus wheels. Testimony revealed that the bus was not in its usual loading spot and that adequate supervision was lacking. In the New York case of *Cross*,[18] a bus left the road after failing to negotiate a curve. Testimony revealed that the driver had said he was sleepy, had asked students to talk to him, and that he was seen rubbing his eyes and yawning. Many other transportation liability cases also exist involving violence, drugs, and unruly activity, and questions of governmental immunity under individual states' laws may apply, as in the Texas case of *King*,[19] where a girl was struck by a car as she crossed the road after being dropped at a school bus stop. According to the bus driver, the girl and her friends routinely walked along the drop-point side of the road for some distance after exiting the bus, and consequently the driver regularly left the location rather than waiting several minutes for the girls to eventually cross the road. The court held for the defendant school district, ruling that since several minutes had lapsed between the time of bus stop departure and the time of accident that the state's statutory immunity against tort claims applied and that any waiver of immunity would have required conditions similar to those in a sister case of *Hitchcock*,[20] where the state's immunity was waived given that the child in *Hitchcock* was struck immediately on exiting the school bus.

The specifics of each case, requirements of individual state law, and applicability of standard of care based on the age of the child are controlling, so that exhaustive discussion is not feasible. What matters is that school districts often have been held negligent in the arena of pupil transportation. In such cases, evidence showed that the potential for injury was foreseeable and that actions by the board or its agent did not meet the minimum standard of care. As we will see in Chapter 11, failure to protect students may be the causal factor leading to injury, and districts and personnel may be held liable. Under these conditions, the transportation function and the law have become constant companions in the modern world.

How Is Transportation Funded?

Growth in school transportation systems in the United States since the turn of the twentieth century has resulted in vast numbers of children carried in school vehicles at public expense. Costs are even larger than noted at the outset of this chapter, in that no single agency fully tracks "other" transportation costs in schools that fall outside uniform state reporting for instructional programs; that is, because many states exclude extracurricular activities from transportation aid formulas, a sizable part of the true cost of pupil transportation goes unreported centrally.

At the start of the new millennium, almost every state provided some form of aid to local school districts for regular pupil transportation purposes (Fig. 10.1). Like

---

17   161 S.E.2d 645 (N.C. 1968).
18   371 N.Y.S.2d 179 (N.Y. App. Div. 1975).
19   *King v. Manor Indep. Sch. Dist.,* No. 03–02–00473-CV, Court of Appeals of Texas, Third District, Austin, Tex. App. Lexis 6346 (2003).
20   *Hitchcock v. Garvin,* 738 S.W.2d 34 (Tex. App. Dallas 1987).

Figure 10.1. Transportation Formulas

State	Aid	Transportation Program	Nonpublic Pupils
AL	6%	Fully state funded categorical aid for students 2 miles or more from school.	N
AK	na	State provides 90% of funding, including air travel or ground transportation to athletic and cultural events.	N
AZ	na	Included in basic program, aids daily route miles; additional funding for vocational, technical, athletic programs.	N
AR	<1%	Expenses divided by ADM with costs of $117 or above receiving aid.	N
CA	2%	Aid for regular and special education through 'mega-item' funding of 32 categorical programs.	N
CO	2%	State pays approved costs at $0.3787 per mile plus 33.87% of excess costs up to 90%.	N
CT	2%	State pays equalized funding 0-60% of eligible costs, minimum $1,000 grant.	Y
DE	8%	State pays full funding, including school choice costs based on miles, fuel and insurance and CPI.	Y
FL	5%	State aid for expenses, bus replacement, density, and route mileage, 2 or more miles or hazardous walking conditions.	N
GA	3%	Aid for special education and regular education pupils more than 1.5 miles based on state determined minimum cost.	N
HI	2%	Transportation provided to all through state or private vendors.	N
ID	5%	State reimburses 85% of allowable previous year costs, including curriculum-related activities.	N
IL	6%	State reimburses over 1.5 miles or more or in hazard areas; reimbursement varies by grade level.	Y
IN	<1%	State pays $280 - ($20 x [eligible pupils + total roundtrip mileage]) over 1 mile. Total aid = per pupil amount times eligible pupils less local cost of $0.43 per $100AV. State pays 80% special and vocational education.	N
IA	na	Included in basic cost.	Y
KS	3%	Included in general state aid as weighted factor.	Y
KY	6%	State pays approved costs for students 1 mile or more from school with density adjustments.	N
LA	na	Included in basic support program.	Y
ME	5%	State pays base year costs plus CPI increase.	N
MD	4%	Previous year's allocation plus lesser of 8% or CPI increase, with guaranteed 3% minimum.	N
MA	3%	State pays 28% aid over 1.5 miles from school. Regional districts receive 80%.	Y
MI	<1%	Included in basic program; partial reimbursement for driver training.	Y
MN	8%	Most funding is provided through the general education revenue program.	Y
MS	nr	Add-on to basic program.	N
MO	4%	State reimburses 75% of approved costs but formula is not fully funded. Districts not exceeding 105% of predicted costs receive 67%; above 105% may receive as low as 56%.	N
MT	2%	State reimburses minimum of $0.85 per mile, extra funding for buses with 45+ capacity; reduced if <50% capacity.	N

State	Aid	Transportation Program	Nonpublic Pupils
NE	2%	Lesser of actual costs or calculated amount on miles transported, in lieu of mileage to parents.	N
NV	nr	Funded through basic support program, 85% of allowable expenditures.	N
NH	nr	State aid only for vocational transportation.	N
NJ	4%	Per-pupil allocations adjusted for average distance pupils reside from school and an incentive factor.	Y
NM	6%	State variably aids average cost per student for each district. Add-on for unpaved and unimproved roads; hold harmless.	Y
NY	7%	Equalized aid to public and non-public school students over 1.5 miles. Sparsity and grade level weightings.	Y
NC	4%	Aid based on pupils transported, eligible expenditures, and number of buses; inefficiency penalty.	N
ND	7%	Maximum 90% reimbursement based on miles, pupils, days, vehicles, distance, and rural/urban setting.	N
OH	5%	Categorical aid provides 50% of costs based on statewide history, adjusted for unique geography.	Y
OK	1%	Supplement to the foundation formula based on Average Daily Haul over 1.5 miles times per capita allowance times factor.	nr
OR	nr	State provides 70% of approved costs over 1 mile for elementary pupils, 1.5 miles for high school students.	N
PA	5%	Subsidy for public and non-public students based on vehicle capacity, mileage, congested areas, service type.	Y
RI	na	Funded through basic support program.	N
SC	4%	State has overall supervision of transportation, including vehicle acquisition, maintenance, training, operational costs.	N
SD	nr	Included in basic support formula.	N
TN	na	Included in basic support formula.	N
TX	na	Maximum rate per mile set by appropriation based on daily cost, maintenance, density, geography.	N
UT	4%	State aids route mileage, transport time, and equipment costs over 1.5 miles grades K-6, 2 miles 7-12.	N
VT	2%	Schools providing transportation eligible for up to 50% reimbursement.	N
VA	nr	Basic support formula considers land area, number of pupils transported, and estimated costs.	N
WA	4%	Based on number of pupils, distance, unique costs, special education, small fleet, special vehicles.	N
WI	<1%	Flat amount per pupil based on distance each pupil is transported.	Y
WY	10%	State pays 100% of transportation and maintenance expenditures for the preceding year and 100% of leases or purchases.	N

nr=not reported; na=not applicable, included in general formula

Source: Catherine C. Sielke and C. Thomas Holmes, Table 4.1 (data excerpted and modified), in *The American Education Finance Association's School Finance Programs of the United States and Canada, 1998–1999,* eds. Catherine C. Sielke, John Dayton, C. Thomas Holmes, Anne L. Jefferson, and William J. Fowler, Jr. (Washington, DC: United States Department of Education, National Center for Education Statistics, 2000).

other forms of state school aid, transportation aid varies widely in amount and distribution method among the states. Transportation aid formulas include a wide variety of features, with factors such as expenditures per pupil, population density, bus capacities, matching grants, or some combination of these variables as common denominators. Transportation aid formula operation is often highly complex; for example, many states use a population-density formula based on an index consisting of the number of pupils transported divided by the eligible bus route mileage. Additionally, many states have an allowable per-pupil cost, which is often the actual calculated cost of daily transportation plus the cost of bus replacement divided by the number of eligible students in a district. In such cases, this amount may then be plotted against a population-density ratio, yielding an allowable cost per pupil as state transportation aid.

Beyond these broad generalizations, transportation aid formulas differ widely on a state-by-state basis. Some states provide a transportation allowance based on hazardous walking conditions, so that students who live close to school can still be transported with the help of state aid. In other states, transportation aid flows through the general fund formula, so that there is a relationship between the philosophy that underlies regular education funding and the financing of transportation. In still other states, there appears to be no reason why the state may equalize the general fund while aiding transportation via a system of unequalized grants. The bottom line is that once basic funding formula similarities are noted, the only other commonality is that in most states' aid almost never covers the entire cost of the transportation function in schools.

Although each state calculates transportation aid using its own unique formula, many states use a concept similar to the example shown in Fig. 10.2. The underlying philosophical basis for Fig. 10.2 is pupil density costs—that is, the ratio of pupils in the district to the district's geographic size. Transportation aid is thus calculated by following each step in the aid formula based on an index of density. In this example, an important point is that while actual transported head count is 583 pupils, yielding a density of 3.81 students per square mile (density table not shown), the effect is to weight the pupils in this district higher for transportation aid purposes than would be true for a district where the number of pupils is large enough to generate a higher density factor. When the density factor is tied to the general fund formula in this example (see Line 5), the actual number of students claimed for transportation aid would be the 583 head count *plus* 79 more students—in effect yielding extra aid for each of those "ghost" pupils because the density index is linearly tied to miles traveled and number of children transported. If the effect of this weighting formula were analyzed, it would be seen that in this example, the density index grants an extra $316,000 in transportation aid ($4,000 base general aid per pupil times 79 extra transportation-weighted pupils) that would *not* have been received if the formula had been distributed on an actual head count basis.

Figure 10.2. Sample Transportation Aid Formula

Area of district in square miles September 20	=	153.0
All pupils transported living 2.5 miles or more from school	=	583.0
Index of density (Line 2 ÷ Line 1)	=	3.81
Factor from density table (not shown)	=	0.1355
Weighted pupil count 583.0 × 0.1355 factor (to General Fund)	=	79.0

In every state, transportation aid calculation is always an outcome of the legislative process. The first legislative act is adoption of a transportation philosophy. If the state has a high commitment to transporting students, state aid will be higher than in states where other priorities have been agreed upon. The second legislative act is adoption of a state aid formula reflecting that philosophy. The third legislative act is a product of the first two choices, wherein an amount of funding is appropriated for the aid formula. In practice, available resources will determine the amount of earmarked aid by "backing into the formula." This means that the formula will be fully funded each year, although full funding could be less than in the prior year because the amount of legislative appropriation for any formula is equal to 100% of available resources, even if less money becomes available. While this may seem like semantics, it is reality in an imperfect world in which tax revenues are finite.

In every state, transportation-aid formulas grant money to school districts based on audited records substantiating the claims districts make for transportation aid. Aid qualification requires good recordkeeping because most states closely audit for transportation overpayment. A set of records for state transportation aid purposes often includes the following:

- Area maps and bus route information;
- Address and destination of all students claimed for aid;
- List of students using more than one kind of transportation (e.g., vocational or special education);
- List of nonpublic school students transported, if claimed;
- Evidence of bus seating capacity for each child claimed;
- Evidence of bridge or road condemnation or construction if the most direct route from home to school is inaccessible;
- Evidence of mileage driven on all routes by all buses;
- Basis and work paper showing calculation for prorated costs;
- Summary and original documents for all pupil transportation for regular routes, special and vocational education, or other eligible transportation;

♦ Claims for payments in lieu of pupil transportation showing dates, mileage, rates, and total payments;

♦ Evidence of insurance costs for vehicles;

♦ Evidence of price of buses and depreciation history;

♦ List of leased or lease-purchase buses, and dates of lease;

♦ Other as required by state-specific statute.

Without accurate records, reimbursement problems arise. Problems range from denial of state aid to liability for malfeasance, fraud, or even negligence if questions about fiscal impropriety or injury ever occur.

Within this general policy framework, the key features of transportation state aid plans can be stated succinctly. First, almost every state transports students at public expense. Second, transportation aid has become a huge cost to states in the belief that children must get to school in order to receive their full entitlement to education. Third, state transportation aid plans generally are tied to population density or sparsity of school district attendance areas. Fourth, there is usually some attempt by the state to judge the fiscal ability of districts to pay for transportation services, either by tying transportation aid to general fund aid or by funding transportation categorically. Fifth, state aid almost always is locally supplemented. Sixth, to qualify for transportation aid, states require extensive documentation by the school district. Seventh, and finally, all these tasks emphasize the value of well-managed transportation systems, from both liability and sound financial perspectives.

What Other Issues Are Relevant?

Several other important transportation considerations should be briefly addressed before leaving this topic. These include the concepts of whether school districts should own their bus fleets or whether they should outsource transportation services; computerization of appropriate transportation operations; elements of bus purchasing; and planning for maintenance and safety.

Owning or Outsourcing

The benefits and disadvantages of district ownership of the transportation fleet versus outsourcing constitute an ongoing debate. On one side of the argument are school districts that claim to have saved money and time by outsourcing transportation services to for-profit companies. There are reasons why these districts may be correct. First, there may be logic to outsourcing bus services for districts with cash flow problems because outsourcing avoids the prohibitive cost of buying buses. The average rural school district runs ten to 20 buses ranging from 15-passenger to 66-passenger units or larger. The average urban district runs hundreds of such bus units. At an average cost of $70,000 or more per bus, purchasing a bus fleet is a huge drain on cash reserves. Second, districts may benefit from outsourcing because they may not be able to afford a schedule of rotating new buses into their fleet, and the high maintenance costs of older buses are not a cash outlay problem if the district does not actually own the fleet. Third, while state laws on bus purchases vary widely, in many cases states require cash purchase. For example, in some states buses can only be bought from capital outlay or transportation funds, in effect putting the total cost on the local tax base unless these funds are equalized or otherwise state-aided for the specific purpose of managing bus purchase costs.

Other arguments also favor outsourcing transportation services. These argue that outsourcing lowers capitalization costs, reduces personnel and administration costs, and provides efficiency through market-savvy contractors whose sole business is transportation and customer satisfaction. Counterarguments, however, include how to ensure quality performance by a private contractor when the school district no longer controls the public relations aspect of the contractor's behavior and the need for insuring against liability for acts of contractors under such conditions. All these issues underscore the need for careful legal and community analysis as part of a decision about outsourcing transportation services.

In contrast, there are persuasive arguments favoring district ownership of a transportation fleet. Advocates argue that district ownership provides more flexibility, allows for inhouse selection, training, and supervision of transportation employees, and ensures greater control over operational costs. In the end analysis, it may be that there is no one best option, as the right choice may depend on a district's financial position and the community's attitude toward this vital service. What must be clearly understood is that, if outsourcing is chosen, written agreements should specify that the contractor is an independent agent and must fully and willingly comply with all federal and state statutes, rules, and regulations. It must also be agreed that the contractor provide appropriate insurance for property damage and bodily and personal injury, although the district must still continue to insure itself.

Computerizing Transportation Services

As school system size has grown and as technology has engulfed the scene, computerization of transportation services has become the standard. Every year more districts move to computerized routing, including many smaller districts. These plans are more cost-effective in that they can apply mathematical formulas for routing efficiency. For many districts, especially large ones with mazes of streets to travel, bus routing systems have reduced costs by 15% or more. Software is available to preplan transportation routes in undeveloped areas in advance of actual population shifts, and these tools combine with other forecasting techniques to help districts more economically purchase school sites years before construction begins. Computerized transportation routing systems are complex and expensive, thereby requiring some cost-to-benefit analysis to justify their purchase. The benefit, however, is vastly improved efficiency.

Although computer routing may not be suited for every district, computerized fleet maintenance databases are common. Such programs incorporate garage operations, vehicle replacement, mechanical repair and maintenance, and fuel consumption records into databases to reveal the relationship between preventive maintenance and emergency repairs. Additionally, the number and type of repairs for each vehicle, operating cost per mile, and cost per individual vehicle repair is tracked. Item and total costs are accounted for and used to inform decisions about continued maintenance or disposal. For example, a district might find that maintenance for one particular bus was $500 in the first year, while the same bus consumed $5,117 in its fifth year. This information can be joined with other costs, such as labor and vehicle down-time, to determine the true cost of a replacement bus purchase. State transportation reports are often prepared using such data management programs as well. The benefit is sizable, in that records can be quickly gathered and analyzed, saving many human hours compared to manual collation or lack of extensive data altogether.

Purchasing Buses

Our discussion about owning, outsourcing, and using cost-to-benefit analysis emanates from the enormity of school bus costs. The price of a typical bus may average more than $70,000, but the purchase of a bus with a wheelchair lift adds many more thousands of dollars. Such large outlays require care to avoid even more problems at vehicle delivery time that could arise from failure to write tight bid specifications or from failure to follow state-specific purchasing laws.

Purchase of large-ticket items like buses is normally performed by the local school district, using written bid specifications to detail the desired vehicle features. Large purchases of any type are usually subject to mandatory state bid laws. In a few states, a state agency prepares the bid specifications, awards the bids, and provides buses to school districts. This is not typical, however, meaning that school district personnel must be skilled at these duties. Buying buses is especially complicated because new buses are generally purchased with separate chassis and body bids. That is, the local district bids these items separately, and the body manufacturer provides a body to fit the chassis at another factory. Although seemingly complex, this method provides greater economy and specialization because bus body manufacturers can mass produce for approximately four standard chassis. Type of motor—diesel or gasoline, and horsepower rating—can also be bid so that the bus meets local preferences. In general, most school districts find a combination of bus sizes is appropriate. Larger buses are more versatile, which, in turn, reduces the number of bus units and number of drivers. Smaller buses are most useful in sparsely inhabited areas or inner cities on crowded streets, and they provide a cost-effective alternative for transporting smaller groups of students for field trips and extracurricular activities.

As indicated, most states have competitive bid laws that apply to large purchases, including buses. The purpose of bidding is to force competition in the awarding of bids because there are only a few bus manufacturers in the country, making it possible for lack of competition to drive prices up. Another reason for laws is that it is tempting for government agencies to develop relationships with favorite vendors who would be thereby advantaged if not forced to compete for large lucrative contracts. Consequently, many states require school districts, as government agencies, to accept the lowest responsible bid for comparable products. As a rule, most bid laws set a threshold purchase price (e.g., $10,000) above which open bids must be taken using a set of statutory bid requirements: for example, how notice of bids must be published, how bids will be opened, how the lowest responsible bid will be determined, how errors in bids will be handled, and so forth.

Maintenance and Safety

The importance of bid laws, rising bus costs, and other concerns about liability have increased the amount of time and energy school districts devote to issues of safety and maintenance of school vehicles. The National Transportation Highway and Safety Administration (NTHSA) passed new regulations in 1977, which were meant to make buses safer in event of collisions, including requirements for padding the backs and sides of bus seats. More recently, new federal regulations required three-point lap/shoulder occupant restraint systems on all newly manufactured small school buses (under 10,000 pounds vehicle weight). Transportation law in the various states presently finds seven states mandating the actual use of three-point systems, and three other states currently requiring installation of two-point lap belts on large buses (over 10,000 pounds vehicle weight).[21] With nearly 50,000 new buses built each year, the transportation safety scene is changing rapidly as old buses are replaced and as all manufacturers of small school buses now routinely install lap/shoulder belt restraint systems on their buses.

Although safe equipment is an essential aspect of a good transportation system, it must be emphasized that vehicle maintenance and staff training are critical to any discussion of funding pupil transportation services. Obviously, good drivers cannot offset bad buses, nor can new equipment offset bad drivers. Consequently, issues of liability underscore the relationship of safety, maintenance, and personnel so that equipment maintenance and staff training become invaluable safety aids by saving lives and prolonging bus life. Safety includes being certain that loading and unloading zones are protected from moving traffic, that students have time to cross streets, that training is required for all staff, and that bus safety information for parents and community members is widely distributed. Maintenance includes drivers' daily vehicle inspections, including walkaround for fluid leaks or tire problems, inoperative lights, flashers, stop arms, and so forth. The director of transportation should establish a regular maintenance schedule that includes oil changes, brake inspections, and all types of maintenance to ensure safety and equipment life. In the worst case, accidents will be avoided; in the best case, buses will last longer—both are excellent outcomes to maintenance and safety programs. But, obviously, all these precautions come at a cost, making transportation a significant demand on the budgeting process.

THE FOOD SERVICE FUNCTION

Like transportation, the food service function plays a critical role in effective and efficient operation of schools by providing a vital support system for the instructional process. It takes knowledge and skill to plan and conduct a system that meets the nutritional needs of children and—as we said at the outset to this chapter—it makes no sense to argue for equal educational opportunity if children come to school hungry. As a result, a brief review of the food service function is needed in order to understand how it operates, how meal prices are set under federal, state, and local participation, and how revenues and expenditures in food service budgets are effectuated.

---

21 *School Transportation News.* (Updated February 2007). *http://www.stnonline.com.*

What Are the General Issues?

As we indicated earlier, the importance of the food service function cannot be overemphasized because the role of nutrition in schools is fundamental common sense. Data from earlier sections of this book suggest that schools face tremendous problems, beginning in the home, that serve as formidable barriers to effective teaching and learning. Most striking among those barriers is evidence that poverty affects large numbers of schoolchildren today, in highly predictable ways. The data show that many children come to school from impoverished homes, with nearly 13 million American children living in families with incomes below poverty level—a number that grew by more than 1.3 million (+11%) in the five years following the turn of the new millennium. Race, immigrant status, and age correlate closely to poverty data, with as many as 35% of minority children and as many as 40% of immigrant children affected by poverty, along with as many as 20% of all children younger than age six years. And the data do not stop at that point, as millions more children who do not officially qualify for poverty income designation are affected by lack of affordable housing, food insecurity, or other economic hardship—in all, more than 28 million (39%) of all children live in low income families.[22]

These and other data linking academic performance to nutrition and social issues have long sparked interest at federal, state, and local levels. Debate over an appropriate role for government has raged for decades, with government aiding health and nutrition in various ways ranging from cash aid to surplus commodity distributions meant to benefit different segments of society and the economy. The role of food service in schools has only increased over time, with most schools now serving both breakfast and lunch because many children are undernourished. While food service cannot solve all of society's problems, it can be a positive force by making school a better experience for children.

How Is Food Service Funded?

Food service programs in schools have a long history of federal, state, and local subsidies to supplement meal prices paid by children. All these sources make up the revenue side of food service operations and are highly interdependent.

Federal Support

The first federal legislation granting aid to general nutrition grew out of very practical economic interests during the Great Depression. In 1935, the *Bankhead-Jones Act* (PL 74–182) was an act in federal legislation making grants to states for creation of agricultural experiment stations. In the same year, Congress approved the *Agricultural Adjustment Act* (PL 74–320) authorizing 30% of customs receipts for encouragement of exportation and domestic consumption of surplus food commodities. The effect was that surplus commodities first began to be used in school lunch programs in 1936, wherein both agriculture and schools benefited in that a school

---

22   National Center for Children in Poverty. (New York: Columbia University Mailman School of Public Health, December 2006). *www.nccp.org*

nutrition agenda was linked to an expanded market for farm commodities. Not long afterward, Congress enacted the *National School Lunch Act* (PL 79–396) authorizing grants to states to help provide food and facilities for nonprofit school lunch programs. By 1954, Congress had passed the *School Milk Program Act* (PL 83–597), providing federal funds to buy school milk. The School Breakfast Program followed. Beginning with a federal pilot project in 1968, the program was then written into federal law in 1975.[23] Less-well known is the federal Summer Food Service Program, which was created around the same time as the breakfast program to provide meals to low income students over the summer when school was not in session.[24] The most recent addition to federal support for school food services took place in 1998 with the enactment of *Child Nutrition Reauthorization Act of 1998* (Public Law 105–336), which expanded the National School Lunch Program to include snacks to students involved in certain afterschool activities.[25] Although the original economic conditions spurring a federal role are long past, federal interest has persisted as Congress continues to support farm prices and as it has broadly promoted affordable nutrition in schools.

As we have seen, federal involvement in education has been substantial and wide-ranging, taking in an array of national social and economic interests. Total federal support for education in Fiscal Year 2005 was estimated at $141.8 billion, of which approximately $71 billion was overseen by the U.S. Department of Education (DOE). DOE interest has been broad and has included programs in the areas of Chapter 1, educational improvement, special education, vocational and adult education, impact aid, higher education, and other special Congressional interests. The total of all federal monies for education, however, has not come only from the DOE. Large amounts of money also originate in the U.S. Department of Health and Human Services, the U.S. Department of Agriculture, the U.S. Department of Labor, and so on. In a highly complex federal outlay of many billions of dollars, school food service has benefited too, as in 2006 federal aid totaled $9.4 billion in cash plus another $802 million in commodity costs, for a total of $10.2 billion—a significant amount of aid to the millions of meals served in schools across the nation.[26]

State Support

A second unit of government that has long been involved in school food services is the individual states themselves. In most cases, state participation has stemmed from a couple of choices states have had to confront. One choice is whether the state even wishes to participate in the National School Lunch Act of 1946, a federal law requiring state funds in order to be eligible to receive federal lunch funding. If a state

---

23 See "School Breakfast Program," *www.fns.usda.gov/cnd/Breakfast/AboutBFast/bfastfacts. htm*

24 See "Summer Food Service Program," *http://www.fns.usda.gov/cnd/summer/about/index. html*

25 See "National School Lunch Program" *http://www.fns.usda.gov/cnd/Afterschool/NSLP_ QA.htm*

26 *http://www.fns.usda.gov/pd/cncosts.htm.*

declined to participate, important federal funding would be lost—a reality leading to another choice about whether, in such cases, the state would participate at all in local food service programs. State support, then, has been both voluntary and compulsory in the sense that options are available; however, states always have a politically difficult time refusing federal aid of any kind.

Individual states' participation in school food service funding is difficult to summarize as each state is free to control its level of involvement. Although most states have chosen to receive federal school food aid, no uniform method of state funding has followed. Any review of current state legislation always reveals a wide range in food service program participation, with the major feature being relatively little uniformity in approach or level of support. Without doubt, the most meaningful observation about the states' role in school food programs is that, while such aid is very important, state funding is typically quite small compared to the federal contribution and especially small when compared to the proportion of total spending for school food services that occurs in the United States.

The Local Role

If it is difficult to generalize about state participation in school food service funding, it is impossible to characterize "typical" funding patterns among local units of government (i.e., school districts). The range of local participation in school food service costs varies widely, so that the local contribution may be said to be great or relatively small. The perspective that the local role is minor flows from the fact that, because the federal government is the largest contributor (with cost-sharing by states in some lesser proportion), the local share is that remaining unfunded portion of total food service costs after cash food sales are accounted for—that is, a presumption that few, if any, school districts absorb the entire remaining costs after federal and state food aid is received. For example, if federal reimbursement for regular paid meals is $0.4152 (41.52¢) and if the state agrees to fund $0.045 (4.5¢), then the unfunded portion of a regular meal is $2.49 (if the local school district sets the meal price at $2.95). Unless the local district's budget absorbs a large proportion of the unfunded cost, the district's role in funding food services will be very minor in impact.

The opposite side of that same perspective proposes that the local school district is a major participant in food service funding. This view argues that the local role is critical because the district's decision about whether to further subsidize meal costs has both financial and moral consequences. If the district decides to become a meaningful player in food service funding, it can do so only by shifting local tax revenue from the other budgeted areas to the food service fund—a decision some people say robs instructional programs. If, on the other hand, the district channels the majority of unfunded costs to consumers, it is inevitable that some children will not receive the intended benefit of food service programs. Fortunately, some of this burden on the local district is made easier because federal aid for free and reduced lunch, breakfast, or milk programs is higher than for regular paid meals; for example, while federal aid for regular paid lunches was set at 41.52¢ for Fiscal Year 2008, reduced price lunch federal reimbursement was set at $2.1852 and free lunch was aided at $2.5852. Under these circumstances, the unfunded local share is greatly reduced—although the gravity of decisions about local food subsidy remains. The biggest problem for local districts often comes as a result of rising costs associated with buying and preparing food such as supplier price increases, local labor costs, and equipment and facilities—all of which are locale-dependent and must factor into what the district ultimately charges for meals. Satisfying the goal of making food service a self-funded program is difficult, and choices between competing ideas must be made. As seen in Fig. 10.3 (p. 320), local costs, efficiencies, and all other aspects of food service operations are a function of district size and management skill.

What Other Issues Are Relevant?

Although entire books exist on managing food service operations, three additional topics need examination here. A short look at broad compliance requirements, organizing for food service, and financial management round out this chapter.

Broad Compliance Requirements

Compliance with regulations and standards is a common concern any time outside aid is provided to school programs. Granting agencies want assurances that programs align with the grantor's intent, and in the case of food service those assurances are required by the federal government in return for dollars and commodities. School districts also must assure individual states of compliance so that the state can provide its own assurances to the federal government. Likewise, when states also aid food service the states themselves inevitably want separate compliance monitoring.

Eligibility for federal aid has been based on federal rules and regulations. Historically, schools and states have had to agree to:

- *Operate a nonprofit program.* Only three-month's operating balance may be kept on hand and still be nonprofit.

- *Serve meals that meet nutrition requirements.* Programs can offer single menu, fast food choice menu, or á la carte menu.

- *Price meals as a unit.* To count as reimbursable, meals must be priced as a unit. This does not prohibit single item sales.

- *Supply free and reduced meals* to eligible needy children.

- *Agree to avoid discrimination.* No child may be refused because of inability to pay, race, sex, or national origin.

- *Keep accurate records of income and expenditures.* Records are subject to intensive state and federal audits.

- *Complete a formal reimbursement claim.* Claims must be sent on a timely basis to the state.

- *Distribute applications for free and reduced meals.* Districts must actively inform each student of the program.

- *Review and act on free and reduced applications.* Parents or guardians must be notified regarding decisions.

- *Develop and implement verification procedures.* A method of verifying accuracy of applications must be followed.

Figure 10.3. Sample Food Service Revenue Calculation
Fiscal Year 2008

	TOTAL ANNUAL MEALS	FEDERAL		STATE		DISTRICT LOCAL		TOTAL 7-1-03 to 6-30-04
		RATE	Reimbursement	RATE	Reimbursement	PRICE	REVENUE	
LUNCHES								
Paid Elem	64,000	.4152	$26,573	.0450	$2,880	2.49	$159,360	$188,813
Jr. High	35,000	.4152	$14,532	.0450	$1,575	2.79	$97,650	$113,757
Sr. High	33,000	.4152	$13,702	.0450	$1,485	2.95	$97,350	$112,537
Free	20,000	2.5852	$51,704	.0450	$900			$57,404
Reduced	12,000	2.1852	$26,222	.0450	$540	0.40	$4,800	$31,562
Adult	5,000					3.49	$17,450	$17,450
TOTAL	169,000		$132,733		$7,380		$376,610	$516,723
BREAKFAST								
Paid Elem	6,000	.2400	$1,440				$0	$1,440
Jr. High	3,500	.2400	$840				$0	$840
Sr. High	2,000	.2400	$480				$0	$480
Free	1,800	1.3100	$2,358					$2,358
Reduced	900	1.0100	$909			0.30	$270	$1,179
Adult							$0	$0
TOTAL	14,200		$6,027				$270	$6,297
SNACKS								
Paid Elem	64,000	.0600	$3,840				$0	$3,840
Jr. High		.0600	$0				$0	$0
Sr. High		.0600	$0				$0	$0
Free	20,000	.6500	$13,000					$13,000
Reduced	12,000	.3200	$3,840			0.15	$1,800	$5,640
Adult							$0	$0
TOTAL	96,000		$20,680				$1,800	$22,480
KINDERGARTEN								
MILK								
Paid		.1450	$0				$0	$0
Free-Avg Dealer Cost			$0					$0
TOTAL	0		$0				$0	$0
OTHER CASH								
Sales/Income								$0
12 Months								
Total Income			$159,440		$7,380		$378,680	$545,500

- *Maintain accurate participation records.* The district must establish procedures for obtaining accurate meal counts.

- *Establish and implement purchasing procedures.* Purchasing procedures must comply with state and federal regulations.

- *Use federally donated foods or commodities.* This includes the ability to store commodities properly without spoilage.

Federal law has also long required food service programs to comply with other regulations in order to ensure that approved programs provide meals based on daily nutritional requirements. These requirements are part of the National School Lunch and Child Nutrition programs, which must provide approximately one-third of the Recommended Dietary Allowance (RDA). To qualify for reimbursement, a lunch must contain a set of menu items and specified components, where components are *meat* or *meat alternate, vegetable* and/or *fruit, bread* or *bread alternate,* and *milk.* Similar regulations apply to breakfast programs. The goal is a balanced diet in exchange for financial aid—a goal that has not wavered since the program's inception in the 1940s.

Organizing for Food Service

The growing complexity and sophistication of school food service programs has led to cost analyses of how districts can better manage programs and expenses. Organizing has centered on types of management systems best suited to a district's unique needs, along with how to effectively manage food service budgets. This has primarily resulted in choosing between contracts for outside management, centralized in-house operations, or decentralized in-house food service systems, all with attendant benefits and drawbacks.

For-Profit Management Companies

Use of outside management companies has arisen from analysis involving whether it is more cost-effective to outsource for food services or to handle operations in-house. Although school districts make different choices based on local circumstances, many have decided to outsource food services. The main reason has been benefits stemming from fiscal and managerial efficiency. Districts that have moved to food service contracts have reported benefits, including increased and expanded menus, elimination of the deficits that have long plagued food service, and improved public perception because of the aggressive market responsiveness of vendors who should be more sensitive to clientele demands. The literature reports many instances of districts that believe that outsourcing food service operations has proved more efficient and less costly. Specifically, advocates have reported five benefits to outsourcing:

- Administrators have more time to devote to instructional matters;

- Food service wage and benefit costs, disputes, and grievances have been reduced because the district no longer handles the operation;

- Menu planning is improved by use of food professionals;

- In-house record-keeping requirements are reduced; and

♦ There is incentive for food service to become a profit center with high client satisfaction.

For school districts considering outsourcing food services, the literature suggests that districts should choose from a list of reputable and experienced firms and should act based on a set of carefully prepared bid specifications meant to assist bidders in deciding whether to bid on the local contract. Because a contractual relationship is likely to last for some time and because much public harm can be done by choosing an unsatisfactory food service provider, careful pursuit of the best bid will serve the school district well.

In-House Operations

For districts not choosing outsourcing, the only remaining option is to provide this function in-house. There are two choices within this option: to centralize or decentralize food services. Careful cost analysis should be the basis for choosing, as each option has its own benefits and drawbacks.

The basis for in-house drawbacks lies in the complexity of running a food service program. There is so much reporting and supervision that districts operating in-house food service programs usually are forced to hire a full-time director. This person must be highly trained to assure the efficient and cost-effective operation of modern support services. Normally, this person is a certified dietitian who also needs skills in working closely with principals and central office staff, as well as taking responsibility for supervising food service workers. The position is one of planning, doing, and comparing results because this person is responsible for a full range of menu planning, food purchasing, hiring and dismissal of staff, and—of course—the program's financial stability.

A critical organizing element for in-house programs is consideration for efficiency and cost-effectiveness. This consideration is often the driving force behind how food service is structured locally and is most apparent as districts choose between centralized and decentralized operations. The debate involves onsite food preparation versus satelliting from central kitchens, fixed versus free choice menus, and a host of other issues. Satelliting means delivering centrally precooked food with finishing kitchens at each school, in contrast to onsite raw food preparation. Central kitchens have proved cost-effective for many districts because the major benefit is mass preparation and nonduplication of full facilities at each school site. In well-managed central kitchens, productivity has been shown to increase by large margins. Costs must be carefully watched, however, because the expense of specialized vehicles to transport meals to sites, finishing kitchen equipment, and the use of specialized freezers for storage can be expensive. But proponents note that if properly managed, capitalization costs are spread over a greater number of schools, with lower end cost. Central operations are not without disadvantage, however, as critics point out that effectiveness may be hurt because site control is lower and because rigidity, overstandardization, and nonresponsiveness may follow in a large centralized operation. In either case, a related in-house problem is personnel, as food service operations face a dilemma of low pay and high labor cost—that is, many private-sector positions pay more for similar work, while at the same time labor costs are a major part of total overhead for in-house food service operations.

Financial Management

Finally, no discussion of the food service function in schools is complete without consideration for the complexity of budgeting. Unless the food service director is well trained, food service budgeting can be overwhelming because of the number of school sites and food programs. Generally, the food service manager, in cooperation with the district's budget director, must establish receipts and disbursements for each school site as part of the budget process and provide key leadership in setting affordable meal prices. This process requires knowledge and organizational skills, including ability to analyze historic data and forecast revenues and expenditures. Complexity further arises in that each school site must be evaluated for the impact of changes in enrollments, food and labor costs, menu, meal prices, and so forth. This is difficult and precise work because food service budgeting is theoretically a cash operation—a fact that makes projection of revenue and expenditures different from other budgeting. As a result, the food service operation must take into account a variety of factors including historical data, demographic changes, school openings or closings, projected enrollments, effects of menu changes, changes in operating procedures, changes in food and labor costs, meal price changes, and state and federal guidelines.

The goal of food service management is accuracy of records and reliability of predictions. The process calls for budget items to be reduced to subcategories, and finally to monthly projections. Potential trouble spots can be identified in this manner, and plans can be made for the entire year. As with every budget in the school district, monthly food service projections are assembled into an annual budget wherein revenue and expenditure must balance. The food service budget then becomes an integral part of the overall school district budget exactly like budgets for other support services. Our discussion of local choices reenters at this point, as actual program cost minus federal and state aid yields the cost per meal that must be charged or, alternatively, locally supplemented. For example, our district earlier in Fig. 10.3 (p. 320) served 64,000 paid elementary meals, for which it received 41.52¢ federal reimbursement and 4.5¢ state aid. According to Fig. 10.3 the district is charging $2.49 per elementary meal (and so on) based on its true costs, which it may subsidize if it chooses. If, when preparing next year's budget, it is believed that costs will go up, the district will have to decide whether to (a) raise prices, (b) shift local tax dollars to the food service fund, or (c) seek new efficiencies such as analyzing outsourced versus in-house services. The interrelatedness and circularity of the budget process is clear in this example—in other words, we began this section by discussing cost-to-benefit regarding outsourcing versus in-house, and we have ended the same discussion by circling back to the same decision with the ever-present goal of low-priced high-quality meals.

The budgeting side of food service can be very frustrating because school districts have no way to reduce costs beyond the limited options of outsourcing versus in-house, maximizing efficiency through designs such as central kitchens, and a few other options such as multidistrict cooperative bulk purchasing or other interdistrict collaborations. Particularly troublesome is that if food service costs rise, districts have no choice other than to take money from other programs to subsidize meals *or* put the cost back on students. At the same time, it must be remembered that the heart of a school food service operation is to support learning. A companion goal is to encourage maximum student participation, while operating as close as possible to a break-even financial position. Although difficult, this is enhanced through good management—that is, effective short- and long-range plans, an operations manager who is visible and involved, and a program supported by committed and knowledgeable boards, staffs, and other stakeholders who understand and value the relationship between food service and student success in school.

WRAP-UP

Our discussion in this chapter underscores the vital contribution of auxiliary services to desirable educational outcomes. It is only sensible to know that equal opportunity is not served if children cannot get to school or if they come to school hungry. Although lacking in glamour, transportation and food service represent vast expenditure outlays and significant liability. The result of our exploration is to again observe the intricately interrelated parts of a complete educational system, wherein each piece makes a vital contribution and cannot be slighted without significant harm to children. Given the demographic data earlier in this book, transportation and food services will only grow in importance as schools become even greater caretakers and providers for children in the future.

pointcounterpoint

Point

Schools today have been asked to take on too many responsibilities that actually belong to parents or to other social welfare agencies. Diverting limited instructional funds to subsidize school meals, particularly breakfast and afterschool snacks, is misdirected social policy, especially in an era of such high-stakes educational accountability.

Counterpoint

With more than 28 million children living in low-income households and with dispiriting evidence that making ends meet now requires an income twice the federal poverty level, it is unrealistic to think that families are widely derelict in their duty to child nutrition. The only way to raise test scores is to care for the whole child, starting with physical well-being.

Questions

- ◆ Which of these two starkly opposing views best represents your personal beliefs and experiences? Why? On what evidence do you base your beliefs?
- ◆ How does your district and school "measure up" on child-based nutrition issues?

♦ How aggressively does your local school district aid nutrition programs?

CASE STUDY

As business manager of your geographically large suburban school district, you have seen transportation costs and problems increase continuously over the last four years. Chief among your concerns have been skyrocketing fuel prices, local pressure to address environmental concerns aimed mostly at the district's large diesel fleet, and safety concerns following a recent bus crash and other violence-related community issues. In fact, the superintendent was quoted recently in the local press, indicating that the district intended to make significant investment in these matters and that he was certain long-term benefits and savings would accrue from these new expenditures. Although no details had been given in the press, you later learned that his goal was to reduce bus route travel time and costs through routing efficiencies and cheaper vehicle operation and to engage new technologies to help with safety concerns. When you met with him later about these ideas, he indicated that he expected you to prepare an analysis of options and costs that would meet with board and community approval.

Back in your office, you reflected on your efforts over the last four years. You had already worked on these problems, but to no dramatic avail—lack of fuel storage tanks had prevented bulk purchasing that would help hedge against rising prices; aging buses were expensive to replace in quantity; and other efforts, such as hiring bus monitors and installing active and dummy video cameras on the district's school buses, had not reduced safety and security anxieties. As you pondered the situation, you realized that the good news was that the superintendent had indicated openness to sizable expenditure in search of long-term solutions; the problem, however, was that you needed to identify and price "solutions" that might work in your situation.

As you strategized, a plan began to emerge. You had recently attended a national conference on transportation and had visited vendor displays hawking new innovations in route management and tracking, safety and security, and fuel cost and operational savings. You recalled that you had seen software designed to optimally match smaller buses to routes in order to use less fuel; the use of global positioning systems to track bus real-time locations and stops and to remotely monitor vehicle performance; the use of alternative fuels to save money and reduce emissions; and ways to retrofit existing vehicles for fuel efficiency and emissions. You also recalled advances in safety and security that might upgrade your district's video camera system, as well as other new technologies, including heat-sensing devices to improve pedestrian safety around school buses and the use of other software to aid in routing considerations such as locating bus stops away from registered sexual predators' domiciles. It might work, you thought—the key was how much would it cost to engage these efficiencies and savings.

Below is a set of questions. As you respond, consider your learning in this chapter and apply your knowledge and experiences to the situation:

Questions

- In your estimation, which of the options being considered by the business manager deserves the highest priority? Why?

- Consider the potential costs and benefits associated with each of the proposed options and classify each along two dimensions: high, medium, or low cost; and high, medium, or low benefit.

- What cost efficiencies and security measures have been taken in your own school district? How much money has been invested in these concerns? How successful have these initiatives been in addressing cost/safety/security issues?

- Do you believe most school staffs (teachers, principals, etc.) will agree that money spent in search of these improvements is worthwhile, even if at the expense of instruction? Why or why not?

FOLLOW-UP ACTIVITIES

- Identify how transportation is funded in your state. Analyze the state funding formula to determine how many dollars are available and the relative emphasis on transportation in your state. Learn how the unaided portion of the transportation budget is met in your local district.

- Discuss with your school district's transportation director how services are structured in your district. Include issues related to decisions about owning versus outsourcing, purchasing, bid laws, maintenance and safety, driver training, and so on. Learn how transportation routing is carried out in your district.

- Identify how food service is funded in your state. Determine the mix of federal, state, and local aid to food service. Learn how meal prices are set and the philosophy that drives the local contribution to the food service fund.

- Meet with your district's food service director to learn how the district has structured this operation. Include issues such as compliance with federal and state requirements and local decisions about in-house and outsourced services, satelliting versus central kitchens, and so on. Discuss the qualifications of a food service director, the basis for approved menus, and other aspects of financial management.

WEB RESOURCES

Action for Healthy Kids, www.actionforhealthykids.org
American Association of School Administrators, www.aasa.org
Association of School Business Officials International, www.asbointl.org
Center for the Prevention of School Violence, www.cpsv.org
Education Commission of the States, www.ecs.org
Food Research and Action Center, www.frac.org

International Green Fuel, www.greendieseltechnology.com
National Alliance for Safe Schools, www.safeschools.org
National Association for Pupil Transportation, www.napt.org
National Business Officers Association, www.nboa.net
National Center for Education Statistics, www.nces.ed.gov
National Conference of State Legislatures, www.ncsl.org
National Education Association, www.nea.org
National Resource Center for Safe Schools, www.safetyzone.org
Pupil Transportation Safety Institute, www.ptsi.org
School Nutrition Association, www.schoolnutrition.org
USDA Food and Nutrition Service, School Meals, www.fns.usda.gov/cnd/
U.S. Department of Education, www.ed.gov

RECOMMENDED READINGS

Association of School Business Officials International. *School Business Affairs.* Reston, VA: Author, 1997–2007. Multiple volumes, issues, and articles on transportation and food services.

Attkisson, Sherry. *School Foodservice Handbook: A Guide for School Administrators.* Lanham, MD: Rowman & Littlefield Education, 1999.

Center on Hunger, Poverty and Nutrition Policy. *Statement on the Link Between Nutrition and Cognitive Development in Children.* Medford MA: Tufts University, 1998.

National Learning Corporation, ed. *School Transportation Coordinator.* New York: Author, 2005.

Parker, Philip M. *The 2007–2012 Outlook for School Food Service in the United States.* San Diego, CA: The ICON Group Intl, 2006.

Ray, John, I. Carl Candioli, and Walter G. Hack. *School Business Administration: A Planning Approach.* 8th ed. Boston: Allyn & Bacon, 2005.

Rudman, Jack. *School Food Service Supervisor.* New York: National Learning Corp., 2002.

Wood, R. Craig, David C. Thompson, and Lawrence O. Picus. *Principles of School Business Management.* 3rd ed. Reston, VA: ASBO, 2008.

LEGAL LIABILITY AND RISK MANAGEMENT

THE CHALLENGE

Of the 55 million pupils enrolled in public schools in 2005, students ages 12 to 18 years were victims of 1.4 million crimes at school, including 583,000 violent crimes. Fully 7% of teachers reported being threatened and another 4% reported being attacked at school. With 46% of schools taking at least one serious disciplinary action each year, 4% taking action for student-related firearms/explosives offenses, and 36% providing access to school grounds only through locked or monitored gates, there is a real concern for discipline, safety, and security—a concern only worsened by liability, as growth in tort-based lawsuits has exceeded growth in GNP for the past 50 years.

Data compiled from NCES Indicators
of School Crime and Safety: 2006 (2007)
and the American Tort Reform
Association (2005).

CHAPTER DRIVERS

At the close of this chapter, you will have reflected upon these questions:

- What is the relationship of schools to the law?
- How do schools derive legal authority?
- What is the origin and nature of legal liability?
- What is immunity, and how does it apply to schools?
- What is tort liability?
- What other kinds of liability arise in schools?
- What do legal liability and risk management mean in the context of school funding today?

MODERN REALITIES

From the outset, this textbook has offered an unvarnished worldview. We have made blunt statements about what schools may become in the future, and we have been critical of people who devalue the contribution of schools to the economic and social lifestyle Americans enjoy. We would be remiss in this book if we failed to also take a realistic view of legal liability and risk management in schools because no one associated with education is entirely immune to the far-reaching influence of law.

Once again, our goals in this chapter are driven by a practical need for information and application. We begin from the broadest perspective by considering the relationship of law to public schools, including how schools are granted authority and how liability issues enter into play. The discussion then deepens, turning to how immunity and liability affect common school interests such as civil rights, defamation, educational malpractice, and contractual liability. Finally, the chapter closes with consideration for how legal liability and risk management should affect the decisions and actions of education's stakeholders. In sum, the issues in this chapter are hard and unpleasant, but we live in an era of unparalleled legal risk where schools are often seen as deep pockets and as the means to right all the wrongs of history. As a result, this chapter provides a fitting conclusion to Part II of this text by warning that liability represents a significant obligation against education's financial assets.

WHAT DOES THE LAW HAVE TO DO WITH SCHOOLS?

Association of the law with public schools is older than the nation itself. Earlier discussion in this text noted that the early colonies passed laws requiring establishment of schools such as the *Ye Old Deluder Satan Act of 1647* in the Massachusetts colony, and the nation's first compulsory education law was passed in that same state in 1852. Such laws were obviously designed to force compliance, and it stands to reason that some people did not obey and were likely held accountable under the law. Although a grim perspective on what lawmaking can be about, laws are meant to apply first to lawless people, with the remainder established to authorize improvement of the social order and for other regulatory purposes.

The relationship of law to schools today so far exceeds the first colonial laws that it is staggering. Schools must be concerned with the legal rights of children, equal access to educational programs, special programs for the underprivileged, fair funding, and a host of other issues relating to constitutional and statutory protections. Legal rights extend to employment, with complex laws governing the rights of employees and employers so that schools are constantly embroiled in political turmoil over who holds the biggest legal stick. As we saw in Chapter 4 on the topic of accounting, the fiscal affairs of schools are tightly controlled by law because even the faintest hint of wrongdoing results in suspicion and may lead to dismissal. The concept of legal liability overarches all transactions and relationships in schools—that is, it is fundamental to say that school districts and every person associated with schools may be jointly and severally liable for wrongful acts and omissions.

The law and schools is thus a two-part relationship. One part of the relationship focuses on regulation for organizational purposes, while the other part focuses on liability for wrongful acts or omissions. Much of this book has related to the regulatory aspect of law because most chapters are deeply rooted in legal prescription for carrying out the educational mission. Our attention in this chapter, however, goes to the other part of the law—that is, respecting the risks and costs of liability because the law and schools have become close partners, with profound budget implications.

The Derivation of School Authority

Everyone associated with education believes that schools enjoy significant authority and control over educational matters. Fewer people, however, understand that such authority is both broadly derived and at the same time limited. As a preface to all issues in this chapter, it is important to identify the sources and limitations of schools' legal authority in order to gain a foundational understanding of the relationship between schools and the law.

Schools derive their legal authority from both constitutional and statutory roots. These sources are complex and interrelated. An overarching view notes that school authority originates in the federal Constitution, the United States Congress, the federal judiciary, the constitutions of the individual states, state legislatures, state courts, and state boards of education. Each source has had a significant influence on the educational enterprise, so much so that the very existence of the local school district, its board of education, and its educational mission are derived from the combination of these powerful forces.

Federal Constitution

Involvement of the federal government in education has been both peripheral and influential. Starting with early federal interest through land grants to newly formed states to be used for educational purposes, federal involvement in schools has grown to be a significant force. The federal path has been indirect because the U.S. Constitution is a document of limited powers, meaning Congress cannot assume powers absent specific authorization in the Constitution. As we noted earlier, the Constitution is silent regarding a federal education role. In the absence of authority, Congress has had to find other ways to affect education because only a Constitutional amendment could establish a direct federal role in schools. In the context of this chapter, the U.S. Constitution both grants authority and creates liability for schools by endowing certain rights to citizens relating to education, while leaving direct responsibility for education to the states.

Congress

Given only limited Constitutional powers, Congress itself has had to become the vehicle for federal involvement in schools. Although having no direct education role, Congress has found a loophole through the General Welfare clause of the Constitution, which Congress has used to pass many laws affecting schools by interpreting general welfare benevolently and broadly. Under this banner, Congress has created a huge federal education bureaucracy that grants billions in aid to hundreds of programs in elementary and secondary schools and higher education. In related actions, Congress has found other ways to indirectly drive education policy by tying seemingly unrelated federal monies to education in order to pressure states to bow to federal education policy. For example, Congress has often tied federal revenue sharing for such projects as highways to Congressional educational interests by threatening withdrawal of highway funds if states do not adopt federal education goals. Likewise, federal laws affecting special education and civil rights powerfully impact schools, as do other laws such as *No Child Left Behind* and its subsequent reauthorization. In the context of this chapter, Congress both grants authority to schools and creates liability by passing laws supporting certain educational initiatives that result in both benefit and liability.

Federal Judiciary

A significant source of authority in schools also rests with the federal courts. In a complex hierarchical legal system, federal rulings may take precedence over state courts, as in the familiar appeal to the U.S. Supreme Court as the court of last resort. In essence, federal courts have held great sway over education by applying federal Constitutional requirements to schools. Racial integration, educational deprivation, special and compensatory education, and countless other educational programs are examples of the result of federal courts' interest in education issues. Congress's involvement at this level has been felt, too, as Congress has exerted enormous control over education through the courts by virtue of its role in appointing federal judges who Congress hopes will take a supportive view of federal interests, including federal goals for education. Similarly, Congress has been responsible for writing most of the laws tested in federal courts. The upshot is that although the federal government cannot assume a direct role in education, its influence has been highly disproportionate via the General Welfare clause, by linking unrelated subsidies to federal educational interests, and by appointing federal judges who in turn rule on questions affecting schools. In the context of this chapter, federal courts both grant authority and create liability for schools by virtue of their politically appointed nature and by their legitimate role as guardians of the law.

State Constitutions

The same authority that prevents a strong federal role in education conversely grants full power over schools to the individual states. The constitutional conventions of each state almost invariably mentioned education, writing into their earliest charters an active role for states. Indeed, school finance litigation today always turns first to the states' constitutional framers' intent to test whether state legislatures are meeting their constitutional obligations. The language of a state constitution's references to education can be a powerful influence on educational policy, granting sweeping power to the state or significantly limiting state responsibility. In essence, states have plenary power over schools, subject only to higher federal protections such as Fourteenth Amendment due process. In fact, all sources of law at the state level regarding education derive from individual state constitutional authorization to its legislature. In the context of this chapter, state constitutions both grant authority and create liability for schools by requiring legislatures to devise enabling educational statutes, which in turn result in both authority and liability.

State Legislatures

Short of constitutional proscription, a state legislature has authority to write any law affecting schools that it chooses. In essence, state legislatures hold absolute power and are bound only by the duties and constraints interpreted by courts based on the applicable constitution. Although those duties and constraints are formidable given federal and state education laws and constitutional requirements for educational equity, state legislatures have plenary control over schools. For example, nothing in federal or state constitutions typically forbids a legislature from creating or abolishing a state department of education, consolidating or reorganizing school districts, increasing or decreasing state financial support for education, or a host of other far-reaching reforms. The source of such power and restrictions rests in each state's constitution and in its relationship to the courts, which interpret the constitutionality of legislative actions. In essence, states control the statutes governing schools and may create or abolish educational structures at will, limited only by the constitutionality of their actions. In the context of this chapter, state legislatures are the ultimate source of authority and liability in schools.

State Judiciary

The system of checks and balances in American government calls for separation of the executive, legislative, and judicial branches. State courts frequently have been asked to test the limits of state legislative power, thereby creating one of the very few checks on legislative prerogative. In the context of this chapter, state courts guard the legality of state acts under the state constitution, making state courts a source of authority and the evaluator of liability in schools.

State Boards of Education

Although state legislatures have full power over schools, most states have delegated responsibility for conducting education to a state school board. State boards are arms of the state, usually created in statute and subject to legislative will. Alternatively, state boards may be constitutional creations, but usually are still under legislative control. As such, schools are legislatively based, with authority passed to lower administrative units. In the context of this chapter, state boards both grant authority and create liability for schools by virtue of the rules and regulations they promulgate and administer.

Local Authority to Act

At the bottom of the hierarchy are local school boards, to which states have delegated daily operation of schools. As such, local school districts are subject to legislative control and may be organized as determined by the legislature and state board. In essence, local districts serve at the pleasure of some higher unit of government and are subject to all laws and regulations—in effect, school districts are ordered to actually carry out the state's educational duties. In the context of this chapter, local school boards function in a constitutionally limited context of state and federal laws under the watchful eye of a state legislature and state board of education—an environment that passes significant responsibility and liability to the firing line of local schools.

WHAT IS THE ORIGIN OF LIABILITY?

The concept of liability is deeply rooted in this nation's history. Many excellent sources detail development of American jurisprudence, but all such sources begin with our inheritance from English law. Among those imported precepts are the key elements of sovereign immunity and tort law. Although many other aspects of law, including criminal law, at times apply to schools, issues involving torts and immunity arise most often and may place public and personal financial resources at jeopardy.

Sovereign Immunity

Sovereign immunity refers to a precept from English law that literally argued "the king can do no wrong." The importance of this concept is immediately apparent because law is often based on following certain logic to an obvious conclusion. If courts accepted that the king could do no wrong and that a king is the head of state, then the state could do no wrong. The ramification is obvious—that is, government is immune in its acts or omissions, a concept not greatly at odds with other sovereign views such as the divine right of kings.

Although Americans today might ponder sovereign immunity and ask how anyone ever tolerated such raw power, it is the case that sovereign immunity was unquestioningly transported into colonial law. The impact of English law on government was seen quickly in the new nation, as the 1812 Massachusetts case of *Mower*[1] held that the state was not liable for its acts. Sovereign immunity in *Mower* and subsequent cases was based on four distinct viewpoints that actually make good sense. One viewpoint argued that the government has limited resources so that proliferation of lawsuits stemming from a ruling, even for limited liability, would be detrimental to the public treasury. A second view held that government must be free from fear of liability because any act of law does not carry equal benefit for each citizen. A third view held that government is the people, especially in a democracy, such that it follows that suit against government is a suit against oneself. A fourth view also held that committing an illegal act is never within the authority of government, so that a wrongful act exceeds any legal authority. This logic also became integral to many U.S. Supreme Court decisions, with the Court noting as early as 1869 that, "[e]very government has an inherent right to protect itself against suits..." and that "the principle is fundamental and applies to every sovereign power."[2] Although we again note that Americans today would view such logic askance and further note that sovereign immunity is now much maligned, it survived nearly unquestioned in this nation until only recently. This is not to say that sovereign immunity has been abandoned, but rather that gradual chipping away has occurred.

Erosion of sovereign immunity was especially aided by two related events. The first event was Congressional enactment in 1946 of the Federal Tort Claims Act, establishing liability for acts by the federal government. In passing the act, Congress agreed that absolute sovereign immunity was no longer viable federal policy and

---

1   *Mower v. The Inhabitants of Leicester*, 9 Mass. 247 (1812).
2   *Nichols v. United States*, 74 U.S. 122 (1869).

thereby opened the door to lawsuits where previously no recourse had existed. But even yet, old concepts held sway as the act actually established only limited liability and preserved immunity for intentional torts and errors of omission by employees acting within their discretionary functions. The second event followed as states adopted similar legislation, again providing at least some recourse against potential abuses of government. The result of these two events led naturally to numerous suits in equity and made possible claims against the financial assets of federal, state, and local governments.

Although federal and state case law is vast when tracing the assault on sovereign immunity, *Molitor*[3] illustrates the fundamental logic underlying all such attacks. In this 1959 case, the state supreme court of Illinois traced the origins of sovereign immunity and its adoption into state law via two other cases styled as *Waltham*[4] and *Kinnare*.[5] Sovereign immunity had been established in Illinois for towns and counties in *Waltham* and had been extended to school districts in *Kinnare,* wherein it was held that a school board was not liable for the death of a laborer who fell from a rooftop, even though the district had not provided safety measures such as scaffolding. Many years later, *Molitor* reversed on the immunity ruling, as the court held a school district liable for injury to a student when a school bus hit a culvert and exploded. The court rejected the traditional argument that permitting liability required wrongful use of public funds to settle claims and further held that depletion of the state treasury was no longer a good defense. The Illinois court quoted a New Mexico case, taking that view as its own, saying, "The whole doctrine of governmental immunity from liability for tort rests on a rotten foundation. It is almost incredible that in this modern age of comparative sociological enlightenment, and in a republic, the medieval absolutism supposed to be implicit in the maxim, 'the King can do no wrong' should exempt the various branches of government from liability for their torts."[6]

Through a long and tortuous history, the concept of governmental liability has taken on new importance. Federal, state, and local governments may now be liable under certain conditions, and employees face the same risk because acting in official capacity is no longer an automatic pass. Of particular importance are the established exceptions to sovereign immunity, as it is decided that liability may apply to proprietary acts, nuisances, and Eleventh Amendment issues, along with other exposure relating to constitutional infringements. In sum, the cracks in immunity defenses have opened all units of government, including schools and school officials, to liability exposure, wherein the outcome of a liability claim will depend on statute and facts and venue—conditions requiring careful management to minimize the financial impact of successful claims.

---

3   *Molitor v. Kaneland Comm. Unit Dist.,* 18 Ill.2d 11, 163 N.E.2d 89 (Ill. 1959).

4   *Town of Waltham v. Kemper,* 55 Ill. 346 (Northern Grand Division 1870).

5   *Kinnare v. City of Chicago,* 171 Ill. 332, 49 N.E. 536 (Northern Grand Division 1898).

6   *Barker v. City of Santa Fe,* 47 N.M. 85, 136 P.2d at 482.

Proprietary Acts Exception

Growing unwillingness of some courts to accept unlimited sovereign immunity has resulted in several exceptions. One of the more widely sympathetic exceptions to immunity involves proprietary acts. This exception occurs as a court determines whether the act at trial was governmental or proprietary in nature. The distinction rests in a governmental function being defined as exercise of police power or a constitutional, legislative, administrative, or judicial power conferred upon federal, state, or local government and its agents; in contrast, proprietary acts are outside the primary scope of the governmental unit itself.

In the context of schools, the difference comes by distinguishing educational activities from other school-sponsored events not central to the educational mission. For example, athletic events outside school time or other voluntary events may invoke a different liability threshold than class field trips. Rulings on such distinctions are inconsistent, however, even given similar circumstances. For example, a spectator in *Sawaya*[7] was injured when a bleacher railing failed at a game where two districts had rented a football stadium from a third district. The state supreme court of Arizona held the third district liable, finding the event to be proprietary. In contrast, in an identical case of *Richards*[8] a Michigan court found no liability, holding that the district did not intend to make a profit from the event and was merely providing an educational activity. The controlling feature seems to be how individual states have ruled on immunity, as illustrated by a Michigan court in *Ross*,[9] which said: "When a governmental agency engages in mandated or authorized activities, it is immune from tort liability unless the activity is proprietary in nature." In contrast, a Texas court said in *Stout*,[10] "Since a school district is purely a governmental agency...it performs no proprietary functions separate from governmental functions." Thus liability for proprietary acts is subject to interpretation of state legislative intent in abrogating immunity and further subject to state courts' attitude toward governmental immunity and liability.

Nuisance Exception

A more familiar immunity exception rests in nuisances. A nuisance allows a condition that injures or endangers health, safety, or welfare. When a nuisance claim arises, it is nearly always in the context that the nuisance was knowable and that there was no attempt or only inadequate effort to prevent an injury. Probably the most common nuisance claim relates to attractive nuisances, which require higher levels of care because the nuisance may be expected to create problems. In the context of schools, a classic example is seen in the Michigan case of *Hendricks*[11] where the court held that a school district had not created or maintained a nuisance when it piled snow on a

---

7 *Sawaya v. Tucson High Sch. Dist.*, 78 Ariz. 389, 281 P.2d 105 (1955).

8 *Richards v. School Dist. of City of Birmingham*, 348 Mich. 490, 83 N.W.2d 643 (1957).

9 *Ross v. Consumers Power Co.*, 420 Mich. 567, 363 N.W.2d 641 (1984).

10 *Stout v. Grand Prairie Sch. Dist.*, 733 S.W.2d at 296 (Tex. App. 1987).

11 *Hendricks v. Southfield Public Schools*, 178 Mich. App. 672, 444 N.W.2d 143 (1989).

playground, resulting in a climbing injury to a child. The court said that to establish a claim of intentional nuisance against a governmental agency, a plaintiff must show that there is a genuine nuisance condition and that the agency intended to create a hazard. Importantly, though, case law is replete with challenges reaching an opposite conclusion.

Although nuisance liability is unpredictable in that establishing liability depends on specific laws and jurisdictions and the unique facts of each case, the concept of nuisance represents another instance in which exception to governmental immunity has been successful in modern context. Clearly, in the case of schools a finding for liability relies heavily on the standard of care required for the particular age of injured persons—and as a matter of prudence, it is also clear that prevention is advisable to safeguard against liability.

Eleventh Amendment Exception

A special situation relates to a third area in which governmental immunity has been at least partially overturned. The Eleventh Amendment to the U.S. Constitution, ratified in 1795, provides that, "...the judicial power of the United States shall not be construed to extend to any suit in law or equity, commenced or prosecuted against one of the United States by citizens of another State, or by citizens or subjects of any foreign state." The Eleventh Amendment was a response to two lawsuits in 1791 and 1792, in which claims against states were brought in Maryland and Georgia. In *Vanstophorst*,[12] foreign residents had brought suit against the state of Maryland for recovery of bad debts. In *Chisholm*,[13] residents of South Carolina had sought a judgment against the state of Georgia. The potential for federal liability spurred passage of the Eleventh Amendment to deny recourse under applicable constitutional protections.

The Eleventh Amendment closed off an opportunity for litigants. This basis of immunity was successful for years, as the U.S. Supreme Court ruled repeatedly that the intent of the amendment was express, including barring suit against a state by citizens of another state and prohibiting citizens from bringing federal suit against their own states. Schools have enjoyed Eleventh Amendment immunity as well under the assumption that the state was implicated to such an extent that liability would extend to schools as arms of the state.

Limits on immunity under the Eleventh Amendment, however, have been established. In some cases, states have voluntarily waived their right to Eleventh Amendment immunity. Usually, waiver is available only when the state explicitly permits and sets forth its intent to allow suit against itself as in *Edelman*.[14] Congress has additionally and purposely limited other Eleventh Amendment immunity, as in the *Individuals with Disabilities Education Act* (IDEA) where Congress specifically denied immunity to states from federal suits for violations of IDEA. Similarly, because Congress has granted itself power to write legislation invoking penalties for successful

---

12 *Vanstophorst v. Maryland*, 2 U.S. (2 Dall.) 401 (1791).
13 *Chisholm v. Georgia*, 2 U.S. (2 Dall.) 419 (1792).
14 *Edelman v Jordan*, 415 U.S. 651, 94 S. Ct. 1347 (1974).

equal protection claims, Eleventh Amendment immunity is unavailable when such a violation occurs. A final limitation is important for schools because Eleventh Amendment immunity may depend on whether courts see schools as a direct arm of the state. This distinction was made in *Mt. Healthy*,[15] as the U.S. Supreme Court held local school districts in a similar light to city and county governments, rather than in the traditional context of seeing schools as an arm or extension of the state. In this case, liability was present because the Court saw schools as political subdivisions of the state as a consequence of their taxing power and autonomy.

In the overall modern context of sovereign immunity, governments still enjoy significant protection from liability, but exceptions and changing attitudes have severely limited what was once absolute immunity. Federal statutory limits on immunity have been an important catalyst for increased liability, especially in context of the Federal Tort Claims Act and the Eleventh Amendment. Enactment of state tort claims acts likewise has meaningfully limited immunity defenses. Doctrinal modifications by courts distinguishing proprietary acts and nuisances have given further footholds to claimants. The result of a complicated historical erosion is that neither absolute immunity nor absolute liability is the unquestioned eventuality today, so that school districts and officials must regard liability—and its potential claim against district and personal resources—as an ever-present companion.[16]

Tort Liability

With no assurance of immunity, all units of government now have potential liability for a wide variety of acts and omissions. As a result, a huge body of statutes and case law has sprung up around issues of liability.

Most governmental liability arises from the law of torts. A tort is a wrongful act other than a breach of contract for which relief may be obtained in the form of damages or an injunction. A claim for tort liability is thus broad, taking in a great many wrongs affecting nearly every aspect of human existence. Torts may arise from defamation, civil rights, negligence, and so on. Although the scope of claims is great, most torts fall into one of three categories: *intentional* torts, torts involving *negligence,* and *strict liability* torts. The law of torts applies to schools as governmental agencies, and individual personal liability may be a concern as well. For our purposes, intentional torts and negligence are most relevant to schools.

Intentional Torts

An intentional tort is defined as a wrong by someone who intends to do something the law has declared wrong. Such torts involve intent or malice, but malice may be simple indifference. Most such cases in schools probably do not involve true intent

---

15 *Mt. Healthy City Sch. Dist. Bd. of Educ. v. Dole*, 429 U.S. 274, 97 S. Ct. 568 (1977).

16 Although governmental immunity is largely "settled" as described in this chapter's discussion, questions of immunity continue to recur as illustrated by the fact that in the period since the last edition of this book four such claims reached the U.S. Supreme Court and nine such claims drew the Court's interest in the last 5 years. See, e.g., *Northern Ins. Co. v. Chatham County*, 547 U.S. 189, 126 S. Ct. 1689 (2006).

or malice, but there are many opportunities for intentional tort claims wherein it is alleged that some act crossed the line of intent and was accompanied by reasonable expectation of harm.

One of the more frequent intentional tort claims in schools relates to corporal punishment, as school personnel are sometimes charged with having crossed the intent line. Such cases usually allege assault and battery. Assault is any threat to inflict injury which, when coupled with a display of force, would give a victim reason to fear bodily harm. Battery is usually filed in such cases too, as it is defined as the touching threatened by assault. While as a rule courts have been unwilling to outlaw corporal punishment and the U.S. Supreme Court clearly said in *Ingraham*[17] that there is no violation of the Eighth Amendment's prohibition against cruel and unusual punishment, there is a vast record of intentional tort claims against schools over this issue. These claims should give rise to considerable caution on the part of school personnel from both moral and legal perspectives. For example, cases have involved students who were beaten severely enough to produce medical trauma, as in *Ingraham,* which resulted in a hematoma, or as in *Mathis,*[18] which claimed posttraumatic stress disorder, and other bizarre acts such as a teacher kicking a disobedient student.[19] Although these cases did not find schools liable, other cases have found oppositely. For example, a teacher was convicted of assault and battery for having broken a student's arm by shaking and dropping him to the floor.[20] Likewise, a teacher was liable for breaking a pupil's collarbone upon throwing him into a wall.[21] Liability was also found when a third-grader was held upside down by her ankles while the principal whipped her with a paddle.[22] Similarly, liability was found when a physical education teacher allowed a student to drown, thinking the child was joking and sent students into the water instead of rescuing the child himself.[23] Although these cases seem outrageous, their existence indicates that common sense does not characterize everyone who works in schools. Intentional torts make up a big part of liability case law, and it is certain that schools will continue to face such claims. Obviously, there is a real possibility that wrongful acts in schools may also end up in criminal court—again, a concept not entirely foreign to schools.

Negligence

Another frequent tort action in schools is a negligence claim. Negligence is defined as conduct falling below a legally established standard of care, resulting in harm. In examining such claims, liability depends on the facts regarding breach of duty, proximate cause, and actual harm.

---

17 *Ingraham v. Wright,* 430 U.S. 651, 97 S. Ct. 1401 (1977).

18 *Mathis v. Berrien County Sch. Dist.,* 378 S.E.2d 505 (Ga. App. 1989).

19 *Thompson v. Iberville Parish Sch. Bd.,* 372 So.2d 642 (La. Ct. App. 1979), *writ denied,* 374 So.2d 650 (La. 1979).

20 *Frank v. Orleans Parish Sch. Bd.,* 195 So.2d 451 (La. Ct. App. 1967).

21 *Sansone v. Bechtel,* 429 A.2d 820 (Conn. 1980).

22 *Garcia v. Miera,* 817 F.2d 650 (10th Circ. 1987).

23 *Thompson v. Bagley,* 835 NE2d (Ohio Ct. App. 2005).

Duty refers to proof that the actor had a responsibility to the injured party. A duty can arise from statute or even common sense. Inadequate supervision is probably the most common allegation for breach of duty in schools, followed by claims involving lack of proper instruction and failure to maintain a safe environment. The standard most often applied is the "reasonable person" test, whereby a defendant's actions are compared to the prudence and skill that would be applied by a reasonable person in the same or similar circumstance. Because our interest relates to school-based liability, the added dimension of superior skill or knowledge is key, so that the reasonableness test takes on the crucial characteristic of the behavior of a professional under the same or similar circumstance. Proximate cause relates to whether the action in fact caused the injury because there is no liability if there is no unbroken chain of events leading to the defendant. Furthermore, the negligence must be substantial—that is, negligence, while easily claimed, must meet a threshold of impact.

The issue of negligence in schools arises from a duty to protect students from foreseeable harm. Under the *in loco parentis* doctrine, this duty is broad as illustrated by *Garcia*,[24] where a five-year-old boy was sexually molested when he was sent to the bathroom alone in violation of the school's written guidelines. The court found that the assault was preventable by proper supervision, which was defined as the degree of supervision a parent of ordinary prudence would take in comparable circumstance. Although the court agreed that a school cannot foresee and take precautions against sudden spontaneous acts by other students and that while the school had no history of similar incidents, liability still applied based on the school's knowledge of danger to unattended students; that is, knowledge implied via the school's written security policies and via the principal's testimony admitting the risks to unescorted students in hallways and bathrooms. Similarly, the U.S. Supreme Court spoke in *Davis*[25] to the duty of educators to guard against student violence and harassment. The victim was a fifth-grade girl who had been sexually harassed by another student. She reported the events to teachers, but the school still took no action. Charges were filed, with the defendant admitting to sexual battery, whereupon the victim's mother sued the board of education and school leaders for damages under Title IX of the *Education Amendments of 1972*. The Court found for plaintiffs, stating that educators are on notice that they may be liable for their failure to protect students from the tortious acts of third parties. The Court further noted that state courts routinely uphold claims alleging that schools have been negligent in failing to protect students from their peers—notably, the Court cited cases from 1953, 1979, and 1982 in long-standing support for its ruling.

Case law is by no means unanimous, however, in fixing liability on schools at the state level, in part because of the question of immunity.[26] State rulings favoring immunity have led to suits in federal court, asserting that schools have a federal con-

---

24 *Garcia v. City of New York,* 646 N.Y.S.2d 508 (App. Div. 1996).

25 *Davis v. Monroe County Board of Education*, 119 S. Ct. 1661 (1999).

26 For example, see *Chesshir v. Sharp,* 19 S.W.3d 502 (Tex. App.–Amarillo 2000) where state statutory immunity protected a teacher when a 5-year-old boy splattered hot grease on his face from a hot frying pan in the classroom.

stitutional duty to protect students from danger.[27] These causes of action, known as civil rights torts, are typically filed under 42 U.S.C. §1983, which allows plaintiffs to seek compensatory and punitive damages when liability can be successfully established.

Several cases illustrate the liability issues at stake. In *Leffal*,[28] an 18-year-old student was killed by random gunfire in a school parking lot after a school dance. The issue was whether the student's constitutional rights were violated by the decision of the school district to sponsor the dance even after being asked by local police to stop sponsoring such events until adequate security could be provided. Only two unarmed guards were assigned to the dance and were unable to prevent the violence. Notwithstanding prior knowledge of danger, the court noted that although students are required to attend school, they are not required to attend dances so that the state's failure to protect against violence did not violate the Constitution. The court noted that the standard under §1983 is a "deliberate indifference" standard where the plaintiff must show that (a) an unusually serious risk of harm existed, (b) the defendant had actual knowledge, or was willfully blind to, the elevated risk, and (c) the defendant failed to take obvious steps to address the risk.[29] Similar results followed in *Rudd*,[30] when a student warned his teachers that another student had brought a gun to school. Officials failed to find the weapon despite a thorough search, whereupon later in the day the suspect pulled out the hidden gun and killed another student on his school bus. The state supreme court held that the district was not liable under the Arkansas Civil Rights Act and further enjoyed immunity from tort liability.

The difficult nature of liability claims is illustrated by the fact that courts have exercised considerable caution when limiting broad constitutional freedoms in the name of safety. In 1999, the U.S. Supreme Court noted that the maintenance of discipline in schools requires that students be restrained from assaulting one another, abusing drugs and alcohol, and committing other crimes.[31] But a heavy burden is still present for school officials when deciding to potentially infringe on constitutional rights. The controlling authority has continued to be *TLO*,[32] where the Court provided a two-part test for reasonableness in school contraband searches, including weapons. The Court held in *TLO* that a search first must be justified at its inception, and second, that it must be permissible in scope so as to not excessively intrude in light of the age and gender of the student and the nature of the infraction.[33] Today, courts are considering school violence and reaching different results as these issues sometimes cross over into freedom of expression. For example, courts have examined First Amendment protections in cases of threats of violence. Although "fighting words" and

---

27 See, e.g., *Graham v. Independent School District No. I-89*, 22 F.3d 991 (10th Cir. 1994).
28 *Leffal v. Dallas Independent School District*, 28 F.3d 521 (5th Cir. 1994).
29 *Leffal*, 28 F.3d at 531.
30 *Rudd v. Pulaski County Special School District*, 20 S.W.3d 310 (Ark. 2000).
31 *Davis v. Monroe County Board of Education*, 119 S. Ct. 1661 (1999).
32 *New Jersey v. TLO*, 469 U.S. 325 (1985).
33 See, e.g., *Vernonia School District 47 v. Acton*, 515 U.S. 646 (1995); see also *Smith v. McGlothlin*, 119 F.3d 766 (9th Cir. 1997).

threats presenting a clear and present danger historically have not enjoyed First Amendment protection, courts have taken into consideration whether such statements made in school settings are believable. For example, in *Lovell*[34] the lower court considered the suspension of a student after she threatened to shoot a counselor over a disagreement involving a class schedule change. The lower court held that boundaries may be imposed on the right to free speech by prohibiting threats of physical injury; however, the court also said that what constitutes a threat is subject to the First Amendment, so that punishable threats are limited to those statements which convey "…a gravity of purpose and likelihood of execution."[35]

The cases presented here for illustration lead to the conclusion that liability is a serious issue for school districts and staffs. The data alone are enough to stir anxieties and to leave school leaders without a clear roadmap on how to deal with keeping schools both safe and free. One line of court cases leads to the view that schools may restrict student behavior in the name of safety without fear of liability, while another line of cases warns that courts will not be sympathetic to trampling of constitutional freedoms. In actuality, middle-ground perspectives provide the best course of action. First, there is a strong duty to exercise the reasonable person rule, consistently applying it to all issues ranging from freedom of speech to search and seizure under reasonable suspicion of safety concerns. Second, school leaders should not fear liability for having acted affirmatively, inasmuch as they might otherwise be held liable for failing to exercise appropriate care. Third, courts generally do not hold educators liable for injuries resulting from spontaneous acts of violence if these acts are unforeseeable—as a rule, this includes injuries caused by nonstudent assailants. However, school leaders are expected to be watchful, as a significant duty exists when the assailant is a student because courts will consider a student's prior conduct so that if evidence of antisocial behavior is shown, the student's future violent acts may have been predictable. Fourth, there is a significant responsibility for preparedness, including evidence of sound risk management training. The reasoning of courts in student suicide cases may be applied analogously to all these issues and particularly to school violence; that is, without adequate training, school employees may underestimate threats of violence. In essence, training in risk prevention may soon become a standard of care for educators.

The discussion in this section clearly indicates that the potential for negligence claims against school districts and persons in their official and individual capacities is great. Of particular concern is that damages may apply if negligence is established. Damages may be compensatory or punitive, depending on whether they are awarded as compensation for actual loss or as punishment for negligence. Compensation may include medical bills and loss of earnings, and may also be given for injuries such as emotional distress or pain and suffering. Other monetary judgments may be assessed too, including exemplary damages meant to make an example of negligent behavior in order to reduce its likelihood of reoccurrence. But for school districts and staff, the issue is clear: liability represents a significant potential claim against financial

---

34 *Lovell v. Poway Unified School District,* 847 F. Supp. 780 (S.D. Cal. 1994).

35 *Lovell* at 784.

assets—either by personal vulnerability or by having to budget school district monies in anticipation of potential liability claims.

Civil Rights

Of all the areas of potential liability faced by school districts, in historical perspective none has garnered more press than civil rights litigation. Stemming from the *Civil Rights Act of 1875* and extending today to embrace a vast body of constitutional and statutory protections against all kinds of discrimination, civil rights have come to represent a constant liability concern for schools.

Civil rights litigation has been present in the nation almost since its birth. The *Civil Rights Act of 1875*, however, opened a new era by seeking to prevent both lawful and unlawful racial discrimination following the Civil War. Because federal law is usually controlling on states, it was reasonable to turn first to federal courts in an attempt to more broadly construe liability beyond simply strict racial discrimination. Consequently, the *Civil Rights Act of 1875* was the legal premise underlying much subsequent litigation, including the famous *Brown v. Board of Education*[36] decision in 1954, which marked the end of "separate but equal" educational provisions in the United States. The basic concept of liability under this federal act was thereby extended to include personal liability of public officials who violate the federal constitutional or statutory civil rights of another individual. This law, usually referred to in relevant part as §1983, denied immunity from liability when it stated:

> Every person who, under color of any statute, ordinance, regulation, custom, or usage, of any State or Territory, subjects, or causes to be subjected, any citizen of the United States or other person within the jurisdiction thereof to the deprivation of any rights, privileges, or immunities secured by the Constitution and laws, shall be liable to the party injured in an action at law, set in equity, or other proper proceeding for redress.

Given such strong language, the struggle over civil rights became even more intense in all corners of society and has had especial importance for schools. Recognizing that every governmental and private action could be closely scrutinized for intent and effect, school officials have been required to be vigilant in making certain that their acts are honorable and above reproach. The fundamental question of liability for acts of school officials was reviewed in *Wood*,[37] which examined school board members' liability risk. Although the U.S. Supreme Court has generally held for officials' immunity when acting in good faith, the Court noted in *Wood* that a board member is not immune under §1983 if that board member knew or reasonably should have known that an action taken within a sphere of official responsibility would violate constitutional rights, or if an act intended a deprivation of constitutional rights. As a consequence, *Wood* set a new standard of "qualified good faith" immunity, wherein liability may arise under three specific conditions. First, board members are legally bound to make decisions within current law. Second, ignorance of the law is no

---

36 374 U.S. 483 (1954).
37 *Wood v. Strickland,* 420 U.S. 308 (1975).

excuse. Third, immunity is forfeited if it is shown that the violator intended harm or if those actions originated in vindictiveness or spite.

A significant burden has thus been placed on schools by §1983—a weighty and expansive burden because of the vast range of possible wrongs. As that door has opened, civil rights legislation has abounded and interpretation of the law has become a career for legislatures, courts, and litigants. The range of liability now takes in a panorama of possible grievances, with governmental units—including schools— required to clearly state and meticulously observe compliance with nondiscrimination. Yet despite the weightiness of §1983 and related law, a judgment for plaintiffs is not an automatic outcome of a civil rights allegation. Liability usually revolves around an indifference standard; for example, if a school official acts callously toward the rights of an individual, liability may arise in both official and individual capacities and can be very costly because §1983 provides that actual and compensatory damages as well as attorney fees may be assigned to the defendant. Civil rights liability has therefore generated a justifiably high level of anxiety. For example, in *Kinsey*[38] a superintendent won $250,000 for mental anguish and loss to his reputation when he was fired after supporting certain candidates in a school board election. Likewise, punitive damages have been awarded, as in *Fishman*[39] when a school district fired a teacher over First Amendment free speech claims. These awards are not especially large, particularly in the context of recent litigation involving such issues as sexual harassment or special education; rather, the cases cited here are purposely chosen to represent the *less*-flamboyant claims arising under civil rights. As a result, many civil rights claims are settled out of court without regard to fault because the cost of defense may be higher than the cost of settlement—a cost that diminishes the district's resources in either event.

Defamation

Still another liability concern relates to defamation. In most instances affecting schools, defamation attaches to faculty and students, with claims most often relating to student records. Schools by their nature accumulate and report data on staff and students, a trend that has only increased with accountability and performance-based school reforms. For example, administrators and boards must evaluate teachers and are at times required to dismiss undesirable or incompetent staff. Likewise, the whole educational process consists of gathering and analyzing data on students and preserving it in perpetuity. While these are among the fundamental duties of schools, they are ripe opportunities for liability if improperly carried out.

Defamation may be libel, in which case harm is done to another person in writing. Defamation also may be slander, in which case the harm is done verbally. In either case, defamation may be *per se* or *per quod*. Defamation *per se* is words requiring no proof of harm beyond their clear meaning. Defamation *per quod* requires an examination of facts. Either form is an actionable tort that may invoke liability, and for

---

38   *Kinsey v. Saldo Indep. Sch. Dist.*, 916 F.2d 273 (5th Cir. 1990), *reh. en banc*, 925 F.2d 118 (5th Cir. 1991).

39   *Fishman v. Clancy*, 763 F.2d 485 (1st Cir. 1985).

which the only defenses are privilege and good faith. In all cases, schools and staffs are vulnerable to defamation claims given such a record-intensive environment.

The defenses of privilege and good faith are important in that they are the basis for schools to conduct the business of preparing and distributing information about pupils and staff. Although these are the only defenses against defamation, they are not inconsequential in that they make it possible to prepare student transcripts and teacher employment records. Care is required, however, because the gravity of permanent records has resulted in only a qualified immunity privilege that holds these records to a higher standard than is true in most other instances. In particular, a defense of privilege in schools is more difficult than for other public officials—for example, justices and state officers have absolute privilege as long as they act officially, and that same privilege extends to anyone involved in judicial or legislative acts such as testimony. In contrast, schools have only a qualified privilege in that they are protected only when carrying out duties common to such organizations and provided that they are acting in good faith. Qualified privilege is further restricted in that even truthful statements lacking good intent, or statements thought to be true, are actionable. Countless examples of this limitation abound, as in an oft-quoted case when a teacher described a student as "…ruined by tobacco and whiskey."[40] To be safe, statements must be made in good faith and may not go further than to state the facts.

Schools may also readily encounter defamation issues when making statements about teachers' fitness to teach and in performance evaluations, although courts are slow to act except in clear factual instances. As noted in *Malia*,[41] qualified immunity is the rule except when it is clearly shown that comments were motivated by personal malice or animosity, or when the evidence against privilege and good faith is overwhelming. A similar opportunity for problems arises in permanent or anecdotal student records, particularly given accessibility under the *Family Educational Rights and Privacy Act* (FERPA) passed by Congress in 1974. This act stipulated which records must be available to parents and students and laid out rules regarding which parts of school information are public or confidential. Under FERPA, student records may not be released without written consent of the parent; pupil records must be open to parents of children younger than age 18 years and to the child once age 18 years is reached; a record must be kept of anyone examining school records; contents of files may be challenged; and public directory information must be identified in advance of publication. As a consequence, school records maintenance may leave a trail leading to a successful defamation claim, with liability attaching for schools and individuals. As always, avoiding liability requires sound policies based on competent legal advice.

Educational Malpractice

Another liability concern for schools has been the matter of educational malpractice. Although very broad-based in its potential implications, the general issue has

---

40 *Dawkins v. Billingsley,* 172 P. 69 (Okla. S. Ct. 1918).

41 *Malia v. Monchak,* 543 A.2d 184 (Pa. Commwlth. Ct. 1988).

been the relationship between student achievement and quality of instruction—an issue undoubtedly destined to become more important as accountability pressures on schools escalate. The issue is not new, as since the 1970s schools have feared that malpractice claims would eventually find traction.

Educational malpractice seeks to apply tort law to student academic failure. Malpractice might be seen as an intentional tort or as negligence. Claims have been hard to prove, however, as an intentional tort would need to show that a school maliciously sought to impede a child's progress. A claim for negligence has been more common. Early malpractice cases raised the question of whether students have the right to a particular achievement level under compulsory attendance laws, while more recent cases have asked whether schools have been negligent in diagnosing educational needs. The leading case continues to date back to 1976 when *Peter W*[42] tested the claim that a student receiving a high school diploma under a California statute requiring graduates to be able to read at the eighth grade level had been the victim of malpractice because his reading level never surpassed fifth grade. The student alleged negligence and argued that his parents were not informed about his deficiencies. The lower court dismissed and was upheld on appeal. The appeals court discussed at length the duty requirement, finding no duty on which to base an action because of inability to articulate a workable standard of care, noting that teaching involves many different and conflicting theories of how or what a child should be taught. The primary basis for the court's logic, however, lay in public policy considerations given the burdensome litigation that would be generated by a successful lawsuit. As the court noted, holding schools accountable for all academic functions would expose them to tort claims—real or imagined—by disaffected students and parents in countless numbers. A similar view was taken by a New York court of appeals in a case brought by a learning-disabled student who argued that he could not cope with filling out simple job applications. In dismissing the $5 million negligence suit, the appeals court in *Donohue*[43] also cited public policy, noting that solutions would require judicial monitoring of day-to-day implementation of educational policy.

Recent cases have generally followed this trend, as in *Ross*,[44] when a high school basketball star was recruited to a university that promised support for academic deficiencies. The student sued for negligence and breach of contract based on malpractice and negligent admission. A federal district court dismissed, and on appeal the court stated that malpractice claims have been widely rejected, largely as a result of a lack of a satisfactory standard by which to evaluate and because of the potential torrent of malpractice litigation. Other courts have noted the pervasive difficulties that could arise in managing a successful malpractice claim given the impreciseness of measuring damages and further pointing out that parents are not helpless bystanders because they have recourse through local school districts and state education agencies.[45] But notwithstanding, malpractice will continue to be an area of watchfulness, especially

---

42 *Peter W. v. San Francisco Unif. Sch. Dist.,* 60 C.A.3d 814, 131 Cal. Rptr. 854 (1976).

43 *Donohue v. Copiague Union Free Sch. Dist.,* 47 N.Y.2d 440, 418 N.Y.L.Q.2d 375 (1979).

44 *Ross v. Creighton Univ.,* 957 F.2d 410 (7th Cir. 1992).

45 See, e.g., *Christensen v. Southern Normal School,* 790 S.2d 252 (Ala. 2001).

in light of *No Child Left Behind* and other accountability standards that are increasingly attracting public scrutiny, along with equal access issues.[46]

Contracts

Finally, but not surprisingly, school districts should be concerned for liability involving contracts. Districts in all states are authorized to enter into contracts for hiring staff, buying supplies and equipment, and carrying out facility projects. As such, school districts are liable for contractual performance, including breach of contract. Liability by either party to a contract usually relates to bad faith or failure to observe one or more of the basic elements of contracts. To be valid, a contract must have mutual consent including offer and acceptance; have consideration in the form of inducement to enter into the contract; must be entered by competent parties; must serve a lawful purpose; and must conform to any other requirements of law. Most contracts in school districts do not present problems, but some special cases occur where a greater risk of liability may be present.

Most contractual problems involving school districts arise around authority to enter into a contract, and such problems are defined by the state-specific nature of contract law. As a rule, only boards of education may enter into contracts for the district, although agency is often granted to administrators to initiate contracts on behalf of the board. Contracts by agents still must be ratified by the board, and many of the challenges involving contracts have centered on whether a contract is enforceable when a board wishes to nullify a contract by agency. Opposite rulings may be found. For example, in *Community Projects*[47] the court held that only a board has contractual power and that an agreement to purchase goods signed by a principal was invalid. An opposite finding came in *Hebert*,[48] as the court held that because the board had ultimate power to contract and had given power to a principal over extracurricular activities that led to a contract, it had granted an implied power to contract. The key to contractual authority lies in the concept of ministerial duties versus discretionary duties of school boards. Ministerial duties are those duties of a board that it may choose not to perform for itself—for example, supervision of playgrounds, curriculum management, and so forth. Discretionary duties are those other duties the board was elected to carry out itself, such as evaluating the superintendent or approving the budget. While ministerial duties may be delegated, discretionary duties cannot. Contracts by board agents (e.g., administrators) are controlled within this distinction, in that expenditure is a discretionary power and may not be delegated. Notwithstanding, school boards often appoint an agent to deal with contracts, therein creating a level of risk by appointing someone who does not have legal authority to actually make a contract. Under these conditions, a district is not legally bound if it refuses to ratify the contract; conversely, though, the board may choose to ratify an invalid contract.

---

46 For example, more than 30 malpractice suits have been decided in federal and state courts since the year 2000.

47 *Community Projects for Students v. Wilder*, 298 S.E.2d 434 (N.C. App. 1982).

48 *Hebert v. Livingston Parish School Bd.*, 438 So.2d 1141 (La. App. 1983).

Under these conditions, disputes about recovery arise if one party claims the other party has breached a contract. The likely scenario is that at least one party to a contract acted in the belief that a valid contract existed and provided products or services, while the other party failed to pay the bill. Recovery may involve damages, or return of actual products may be sought. The two issues of greatest concern in such situations are whether there is an express or an implied contract, and whether it can be shown that the contract itself was invalid for any reason. An express contract is one in which the duties and rights are expressly agreed upon by all parties. An implied contract is one in which at least one party has acted to read a contract into the actions of both parties, even though there was no express agreement. The difference is not trivial. In the case of an implied contract, the court must consider the value of goods or services so that a fair value can be established because—if recovery is permitted—recovery is limited to the reasonable value of goods or services. In the case of an express contract, however, recovery is controlled by the value expressly agreed to without concern for whether the amount is reasonable. In the latter instance, it is particularly prudent to avoid contracts that are unreasonable, as courts will generally bind both parties to an improvident contract if the contract is determined to be both valid and express.

In some instances, however, the contract itself may be invalid. As discussed earlier, an invalid contract is one that fails to conform to all required elements. For example, no contract could exist if mutual acceptance were lacking or if one party was legally incompetent, including lack of authority to enter into contracts or when the contract's purpose is outside the law. Similarly, lack of consideration voids a contract, as gifts or free services do not meet the consideration test. Furthermore, contracts may be invalid because of failure to follow a prescribed form. For example, a contract required to be in writing, but made orally, is invalid. These instances create particular problems under recovery claims in that services or products may have already been rendered and consumed before the dispute is known, making an equitable claim more difficult by asking a court to either relax the statutory requirement or to allow uncompensated benefit to one party. While each case is unique, the general rule has been that if all other elements of a contract were satisfied and if the district had express authority to contract, then it will be liable under implied contract so long as the form or requirements of the contract do not violate other statutory provisions. To some extent, the outcome depends on the court's attitude toward the question of whether equity or strict statutory application is more important when dealing with issues of public policy.

Case law involving contract recovery is legion. One of the areas of frequent dispute involves additional work by one party beyond the expectations of the other party. This situation often arises in construction projects. For example, the court held against a school district in *Flower City*,[49] where a contractor who was hired to remove asbestos from a school also cleaned up and repaired fire damage, whereon the district refused to pay for extra services. In contrast, the court ruled for the school board in

---

[49] *Flower City Insulations v. Board of Educ.*, 594 N.Y.S.2d 473 (N.Y. App. Div. 1993).

Owners Realty[50] when a contractor performed additional work while removing asbestos. The court reasoned that no other recourse was available in that the written contract barred claims for additional compensation. Absent such specifics or in tandem, however, courts also consider broader principles. In general, if it is found that cause exists for a claim against a public body, the first issue is whether the goods are returnable or if they have been consumed—if the goods can be returned, courts usually permit physical recovery. The second issue is whether an implied contract will be found if it is determined that no express contract existed. The third issue is equity—that is, boards may not abuse their power in voiding contracts, and vendors may not raid the public treasury by misusing contract law.

Contract law is complex. Yet an overarching umbrella of common sense is easily applied. First, school districts do have contractual authority. Second, the required elements of contracts apply, and school boards are expected to protect the public treasury through economy and compliance. Third, contract law may differ among the states, making it important to know local requirements. Fourth, boards may appoint agents, but they may not delegate their discretionary duties, and contracts and expenditure of funds are discretionary duties. Fifth, courts tend to guard the treasury at the expense of outside parties. Sixth, boards may not abuse their preferential treatment by taking advantage of the law's protectiveness toward the public treasury. Seventh, contracts are unassailable if in proper form. Under these conditions, schools and school leaders can avoid serious contractual problems.

WHAT DOES ALL THIS MEAN?

The relationship of public schools and the law in the United States has been in place for centuries, with signs of ever-increasing entanglement. Educational policy and process are topics that stir public interest, and the modern desire to do battle in court has accelerated what was already an adversarial relationship defined by many groups taking interest and responsibility for the educational enterprise. It is not surprising, then, that all actions in schools including personnel matters, civil rights, application of educational policy, and constitutional responsibility for education have been tested in the courts.

As we noted at the outset, this chapter did not try to exhaustively review every area of risk and liability that schools may encounter. Instead, we argued that it is not necessary to be a lawyer to understand and obey the law, and that the paramount duty is to assess and minimize risks and to act as a reasonable person would act under the same conditions given the same level of skill and knowledge presumed to the position. This charge strongly asserts that local school districts and individual school sites should enact formal risk management plans[51] as the first line of defense, wherein legal risks are systematically predicted and reduced through well-constructed poli-

---

50 *Owners Realty Management v. Board of Educ. of New York,* 596 N.Y.S.2d 416 (N.Y. App. Div. 1993).

51 Dennis R. Dunklee and Robert J. Shoop, *A Primer for School Risk Management: Creating and Maintaining District and Site-Based Liability Prevention Programs* (Needham Heights, MA: Allyn and Bacon, 1993).

cies, procedures, and practices. Only then should risk management turn to insuring against liability and loss—that is, insurance plays an indispensable role by serving as the second line of defense by protecting against unforeseen risk, but school districts should not substitute insurance for methodical risk prevention. In sum, planning for risk and liability is an act of budget stewardship—an act calling for managing the inevitable risks every district faces.

pointcounterpoint

Point

Schools today have taken on many earmarks of prisons, with fences, metal detectors, guards, and remote monitoring devices that rob children of their carefree years. The ominous cloud of potential rights violations has greatly aided miscreants' free reign in schools by tying officials' hands when attempting to deal with unacceptable behavior.

Counterpoint

Although schools today must be more cautious in dealing with potential liability, the problem is overblown because most schools are effective sites of learning and prepare children for productive lives. While the media may demonize schools as places where the inmates are in control of the prison, good school leaders have sufficient power to effectively manage the learning environment as evidenced by the success most schools enjoy.

Questions

♦ Which of these two opposing views best represents your personal beliefs and experiences?

♦ What security measures exist in your school? Why were these measures enacted? How effective have these measures been? Are there areas that could be improved? If so, how?

♦ Given the reading and your own personal experiences, how can schools reduce liability risks without taking on more prison-like characteristics?

CASE STUDY

As the assistant high school principal in charge of student discipline, you were not surprised at yesterday's school administrative team meeting to hear the head principal address concerns about student conduct. As in most high schools, staying on top of an energetic bunch of teenagers was a challenge, but you had a full understanding and even sympathy for why student conduct currently was high on the radar screen. More specifically, in the last few weeks several boys had reported instances of bullying in locker rooms and hallways, and several girls had indicated they were seriously considering filing sexual harassment charges against other pupils. In addition, there had been instances of fights and vandalism at school-sponsored night activities, and the local media reports of school news seemed to be taking on a police log tone. Judging from news stories, these events had attracted the attention of both the superintendent and the school board, and you had heard that there had been informal discussion at that level about "...what's the problem and what can be done about it." In their estimation, the types and numbers of incidents had escalated from typical daily discipline issues to a serious matter with potential legal liability for the district, which not only was bad publicity but also could be costly. At yesterday's school administrative team meeting, the principal indicated that the board would soon ask all high schools in the district to undertake a self-assessment on management of student discipline, as well as the security and safety of students and staff during the school day and at cocurricular events; and that the superintendent had already instructed principals to initiate assessments that would result in individualized building-based risk management plans.

Because your primary job assignment dealt with discipline issues, you fully expected to play a big part in these events. True to form, the principal asked you to head up a task force to develop a building-level comprehensive risk management plan. Although the principal left it to you to determine committee structure and scope of the management plan, it was made clear that the end product should be guided by best practices and should carefully assess current conditions, current and prospective needs, and offer actionable recommendations for site-level improvements. Upon the meeting's conclusion, you knew you had a big task ahead and that you would need to engage in significant research and enlist a dedicated and creative committee.

Below is a set of questions. As you respond, consider your learning in this chapter and apply your knowledge and instincts to the situation:

Questions

- What questions need answers before you engage other persons in this process?
- Where will you turn for information on best practices?
- What are the elements of risk assessment and risk management that should be applied to this situation?
- Who will you ask to serve on the site committee? Why?

FOLLOW-UP ACTIVITIES

- Conduct a search of major newspapers in your state for articles involving schools, lawsuits, and liability—you may need to search several years. Using your learning from this chapter, analyze the allegations and make a judgment on the merits of the claims.
- Contact the superintendent's office or the business director in your school district and discuss how the district approaches risk management from a philosophical and operational perspective. Ask whether the dis-

trict has a written risk management plan. Obtain a copy and review what the district believes is important and the preventive measures described in it.

◆ Talk to your principal about what your school does to assess risk and to protect against liability. Probe the scope of risk management and liability as understood by your principal and the general issues that are relevant on a daily basis in your school.

WEB RESOURCES

American Association of School Administrators, www.aasa.org
American Federation of Teachers, www.aft.org
Association of School Business Officials International, www.asbointl.org
Center for the Prevention of School Violence, www.cpsv.org
Council of Chief State School Officers, www.ccsso.org
Education Commission of the States, www.ecs.org
National Alliance for Safe Schools, www.safeschools.org
National Center for Education Statistics, www.nces.ed.gov
National Conference of State Legislatures, www.ncsl.org
National Education Association, www.nea.org
National Resource Center for Safe Schools, www.safetyzone.org
U.S. Department of Education, www.ed.gov

RECOMMENDED READINGS

Association of School Business Officials International. *School business affairs.* Reston, VA: Author, 1997–2007. Multiple volumes, issues, and articles on legal issues, liability, and risk management.

Russo, Charles J. *Reutter's the Law of Public Education.* 6th ed. New York: Foundation Press, 2006.

Russo, Charles J., Harvey Polansky, and R. Craig Wood. *Primer on Legal Affairs for the School Business Official.* Reston, VA: ASBO, 2001.

Russo, Charles, ed. *Key Legal Issues for Schools: The Ultimate Resource for School Business Officials.* Reston, VA: ASBO, 2005.

Wood, R. Craig, David C. Thompson, and Lawrence O. Picus. *Principles of School Business Management.* 3rd ed. Reston, VA: ASBO, 2008.

A View of the Future

SITE-BASED LEADERSHIP

THE CHALLENGE

School leadership is an important education policy issue because research demonstrates that it is second only to teacher quality in its impact on student achievement. Leadership is widely regarded as a key factor in accounting for the difference between underperforming schools and schools that foster student learning. Today's schools require dynamic, well-trained, talented leaders who understand the social, economic and political forces that influence education; who are committed to fresh ideas and solutions and willing to take risks to implement them; and who have a 21st-century view of education management.

National Conference of State Legislatures (2007)

CHAPTER DRIVERS

At the close of this chapter, you will have reflected upon these questions:

♦ What is the strategic concept involved in site-based leadership?

♦ What are the roles of principals, central office staff, school site councils, and others in site-based leadership?

♦ How do issues of organization, areas of legitimate control, and data access affect site-based leadership?

♦ What budget issues are involved in site-based leadership?

♦ How does this entire book come together around site-based leadership?

PULLING IT TOGETHER

Throughout this textbook, site-based leadership has been mentioned frequently. At times our treatment of the concept has been direct, but most often it has only hinted at the growing role of school-based leadership and mostly has intended to provoke deeper thought beyond our topics of the moment. A companion purpose, though, has been to imbue site-based leadership into our entire discussion in a very unassuming fashion—as if its prevalence is a *fait accompli*. As we near the end of our introduction to school finance and resource management, the issue of site-based leadership should be addressed head-on, and we should explain more fully why it is so important to this book. Our interest has nothing to do with zealotry; rather, it comes from seeing site-based leadership as critically important to the demands of the future. As a result, we use site-based leadership to pull together the many parts of this book as tomorrow becomes today.

We begin by first reviewing the strategic concept underlying site-based leadership in order to establish an operational framework. Because it is so people-dependent, we then turn to the roles of principals, central office staff, school site councils, and others. These participant roles lead to discussion about membership, organization, areas of legitimate control, and data access—critical aspects if site-based governance is to have an impact. With concepts and roles in place, we arrive at the crux of this chapter by examining the financial implications of shared leadership, including decision making about general site costs, personnel, instruction, facilities, student activities, accountability, and so forth—that is, the key topics from earlier chapters in this textbook are revisited in the context of site-based devolution. In sum, this chapter pulls together all that we have explored in this book and couches it in the context of tomorrow's constituent-based educational organization. In many ways, this chapter is the point of the entire book—the application of money by knowledgeable people who stand on the firing line of schools.

THE SITE CONCEPT

Variously named as site-based management, school-based management, and so on, site-based leadership has enjoyed high visibility on policy agendas in the United States for nearly two decades. Although some form of site-based leadership had been in some schools for many years, school reform and accountability beginning in the 1980s resulted in a broader understanding that instructional and resource decisions should be located closer to where teaching and learning actually take place—the individual school site. The fiercely competitive context in which education now finds itself also has lent a hand to popularizing the site-based concept, as school choice and charter school legislation have forced states and local school districts to scrutinize their instructional and budgetary attitudes. In addition, policy makers were spurred in the 1990s to reconsider school-based leadership because court decisions on school funding in Kentucky and New Jersey profoundly affected the educational establishment. In the case of Kentucky, the *Rose*[1] decision forced redesign of the entire educational system to include strong school-based management, sparking similar legislation in several other states as well. In the case of New Jersey, the long-embattled state education system was overturned in multiple iterations of *Abbott*,[2] requiring that the state equalize funding between the wealthiest and poorest school districts and requiring districts to reallocate funding to individual schools in ways that make each school site accountable.

The site-based trend, arguably begun in modern form by *Rose,* has spread widely. In 2005, the Education Commission of the States (ECS) noted that school districts engage site-based management to some extent in virtually every state and that 34 states have statutes on the books related to site-based decision making. ECS further noted that 17 states have mandated site-based management statewide in some form and that three states have mandated it in specific districts.[3] Legislative interest continues today, as 36 bills on the topic of school-based management were signed into law in 17 states in the period 2000 to 2007.[4] While laws among the states vary widely in scope, the net effect is that site-based leadership, including some degree of resource control at the school level, is entrenched and growing.

At the root of the site-based concept is the premise that individual schools should be given real responsibility for curriculum, staffing, and budget decisions. Individual schools should be allocated a budget to carry out their educational programs, and each school must set goals and conduct performance assessments with genuine consequences for success or failure. The premise rests on a strong conviction that decisions made closest to where students are located are better than decisions made at higher levels that are more removed from the daily operation of schools. Although actual practice has varied, all site-based designs have sought to transfer data, money, and authority to the school site in order to involve parents, teachers, and other stakeholders in meaningful decision making. In sum, the site-based concept risks much on a belief that people in the trenches need real authority over budget, personnel, and curriculum if optimal student success is to be achieved. Under these circumstances, stakeholders in schools are faced with developing new skills because responsibility for learner outcomes is a very serious matter.

1   *Rose v. Council for Better Education,* 790 S.W.2d 186 (Ky. 1989).

2   *Abbott v. Burke,* 575 A.2d 359 (N.J. 1990) and continuing through *Abbott v. Burke*, M-1088 September Term 2006, Supreme Court of New Jersey, 2007 N.J. LEXIS 588, May 24, 2007, Decided.

3   Education Commission of the States, *Site-Based Decisionmaking: State-Level Policies.* (Denver, CO: Author, 2005).

4   Education Commission of the States, *Recent State Policies/Activities: Site-Based Management.* (Denver, CO: Author, 2007).

FRAMEWORK FOR IMPLEMENTATION

According to advocates, the concept of site-based leadership lends weight to its own importance by fostering an improved school site culture that leads to better decisions affecting student achievement.[5] Implementation is complex, however, and demands a framework that carefully accounts for strategic readiness, the legitimate role of various stakeholders, and effective use of newly acquired budget authority—concepts traditionally unfamiliar to individual school sites, but which form the backbone of site-based leadership.

What Is the Strategic Concept?

Our experience in working with school districts throughout the nation has led us to understand that the most difficult task in implementing site-based leadership is creating a basis and culture for dramatic change. Change is unsettling, and people who advocate loudest for change are sometimes the same people who resist most fiercely when the opportunity for meaningful change arises. It is easy to talk a good game or to complain that decisions in schools are too centralized, but the literature on organizational theory clearly indicates that meaningful and lasting change must be brought about planfully. Although it is beyond the scope of this text to develop strategies for change, adopting site-based leadership requires careful preparation based on planning at the district and school levels about how radical change will be introduced and carried out. For example, an autocratic top-down imposition of site-based leadership is likely to be resented and clearly would be ironic. Likewise, a common error is to simply turn decisions over to school site councils without adequate groundwork in philosophy and operational skills. People seek authority and power, but they do not want to make irrelevant decisions or to be given responsibility beyond their skills. Because site-based leadership does not mean abdicating central authority to individual schools, the first part of a useful framework for implementation is a well-designed plan that accounts for the following three critical aspects of transferring power:

- ♦ *Assessing the history and data* on readiness of the individual school site;
- ♦ *Developing strategies for implementation* based on assessment findings;

---

5   It is important to note that there is no solid body of research evidence linking site-based leadership (also referred to as school-based management or school-based leadership) to improved student achievement. See, e.g., David Peterson, "School-Based Management and Student Performance," *ERIC Digest*, No. 62 (Eugene, OR: ERIC Clearinghouse on Educational Management, 1991), and Lori Jo Oswald, "School-Based Management," *ERIC Digest*, No. 99 (Eugene, OR: ERIC Clearinghouse on Educational Management, July 1995). Some have argued that these disappointing results are a result of researchers' use of inconsistent or unclear definitions of the concept, or, conversely schools under study did not fully implement the site-based model as intended. However, even without a solid link to student achievement, the concepts of participatory decision making and parental and community involvement inherent in this leadership model offer many educational benefits as described in this chapter.

♦ *Creating accountability, timelines,* and *costs* for implementing site-based leadership.

Assessment

As we saw in Chapter 7, site-based plans can be elaborate, and it is intuitive that change can be ill-fated if people do not have adequate understanding and training, or if they resent the goals or the process. Avoiding problems for all stakeholders demands careful assessment strategies on two levels, and both levels should be completed before beginning a transfer of central decision making to the school site. The first level consists of organizing an overall site-based leadership plan for each individual school, understanding the historical justification for current practices, assessing the likelihood of success once site-based leadership is enacted, and making an informed choice at each school about how extensively to adopt site-based leadership. The next level consists of determining how the overall site-based plan will look at both district and individual school levels. Although all elements are essential, the most critical task comes when the site-based team that implements the plan assesses the readiness of the individual school and the district. It goes without saying that the assessment stage is no time for posturing about educational faddism because the honesty of all stakeholders and the perceptiveness of the planning team at this juncture will determine how well implementation will work. In sum, assessment is the careful evaluation of the likelihood for success once profound and uncharted change rules the day.

Implementation

Implementation begins directly after assessing readiness for site-based leadership. We have implied that implementation itself must be site-based to be successful, which is to say that an implementation team at each individual school site must be formed to represent all stakeholders of the particular school. Team members should be drawn from administrators, teachers, students, and parents, as well as the community's many constituent groups such as business, industry, professionals, and older citizens. The implementation team should represent many viewpoints and must be extensively helped to focus on how site-based leadership should work at the individual school level. The eventual makeup and work of individual school site councils should be an outgrowth of planning by the implementation team. In sum, implementation is the act of building on assessment of readiness in preparation for the accountability structures that support site-based leadership.

Accountability

The implementation team and the newly formed school site council need to devote much energy to developing an overall site-based leadership plan, with controls specific to each school. Parameters of each site-based plan must be determined, timelines must be set, and accountability strategies must be agreed upon. The goal of these activities is not only to structure how site-based leadership and constituent-based decisionmaking will occur, but also to reach key agreement on the mission, goals, and appropriate responsibility of the many participants. For example, frustrations arise when people are involved in decisions that are beyond their skills, exceed their authority, or infringe on other prerogatives or legal restrictions. Implementation plans need good counsel during the development stage and should reflect the detailed parameters of the overall project, show timelines, and set procedures and accountability standards. In essence, the planning model for implementation at the individual school site must create a vision addressing the following:

- Beliefs
- Mission
- Climate
- Objectives
- Policy
- Preliminary planning document
- Collective bargaining and legal issues

Beliefs articulated in the school site leadership plan must be based on sound educational research, theory and best practice. These statements should be simple and declarative, communicating a positive message of wide involvement. Belief statements should be generated by each stakeholder group and merged in a cooperative process that builds teaming. For example, the following teacher beliefs are taken from districts using site-based leadership to build positive school-based culture:

Teachers in this building believe:

- students learn basic skills as a consequence of how teachers teach.
- expecting students to be successful will make it happen.
- success is more important than failure.
- sharing ideas increases student performance.
- in working together to coordinate programs within teams and across grades.
- in a positive attitude toward change.
- the student is at the center of the educational process.

A similar process should be used for developing mission statements at the school site level. Mission statements should be simple and clear. It is important that the focus be on the direct educational experiences of every student because mission statements declare actionable intent. Examples of mission statements include the following:

- *This school will graduate* persons who will become productive, responsible citizens.
- *This school will teach* students to think as individuals and to think critically.
- *This school will empower* those individuals who accept the responsibility for student learning.

Mission statements should also be supported by goals and objectives. Goals and objectives provide greater specificity and yield measurable outcomes. Several states have enacted performance-based achievement plans that can serve as good models for implementation teams. Goals and objectives might be stated in terms of student knowledge, dispositions, and performance; for example, the following statements could be adopted by a school site:

- Students will *know* where and how to access materials for conducting science investigations (*knowledge*).
- Students will show *enthusiasm* for science (*disposition*).
- Students will be able to locate resources and *apply* them to a problem (*outcome*).

Successfully implementing site-based leadership also depends significantly on consensus for a positive school climate. Climate is a condition that is deliberately built and requires stakeholder participation. Climate is complex and includes the following concepts:

- There is a stimulating *supportive environment.*
- There are *positive expectations* for staff.
- There is *constant feedback*—positive and negative—that is always constructive.
- There are *rewards and punishments* articulated for all levels of the educational program.
- There is a *feeling of family.*
- *Open communication* is the rule and not the exception.
- *Achievement and growth* of students and staff is the reason for the school to exist.
- There is *closeness* among parents, community, and principal.

The outcome of agreement on beliefs, mission, goals and objectives, and climate should lead to formulation of site-based leadership policy and the implementation phase. These concepts go far toward establishing accountability for outcomes. Belief statements and so on should be adopted as policy, and implementation is the process of carrying out these aims. A guiding document should result from preparing for implementation. The document should set out everything discussed thus far, with additional caution that it should not infringe on collective bargaining or legal issues—that is, all plans should be carefully checked against state statutes and have the benefit of legal counsel.

Implementing site-based leadership must be fully inclusive of principals, site councils, staff, and parents who are charged with important, relevant, and substantive issues for which they will be held accountable. These issues comprise the real ongoing work at each school once implementation is complete. The value is self-evident, as site-based leadership participants can reasonably be expected to work with the following:

- Instruction
- Student achievement and growth
- Student socialization

- ◆ Critical thinking skills
- ◆ Innovation
- ◆ Attendance
- ◆ Budgets
- ◆ Completion or graduation

What Is the Role of the Principal?

Success in implementing and operating a site-based leadership plan is in large part a function of how well roles are carried out. A clear understanding of powers and limitations is essential to cooperative and productive relationships. As indicated in the opening quotation to this chapter, research points convincingly to the critical role of principals in successful school-based reforms, if for no other reason than because a lead person must provide the rallying point and a procedural knowledge base. School principals are perfectly situated for such leadership by virtue of legal and positional authority. As a result, site-based designs cannot work unless principals understand and value shared decision making.

Site-based leadership requires principals to take the lead, delegating decisions to appropriate levels. This is harder than it sounds, because the very first leadership act is to surrender the control and efficiency of functions formerly housed in the principal's office or at some higher level. Schools successfully engaging site-based leadership have strong principals who are unthreatened by control issues—in fact, these persons are typically stronger professionals because they must work harder and more effectively than their more traditional colleagues in order to achieve broad-based consensus. A key concept, however, is that delegation of authority must be realistic. Site council members should not be asked to make inappropriate decisions or to engage in work beyond their expertise. The balance is a fine line because resentment follows when the work of site teams is viewed as trivial or as abdicating administrative responsibility. Principals also walk a fine line because they must support decisions made by others if at all possible. The principal fundamentally takes the role of leader, counselor, supporter, and encourager of the site council. Within this framework, delegation is not abdication of power, as the principal must become an advocate for the persons making decisions to ensure their effective implementation.

The flip side of delegation is accountability because site-based leadership actually raises the performance standard for each person. As we saw throughout various parts of this book, demands for accountability are increasing, and the primary rationale of policy makers in mandating a shared decision making model is to increase school effectiveness. Discussion earlier in this chapter raised the issue of measurable outcomes, and the school site is where this accountability is envisioned and acted on most effectively. The role of the principal is to lead and model accountability, both by personal commitment and by exhorting others to adopt the organizational structures that will enhance school outcomes.

At the end of the day, successful site-based designs are driven by strong principal leadership. As titular and functional head of the school, it is the principal who can most effectively initiate and guide school growth. The principal is the central link between the district, the individual school, and the community and is further the position-holder with the legal and (hopefully) moral authority to effectuate change. This does not lessen the contribution of the site council or staff, but it underscores how all effective organizations rely on a key leader to mobilize others.

What Is the Role of Central Office?

A common misperception is that decentralization reduces the role and importance of central administration. Although relationships are changed, the central office becomes even more important because all school site powers flow from central office actions that enable and support site leadership. The issue of central support is critical because this level must genuinely relinquish many decisions to individual school sites, including power to make budget decisions. It is always difficult to give up power, and in this case it is even harder because central office accountability to higher units of government and the community is still a major force.

Because the role of principals is critical to all good site-based plans, principals are paralyzed without the support of the central office and the board of education. The central office must educate principals and other stakeholders about decentralization, making the role of central administration vital to implementing site leadership. Starting at the board level and working down through all central office ranks, organizational and financial structures must be created and publicly supported in order to send a message of enthusiasm and genuineness. The central office must take the lead in transferring many decisions to the school site level and must take a leadership role in training people about sources of power, authority, revenue, expenditures, curriculum—that is, the many topics explored in this book. Experience shows that when the central office moves from a position of control to an advocacy/support role, site plans are genuinely empowered. Conversely, districts that pay only lip service to school site leadership without relinquishing the necessary controls engender skepticism and resentment. Changes in central office behavior are hard to enact and—in a majority of school districts—take time. Literally, an entirely new set of roles, relationships, and behaviors must be forged between central office, principals, teachers, council members, and the community. The literature suggests four kinds of knowledge and skills that the central office must develop when restructuring for school site leadership:

- *Interpersonal and team skills* for working together effectively;
- *Technical knowledge and skills* for providing services;
- *Breadth skills for engaging in multiple tasks,* especially the tasks decentralized to the site council as a result of a flattened organizational structure; and
- *Business knowledge and skills* for managing the financial aspects of the school site.

What Is the Role of the Site Council?

The philosophical and operational shifts following from site-based leadership are significant. Issues of legitimate control, access to data, and budget join to form a very different way of life as site councils begin to govern the operation of schools. In short, site councils assume many tasks formerly reserved to administrative ranks; that is, site councils have the potential to have a powerful impact on the basic organizational design including site costs, personnel, student activities, and so on. These concepts form the remainder of this chapter.

Organization

Although states legislating site-based leadership have frequently mandated key organizational and membership issues, the general intent is that site councils should be organized around the goals of the individual school after consideration for overall district structure. Concern for readiness of site councils to deal with the issues under their purview is usually evident, so that states often require an information and training phase, lasting in some cases as long as one year. The driving force behind organizing should be singular—expectations must be realistic, and the site council must have clear direction from the district. Stated simply, can the site-based leadership plan realistically be accomplished? At the outset, organizational questions should be raised, among which the most important are the following:

- *How* is membership on the site council determined?
- *What* matters should the site council consider?
- *Who* has formal decision-making authority?

These questions set the tone for all site council relationships. Clearly, it is easiest to deal only with beliefs, vision, and policy, but site-based leadership intends to go much farther. Generally, site councils are empowered to address funding, instruction, and assessment of programs at individual sites. But importantly, the degree of specificity for these roles has the potential for great benefit or misunderstanding.

Membership

Although both organizational and membership structures are often mandated, experience indicates that certain site council designs work better. Groups that are too large, too small, or that do not represent the community have a hard time making decisions and gaining external support. The success of councils has varied from school to school based on a host of issues, with data showing increased likelihood for smooth operation when the following structures are in place:

- *The most manageable group size* is approximately ten to 12.
- *Composition of the council* should reflect the intent of the strategic objectives and preliminary planning goals.
- *The council should consist* of the principal, lead teachers, support staff, parents, and interested community members.
- *Members should have a broad perspective* on public schools.
- *The council must avoid* individual platforms and agendas.

The organizational design should establish the principal as leader of the site council. This requires the principal to be a visionary, facilitator, organizer, motivator, resource for information and procedure, and risk taker. Again, realistic expectations should rule—that is, principals must assess their own strengths and weaknesses and help the group understand its own characteristics. A weakness in many site plans is failure to conduct realistic self-assessments, and a failure of districts lies in not providing leadership development opportunities to principals. Assessment should ask at least the following questions:

- Does the principal have the energy to work with the council?
- Is the principal willing to delegate responsibility to others?
- Does the principal manage time well?
- Is the principal receptive to new ideas?
- Is the principal confident in the role as leader?
- Does the principal work well with groups?
- Does the principal have confidence in the ability of teachers and others?

Along with assessing the principal's readiness, membership on the site council means that professional staff also must be prepared to lead. Teachers need skills in two areas to make meaningful contributions: that is, the instructional domain and the managerial domain. Teachers are usually expert in the former and unskilled in the latter. Yet these are the areas of legitimate site-based leadership responsibility and the source of most frustrations when implementing site-based plans. Questions to be addressed include the following:

- Do teachers see the value of site-based leadership?
- Are teacher perceptions of site-based leadership accurate?
- Are teachers ready to accept new tasks without more pay?
- Are teachers ready to share control of their classrooms?
- Are teachers ready to accept decisions of the site council?
- Are teachers ready to take direction from peers?
- Do teachers believe they should be involved in management?

Membership on the council must also include parents and community members. Although wide representation is important, members must be able and willing to make contributions. Lay members should be interested in the school, and there should be a balance among parents and community stakeholders. Although all viewpoints are valued, there must be evidence of ability to work effectively in groups. Each of the questions we asked about principal and teacher readiness can be applied to laypersons as well. For example:

- Do laypersons see the value of site-based leadership?
- Are lay perceptions of site-based leadership accurate?
- Are laypersons ready to commit extensive time and energy?
- Do laypersons accept that some areas are legally off-limits?
- Do laypersons have the necessary interest in management?

Once site council members have been selected on the basis of knowledge and disposition, the site council will need to meet regularly. The principal should chair the group, at least for the first year. Initial meetings should focus on reaching consensus among members on organization and process. It is important for the principal to allow everyone a voice in the decision-making process. The principal should lead the discussion concerning beliefs, vision, mission, and policies of the council. The initial process should focus on working collaboratively before trying to resolve any actual problems of the school.

Legitimate Control

Identifying the proper boundaries of site council control is crucial, as frustration and overreaching can easily occur. Legal problems also may arise if the council strays into constitutional, statutory, or other protected areas such as negotiated contract items. Most likely, the school site council will concern itself primarily with instruction and budget issues, at least in the early stages, making it important for everyone to be well informed and willing to share power.

Working with instructional issues requires deep knowledge on the part of all site council participants. Members must broadly understand the instructional program at both school and district levels, and the team must understand any state curriculum requirements as well. The council will need access to data, with great care taken not to violate privacy laws. Very important is training regarding the implications of each decision the council makes; for example, improper access to data may violate the *Family Educational Rights and Privacy Act* (FERPA), and the legal and ethical implications of decisions about tracking students into college and vocational programs are significant. Nonetheless, site councils need data to make guided decisions.

Site councils work best when they have the following types of data by grade levels and programs:

- ◆ Enrollment data.
- ◆ Attendance data.
- ◆ Student achievement data.
- ◆ Promotion and retention data.
- ◆ Discipline counts, issues, and dispositions.
- ◆ Dropout data.
- ◆ Elementary, middle, and high school program offerings.
- ◆ Special education, vocational, and early childhood data.
- ◆ Library and resource data.
- ◆ Student demographic data such as single parent, free and reduced price meals, English Language Learners (ELL), and so on.
- ◆ Other reports such as use of technology in schools, accreditation, curriculum planning, and so on.

These data are useful when examining district and school site structure, client satisfaction, internal and external comparisons for benchmarking purposes, and work environments. The data are integrated in many ways, in that they affect decisions about mission, goals, objectives, and programs while simultaneously providing feedback to help make strategic adjustments. For example, data might be used to determine that the school needs to adopt a new goal of increasing attendance to the 95%

level, or that growth in instructional costs will be no more than 2% each year. Student assessment data (when combined with budget data discussed next) might also be used in deciding to hire another primary grade teacher to reduce class size at a particular school. Conversely, the council might use the same data to decide to use the money freed up from a retiring staff member to hire additional classroom aides instead of filling the teaching vacancy. Uses of data are limited mostly by creativity, legality, and reality, while lack of data severely restricts the power of informed site-based decision making.

Legitimate control is an area needing very clear definition at both district and school-site levels before site councils are actually empowered. Too much control is as bad as not enough. Control is bounded by the reality of all chapters in this text, in that *all genuine power rests in the ability to control and direct staff and money*. Token councils spark deep resentment, and overreaching councils create equally complex problems. In sum, appropriately empowering site councils is an act of genuine leadership and a rich resource in itself.

What Are the Budget Issues?

There would be no reason to discuss site-based structures in this text if it were not for the increasing relationship between school-based leadership and school-based budgets. The power of site-based budgeting is secured when it is realized that budget, staffing, and curriculum are the cornerstones of all educational productivity. In fact, everything that matters in schools is wrapped up in these issues, as fully 80% to 85% of a district's budget is devoted to personnel and direct instruction—indeed, 100% when support services are understood in the context of instruction.[6] The relationship of site-based leadership to the budget is therefore one of empowering site councils to increase student achievement through a spending plan. As a rule, the budget issues relevant to individual school sites are *basic knowledge* relating to overall context and *site knowledge* relating to general site costs, staffing issues, instruction, facilities, and student activities.

Basic Knowledge

The primary budget responsibility of a site council is for costs associated with the individual school site. However, the council needs a general understanding of overall budget structure in order to avoid an information hole wherein people see only a small part of the big picture. The site council should examine overall budget issues before attempting to work with individual site budgets.

This textbook lays out the basic knowledge needed by administrators, teachers, board members and laypersons who are likely to serve on site councils. Although the knowledge in this book affects participants at different levels and is often deeper than laypeople might wish to go, the entire site council needs to broadly understand reve-

---

6   Some states have promoted a "65% solution" that would require at least 65% of budget authority must go to direct instruction. Interest is not limited to the United States, as some proposals (e.g., England and Australia) have considered upward of 90% school-based funding.

nue sources, the formula by which the local district receives funding, and the school site budget and various cost categories—that is, the issues making up this textbook! Without basic knowledge, the site council is unable to make good decisions about instruction, staffing, supplies, capital outlay, maintenance, and a host of other highly complex issues. Specifically, the site council must gather an appreciation for the entire fiscal picture of the school district and for individual site costs in terms of the following:

- Sources of revenue to the district and methods of taxation
- State revenue sources
- Local revenue sources
- State-aid formula
- State accounting and reporting requirements

Early meetings of the site council should focus on gaining this basic knowledge. Discussions should address all bulleted areas in this chapter and should also describe funding for special education, transportation, and other categorical programs—all in context of the relationship between programs and revenue within the constraints of fiscal realities. The goal is to have all site council members understand the flow of money to the district and to individual schools, while conceptually connecting funding to mission, goals, and so on.

Site Knowledge

Because the site council will spend significant time on budget matters, it is important for members to see that some costs are beyond the control of individual schools (indirect costs) while other costs are within control (direct costs). A useful way of viewing indirect and direct costs is to see all costs that are not site-specific as indirect costs, and all costs specific to instruction and annual operations as direct costs. For example, bonding for new facilities is an indirect cost because bonding is beyond the scope of a school site council, although it should help take the lead in identifying infrastructure deficits and improvements at the school level. A related concept is fixed costs. Fixed costs are those that do not change despite fluctuations in a given level of activity. Fixed costs may be direct or indirect, but they tend to be overhead costs regardless of the educational programs that go on within an individual school. Variable costs are the opposite of fixed costs—that is, they are expenses that vary in tandem with level of service. Finally, marginal costs are those that change if the school adds a level of service. Site councils have little control over fixed and some indirect costs, but they have greater control over direct, variable, and marginal costs, depending on how the district has organized its site-based funding plan. The concept is important because it signals the boundaries of site councils. Examples of how various costs might be viewed in a given school district include the following:

Budget Items	Cost
Teacher salaries	Direct, variable
School administration costs	Direct, variable
Capital outlay	Indirect, fixed
Social services	Direct, variable
Maintenance—custodial	Indirect, fixed
Central office salaries	Indirect, fixed
Transportation	Indirect, variable
Food services	Indirect, variable
Purchasing operation	Direct, variable
Maintenance of facility	Indirect, variable
Utility costs	Direct, variable
Learning programs	Marginal, variable
Activities	Direct, variable

The classification scheme outlined here is based on certain judgments that would change substantially if site-based leadership were conceptualized differently in the target district. For example, the chart above makes value judgments—that is, that at some point in time cost-benefit analysis showed efficiencies related to district-wide maintenance and transportation programs, and that teacher and administrative salary costs should be placed under the control of the individual site. Completely opposing values would create an entirely different design—for example, the most obvious opposite view is placing teacher and administrative costs on a districtwide basis with district right-of-assignment retained, so that the only impact of the site council on personnel costs would relate to decisions about hiring or replacement. Likewise, the site council could be given a transportation budget (see the example of a site-based budget in Chapter 7), while retaining other transportation functions at the district level. In other words, structural decisions about site-based leadership/budgeting drive everything, including whether a cost is viewed as direct, indirect, fixed, or variable.

The issue of control versus no control is illustrated by utility costs because there is a basic need for heating, cooling, and lighting school buildings. One view is to place these costs at the district level as uncontrolled overhead costs. A different way is to rebate back to the school any unspent utility funds as a bonus for energy efficiency and conservation. Because site councils are involved with all expenditures in the school, energy conservation then becomes of direct interest to the council and actually injects a measure of control where none would otherwise be present. In this scenario, the site council might develop an energy monitoring system. The same line of thinking might be applied to school facilities, with the site council monitoring the condition of the facility with primary concern for its instructional adequacy. In this example, the site council should make the district aware of ongoing infrastructure needs, maintenance and repair, and help maximize efficiencies by feeding details of the site plan into an overall school district capital improvement plan.

Taken together, the many topics in this textbook are valid areas for development under site-based leadership. Basic and site knowledge takes in a broad scope of legitimate control, and the effectiveness of site-based leadership should be judged by how well the site council holds itself accountable for both knowledge and results. Councils should be trained to give thoughtful answers to the following questions:

- What are our schools becoming?
- What should our schools be doing?
- What are our schools capable of doing?
- What is the effect of money on schools?
- What happens when our schools get more or less money?
- How does school money get tracked?
- What is a fair aid formula, and how does our state compare?
- How should we organize for budgeting in our district?
- How is each school in our district funded?
- How do we recruit and select staff?
- How does due process affect our council?
- What are instructional budgets?
- What is the role of student activities?
- What is the role of capital outlay, maintenance, and operations?
- What is accountability?
- How are districts in our state funded?
- Do we understand liability, and have we prepared a risk management plan?
- What is the budget process, both generally and in our district?
- How do we determine staffing needs?
- What are our compensation policies?
- What is instructional planning?
- How do we budget for instruction?
- What are activity funds?
- How do transportation and food service work in our district?

Revisiting a Sample School District

Our discussion in Chapter 7 of school-based reform and the growing importance of site-based leadership does not need repeating here, but from the list above it is clear that we believe school site councils should have significant input into all budget issues. For example, it is reasonable for each school to decide how to allocate teaching and nonteaching staff to meet the school's mission, goals, and objectives. One school might eliminate a vice principal in favor of an additional teacher to reduce class size, while another school might choose larger classes in exchange for providing aides in each classroom. A third school might trade a teaching position for a guidance counselor to help troubled students. Similarly, the site council might choose to implement new curricula at the expense of student activities, or a council might opt for new cocurricular programs that are carefully justified on the basis of contributing to learner outcomes. The range of possibilities is limited only by good sense and statutory authority—but it is clear that budget, personnel, and curriculum are the key assets of schools and that effective site-based leadership cannot escape dealing with these issues in a coordinated fashion.

The sample school district earlier in Chapter 7 was modeled on this exact concept. As we created the scenario, we raised a series of questions that now provide both review and a solid rationale for site-based leadership. At the outset, we asked the following questions that should be raised regardless of school district organization. Site councils will find these particularly relevant:

+ *Who has responsibility* for establishing the overall level of expenditure in a school district and school building?
+ *Who has responsibility* for establishing expenditures for each major program or organizational unit?
+ *Who has responsibility* for selection of specific resources within the allotted dollar amounts for each program?
+ *Who has responsibility* for curriculum selection?
+ *Who has responsibility* for initiation of new instructional programs or elimination of current programs?
+ *Who establishes* capital outlay budgets and decides how facilities and equipment are allocated?
+ *Who has responsibility* for establishing salaries and benefits?
+ *Who hires* personnel?
+ *Who decides* which items and amounts will be cut if needed?

These are *the* structural and operative issues facing school site councils, going to the heart of how budget, staffing, and curriculum are planned and executed. The sample district in Fig. 7.6 (pp. 226–231) went directly to these issues. Our sample school district chose to *track* instructional budgets using detailed accounting codes to permit accumulation of data by program; *decentralize* many budget tasks; retain some *central* coordination at the board and director levels; *allocate* uniform amounts per pupil for instructional program purposes; *retain* transportation services centrally; *allocate* discretionary transportation budgets to schools; *decentralize* some aspects of capital outlay and equipment purchasing; and *link* expenditures to expected learning outcomes. In effect, our discussion in Chapter 7 described a model school district that has acted to locate genuine program and budget authority at the school site level in the belief that efficiency is gained by district coordination and control of indirect costs like maintenance and construction. School sites, however, were authorized to determine how programs operate—in this particular example, site-based decision making led to a program allocation of approximately $892,000 sited in local school buildings. Accountability was a central feature of our model budget, as the fund accounting structure was designed to produce program and expenditure analysis, with all expenditures justified by expected outcomes.

Although considerably more complex than traditional ways of managing schools, site-based leadership/funding designs have the potential to better integrate district and school goals into a coherent plan that serves the unique needs of each school site. Our questions earlier in Chapter 7 captured the principles and spirit of site-based leadership, in that a good site plan should have ready answers to the following queries:

- What is the district's overall mission?
- What are the district's goal statements?
- What is my school's overall mission?
- What are my school's goal statements?
- What were the results of the district's environmental scan?
- What were the results of my school's environmental scan?
- Does my school's educational plan reflect these needs?
- How can I spend my budget to address these needs?

FINAL COMMENTS

Several comments apply as we end this chapter on site-based leadership. Of primary importance is that the chapter does not blindly advocate for site-based budgeting. Site-based plans are not fully appropriate to every situation, although some elements are automatically meritorious and should be operational in every school. Neither is site-based leadership a clever means by which a local school board can shed its legal and financial responsibility. Nor is it a plan allowing the superintendent to avoid top responsibility for decision making. Rather, site-based leadership is a concept that can improve the efficiency and effectiveness of direct services to students.

As a result, we believe site-based leadership has key elements that must be required of all schools in the modern context. Simply put, why should any legitimate stakeholder be denied a role in the operation of schools? And further, why should any district seek to retain power to itself when it knows that hoarding power only creates resentment among stakeholders? It is our view that these questions have only one answer, and that schools have no choice except to embrace stakeholder participation. The only remaining legitimate issue is to what extent site-based leadership should be enacted locally—a decision with powerful consequence because staffing, curriculum, and budget are the cornerstones of all educational productivity.

pointcounterpoint

Point

The advent of site councils has been of great benefit to local schools by opening the doors to parents and others. These persons often have very useful insights into how schools are perceived and misperceived. Their participation in curriculum and budget matters is particularly helpful, as they often have very creative program/funding ideas and become strong advocates for the school simply by being involved.

Counterpoint

Although the concept behind site councils is well founded, the practical application too often comes up short. Many site councils end up being rightly criticized for elitism, cronyism, favoritism, meddling, and basic ineffectiveness relating to lack of expertise in the conduct of schooling.

Questions

+ Which of these two opposing views best represents your beliefs about or experiences with site councils and the larger issues underlying their existence?

+ If your school district has site councils, how are principals, teachers, and others involved in site council activities? Are their roles similar to or different than those described in this chapter? Describe the similarities or differences.

+ If your school district has site councils, how effective are they in your estimation? Explain. How could their functioning be improved?

CASE STUDY

As a newly hired middle school principal, you were aware that your school district was heavily into site-based management. Coming to your new position from another state, your hiring interview had been a steep learning curve wherein you had learned that the state legislature had enacted extensive site-based management requirements for public schools. As the superintendent fleshed out the broad details of the law and the basics of your local school district's site-based structure, you had gathered a definite sense that site councils were very actively involved in the life of schools in this district. The superintendent had indicated that your effectiveness in working with your school's site council would be important to your overall success because the district took democratic leadership principles very seriously.

Shortly after the school year began, you held your first middle school site council meeting. You had met the council members earlier because the hiring process had also included an interview with that group. The first council meeting of the year went very well, and you were pleased with how the site council chair had organized and conducted the meeting, engaging members in scoping out the year's work agenda. At that meeting, the council had agreed to review both the language arts and biological sciences curriculums, as well as launching a drive to secure funding for a football weight training facility.

Approximately a week later, the site council chair unexpectedly dropped into your office to chat about the agenda. With the next regular meeting only a few weeks away, he indicated you needed some background in order to understand the dynamics that surrounded the site council. As he talked, you became concerned about the facts he presented and about how the council apparently perceived your role. He indicated that several site council members were privately furious that one of the science faculty members had "scoffed" at creationism in classes and that those same council members were also intent on reviewing the language arts curriculum for inappropriate books and ideas. From what you could gather, the site council believed its role was to govern curriculum content for basic decency and age-appropriateness, and that your role was to support their position. As the meeting ended, you were uncertain about the chair's own personal position in these matters, but you were certain that you faced a potentially difficult year. As an afterthought, the chair had added on his way out the door that the site council had secured a donor who had agreed to provide $200,000 in matching funds for the proposed athletic weight room.

Below is a set of questions. As you respond, consider your learning throughout this entire book and apply your knowledge and instincts to the situation:

Questions

♦ What are the fundamental issues in this case study that concern you? Why?

♦ What is your instinctive reaction to the "facts" as presented here? Why? What does this say about you as a leader?

♦ What should be your first action? Why?

♦ How will you approach working with the site council—both in terms of the immediate situation and long-term?

FOLLOW-UP ACTIVITIES

♦ Write a reflection on how leadership is carried out in your school district. Review the many questions posed in Chapters 7 and 12 on who holds power, answering them in light of your own experience. If your reflection identifies some significant evidence of site-based leadership, analyze how this is accomplished, with consideration for your own views on strengths and weaknesses of the model in place in your particular school.

♦ If your state or school district uses school site councils, research the reasons why councils exist, their purpose, scope of authority, and responsibilities. Examine state statutes if relevant, and examine your local board policies. Interview your principal about the duties of the site council and its operation. Ask others about their perceptions of the site council's effectiveness, including teachers, other administrators, laypersons, and staff.

♦ Volunteer to serve on a school site council. Alternatively, ask permission to attend and observe site council meetings.

WEB RESOURCES

American Association of School Administrators, www.aasa.org
American Federation of Teachers, www.aft.org
Association of School Business Officials International, www.asbointl.org
Building Excellent Schools, www.buildingexcellentschools.org
Council of Chief State School Officers, www.ccsso.org
Education Commission of the States, www.ecs.org
National Association of Elementary School Principals, www.naesp.org
National Association of Secondary School Principals, www.nassp.org
National Center for Education Statistics, www.nces.ed.gov
National Conference of State Legislatures, www.ncsl.org
National Education Association, www.nea.org
National Middle School Association, www.nmsa.org
National School Boards Association, www.nsba.org
Public Education Network, www.publiceducation.org
U.S. Department of Education, www.ed.gov

RECOMMENDED READINGS

Association of School Business Officials International. *School Business Affairs*. Reston, VA: Author, 1997–2007. Multiple volumes, issues, and articles.

Crampton, Faith E., and Randall S. Vesely. "Resource Allocation Issues for Educational Leaders," in *Handbook for Excellence in School Leadership*, eds. Stuart C. Smith and Philip K. Piele. 4th ed. Thousand Oaks, CA: Corwin Press, 2006.

Duffy, Frances M. *Power, Politics, and Ethics in School Districts: Dynamic Leadership for Systemic Change*. Lanham, MD: Rowman and Littlefield Education, 2005.

Epstein, Noel, ed. *Who's in Charge Here: The Tangled Web of School Governance and Policy*. Washington, DC: Brookings Institution Press, 2004.

Furman, Susan, and Richard Elmore, eds. *Redesigning Accountability Systems for Education*. New York: Teachers College Press, 2004.

Goertz, Margaret E., and Allan Odden, eds. American Education Finance Association. Annual Yearbook. *School-Based Financing*. Thousand Oaks, CA: Corwin, 1999.

Kedro, James M. *Aligning Resources for Student Outcomes: School-Based Steps to Success*. Lanham, MD: Rowman and Littlefield Education, 2004.

Valesky, Thomas, Dianne Horgan, Carol Etheridge Caughey, and Dennie Smith. *Training for Quality School-Based Decision Making: The Total Teamwork System.* Lanham, MD: Rowman and Littlefield Education, 2003.

Walker, Elaine W. "The politics of school-based management: Understanding the process of devolving authority in urban school districts." *Education Policy Analysis Archives* 10 (August 4, 2002). *epaa.asu.edu/epaa/v10n33.html*

FUTURE TRENDS IN SCHOOL FUNDING

13

THE CHALLENGE

Whatever it is that money may be thought to contribute to the education of children, that commodity is something highly prized by those who enjoy the greatest measure of it. If money is inadequate to improve education, the residents of poor districts should at least have an equal opportunity to be disappointed by its failure.

Coons, Clune, & Sugarman (1970)

CHAPTER DRIVERS

At the close of this chapter, you will have reflected upon these questions:
- What are the lessons that you have drawn from this book?
- What are the future issues in school funding?

THE BIG PICTURE

Our journey in this textbook has provided a broad contextual overview of money and schools. Funding for education is a complex topic, even though we have tried to make it as straightforward as possible. The task has been more difficult in that this book is meant to address many audiences, each with different expectations for depth, style, and exhaustiveness. We introduced concepts at considerable depth, although we know that we have merely provided a foundation for the expertise that comes only with extended study and professional experience. But it is precisely that point which makes this book so relevant for our audiences—by seeing the big picture of school money, stakeholders are better grounded in the many perspectives needed to engage the world of educational decision making.

As we close this book, there is much to be gained from reflecting on lessons learned and by speculating about the future. Reflection anchors our understanding of how the many pieces of school funding fit together, and an eye to the future prepares us to deal with the change that continues to dominate the educational landscape. As traditional roles shift and as lines of authority, power, and influence become increasingly blurred, the future holds both promise and consequence for the choices now being made. Progress and change are, after all, the tools that real leaders use to mold and reshape the context that makes up the big picture of schooling.

WHAT ARE THE ISSUES?

A fundamental theme throughout this book is that schools are facing a crisis of unequaled proportion that encompasses a complex mosaic of society. Schools are changing dramatically, with profound implications for the future. From one perspective, the problem seems simple in that equal educational opportunity must be provided to every child, but in reality the problem is vexing because resolving it requires agreement on diverse goals and substantial new investment of resources *or* dramatic reallocations of existing funds—with the latter creating a new set of winners and losers in school funding. At the very least, resolution will require increased stakeholder participation in schools, along with serious debate about the aims of schooling and the role of equity, adequacy, efficiency, and choice. All these issues are affected by larger concerns for the health of the economy and the nagging question of just how heavily equal educational opportunity actually depends on money. Although we cannot resolve these issues here, the future is framed by these struggles. Our overriding thesis is, of course, that this is a battle that must be engaged by administrators, school boards, teachers, policy makers, and laypersons if our nation is to remain a world leader.

Lessons From this Book

The social, political, and economic context of education discussed in Chapter 1 laid bare a sobering lesson. We examined the condition of schools in social and economic language, finding that schools are a source of both optimism and cynicism.

National reports have long predicted a dismal future as student achievement has declined.[1] Yet Americans have historically clung to the view that education is the key to social and economic mobility, even as research indicates that inequities in distribution of educational rewards is producing anger in increasingly disenfranchised populations, which include those in poverty (including the "working poor") and those who consider themselves solidly middle class. The lessons in this chapter were thus fourfold. First, educational opportunity means different things to different people. Second, everyone wants a better life. Third, there is constant strife over the relationship between schools and socioeconomic class that threatens national unity. Fourth, equal opportunity costs money—that is, *money matters*. We used this line of thinking to propose that schools have many stakeholders who must become involved politically and educationally in ways that serve all children well. In fact, it was our thesis that the remaining chapters in the book would provide important knowledge needed by stakeholders to enable them to become more effective leaders in schools, in both formal and informal capacities.

Chapter 2 built on this view of schools by moving deeper into the world of policy making, exploring the role of education as both an economic and social good. We discovered that education is an enormous enterprise, rooted in the history and richness of American democracy in ways that have shaped our current education system. The lessons in this chapter were several. Of greatest importance was that tradition and policy never develop in a vacuum; that is, everything that exists has roots that have a rational explanation leading to present circumstances. Of equal value were the views of how and why federal, state, and local units of government have settled on their current roles in controlling and funding education, while at the same time realizing that these relationships are not static. The struggles over values in education were again apparent in this chapter, as disagreements over the worth of education and who should pay for schools have continued to play out in educational policy making.

Our knowledge quest next led to Chapter 3 where we discussed basic funding sources for schools. We noted that while taxes have never been popular with the American public, over time massive federal, state, and local tax systems have nonetheless developed, wherefrom schools derive their revenues. The dilemma of funding education in the 50 states was also explored, and it was seen that, absent a significant federal role, equal educational opportunity could not be provided without a strong state role. We noted that each state's school funding system was the product of its unique political and economic history. The lessons learned from this chapter were twofold. First, although no perfect tax system can ever be built—because taxes are the product of political environments wherein infinite desires compete for finite revenues in a context of constituent self-interest—progress has emerged from seeking a more balanced tax system. Second, real gains in equal opportunity have been made through state aid formulas, despite the sometimes ugly politics of school funding. Still, much work remains to be done in many states, with stakeholders having two

---

1   See, for example, National Commission on Educational Excellence, *A Nation at Risk: The Imperative for Educational Reform* (Washington, DC: Author, 2003).

routes to secure greater funding for education and more equitable distribution—either through their legislature or through the courts.

Chapter 4 opened Part II of this textbook by moving from a broad policy perspective into a more detailed analysis of budgeting in schools by examining fiscal accountability and professionalism. We laid out a noble view of the public trust, emphasizing the fiduciary responsibilities of school administrators and staffs and identifying how school revenues and expenditures are structured. Admittedly a difficult topic to present in brief form, the message was that everyone needs at least a basic knowledge of the types of money received by schools, how money can be spent, and how public funds are guarded against error and wrongdoing. Part of the message in this chapter was to instill respect for control of financial assets because we are unswerving in our belief that money and staff are the key control points in schools.

Our examination of the mechanics of school money continued in Chapter 5 as we looked at the concepts and practices underlying budget planning. The first part of the chapter focused on ways to organize for budgeting, while the second half focused on carrying out the process of creating a budget. Implicit were three key arguments. First, we argued that without funds there are no schools. Second, we argued that the purpose of budgeting is to implement equal educational opportunity by converting dollars into programmatic priorities. Finally, we argued that money talks, making a plea to view the budget as the principal planning system by which political and legal approval is secured for providing education to children—a lesson lost, we avowed, when people see budgets only as an accounting tool, rather than as a tool for making informed educational decisions.

We next turned to examining the major cost determinants of budgets. The first step came in Chapter 6, as we looked at the relationship of school money to the personnel function, which represents a major proportion of school budgets. With some schools already in financial crisis but at the same time facing a need to expend greater resources—for example, to hire more staff to respond to state and federal mandates that all students achieve at high levels—it is especially critical for stakeholders to be knowledgeable about staffing issues because at least 80% of an average school district's budget goes to personnel costs.

Chapter 7 moved to the heart of budgeting by exploring instructional costs. Much time was devoted to looking at district and school-based budgeting, including an introduction to the role of site-based leadership. Two key lessons emerged. First, budgeting for instruction is the most important activity in schools because it enables teaching and learning to occur. Second, instructional budgets should reflect the mission and goals of the district and individual school. The focus of the chapter was on choosing among organizational designs to take advantage of stakeholder participation for the purpose of building support for schools and to scrutinize the relationship between spending and student learning.

Chapter 8 turned to budgeting for student activities, an area whose importance in schools is often overlooked. We set out the view that such activities are integral to students becoming well-rounded individuals and noted that many opportunities and pitfalls exist in funding this important dimension of school life. The chapter focused on identifying the many activity fund accounts in a typical district and on appropriate handling of money at the individual school level.

Chapter 9 moved to the topic of budgeting for school infrastructure. The focus was fourfold. First, we emphasized the importance of viewing the physical environment of schools as one of the critical factors in student success. Second, we provided an overview of infrastructure needs and funding methods, noting that at present schools' infrastructure needs are severely underfunded. Third, demographic, capital program, and facility planning skills were analyzed. Fourth, we argued that maintenance and operation of facilities have far-reaching effects on community and student attitudes toward schools. We couched this discussion as a continuation of our view that stakeholders must become more knowledgeable about the importance of school infrastructure and advocate for full and fair funding to remedy the vast inequities that now exist in school facilities. The overarching goal, of course, was to illustrate that all parts of a school funding system must work together to provide an effective learning environment.

The vein of new knowledge and stakeholder participation was continued in Chapter 10, as we examined transportation and food services. We took the position that while the instructional mission of schools rightly receives great attention, it is equally true that instruction is sorely hindered when children are hungry or deprived of the means by which to travel to school. Relatedly, great liability exists for these aspects of school operations. And obviously, neither transportation nor food service could operate successfully without prudent fiscal management. The lesson of this chapter was clear: schools are complex fiscal organizations made up of interrelated parts that aid or obstruct the instructional mission, and stakeholders need to be aware of the important supporting role that programs like food services and transportation play in student success.

Our journey moved in Chapter 11 to legal liability and risk management in school settings. This chapter was based on the idea that prudent stakeholders must understand the sources of authority enjoyed by schools, the nature and limits of immunity, the problems encountered when laws and rights are violated, and the loss of discretionary revenue resulting from liability-related issues. The purpose of the chapter was to inform stakeholders of broad liability principles and to encourage careful planning for risk management. The overriding lesson, of course, was caution in all matters because the law and schools are constant companions.

Finally, Chapter 12 revisited the topic of site-based leadership, taking highlights from each previous chapter to create a unified direction. A theme of this textbook has been that outmoded, ineffective approaches to school budgets must be abandoned, and that stakeholders must be empowered to participate in fiscal decisions and equipped with the leadership skills to effect positive change through fiscal resource allocation. Because we believe the budget is the vital organ that supplies the essential nutrient (money) to an integrated and interdependent organism called schools, it stands self-evident that this book has called for wide participation and for rejection of the view that budgets are off-limits or of no interest to anyone except school administrators. To meet that goal, we developed a framework for implementing site-based leadership, examined the role of stakeholders, and laid out the areas in which administrators, school boards, teachers, and laypersons have a duty to become involved. In many ways, then, this chapter held the most important lesson of the book—if schools are expected to provide equal opportunity, the budget must become a democratic tool for equity and excellence. As a result, general and specific budget knowledge appropriate to each stakeholder's level of participation is badly needed if the goals of public education are to enjoy widespread support.

Future Issues in School Funding

The unsettled and evolving nature of society and schools promises a full slate of issues in the foreseeable future. Major public debate is long-standing on all these issues, but the intensity is increasing as the nation's social fabric continues to experience deep stress. Fundamental change characterizes the new millennium along lines that produced wide rifts in the past. The list is familiar: the *politics* of money; the impact of the *economy* on schools; the enhancement of *equity, adequacy,* and *efficiency* in school funding; the social and economic consequence of efforts to increase educational *choice;* and, of course, the continued devolution of *school governance.* Although we have talked extensively about these issues in the foregoing chapters, a final look with an eye to the future provides appropriate closure to this book.

Politics of Money

To rephrase a popular saying, we would assert that the way to someone's heart is often through their pocketbook. A basic tenet of economics is that a rational person makes choices out of enlightened self-interest, so that philanthropy and altruism are possible only after a hierarchy of personal economic wants and needs are satisfied. It is also the case that economic status remains the only acceptable element along which our society can stratify and segregate itself. The combined effect of self-interest and the human tendency to affiliate with those similar to oneself creates a powerful force in the form of politics of money.

The inescapable human desire to put individual prosperity ahead of absolute equality virtually guarantees continued tension over money and schools. Politics in a representative democracy is exactly what its name implies: that is, citizens elect officials in the belief that their interests will be represented first, so that equality becomes a goal to be achieved only after self-interest is satisfied. Money buys security and privilege, and more money buys even more security and privilege. Capitalist democracy is an odd creature, in that it is uncomfortable with the consequences of brute market forces, so that it becomes capitalism tempered by guilty efforts that resemble charity, justified by a logic of self-help in which democracy and the opportunity for socioeconomic mobility are equated. A more extreme view would argue that even these efforts are suspect, as they are actually underlain by the unspoken knowledge that one of the outcomes of unbridled capitalism is the presence of, and need for, a permanent underclass. The issue, regardless of partisan politics and political philosophy, is simply that money is power—specifically, power to purchase goods, privileges, and influence.

As we have implied throughout this book, the United States has long committed to individual initiative and personal freedom. The strength of these often conflicting national goals has experienced ebb and flow, as a collective social conscience has predominated at times, and as the free market has triumphed at others. One of the great achievements of the United States has been access to socioeconomic mobility, whereby people from poor backgrounds have been able to amass great wealth and power. Many of the current social programs we take for granted today were born out of the poverty and human suffering of the Great Depression in the 1930s, whereas others arose from the social activism of the Great Society in the 1960s. However, trickle-down economics in the Reagan years and government downsizing during the 1980s and 1990s represent the ever-awaiting opposite side of the coin. Many factors go into the politics of money, but it is an undeniable reality that schools' financial fate relies on the conscience and good will of individuals and government, often with conflicting priorities.

A realistic view of the future requires us to concede that money dominates any decision process—in the case of schools, a process driven by money supply and public attitudes and preferences. Scarcity and self-interest have been the rule for the last few decades in many states, beginning with tax relief initiatives such as Proposition 13 in California in 1978 that gutted funding for education and extending to more recent efforts to eliminate or scale back social programs that historically provided an economic safety net for the most vulnerable of our citizens. The roaring economy of the 1990s did little to offset the fierce scrutiny of government, as the overwhelming demand was to return surpluses to individual and business taxpayers rather than to invest in better or more government services. Similarly, the profound reforms of the *No Child Left Behind Act* in 2001 placed new demands on schools for accountability as measured by high stakes testing, imposing economic sanctions on states and school districts with "failing schools" and requiring school choice options for parents and students "trapped" in such schools. In many ways, American society has returned to its roots of independence and self-reliance, as characterized by welfare reform, get-tough criminal reform, distrust of big government, and the elimination or scaling back of many social programs. The mood of the nation has become less charitable and more inclined to embrace personal freedoms that strongly mirror the underlying politics of money. When these views combine with economic conditions and compete with other demands for equity, efficiency, and so forth, a reasonable person is likely to conclude that schools will not experience any sharp revenue increase in the near future.

The Economy

A continuation of the same discussion of the politics of money relates to the condition of the economy. Public economic confidence is closely watched at all levels of government on the assumption that the wellbeing of the nation depends substantially on how people or "consumers" perceive their personal economic prospects at any moment. The old saying that "possession is nine-tenths of the law" could be restated to say that "reality is perception" when speaking of the economy because consumer confidence drives political and economic policy decisions at the highest levels.

A realistic view of the future must acknowledge that school funding is inextricably tied to the health of the economy at local, state, federal, and global levels. Despite the historic growth in school revenue over time, the impact of the economy on schools can be dramatic as seen in many states where in recent years taxpayer attitudes and shifting economic fortunes have led to severe state-imposed tax and expenditure limitations. For example, the economic boom of the 1970s was followed with losses for schools during tight budgets of the 1980s, and the mindset of reductionism carried into the highly prosperous 1990s as Congress and the individual states continued to scale back many costs despite a strong economy. Similarly, the economic downturn at the start of the new millennium has had consequences for schools, with economic instability facing some states far into the future—a dilemma made worse in some cases by deep state structural deficits, some of which were born from the overly-generous tax cuts in the boom years of the 1990s. Clearly, the state of the economy drove attitudes about government spending over the last two decades of the twentieth century and continues to do so today—under these conditions, schools are unlikely to be the beneficiaries of any economic windfall in the near future.

Equity, Excellence, Adequacy, and Efficiency

A close companion of self-interest and economic realism is the unending struggle for equity, excellence, adequacy, and efficiency at all levels of society. As we said earlier, these sometimes conflicting goals are embedded in the American soul, with the result being that our form of government reflects a great and perpetual tension between social conscience and individual freedom. The tension is apparent in a nation that is still uncomfortable with its history of social inequality, trying at times to aggressively use government to remedy past injustice and at other times ignoring its unsavory past. Desegregation of schools in the 1950s, the Great Society of the 1960s, the bitter legal battles in the 1970s over school funding, the rise of racial quotas and preferences in the 1980s, and the weakening of affirmative action and revoking of many entitlements in the 1990s illustrate the nation's painful struggles with questions of equity. The same period has been characterized by calls for excellence and efficiency, as school reform has swept the country following reports of dismal achievement, and as advocates for retrenchment have harshly scrutinized every expenditure of government. And the legacy of such conflict has been certain, as schools and other government agencies now find themselves starved for adequate resources, appealing to a public that—at least until the next shift in national psyche—has little desire to spend more on what it sees as failing schools and "big government."

The result has been a conflicted society, often with bizarre outcomes. For example, the last 40 years produced U.S. Supreme Court decisions barring entanglement of church and state in schools, only to see those rulings overturned or weakened in recent years. Likewise, protracted litigation upheld racial preferences in college admissions, with those decisions also assaulted with sizable success in very recent years. School funding litigation has followed the same uncertain path of victories and reversals, and the psychology of change and unrest has provided fertile ground for critics decrying the lack of student achievement in public schools and leading many states to enact stringent standards, including financial sanctions against low-achieving schools. Efficiency in government has been the motto of watchdog groups protesting every tax or spending increase. As increasingly extreme ideological and advocacy groups have rallied around one or more of these values, bitter social strife has resulted—often to the detriment of the children they claim to serve. For example, extreme advocates of equity who champion the deep needs of students in poverty often demand limitless resources for schools without accountability or even sensitivity to the many other social goods that government must fund. At the other end of the spectrum are ideologues so extreme in their demands for what they define as "efficiency" that they advocate dismantling the nation's public school system in order to let pure market forces prevail and eradicate those inefficiencies. These irreconcilable divides are played out daily in the media and the political arena and, if not moderated, will lead to paralyzing gridlock.

A reasonable view of the future does not see a lessening of these forces. The terms and conditions will change, but the cries will continue and become more strident. Schools are often caught in the middle because they cannot fully satisfy one constituency without offending another. A realistic view sees only continued strife, with persistent calls for greater choice in schooling and further devolution of government as solutions to incompatible social and economic goals.

Educational Choice

An outgrowth of issues raised here has been a greater demand for parental choice in schooling. Educational choice takes many forms such as interdistrict and intradistrict[2] choice, forms of public school choice that actually have existed for many decades in a number of states and have been used quite successfully.[3] In the late 1980s, a new form of public school choice emerged with the charter school movement, which by the 2004–2005 school year had spread to 40 states and the District of Columbia.[4] The original vision of charter schools was as incubators of educational innovation that, once proven effective in this microcosm, could be disseminated more broadly to other public schools. In reality, charter schools have served many purposes and remain a popular form of public school choice in a number of states. Still, altogether they enroll less than 2% of the nation's public school students.[5] The most controversial form of school choice remains private school choice in the form of vouchers that permit public tax money to be sent to private and religious schools that parents select. Unlike supporters of other forms of school choice, voucher advocates are comprised largely of individuals and groups from opposite ends of the socioeconomic spectrum; for example, some poor urban parents of color have supported vouchers as a lifeboat that will save their children from what they perceive to be the sinking ship of failed urban schools riddled with racism and crime. At the opposite end of that spectrum are wealthy white conservatives who see public schools as a failed monopoly; they believe that in a capitalistic society the market always works better and more cheaply than government. Other core advocates of vouchers have been Christian conservatives and others who prefer a faith-based education for their children. Ironically, all these groups share an interest in the politics of money. If money were no object, poor urban parents would move to more affluent communities with better schools. Wealthy white conservatives who support vouchers believe that

---

2   Intradistrict school choice today also includes magnet schools, although magnet schools emerged in the 1960s to encourage voluntary desegregation.

3   Interdistrict and intradistrict public school choice are also often referred to as "open enrollment."

4   U.S. Department of Education. "Contexts of Elementary and Secondary Education: School Choice." *Indicator* (2007): 32.

5   *School Choice* (2007). Percentage calculated from student enrollments in Table 32–1.

dismantling what they view as an inefficient public school system would free up tax dollars for a better educational system for all, with money left over to reduce taxes. Those with preferences for faith-based education often believe their tax dollars have already paid for schools, just not the one they want for their children and hence paying taxes and private religious school tuition is "double taxation."

More radical forms of school choice, like vouchers, have become a flash point in the politics of education, incorporating elements of equity, excellence, adequacy, and efficiency in a context that bears heavily on future funding for public schools. Research in this area must be viewed with caution as it is sometimes tainted by personal ideologies, conservative and liberal, rather than being objective analyses of solid data. To further complicate matters, federal and state courts have not been unanimous in their views of voucher plans. As always, the language of federal and state constitutions, as well as state law, powerfully affects the outcome of such struggles. For example, the U.S. Supreme Court upheld the Cleveland voucher program in 2002, while the Florida Supreme Court struck down a statewide voucher program in 2006. Less-controversial forms of private school choice, such as tax credits and tax deductions for private school tuition used in a handful of states, have for the most part survived court scrutiny. However, these plans have been open to the criticism that they still benefit mostly middle and upper income families because parents usually must pay their child's tuition upfront and then wait several months to file for the tax credit or tax deduction. For many low income parents, this is an insurmountable barrier. Furthermore, the poorest of families may not be required to file a tax return and hence cannot gain any advantage from this opportunity.

It is clear that Americans like choice, whether choosing consumer products or choosing schools for their children. So there is no evidence to suggest any of the forms of educational choice discussed here will fade away. In fact, new forms of educational choice continue to emerge, like virtual or "cyber" schools, that are often accommodated either through existing charter school or open enrollment laws.[6] In addition, private virtual schools are readily available. Virtual schools have had broad appeal to parents who previously home-schooled their children, yet another form of educational choice. However, funding issues related to virtual schools have become contentious in some states and have even led to litigation, as in Pennsylvania and Wisconsin. A frequent source of dispute is that the state aid received by virtual schools is equal to that received by schools housed in actual buildings requiring maintenance and upkeep, while virtual schools do not incur similar expenses. Furthermore, the addition of previously home-schooled students to public school rolls via virtual schools represents a new and largely unforeseen expense to many state school aid systems.

A realistic view sees at best stable demand for school choice and at worst continued growth, as religious and nonsectarian private schools increasingly must compete for enrollments alongside new for-profit enterprises that have come to see school

---

6   Rapp, Kelly E., Suzanne E. Eckes, and Jonathan Plucher. "Cyber Charter Schools in Indiana: Policy Implications of the Current Statutory Language," *Education Policy Brief* 4 (2006).

choice as a growth industry. Although not yet universal, education is becoming a consumer's marketplace, with public schools being forced to join in the competition for enrollment-driven funding.

Devolution of Governance

Finally, all these issues come together under the aegis of devolution in governance. Our discussion of site-based leadership in earlier chapters courted this issue, as people need and want to return government—including schools—to more manageable, visible levels. Devolution has swept the nation from the highest levels down, as exemplified by Congressional efforts in the 1990s to delegate many social programs to the states. States, in turn, have delegated some previously state-funded programs and responsibilities to local units of government. Schools are being affected, if for no other reason than state resources are continually strained by new responsibilities. Demands on schools will only increase under these circumstances, particularly as states and the federal government relentlessly continue to control student outcomes through standards-based legislation and as interest grows in school-based accountability measures.

A realistic view of the future does not foresee a dramatic shift in economic policy or personal attitudes toward growth in government, social justice, or school choice. The economy drives attitudes from a viewpoint of self-interest, mitigated only by a sense of basic human dignity that manifests itself in a modest degree of social responsibility. Americans prefer personal liberty and economic competition, but they curb their innate capitalist inclinations via limited support for limited social programs. The question for the future is whether Americans will choose to expand or restrict the boundaries of those social programs based on the economic and social changes continually predicted by economists and demographers. *In the end only one thing is certain—money drives everything, including the future of schools.*

A FINAL WORD

Although this chapter might easily leave the impression that the future is bleak, it is only the case that we have been brutally honest in assessing the challenges facing public school funding. The United States has always been a land of enormous opportunity, and we sincerely believe it will continue on its great course and successfully meet the challenges of the future. Our hope, however, does not lead us to be blind to the fact that the nation is at a crossroads, with one path leading to renewed greatness and the other path leading to partisan demise arising from lack of national unity. Given history and the massive change drivers now propelling the nation, continued greatness is possible only if the difficult economic and social problems we have outlined are resolved through equal educational opportunity.

The Interstate School Leaders Licensure Consortium (ISLLC) professional standards identified in the foreword to this textbook take on new meaning when considering money and schools. Education needs great leaders who understand the relationship between money and equal educational opportunity, and the technical knowledge required to provide a bright future for children is exceeded only by the strength of character that will be needed to lead the United States to its great potential. *Schools need leaders who promote the success of all students by understanding, responding to, and influencing the larger political, social, economic, legal, and cultural context in which education is so deeply imbedded.* In other words, money matters, so that good schools depend entirely on stakeholders who understand and use money to create equal educational opportunity: administrators, boards, teachers, and laypersons joining hands to bring the United States together around our common hope—our children.

pointcounterpoint

Point

A substantial body of research demonstrates that students in poverty, as well as other students commonly defined as "at-risk," need greater resources to be academically successful. It is clearly a matter of equity and access to equal educational opportunity that states should provide the additional funding for these students, no matter how much it costs. If these children are not successful, that is, drop out of school, they become a permanent tax burden for the rest of society given their greater unemployability and use of social services.

Counterpoint

The federal government already provides significant funding for poor students as well as others categorized as "at-risk"—for example, funding for special education, bilingual education, and so forth. Almost every state also provides some extra funding for these same students. With all these "special" aids, it is the average student who is short-changed by being placed in large classes with little individual attention. The real problem is that schools and school districts are not using their funding efficiently.

Questions

♦ Given your experience and the readings in this text, which position seems more accurate? Why?

♦ In your view, can schools provide equal educational opportunity to all students and still be efficient? Explain.

CASE STUDY

At the start of your second year as an urban school superintendent, you were shocked to read this morning's local headline captioned "Parental Satisfaction with Local Schools at All Time Low." Apparently, a nationally known conservative think-tank had conducted a survey of parents in the district, unbeknownst to you and the school board, and had released the highly critical report to the media. One of the major areas of discontent, according to the news account, was what parents perceived as arbitrary assignment of their children to schools. If the media had accurately reported parental attitudes, patrons were demanding not only to choose their children's school but also to have a wider array of choices, like specialty schools, alternative schools, and even virtual schools.

While you would not have welcomed the news at any point, you were especially concerned about the timing of negative press. The headline had hit just as you were in the midst of your contract renewal with the board, and the combination of these factors was unsettling because this was your first contract renewal and you knew there were tensions within the board about your performance. For example, this year's student test scores, while showing some improvement, were not as high as expected, and several schools in the district were facing state and federal sanctions for failing to make adequate yearly progress—an unwelcome bit of news that had already received unflattering local media coverage. To make matters worse, the state legislature was now considering a bill to permit vouchers in all urban districts in the state which you feared would skim off the best and brightest students and their attendant funding, leaving your district to educate an increasingly expensive and challenging student body.

Immediately upon arriving at your office this morning, you called an emergency administrative cabinet meeting. You announced that you were creating a task force to draft a decisive response to the study, with the charge to develop low or no-cost options that would satisfy parental demands. You indicated that the task force would need to find ways around the financial barriers most urban school districts, including yours, typically face—for example, a budget able to cover only the bare necessities of instruction, a long list of problems like much needed maintenance and repairs, and so on. As you summed up the charge, you emphasized the need for thinking outside the box by saying that the district needed to consider some significant restructuring to meet these demands because rearranging resources was the primary way out of this situation.

Because the headlines and your contract negotiations were hitting simultaneously, you announced that you would personally chair the task force and that you would select about a dozen individuals to serve with you. As you closed the meeting, you indicated that some members of your administrative cabinet would be appointed to the task force and that a rigorous meeting schedule would follow because you expected to form a response in three months or less. Back in your office, you wondered about the risk inherent to your actions, but under the circumstances you knew you needed to be seen as a proactive problem solver.

Below is a set of questions. As you respond, consider your learning throughout this book and apply your new knowledge to the situation:

- ◆ Who will you select to join you on this task force? Explain your rationale.

- ◆ Brainstorm the options you might present in your final report. Detail the costs, if any, of each option as well as the potential educational benefits.

- ◆ In addition to the task force, are there other responses or initiatives the school district might undertake to empower parents?

- ◆ Are there any assumptions, beliefs, tactical errors, and so on in this case study that give you cause for concern? Why?

FOLLOW-UP ACTIVITIES

- Identify three major educational issues at national or state levels and provide your rationale for selecting them. Discuss how funding is associated with each and indicate whether you believe (based on your readings here and other research) that sufficient funding is available. Discuss how greater funding might be secured. Be as specific as possible—for example, would additional funding come from local, state, or federal levels, or some combination?

- Prepare a report on education policy issues in your state such as the political environment for school funding, the condition of the economy, the impact of school choice, and demands for equity, adequacy, and excellence. Use resources such as local newspaper articles and publications of local or state think-tanks and stakeholder groups like teacher unions, taxpayer associations, and so forth.

WEB RESOURCES

American Federation of Teachers, www.aft.org
Brown Center on Education Policy, www.brookings.edu/gs/brown/brownhp.htm
Center on Budget and Policy Priorities, www.cbpp.org
Center on Education Policy, www.cep-dc.org
Council of Chief State School Officers, www.ccsso.org
Economic Policy Institute, www.epi.org
Education Commission of the States, www.ecs.org
Education Next, www.educationnext.org
Education Policy Analysis Archives, http://epaa.asu.edu
National Center for the Study of Privatization in Education, www.ncspe.org
National Conference of State Legislatures, www.ncsl.org
National Education Association, www.nea.org
National Governors Association, www.nga.org
National School Boards Association, www.nsba.org
The Program on Education Policy and Governance, www.ksg.harvard.edu/pepg
United States Government Accountability Office, www.gao.gov

RECOMMENDED READINGS

American Federation of Teachers. *Do charter Schools Measure Up? The Charter School Experiment after 10 Years*. Washington, DC: Author, 2002.

Anyon, Jean. *Radical Possibilities: Public Policy, Urban Education, and the New Social Movement*. New York: Routledge, 2005.

Belfield, Clive R., and Henry M. Levin. 2005. *Privatizing Educational Choice: Consequences for Parents, Schools, and Public Policy*. Boulder, CO: Paradigm Publishers, 2005.

Callahan, Raymond. *Education and the Cult of Efficiency: A Study of the Social Forces that have Shaped the Administration of Public Schools.* Chicago, IL: University of Chicago Press, 1962.

Center on Educational Policy. *Educational Architects: Do State Education Agencies have the Tools Necessary to Implement NCLB?* Washington, DC: Author, 2007.

Chaikind, Stephen, and William J. Fowler, eds. American Education Finance Association. Annual Yearbook. *Education Finance in the New Millennium.* Larchmont, NY: Eye On Education, 2001.

Chubb, John E., and Terry M. Moe. *Politics, Markets, and Schools.* Washington, DC: Brookings Institution Press, 1990.

Crampton, Faith E., ed. "Education Finance Issues of National Importance in the 21st Century." *Educational Considerations* (2000).

Ladd, Helen F., Rosemary, Chalk, and Janet S. Hansen, eds. *Equity and Adequacy in Education Finance: Issues and Perspectives.* Washington, DC: National Academy Press, 1999.

Levin, Henry M., and Patrick J. McEwan, eds. American Education Finance Association. Annual Yearbook. *Cost-effectiveness and Educational Policy.* Larchmont, NY: Eye On Education, 2002.

United States Government Accountability Office. *No Child Left Behind Act.* GAO-05–79. Washington, DC: Author, 2005.

Wise, Arthur E. *Rich Schools, Poor Schools: The Promise of Equal Educational Opportunity.* Chicago: University of Chicago Press, 1968.

Witte, John F. *The Market Approach to Education.* Princeton, NJ: Princeton University Press, 2000.

INDEX

---

1   Page numbers followed by f indicate a figure.

R

S